RIVERSIDE COMMUNITY COLLEGE 1916

D0583930

DATE DUE

JE 17 '94			
MY 22 '00			
JE 10 '00			
JA 24 '02			

DEMCO 38-296

Pitt Series in Policy and Institutional Studies

ARMS FOR THE HORN

U.S. Security Policy in Ethiopia and Somalia 1953–1991

Jeffrey A. Lefebvre

University of Pittsburgh Press

Riverside Community College
Library
4800 Magnolia Avenue
Riverside, California 92506

Published by the University of Pittsburgh Press, Pittsburgh, Pa., 15260

Copyright © 1991, University of Pittsburgh Press

All rights reserved

Eurospan, London

Manufactured in the United States of America

Library of Congress Cataloging-in-Publication Data

Lefebvre. Jeffrey Alan.

Arms for the Horn : U.S. security policy in Ethiopia and Somalia, 1953–1991 / Jeffrey A. Lefebvre.

p. c. — (Pitt series in policy and institutional studies)

Includes index.

ISBN 0-8229-3680-1

1. United States—Military relations—Ethiopia. 2. Ethiopia—Military relations—United States. 3. United States—Military relations—Somalia. 4. Somalia—Military relations—United States. 5. Munitions—United States. I. Title. II. Series.

E183.8.E8L44 1991

355′.03263—dc20 90-28360

CIP

A CIP catalogue record for this book is available from the British Library.

For my mother and father, and for

Marina and Alexandra

Contents

List of Acronyms

ACR	*African Contemporary Record*
AID	Agency for International Development
AI/TI	arms imports/total imports
APC	armored personnel carriers
ASA	Army Security Agency
AWACS	airborne warning and control aircraft
CENTCOM	Central Command
CINCEUR	commander-in-chief for Europe
CINCMEAFSA	Commander-in-Chief, Middle East, Africa, and South Asia
CINCSPECOMME	Commander-in-Chief, Special Command for the Middle East
DA	development assistance
DIA	Defense Installations Agreement
DoD	Department of Defense
DSC	Defense Satellite Command System
EDU	Ethiopian Democratic Union
ELF	Eritrean Liberation Front
ELM	Eritrean Liberation Movement
EPLF	Eritrean People's Liberation Front
EPRDF	Ethiopian People's Revolutionary Democratic Front
EPRP	Ethiopian People's Revolutionary Party
ESF	Economic Support Funds
EURCOM	European Command
FMS	Foreign Military Sales
FSO	foreign service officers
GCC	Gulf Cooperation Council
HIMS	His Imperial Majesty
IBRD	International Bank for Reconstruction and Development (World Bank)

List of Acronyms

ICA	International Cooperation Agency
ICBM	intercontinental ballistic missile
IEG	Imperial Ethiopian Government
IMETP	International Military Education and Training Program
INF	intermediate-range nuclear force
JCS	Joint Chiefs of Staff
JLPC	Joint Logistics Plans Committee
JSPC	Joint Strategic Plans Committee
MAAG	Military Assistance Advisory Group
MAP	Military Assistance Program
MDAA	Mutual Defense Assistance Agreement
MDAP	Military Defense Assistance Program
MEDO	Middle East Defense Organization
ME/CGE	military expenditure/central government expenditure
MIDEASTFOR	Middle East Force
MOD	Mareehan/Ogadeeni/Dulbahante
MPLA	Popular Movement for the Liberation of Angola
MTT	military training teams
NDF	National Democratic Front
NEA	Bureau for Near Eastern Affairs (Department of State)
NFD	Northern Frontier District
NPP	national policy paper
NSC	National Security Council
NSS	National Security Service
OAU	Organization of African Unity
OLF	Oromo Liberation Front
PD	presidential determination
PDRE	People's Democratic Republic of Ethiopia
PDRY	People's Democratic Republic of Yemen
PKO	Peace-Keeping Operations
PMAC	Provisional Military Administrative Council
POL	petroleum, oil, and lubricants
RDF	Rapid Deployment Force
SAC	Somali Aeronautical Corps
SALF	Somali-Abo Liberation Front
SAP	Security Assistance Program
SCC	Special Coordinating Committee
SDLF	Somali Democratic Liberation Front

SLBM	submarine-launched ballistic missile
SLOC	sea lines of communication
SNA	Somali National Army
SNM	Somali National Movement
SPM	Somali Patriot Movement
SRSP	Somali Revolutionary Socialist Party
SSDF	Somali Salvation Democratic Front
SSF	Somali Salvation Front
STRATCOM	strategic communications
SWP	Somali Workers' party
SYL	Somali Youth League
TPLF	Tigre People's Liberation Front
UAR	United Arab Republic
USC	United Somali Congress
WPE	Workers' Party of Ethiopia
WSLF	Western Somali Liberation Front
YAR	Yemen Arab Republic (North Yemen)

Preface

During the first six months of 1991, dramatic political changes in the Horn of Africa have sparked both hope and fear about the future of this war-ravaged region of the world. In late January, Siad Barre, who had ruled over Somalia since October 1969 and was blamed by many Somalis and foreign observers for exacerbating clan tensions in this already fragile society, for ruining the economy, and for violating human rights on a wide scale, was forced to flee the capital, Mogadishu. Since that time, rival clan-based rebel groups—the Hawiye-based United Somali Congress (USC) and the Ogadeeni-based Somali Patriot Movement (SPM)—involved in the anti-Siad movement have fought each other over control of the capital and surrounding areas. To complicate matters, a Daarood-based Somali National Front (SNF) has emerged and informally aligned itself with the SPM against the USC-dominated "provisional" government established after Siad's defeat. Meanwhile, in the north the Isaaq-based Somali National Movement (SNM) has established its own administration and in May declared the Republic of Somalia—the secession of which would divide Somalia along the lines of the former colonial boundaries established by Great Britain and Italy at the end of the nineteenth century. According to some observers, the deteriorating situation makes Somalia "a total write-off" diplomatically and economically.

Meantime, by April the situation in Ethiopia had grown even more desperate for the central government since its military defeats at the hands of the Tigre People's Liberation Front (TPLF) and loss of the Eritrean port of Massawa to the Eritrean People's Liberation Front (EPLF) the previous year. On May 21, Lt. Col. Mengistu Haile Mariam, the strongman of the Ethiopian revolution since his bloody seizure of power in February 1977, resigned as president and fled to join his family already in Zimbabwe. Mengistu's fall was brought about by the failure of his economic policies, Moscow's strategic disengagement from the Horn of Africa, his failure to bring an end to the war in Eritrea, behind-the-scenes

U.S. pressure, and more important, by the forces of the Ethiopian People's Revolutionary Democratic Front (EPRDF)—a TPLF-dominated umbrella group—who had advanced to within fifty miles of Addis Ababa. Within a week after Mengistu's departure from Ethiopia, his successor, Tesfaye Dinka, surrendered the capital to the EPRDF and lost control of the government's last remaining strongholds in Eritrea to the EPLF—the provincial capital of Asmara and the southern port of Assab. With the EPRDF-dominated provisional government attempting to restore order in the capital and to alleviate the fears of the Amharas who see their traditional hold on power threatened and the country possibly dismembered; with the EPLF declaring its intention to hold a referendum on independence for Eritrea; and with the Oromo Liberation Front (OLF) clamoring for greater autonomy or independence for the Oromo-inhabited areas of the south, Ethiopia too may be on the verge of disintegration or perhaps renewed civil war between center and periphery.

These developments in the Horn, coupled with the presumed end of the cold war between Washington and Moscow, and the U.S.-led coalition war against Iraq in early 1991—in which the Horn of Africa played no significant strategic role—suggest that a four-decade-long era in which the United States used arms transfers to secure its security objectives in the Horn of Africa has come to an end. Unfortunately, that legacy is not so easily erased, as the internal struggles that continue in the Horn of Africa are fueled by billions of dollars' worth of U.S. and Soviet weapons imported over the past forty years. American policy makers, however, now claim that a new era has begun in which the United States will be primarily interested in promoting human rights, democracy, and stability in the Horn by relying upon economic development and humanitarian aid to the exclusion of arms transfers—or all but minimal security assistance. It seems appropriate, therefore, to provide an overview of why Ethiopia and Somalia were armed by the United States (and the Soviet Union), and to write, perhaps, the last chapter on this aspect of U.S. policy in the Horn of Africa.

Thus in this book I attempt to fill two gaps—one theoretical and the other historical. First, I propose a theoretical framework to explain the sources and games of influence in the arms relationships between great-power suppliers and small-power recipients. Second, I intend to provide a comprehensive case study of the internal and external forces that have shaped U.S. security relations with Ethiopia and Somalia over the past four decades. Although in recent years several perceptive books have been written dealing with U.S. policy in the Horn of Africa—Marina Ottaway, *Soviet Influence in the Horn of Africa* (1982); Harold Marcus, *Ethiopia, Great Britain, and the United States, 1941–1974* (1983); John Spencer,

Ethiopia at Bay (1984); David Korn, *Ethiopia, the United States, and the Soviet Union* (1986); Bereket Habte Selassie, *Conflict and Intervention in the Horn of Africa* (1980)—they have either been overtaken by events or their analysis was limited in scope. With few exceptions, most of the literature concerning U.S. policy in the Horn has tended to focus on U.S.-Ethiopian relations, particularly in the years 1974–1977, and devotes little attention to bureaucratic influences or the intrusion of Middle Eastern politics. On the other hand, while much has been written about the development of U.S.-Somali relations between 1977 and 1980, only Korn's *Ethiopia, the United States, and the Soviet Union* takes the story past this point. However, since the U.S.-Somali relationship is not the focal point of his book, Korn does not provide a complete analysis of U.S. policy toward Somalia. Thus *Arms for the Horn* intends to fill a number of historical and analytical gaps in the evolution of U.S.-Horn relations.

In studying the evolution of influence, one must focus on both the supplier and recipient side of an arms relationship. Obviously, there is a drawback in conducting research exclusively in the United States. While the sensitive political nature of this subject might have inhibited meaningful field research, I have attempted to overcome this problem through interviews and by using primary documents to gain an appreciation of the "Horn perspective." Of course, I am fully responsible for all the interpretations in this book.

I take this opportunity to thank many people who have provided guidance, insight, and support throughout this project. While they bear no responsibility for its weaknesses, it is no doubt a far stronger work because of their contributions.

Funding for the preparation of the book manuscript was provided by the University of Connecticut Research Foundation. The staff of the libraries at the University of Connecticut and at Yale University were always pleasant, willing, and able to find and procure documents for me. A Yale/Mellon Visiting Faculty Fellowship for 1987–1988 provided valuable research time and access to the declassified government documents collection housed at Yale University's Seeley Mudd Government Documents Center. During the year I spent at Yale, Bruce Russett was a most gracious host, and arranged for my participation in the International Security and Arms Control seminar. My continuing association with ISAC has proved stimulating, and this work has profited from these sessions.

Officials at the Department of State, Department of Defense, AID, and congressional committee staff members who must remain nameless generously took time from their busy schedules to speak with me. I thank them, along with many others who shared their knowledge and insights. I extend special appreciation to John Loughran, Edward Korry, Richard

Moose, Donald Paradis, and Arthur Richards, who welcomed me into their homes and spent several hours discussing their experiences.

I also extend my appreciation to several of my former professors and current colleagues who reviewed earlier versions of this manuscript. Larry Bowman, my friend and principal critic, introduced me to the Horn of Africa back in 1979. Garry Clifford taught me some of the tricks of the trade in doing historical research. Betty Hanson was instrumental in shaping the theoretical approach underlying this work. My colleagues in the Political Science and History departments at the University of Connecticut at Stamford, Estelle Feinstein, Joel Blatt, and Sarah Morehouse, were a great source of encouragement. Elise Seholster put the first draft on the word processor. Ray Blanchette prepared the maps and figure 1 in the appendix. The staff at the University of Connecticut at Stamford lent their services several times on short notice. Catherine Marshall and Jane Flanders at the University of Pittsburgh Press have patiently answered the naive questions of a novice and, along with the manuscript reviewer, to whom I owe a great debt of gratitude for identifying theoretical and substantive weaknesses, have together offered superb suggestions on how to translate a rough manuscript into a book. Jane Flanders deserves a special note of praise for her patience in allowing me to make this book as current as possible, despite the disruptions. Some of the material in chapters 3–6 appeared in "Donor Dependency and American Arms Transfers to the Horn of Africa: The F-5 Legacy," *Journal of Modern African Studies.*

Finally, it would not have been possible to complete this book without the love, support, and understanding of my family. My Aunt Adrienne was a great cheerleader along the way, as was my mother-in-law Lee Blom. My parents' excitement, continuous encouragement, and refreshing visits to Connecticut made this task much easier. Over the past year my wife Marina accomplished the unbelievable—giving birth to our daughter, graduating with honors from law school, passing the Connecticut bar exam, finding the energy to cheer me along, and jumping in on two occasions to help retype chapters that I had lost in the computer. Our daughter Alexandra made no constructive contribution to the completion of this project except to show great tolerance for her father's work at the word processor and to be a delightful source of distraction and inspiration. To those closest to me I have dedicated this book.

Arms for the Horn

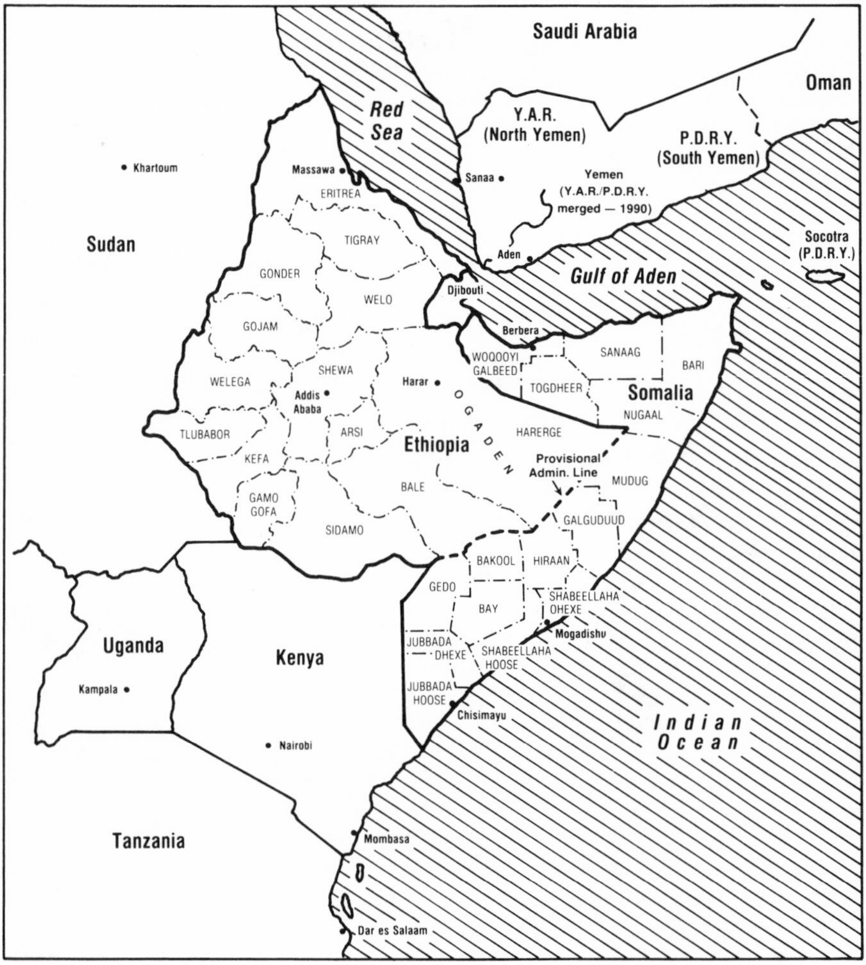

Map 1 The Horn of Africa

Introduction

Nothing is more essential than that permanent, inveterate antipathies against particular nations and passionate attachments for others should be excluded, and that in place of them just and amiable feelings toward all should be cultivated. The nation which indulges toward another an habitual hatred or an habitual fondness is in some degree a slave. It is a slave to its animosity or to its affection, either of which is sufficient to lead it astray from its duty and its interest.

—George Washington, Farewell Address, September 17, 1796

Foreign influence and the "variety of evils" it may produce has been an issue of concern to American leaders since the beginning of the republic. President Washington recommended in his Farewell Address that "the great rule of conduct for us in regard to foreign nations is, in extending our commercial relations to have with them as little *political* connection as possible."[1] Washington went on to warn that sympathy for a favorite nation might facilitate "the illusion of an imaginary common interest in cases where no real common interest exists" and lead the United States into "a participation in the quarrels and wars of the latter without adequate inducement or justification." Another inherent danger was posed by the "ambitious, corrupted, or deluded citizens [who devote themselves to the favorite nation] facility to betray or sacrifice the interests of their own country without odium, sometimes even with popularity." Many opportunities existed for foreign nations "to tamper with domestic factions, to practice the arts of seduction, to mislead public opinion, to influence or awe public councils!" Washington thus cautioned his fellow citizens to "steer clear of permanent alliances with any portion of the foreign world," and advised that "so far as we have already formed engagements let them be fulfilled with perfect good faith. Here let us stop."

Needless to say, since the end of the Second World War George Washington's advice has not been heeded. In 1947 the United States extended military assistance to Greece and Turkey under the aegis of the Truman

Doctrine. By the end of the 1940s the United States had tied itself to a collective defense organization (NATO) to defend Western Europe from communist (Soviet) aggression. During the 1950s U.S. foreign policy assumed a truly global dimension as the United States not only joined in establishing collective defense organizations in regions outside of the Western Hemisphere, but also began to supply military and economic assistance to small and weak countries in the Far East, Africa, and the Middle East.

Whether or not the United States has overextended itself via the numerous political-military commitments it has concluded since the end of the Second World War is not the subject under scrutiny here. Rather, the takeoff point for my analysis draws its inspiration from the great prescience President Washington exhibited in warning about the danger and manner in which foreign powers with whom the United States developed political-military relations would attempt to influence U.S. foreign policy. More specifically, I seek to explore and add a corollary to Washington's depiction of influence in great power-small power relations. After citing the many dangers arising from entangling alliances Washington observed that "such an attachment of a small or weak toward a great and powerful nation dooms the former to be the satellite of the latter." What he neglects to mention is that the very same forces might also subordinate a great and powerful nation to do the bidding of a small or weak nation.

Thus, this is a study about *influence* and how it is wielded in a great power supplier–small power recipient arms transfer relationship. The protagonists starring in this bargaining game of influence are the United States in the role of the great power arms patron and the governments of Ethiopia and Somalia, alternatively, in the role of America's small and weak Third World arms client. What makes the question of influence so intriguing and perplexing in the case of U.S.-Horn relations is that here in Africa's northeast corner reside two of the world's poorest, yet most heavily armed states in the African continent. For more than a quarter century Ethiopia and Somalia have been locked in a cycle of violence that has made the Horn of Africa one of the world's "hot spots."[2] Despite the tragedy of having two countries that can least afford it wasting their scarce resources acquiring weapons and dealing with security problems, over the past four decades Ethiopia and Somalia have received American weapons, spare parts, ammunition, and military training valued at almost $1 billion. Moreover, Soviet arms transfers to Mogadishu and Addis Ababa during just the past two decades have totaled more than $11 billion.[3] This analysis will seek to explain why the United States has transferred military resources and various types of sophisticated weaponry to Ethiopia and Somalia as well as identify the main determinants that have shaped arms negotiations between Washington and its two primary arms clients in the Horn of Africa.

ARMS, INFLUENCE, AND DEPENDENCE

The question of "who influences whom" in a great power–small power arms partnership has been a subject of much debate among scholars, analysts, and government officials for more than two decades. Government proponents, who favor using arms transfers to secure relations between two countries, claim that because both supplier and recipient benefit from this "voluntary" exchange of arms for military-political-economic assets, influence is exerted in a benign fashion.[4] Third World and "radical left" critics argue that arms transfers create a form of client dependence and allow the imperialist Western powers to manipulate and exploit the vulnerable and dependent nations of the Third World.[5] At the end of the 1960s "revisionist" critics affected by the U.S. experience in Vietnam and later dealings with the state of Israel began writing about the "big influence of small allies," "the limits of power," and "reverse leverage," suggesting that arms transfers created a supplier-recipient relationship characterized by donor dependence in which arms clients are able to manipulate and force their patrons to accept undesirable costs or risks.[6] Still others, in noting the trend toward increasing global interdependence, believe that the diffusion of arms to the Third World has been accompanied by a diffusion of influence as well, infusing a quality of mutual dependence that allows both partners to exert influence over the other at a given time.[7] Despite the different conclusions drawn by these models, they do seem to agree that an inverse relationship exists between influence and dependence—as one's relative dependence upon an arms partner increases (or decreases), one's relative influence decreases (or increases).

Influence in supplier-recipient relations becomes important as the result of the inherent competition that arises when two parties seek to maximize benefits and minimize costs and risks.[8] But this is not a static relationship. The relative influence or dependence of each partner is fluid and may shift over time, thereby affecting bargaining outcomes.[9] Arms relationships might be envisioned as in constant flux, moving along a continuum between the two extremes of supplier-dependence and recipient-dependence. Thus, two key questions need to be explored: (1) What are the determinants of supplier and recipient dependence? and (2) What strategies are used by arms partners to translate their relative bargaining strength into influence?

THE MANIPULATION OF WEAKNESS

One bargaining strategy used by arms partners involves the manipulation of weakness. Weakness in this context is derived from a state's perception of external and internal threats, the value of strategic, political, and economic assets offered by its partner, and the vested interests of domestic actors in maintaining a stable partnership. Whereas the "balance of interests" model of conflict resolution confers the bargaining advantage upon the player for whom the stakes (interests) are relatively greater, and is motivated therefore to accept risks and costs shunned by its opponent, the opposite situation seems to pertain in supplier-recipient relations.[10] Interests and threats are sources of bargaining weakness. To the extent that one arms partner requires the services or assets of the other, it is vulnerable to manipulation.

A first source of weakness and vulnerability arises from the need to respond to a real or perceived threat. A great power supplier may feel compelled to transfer arms on less than ideal terms in order to deter, contain, or roll back the attempted intrusions of international rivals seeking to usurp their interests in a client state or in the surrounding region. A recipient who is confronted by hostile neighbors or internal insurrection may accept a less than optimal arms package, sacrifice other interests, or make humiliating concessions so as to keep a potentially critical weapons pipeline open or to avoid antagonizing a great-power benefactor whose extended deterrent protection services might be needed in the near future. The manipulation of weakness in this context involves playing upon the fears of the other country.[11] Thus, a first hypothesis might read that a state's relative influence and ability to manipulate and exploit the weakness of its partner increases (or decreases) as the threat perception of its arms partner increases (or decreases).

A second source of weakness that may be manipulated concerns the value of the assets involved in the quid pro quo exchange between supplier and recipient.[12] A great-power supplier may be willing to pay a high price in the form of military assistance to acquire and maintain access to military bases situated near maritime choke points, resource-rich countries or other strategic locations. Likewise, a recipient may compromise certain interests in order to appease a supplier who can provide desired quantities and various types of sophisticated weapons, or is capable of transferring arms on favorable financial terms, or has demonstrated a willingness to bring its political and military assets to bear in defense of a client's interests. The manipulation of weakness strategy also involves a bit of "look what I can do for you" posturing. Thus, a second hypothesis is that a state's relative influence and ability to manipulate weakness increases (or decreases) as the perceived value of its assets rise (or fall).

A third source of vulnerability arises from the vested interests of influential domestic actors (individuals, groups, and institutions) who define and perceive threats as well as determine the value of the other country's assets.[13] These assessments are often affected by considerations that have little or nothing to do with objective strategic reality. For a multitude of reasons—including the enhancement of personal power and prestige, maintaining control over an unstable political system, attachments built on moral, ethnic, religious, or ideological grounds, the need to appease or impress domestic interest groups, public opinion, or foreign governments, to maintain international credibility, or as the outcome of the implementation of bureaucratic missions and SOPs—influential actors who can significantly affect the decision-making process might oppose policies that threaten to antagonize an arms partner.[14] In short, they have a vested interest in avoiding the disruption or destabilization of relations.[15] These actors, in effect, serve as foreign advocates and undermine the influence of their own government by exerting pressure to meet the demands of an arms partner. Thus, a third hypothesis might suggest that a state's relative influence and ability to manipulate weakness is enhanced (or diminished) where there exist influential domestic actors in the partner state who advocate (or oppose) its cause.

A state may manipulate the weakness of an arms partner by (1) playing upon a partner's fear of a menacing external or internal environment, (2) threatening to impose sanctions or jeopardize access to valued assets, and/or (3) exploiting the services of domestic factions in the partner state to advocate one's cause. However, this strategy does carry certain risks. In particular, the game board may change as threats may recede, alternatives emerge, or interests change. Nonetheless, given the fact that suppliers and recipients share a basic interest, which may vary in intensity, in maintaining the arms connection, the manipulation of weakness will remain a valued bargaining strategy for both partners.

THE THREAT OF DEFECTION

A second strategy used by arms partners to influence bargaining outcomes involves the threat of defection. The ability to threaten defection or to secure valued assets from a third party is a function of time pressures, the availability of viable alternatives, and the willingness of domestic actors to execute such a threat. In contrast to balance-of-power theory, which contends that increasing power reduces constraints and consequently enhances a state's capacity to affect international outcomes, the ability to threaten defection to a third party has less to do with increasing power than with the reduction of constraints.[16] A great power, for example, may have less flexibility or room to maneuver than a small and weak power because of greater constraints on its behavior imposed by external conditions and internal forces.[17] To the extent that a state can make a viable and credible threat of defection, its relative dependence is diminished and influence increased vis-à-vis its arms partner.

A first constraint that may limit a state's ability to make a threat of defection is related to the immediacy of a threat. "Crisis behavior" theory suggests that as the time frame for making a critical decision contracts, actors may assume risks or accept consequences they would typically avoid under less pressured circumstances.[18] A supplier confronted by an immediate threat to its regional interests or position of predominance in a client state may feel coerced into transferring military resources on less than desired terms. Likewise, a recipient state faced with similar circumstances might wish to avoid the logistical problems associated with changing arms partners in the midst of a crisis or war.[19] Although a crisis atmosphere may in fact prompt a desperate arms partner to make such a threat, in and of itself, the immediacy of response required by the burdened state does not necessarily make the *enactment* of the threat viable or believable. Thus, a first hypothesis might read that a state's relative influence and capacity to enact (rather than make) a threat of defection decreases (or increases) where threats are immediate (or latent).

The time-frame problem is intimately linked to a second constraint that directly affects the viability of a threat of defection: the availability of alternatives. Valued assets of an arms partner may be replaced in part or in full by outside parties.[20] Arms suppliers may in fact attempt to diminish their dependence upon any one recipient by developing redundant assets and capabilities in a particular region.[21] Recipients, on the other hand, may seek to diversify their sources of supply in order to decrease their dependence upon and vulnerability to actions taken by suppliers.[22] Thus, a second hypothesis to be proposed under this model is that a state's relative influence and capacity to make a viable threat of defection increases (or decreases) as the number of potential alternative partners offering comparable assets increases (or decreases).

A third constraint affecting the use of a threat of defection involves those internal actors who define the parameters of choice.[23] For the threat of defection to be effective as a weapon of influence it must be credible. It is made credible by the presence of positive and/or negative countervailing pressures in the form of influential individuals, groups, or institutions within the manipulating state.[24] There must be advocates willing to make the case for defecting to another partner, and/or advocates opposed to the terms of the current arms relationship. Essentially, these countervailing forces ensure that the internal debate is not one-sided, and therefore one partner cannot take the other for granted. Thus, a third and final hypothesis is that a state's relative influence and the credibility of a threat of defection will be enhanced (or diminished) by the presence (or absence) of countervailing domestic pressures within its own political system.

The threat of defection is a rather crude and blunt bargaining strategy in which one partner threatens to terminate the exchange of its valued assets to the other and to offer them to a third party willing to meet its demands or play by its rules. This strategy places arms partners in a chilling game of "chicken" or "called bluff," which may leave a very bitter taste in the mouth of the loser.[25] The threat of defection carries several risks that may ultimately backfire and defeat the long-term purpose of this strategy: (1) a state constantly being threatened by the defection of its partner may seek out a new and more dependent supplier or recipient; (2) one's partner may tire of dealing with this threat and opt out of the relationship entirely, thereby forcing the manipulator to carry through with the threat of defection and perhaps be thrust into a more dependent relationship vis-à-vis its new partner; or (3) potential alternative partners who observe this manipulative behavior may decide they do not want to be victimized in the same way. Assuming that states do learn from their own experience and observed experiences of others, the threat of defection should be used sparingly; otherwise it may lose its impact.[26]

SUMMARY: THE SUPPLIER-RECIPIENT BARGAINING MODEL

The supplier-recipient bargaining model, which I will apply to the study of influence in American arms relations in the Horn of Africa, involves two different, though complementary strategies: the manipulation of weakness and the threat of defection. From these two bargaining strategies flow six fundamental questions that will shape the organization and conclusions of this foreign policy analysis. Three questions that fall under the manipulation of weakness strategy will be asked of each partner. (1) Is the external environment perceived as high-risk or threatening? (2) Are the assets being obtained from the arms exchange unique or of high value? (3) Are there influential domestic actors who wish to avoid disruption in the relationship?

Each partner will also be asked three questions derived from the hypotheses developed under the threat of defection strategy. (1) Is the external threat deemed to be immediate or latent? (2) Do viable alternatives exist?

(3) Are there influential domestic actors who will support actions that may cause disruption in the relationship?

The above hypotheses and questions will provide the organizational framework for ten case studies of influence in U.S.-Horn arms bargaining; six cases involve the United States and Ethiopia between 1953 and 1977, and four involve the United States and Somalia between 1977 and 1990. Ideally, the six questions identified as critical to the manipulation of weakness and threat of defection bargaining strategies will prove applicable not only in the case of U.S.-Horn relations, but in any given supplier-recipient arms relationship. This analysis will begin in part I with an overview of the arms transfers policy setting in the United States (chapter 1) and the Horn of Africa (chapter 2). Part II will present the six case studies involving key decision points in the U.S.-Ethiopia arms relationship (chapters 3–8). Part III will pick up the story with an analysis of the four case studies pertaining to U.S.-Somalia arms transfer and security questions (chapters 9–12). My conclusion will explore the usefulness of this supplier-recipient model and what it portends for the future of U.S. arms transfers to the Horn of Africa in light of recent developments.

I

U.S.-Horn Security Calculations

1

U.S. Security Calculation in the Horn of Africa

Arms transfers have generally been considered a highly accurate barometer of U.S. interest in a particular recipient state and region of the world.[1] Perhaps even more so than in the case of FMS cash arms sales, the levels of military resources distributed under the aegis of what is now entitled the Security Assistance Program (SAP) provide a gauge of U.S. interests in dealing with recipient states dependent upon American largesse.[2] Because there are limited financial resources available to meet the security needs and arms demands of the many claimant states, difficult decisions must be made as to who gets how big a slice of the American security assistance pie.[3] The particular types of weapons the U.S. government is willing to provide to an arms recipient also reveals where American interests lie. Both of these considerations will be used to assess the state of U.S. foreign relations in the Horn of Africa.

From 1953 until the termination of the U.S.-Ethiopia military relationship in 1977, Addis Ababa stood at the top of Washington's arms client list for sub-Sahara Africa. During this time the United States provided Ethiopia with over $185 million worth of grant military assistance, approved $36 million in FMS financing credits, concluded FMS cash agreements valued at about $135 million, and spent approximately $22 million training 3,912 Ethiopian military personnel.[4] The fact that Addis Ababa's portion amounted to approximately 0.5 percent of Washington's worldwide security assistance budget for the same period is a poignant statement of Ethiopia's perceived global marginality. But Ethiopia's importance within the Africa regional context is highlighted by the fact that between 1953 and 1977 Addis Ababa received over 80 percent of the Military Assistance Program (MAP), more than 55 percent of the International Military Education and Training Program (IMETP), and about one-fifth of Foreign Military Sales (FMS) financing funds allocated to sub-Sahara Africa.[5] Ethiopia also accounted for approximately one-third of FMS cash arms transfers approved by Washington for Africa.[6] Even with the proliferation of American security assistance programs throughout the African continent during the 1960s and 1970s, more than 45 percent of total U.S. arms transfers to sub-Sahara Africa were designated for Ethiopia.[7]

Although Washington's security assistance investment in Somalia over the past ten years has been significantly larger in absolute terms than in Ethiopia, in relative terms the totals have remained about the same. Through the fall of 1989, when the U.S. Congress forced the suspension of military aid to Mogadishu, the United States had provided Somalia with just under $370 million in security assistance, which included approximately $128 million in MAP funds, $175 million in Economic Support Funds (ESF), $60 million via FMS financing, and about $7.5 million for the IMET program to train almost 400 Somali military students.[8] Washington also approved more than $200 million in FMS cash arms agreements, bringing total arms transfers over this ten-year period above the half-billion dollar mark.[9] In terms of the bigger scheme Mogadishu was perceived in much the same light as Addis Ababa, receiving approximately 0.6 percent of U.S. security assistance funds distributed worldwide. But, unlike Ethiopia, which maintained a steady place at the top of Washington's MAP list for Africa, Somalia's ranking among sub-Sahara Africa SAP recipients moved from fourth (1980–1985) to first in 1986 before falling behind Kenya and being practically banished from the list in 1989. Mogadishu's portion of the regional security assistance pie remained at about 10 percent between 1980 and 1987 and then rose to 20–25 percent—during a time of significant cutbacks in SAP funding levels for sub-Sahara Africa—before the aid suspension.[10] With U.S. arms transfers to the African continent being more widely and evenly distributed today than in the past, American dependence upon Somalia would on the surface appear to be less than it was in the case of Ethiopia.

That Ethiopia and Somalia have not enjoyed the status and privileges afforded to American arms clients such as Israel, Saudi Arabia, and Iran under the shah is further proved by Washington's desire to place not only quantitative restrictions, but qualitative limits on the types and technological sophistication of weapon systems transferred to the Horn.[11] An important part of the story underlying U.S.-Ethiopia military relations involved attempts by Emperor Haile Selassie and the Provisional Military Administrative Council (PMAC) to acquire state-of-the-art American weapons. The U.S.-Somalia security relationship has been framed by Washington's refusal to provide offensive weaponry to Mogadishu. Thus, conflict between the United States and its arms clients in the Horn of Africa has assumed a qualitative as well as a quantitative dimension.

Despite the second-class treatment accorded to Ethiopia and Somalia by the United States, American political-military support has been responsible to a considerable extent for turning them into formidable African powers. For some three and a half decades, U.S. policy makers ascribed to the Horn of Africa a level of political-military value that was used to justify the transfer of approximately $1 billion worth of military equipment, support, and training to the governments of Ethiopia and Somalia. What needs to be explored further is the operative policy setting in which the United States bargained with its arms clients and made critical arms transfer decisions. It appears that Washington's dependence upon, or its vulnerability to manipulation and threats of defection in the conduct of foreign relations with Addis Ababa and Mogadishu has been shaped over the long term by (1) American perceptions of global and regional geopolitical threats, (2) the desire to maintain a military presence in what was viewed as a strategic, but unstable corner of the world, and (3) the intersecting and conflicting interests of domestic actors.

GLOBAL AND REGIONAL GEOPOLITICAL THREATS

If presented with a blank map of the world from which to select geopolitical targets of opportunity, American defense planners would automatically stick a pin in the Horn of Africa.[12] The Horn's location at the southern end of the Red Sea, near the Strait of Bab al-Mandab, and across from the Arabian Peninsula, provides a prime spot from which to project power and provide rear area support for military intervention in the Middle East and the Persian Gulf. The strategic analyst J. Bowyer Bell neatly summarized how the U.S. national security establishment has viewed the Horn of Africa throughout the post–World War II period: "The basic strategic importance of the Horn is not the presence of copper deposits, the fate of democracy, or the future of the Ethiopian monarchy; it is simple geography."[13] Thus, challenges to the United States in the Horn of Africa do not pose direct, but indirect threats to vital U.S. interests lying offshore and across the Red Sea in the Arabian Peninsula. American policy makers have feared that a hostile takeover of the Horn of Africa would enhance the capability of Washington's global or regional rivals to (1) destabilize important pro-Western governments in the Middle East and northeast Africa, (2) interrupt commercial shipping lanes leading out of the Indian Ocean to the West, and (3) cut off Western access to Middle Eastern oil.

For reasons of geography mixed with cold war rationales, the United States has taken threats to stability and America's tenure in the Horn very seriously. The Horn of Africa is located along the two primary shipping routes that link the Persian Gulf, South Asia, and Southeast Asia with the

United States and Western Europe: (1) the Suez Canal route, whereby commerce from these Indian Ocean regions must pass near Somalia's coastline, maneuver through the Strait of Bab al-Mandab, and proceed through the Red Sea, paralleling Ethiopia's coast for some 600 miles on its way north to the Suez Canal before entering the Mediterranean Sea; and (2) the Cape route, whereby commerce must cross the Gulf of Aden and pass near the Somali coast on its way south around the South African cape to the Atlantic Ocean. Its position along the Red Sea also involves the region in the geopolitics of the Middle East and Africa, whereby in certain contingencies the Horn could serve as a staging site for military intervention in neighboring states. A less talked about and appreciated aspect of the Horn of Africa's geopolitical history and potential is its use as a regrouping and rear staging area for a counterinvasion of Europe, à la World War II.[14] The area's geostrategic significance is further magnified by analysts who project that by the mid-1990s more oil will be exported from the Red Sea than from the Persian Gulf.[15] Worst-case scenarios based upon these considerations, therefore, have affected Washington's calculation of threat in the Horn.

Since the beginning of the cold war, the Soviet Union has been viewed as posing the most dangerous geopolitical threat to U.S. global and regional interests.[16] The notion that the Soviet Union was an ideologically motivated, expansionistic power was used to justify American efforts to preempt, deter, and combat the expansion of Soviet influence worldwide.[17] As a consequence of the U.S. policy of containment, the United States has proved most sensitive to the perceived Soviet threat in the Horn. What should be noted, however, is that American perceptions of the degree of threat posed by the Soviet Union have not remained constant and have produced sharp disagreements within the U.S. foreign policy–making community.

American-Soviet competition in the Third World, and its effect upon U.S. threat perceptions in the Horn of Africa, has moved through at least six phases. Between 1946 and 1955, with cold war competition centered in Europe, the Far East, and the Northern Tier of the Middle East, the Soviet threat in the Horn appeared low-level and latent. Although U.S. regional perceptions of threat were heightened following the conclusion of the Soviet-Egyptian arms deal in the fall of 1955, the Soviets were not viewed as serious competitors for influence in the Horn. After another shock occurred in 1963, when Moscow concluded an arms deal with Mogadishu, differences emerged between Washington and the U.S. embassy in Mogadishu on the one hand and the U.S. embassy in Ethiopia over the nature of the threat posed by the Soviet position in Somalia.

American threat perceptions continued to diverge as the result of the massive Soviet-sponsored arms buildup that began in Somalia in 1972, coupled with Russian military construction activities at the Somali port of Berbera, at a time that the United States was pursuing a policy of global détente with the Soviet Union. Subsequently, Soviet and Cuban intervention on the side of Ethiopia during the 1977–1978 Ogaden War in the Horn caused some within the U.S. national security bureaucracy to raise the alarm of an immediate and dangerous Soviet threat, with most of the others coming over to their way of thinking following the USSR's invasion of Afghanistan in December 1979. Finally, since early 1989, in light of the Russian troop withdrawal from Afghanistan, agreement on the disengagement of Cuban troops from Angola and decreasing Soviet involvement in Ethiopia, the Soviet threat to U.S. interests in the Third World appears to be on the wane.

While the Soviet factor has remained a constant in Washington's risk calculation and arms transfers policy equation for the Horn, it has varied in strength and impact. A rough correlation has seemed to exist between U.S. perceptions of threat regarding the Soviet Union at the global level and assessments of the Soviet threat in the Third World.[18] Unstable relations between the two superpowers at the global level have raised the stakes at the regional level. Conversely, a stable U.S.-Soviet global relationship has reduced Washington's incentive to become involved in superpower bidding wars in the Third World.

A secondary challenge to the United States has been the threat from what have been perceived as anti-Western forces operating in the Middle East and northeast Africa.[19] As in the case of the global superpower rivalry, the perceived threat posed by these regional actors has fluctuated over time. At various times between 1955 and 1970 the Egyptian leader Gamal Nasser sought to undermine U.S. influence in the Middle East and the Horn of Africa. In the 1980s the Reagan administration came to view Libya's Muammar Qaddafi as America's archnemesis in northeast Africa. A battle of words and nerves began with the Islamic Republic of Iran in 1979, though it has dissipated somewhat since the death of the Ayatollah Khomeini in 1989.

At the beginning of the 1990s, Iraq emerged as the newest challenger to U.S. regional interests. In January 1991 the United States went to war against Iraq, whose August 1990 invasion of Kuwait was viewed as threatening Western oil supplies and disrupting Washington's proposed post–cold war international order. Until the war with Iraq, this regional challenge to American policy was viewed as occurring at a lower level of potential conflict than that posed by the Soviet Union. West bloc and East bloc arms transfers, however, had turned some countries such as Iraq into formidable regional military powers who can engage in more than harassing activities.

Due to the zero-sum nature of the superpower rivalry, the Soviet threat has generally been given greater weight in the American security calculation. In contrast, regional challenges have been viewed as more limited in scope, presumed easier to handle, and void of broader ramifications that might prove detrimental to U.S. interests elsewhere in the world. Moreover, American policy makers have often tended to assume, and wrongly so, that regional challengers to U.S. interests are simply acting as agents for Moscow rather than independently out of their own concerns.[20] Thus, while the "fire in Washington's belly" has been stirred by the shenanigans of regional antagonists, the United States has proved even more susceptibe to manipulation by the invocation of the Soviet threat.

MILITARY BASES, REGIONAL CONFLICT, AND STRATEGIC REDUNDANCY

Because U.S. arms transfers to the Horn of Africa have been motivated almost exclusively by geopolitical considerations, framed by the global threat posed by the Soviet Union and the lower-level threat identified with radical anti-Western regional forces, Washington's overriding strategic objective has been to acquire and maintain the capability to respond to any military contingency that may threaten U.S. interests in the Middle East, northeast Africa, and the Red Sea arenas. In pursuing its objectives overseas, the United States established intelligence-gathering and power projection facilities in strategic areas throughout the globe. In the case of the Horn, U.S. political-military relations with the governments of Ethiopia and Somalia were based almost exclusively upon Washington's interest in having access to military facilities in the Red Sea region. For twenty-five years the Kagnew communications station located in Ethiopia's northeast province of Eritrea served as the driving force behind U.S. arms transfers to Ethiopia; over the past decade, an agreement granting the United States access to Somali military facilities, most notably the port and airfield at Berbera, provided the incentive for Washington to maintain a military relationship with Mogadishu. The quid pro quo (arms-for-base-access) arrangements arrived at with Addis Ababa and Mogadishu emphasizes that, in the eyes of U.S. defense planners, the principal assets these countries have to offer the United States are geostrategic.

Washington's strategic dependence and its capacity to maneuver for position in the Red Sea arena has been constrained over the years by two regional rivalries: (1) the Ethiopian-Somali conflict, and (2) the Arab-Israeli conflict. In the first instance, the experience of outside powers, who have attempted to gain and consolidate a position of influence in the Horn of Africa over the past three decades, suggests that one cannot be friends with both Ethiopia and Somalia. Those who wish to meddle in the affairs of the Horn must be prepared to choose sides. Addis Ababa and Mogadishu demanded complete fidelity from their primary arms suppliers, who were viewed as holding the key resource (weapons) affecting the ultimate outcome of their dispute. Suppliers resisting, or refusing to adhere to this rule of expected behavior found their stays of residence abruptly terminated. Thus, American as well as Soviet freedom to maneuver between Addis Ababa and Mogadishu was constrained by this regional rivalry.

Despite the Horn of Africa's location at the southern end of the Red Sea, the Arab-Israeli conflict at the northern end of this strategic waterway has continually intruded upon the politics of the area. Seven of the nine states that line the Red Sea—Egypt, Saudi Arabia, Jordan, Yemen (formerly the Yemen Arab Republic [YAR], and the People's Democratic Republic of Yemen [PDRY] which merged in May 1990), Djibouti, Sudan, and Somalia—identify themselves with the Arab/Islamic world.[21] Israel and Ethiopia are seen as outcasts who have found themselves under siege by hostile Arab neighbors and have cooperated with each other at different times over the years.[22] The United States, in turn, has tried to avoid being forced to choose between these two rival camps.

Washington's freedom to maneuver within the Red Sea region has been subject to the fluctuations between antagonistic confrontation and more muted or peaceful competition the United States has experienced in its relations with the leading Arab states, most particularly Egypt.[23] In the immediate post–World War II period, and up until the time of the political falling out between Washington and Cairo in 1955, American relations with the Arab world as a whole were generally quite cordial, in spite of Washington's diplomatic support for the state of Israel. The perceived challenge to American Middle East policies presented by Gamal Nasser's Arab nationalist ideology and the radical overthrow of pro-Western governments in Syria and Iraq in the second half of the 1950s, gave way during the early 1960s to a less hostile and, in some respects, more cooperative relationship. But the antagonism resurfaced, in a more intense form, and more strongly, after the June 1967 Arab-Israeli War; it was exacerbated by the Johnson administration's wholehearted embrace of Israel, coupled with the growing Soviet role in the Middle East. Then in the aftermath of the October 1973 war and termination of the Arab oil embargo against the West, a certain moderation in policies occurred both in Washington and in some Arab capitals. By the end of the 1970s, several of Washington's former antagonists in the Arab world were openly aligning themselves politically and militarily with the United States. Thus, the Middle East conflict has produced roughly two thematic periods for U.S. policy toward the Horn of Africa: (1) the pre-1973 period in which the United States had only the Ethiopian and Israeli security options in the Red Sea area; and (2) the post-1973 period in which Arab options in the region became available to Washington.

The Red Sea is undoubtedly one of the most politically volatile regions of the world. Given the unpredictability of how internal and external events will affect this arena, the wisdom of not putting all of one's eggs (in this case, basing one's strategic policy) in one basket seems apropos. Worst-case analysis leads a power such as the United States, therefore, to attempt to develop strategic redundancy in such an unstable and unpredictable region. But the international conflicts and internal turmoil, which have created opportunities for political-military penetration by external powers, also have limited U.S. options and policy flexibility, either because Washington has been forced to choose sides in a dispute, or because there are no viable alternatives.

However one views the acceptability or unacceptability of certain foreign political-military entanglements—in the case of the Horn of Africa, for example, one's preference for Ethiopia or Somalia—the question still must be asked whether the United States' strategic dependence on either one can be reduced by exploiting opportunities elsewhere in the region. By cultivating a strategic relationship with other states in the area, Washington may attempt to circumvent the Ethiopia-Somalia conflict and, thereby, reduce its strategic dependence. While the United States has never been completely isolated or dependent upon a single state along the Red Sea littoral, Washington's position has been at times quite precarious.[24] Ideally, U.S. defense planners would like to rim the world's sea lanes, and most particularly "choke points," with an American presence and to prop up pro-Western governments for purposes of deterrence and political preemption.[25] Thus, in assessing Washington's political-military relations with the governments of Ethiopia and Somalia, it is important to bear in mind the broader context of the U.S. strategic position throughout the entire Red Sea region as well as near the waterway's southern entrance at the Bab al-Mandab.

Given Washington's primary strategic interest in securing access to military bases in Ethiopia and Somalia, there were several issues American policy makers had to confront in maintaining a presence in the Red Sea region. First, in trading arms for military bases, was the United States contributing to the volatility of the Horn? Second, was an American

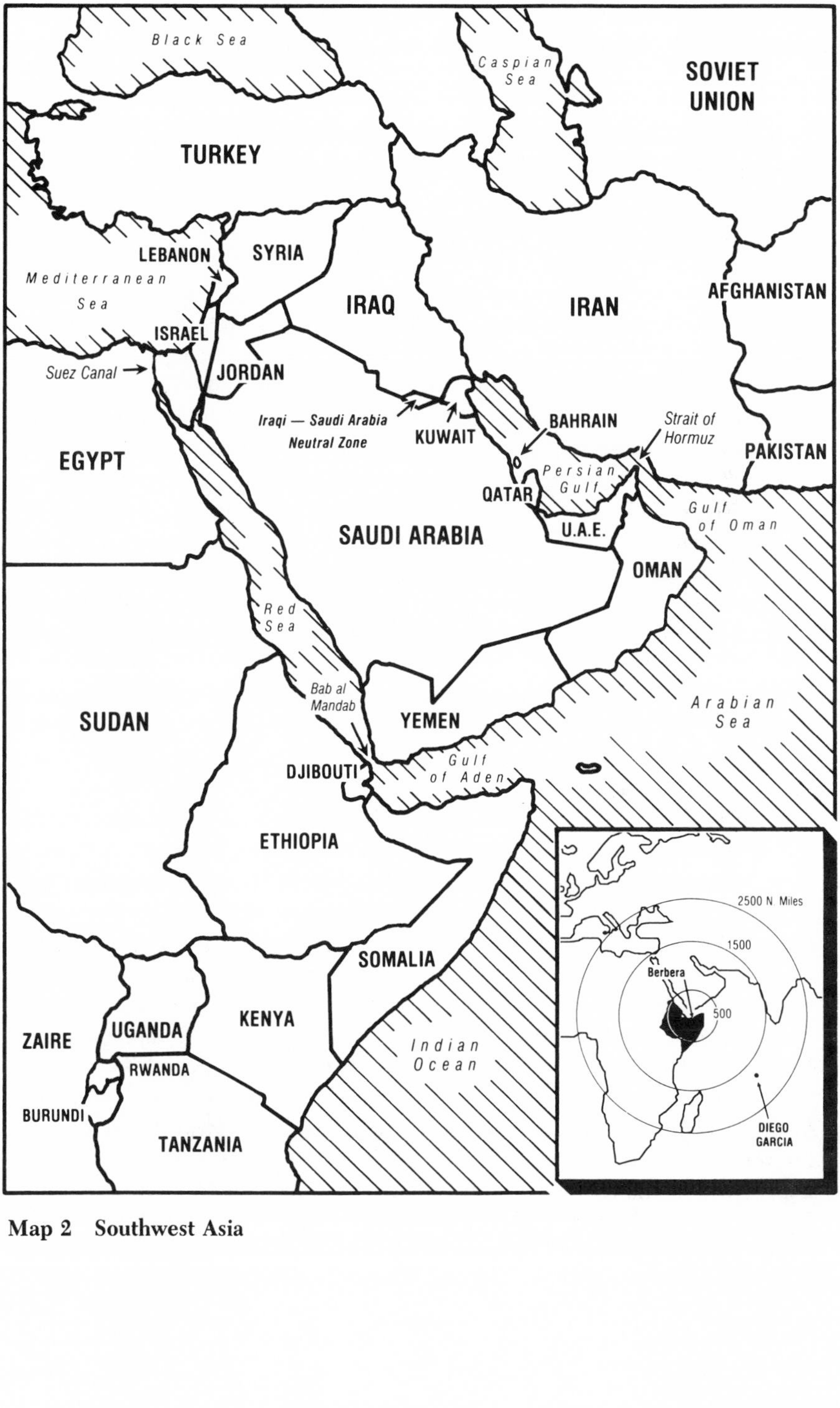

Map 2 Southwest Asia

strategic presence in either Ethiopia or Somalia necessary to maintain a high-profile deterrent, quick-response capability, particularly for military operations at the southern end of the Red Sea or intervention in the Middle East? Third, would it be possible to maintain a positive political relationship with Ethiopia and Somalia simultaneously? Finally, could the formulation of American security policy in the Horn of Africa be screened from the Arab-Israeli conflict and global superpower competition?

DOMESTIC INTERESTS AND PERSPECTIVES

To an extent not found in certain other areas of U.S. foreign policy, the formulation of American policy toward the Horn of Africa has been left largely in the hands of the permanent bureaucracy of the U.S. government. Long-term U.S. interests in the Horn have been shaped by bureaucratic concerns rather than political concerns. Elected officials in Washington have not considered the development of expertise or the expenditure of time and resources on the affairs of the Horn an adequate basis on which to build a political career. Instead, White House and congressional interest and intervention in the formulation of U.S. arms transfer policy toward the Horn of Africa has been indirect, sporadic, and short-lived. The U.S. national security bureaucracy has, for long periods, operated in a political vacuum left by Congress and the White House; as a result, the content and conduct of U.S. policy in the Horn has been largely controlled by mid-level and lower-level officials in the American foreign policy bureaucracy who are guided by institutional operating procedures, rather than by personal or political loyalties and beliefs.

PRESIDENTIAL PRIORITIES

Constitutionally the president of the United States is the pivotal actor in U.S. foreign policy decision making. Because the political life of a president is relatively short, there is a propensity to leave the presidential mark in the field of foreign relations through the enunciation of broad policy guidelines, or doctrines bearing a president's name—the Monroe, Truman, Eisenhower, Nixon, Carter, and Reagan doctrines, and George Bush's "new world order." But presidents may have a more subtle impact on U.S.-bilateral relations through their personal interaction with foreign leaders.[26] U.S. diplomatic interaction in the Horn of Africa presents an interesting case in point where stability and disruption in U.S.-Ethiopia and U.S.-Somalia relations has been partly the result of the existence, or nonexistence, of a personal rapport between the occupant of the Oval Office and the leaders of these two states.

In the case of U.S.-Ethiopia relations, personal relationships between the heads of state have existed at two extremes. During Haile Selassie's forty-four-year reign as emperor, he met with five of the eight men who occupied the Oval Office—Franklin Roosevelt at the Suez Conference in early 1945, Dwight Eisenhower in May 1954, John Kennedy in October 1963, Lyndon Johnson in February 1967, and Richard Nixon in July 1969 and again in May 1973.[27] Presidential relations with Selassie's ultimate successor, Mengistu Haile Mariam and other top-ranking members of the Ethiopian government, have been virtually nonexistent. Thus, the 1974 Ethiopian revolution not only eliminated Emperor Selassie and his advisers, but also destroyed the thin personal bond of friendship that existed between Washington and Addis Ababa, and which to date has not been rekindled. The Bush administration, however, did seem to be setting U.S.-Ethiopia relations on the right track, as high-ranking U.S. officials met with the leader of the EPRDF provisional government, Meles Zenawi, in 1990 and again in 1991 while brokering a change in Ethiopia's government and the end of the civil war.

White House relations with individual Somali leaders have moved along a much more bumpy path. Fifteen months after John Kennedy had welcomed Somalia's Prime Minister Ali Shermaarke to Washington in November 1962, the Somali leadership accused the United States of playing a "sinister" role in the Horn of Africa when fighting broke out along the Ethiopian-Somali border in early 1964.[28] The next U.S.-Somalia heads of state meeting did not occur until March 1968 when Premier Ibrahim Egal met and dined at the White House with Lyndon Johnson. Another fourteen years would lapse before a Somali leader would be personally greeted by an American president. Jimmy Carter's attempt at the beginning of his presidency to establish a personal relationship with Siad Barre fell victim to the outbreak of war in the Ogaden between Ethiopia and Somalia in the summer of 1977. It was not until March 1982, a year and a half after the U.S.-Somalia arms-for-access agreement was concluded, that President Barre traveled to the United States and met with President Reagan for the first and only direct contact between the American and Somali heads of state since the 1969 military coup d'état in Mogadishu. Given the confusion in Somalia since the overthrow of Siad, no one is quite sure whom to deal with in Mogadishu.

American presidents, with few exceptions, have shown little inclination to gain a better understanding of, or devote more time to, issues involving the Horn of Africa. There are several reasons for this, including (1) the African arena's ranking at the bottom of Washington's foreign policy priority list, (2) the absence of a strong and vocal domestic constituency, (3) the fact that none of the past or current leaders of Ethiopia and Somalia has attained the international stature of the Ethiopian emperor, (4) a belief that there has been no ideological compatiblilty with the domestic or foreign policies of these states, and (5) unlike the situation that pertains, for example, in relations with American allies in Europe, whereby the U.S. president meets with these leaders at least once a year, presidential meetings with the leaders of most Third World states have come years apart and typically only once during a presidential term. This absence of regular contact has inhibited the development of a personal rapport and has contributed to an even greater institutionalization of U.S. policy in the Horn.

CONGRESS AND THE NONSECURITY PERSPECTIVE

The Horn of Africa has not gone entirely unnoticed by the U.S. Congress, which over the course of the past two decades has taken a more critical look at American foreign policy in the Third World. Especially now in the post-Vietnam era, Congress has adopted a cautionary view toward U.S. arms transfers to volatile regions of the Third World for fear of the United States being dragged into a foreign conflict.[29] America's current budget deficit problems and heightened sensitivity to concerns about providing weapons to undemocratic governments, particularly those guilty of gross human rights violations, have also generated reservations within the legislative branch about granting security assistance.[30] Because of its oversight role and responsibility for appropriating and authorizing security assistance funding requests presented by the executive branch, Congress does have the power to affect at least indirectly the content and conduct of U.S. arms transfer policy.[31]

The relative lack of interest exhibited by the legislative branch in exercising this power with regard to Ethiopia and Somalia until recent years had much to do with the fact that the primary U.S. interest in the Horn of Africa was geopolitical—maintaining access to military bases. Generally speaking, geopolitical rationales provide little incentive for action within the U.S. Congress. Although members of the specialized congressional committees and subcommittees acquire a certain expertise and appreciation of the geopolitical stakes, a foreign policy issue must have a heavy domestic component if it is to attract the attention of a member of Congress. In short, political arguments, not strategic rationales, generally carry the day on Capitol Hill.[32] For the most part, U.S. policy in the Horn of Africa has lacked this domestic political content.

A second reason why the legislative branch has rarely acted as an advocate for U.S. arms transfers to the countries of the Horn has to do with another domestic political fact of life: congressional careers are not advanced by spending money overseas.[33] U.S. foreign assistance programs are often greeted with cynicism, skepticism, or outright hostility on Capitol Hill. Moreover, even when Congress is not in a budget-slashing mood, the fact that the multibillion dollar security assistance program represents less than 1 percent of the total U.S. budget, or 2–3 percent of the defense budget, has made it a low priority item. Then, when one considers that annual U.S. security assistance to Ethiopia and Somalia amounted to less than 1 percent of the SAP budget, it is no wonder that Congress—an institution noted for rounding off to the nearest $100 million—would not waste time, or expend political capital on a relatively minor budget matter.[34]

Finally, the disinclination of the legislative branch to assume a positive advocacy role in the Horn of Africa results from a domestic constituency void. Arms sales to the financially strapped governments in Addis Ababa and Mogadishu were not on a scale such as found in the Middle East or Europe, for example, that might affect the operations of U.S. defense industries and be of concern to a member of Congress within whose district these industries were located. On occasion, the issues underlying the Middle East conflict spilled over into the Horn and incited the Israeli and Arab lobbies operating in Washington, and their respective home governments, to challenge U.S. policy. The African-American community—the group with the greatest long-term interest and stake in bringing to the fore international issues affecting the continent—has devoted most of its energies over the years attempting to affect American policy toward southern Africa.[35] What interest it has shown in the Horn has been largely superficial, based upon a mythical attachment to Ethiopia's deposed Emperor Haile Selassie; once Selassie was gone from the scene, this interest dissipated.[36] Because the Marxist-Leninist governments in Addis Ababa and Somalia evoked little sympathy within the African-American community, Congress did not feel especially put upon to educate itself or involve itself more actively in the issues at stake in the Horn of Africa.

Therefore, the U.S. Congress might be looked upon as playing more of a counteradvocacy role with regard to the Horn of Africa because of its institutional bias against overseas aid programs. Congress is not necessarily a co-conspirator with the executive branch in making a threat of defection, since this simply means replacing one foreign commitment with another. Congress is more likely to favor a threat of aid reduction or termination rather than defection. Nonetheless, in the specific case of U.S. policy in the Horn of Africa, the legislative branch has acted as a countervailing force to arms transfer advocates.[37]

BUREAUCRATIC MISSIONS AND RIVALRIES

America's security relationships in the Horn of Africa have been relatively free of abrupt shifts and drastic policy changes in spite of the complications caused by regional instability and domestic policy conflicts. The United States maintained an uninterrupted military relationship with Ethiopia from 1953 until 1977, and had done so with Somalia from 1980 until September 1989, and the relationship still continues, if in name only. This constancy in policy is attributable in large part to the institutionalized style of decision making within the executive branch that characterizes the U.S. arms transfer process. These institutions, which live on long after a presidential administration has ended, are able to place their own long-term stamp on American policy—a stamp that emphasizes stability, not disruption or making waves.[38]

While there are many basic areas of agreement among these organizations as to American national security objectives and policy means, policy disputes arise as a result of conflicting interests and inscribed biases, which are endemic in a highly diversified institutionalized setting. These conflicts may exist between different agencies of the executive branch, or within a particular organization. Because each unit and subunit has established its own particuliar set of missions, interests, and operating procedures, it is not surprising that they should perceive different risks and opportunities in association with a certain policy option.[39] With regard to the Third World, the most prominent line of division for inter- and intra-agency disputes has revolved around the degree of globalism, regionalism, and localism that should be expressed in U.S. policy.[40]

In the formulation of U.S. arms transfer policy, the most consequential conflicts at the executive branch interagency level have involved the State Department, the Department of Defense, and the National Security Council. State Department officials have been generally supportive of an approach to Third World affairs that is more sensitive to the regional repercussions of foreign policy decisions. Their diplomatic mission leads them to view an arms transaction as a political act first, geared to a foreign audience. But the State Department is not merely concerned about how to preserve or improve a specific foreign relationship, by extending security assistance or the sale of arms, State's assessment of the desirability of such an action includes whether it would jeopardize relations with other countries. Given the State Department's interest in maintaining friendly relations with foreign governments, as well as its responsibility for providing the political clearance to transfer weapons to other countries, American foreign policy initiatives that are deemed politically provocative and that threaten to disrupt regional bilateral relationships may be opposed and rejected.

Although not oblivious to regional considerations, a globalist mode of thinking has predominated at the Pentagon and National Security Council (NSC). Questions concerning strategy and the global defense mission and needs of the U.S. military have shaped the policy preferences of the Defense Department. Arms transfer issues are judged not so much for their political value, but for their impact on U.S. military missions and capabilities. Military priorities (such as the defense of Western Europe) may be threatened by an overextension of resources, or force commitments to other countries.[41] Broader questions of strategy and policy integration that transcend more specific regional concerns form part of the backdrop for decision making at the National Security Council. Moreover, because the NSC is the president's own personal foreign policy center, and the National Security Adviser acts in a sense as his foreign policy alter ego, policy recommendations made by this agency not only will be more reflective of the president's ideological and personal biases, but also may be affected by domestic political considerations.[42] Despite a shared predisposition to adopt a broader outlook and emphasis on the global ramifications of policy options, the institutional parochialism of the Pentagon and NSC often results in each agency's providing a different set of calculations and policy recommendations.

Having noted the potential for sharp divergences and policy clashes between these executive branch agencies, we should also note that until recently a general consensus had held between them concerning arms transfers, and more specifically U.S. policy toward the Horn of Africa. First, arms transfers were viewed as a vital instrument for securing U.S. foreign policy objectives in the Third World, including the Horn.[43] Second, an American political-military presence in the Horn was considered desirable to facilitate the protection of the sea lines of communication (SLOCs) linking the northern rim of the Indian Ocean with the West. Finally, an arms-for-access to base-rights quid pro quo was recognized as a legitimate exchange and standard operating procedure for guiding the conduct of U.S.-Horn security relations. The globalist-regionalist conflict tended to surface over the more specific question of how much "rent" was appropriate, or what price Washington should pay to maintain a political-military presence in the Horn.

The State Department has acquired the reputation as the executive branch's institutional bastion for taking a regionalist approach to foreign policy; its regional bureaus (Europe, the Near East and South Asia, East Asia and the Pacific, the Latin American Republics, and Africa) are considered the policy-making centers of the department.[44] Sitting at the core of State's decision making, however, has involved these bureaus in three rifts dividing the department: (1) State's globalists (that is, generally top-ranking officials or political appointees who temporarily inhabit the Policy Planning Staff and Political-Military Affairs) versus the regional bureaus; (2) the regional bureaus against each other; and (3) the regional bureaus versus the country specialists (that is, embassy staff and desk officers). These three intradepartmental schisms essentially revolve around the question of who can best determine what American policy should be.[45]

Globalists base their position upon an ability to see the big picture and plan for the long term; their predisposition is to integrate, not isolate, regions of the world. This worldview allows them to give U.S. policy a more coherent and coordinated look—which is something, they argue, the regionalists cannot do.[46] Regionalists contend that because the State Department's regional bureaus conduct foreign policy on a daily basis, they are more apt to be aware of regional realities, and better positioned to produce a policy that will not alienate America's overseas friends and allies.[47]

Despite the regionalists' shared outlook, they are also rivals. Each regional bureau tends to promote its own interests. In the case of arms transfers this self-promotion means ensuring a fair share of the security assistance pie for their clients. Policy disputes between regional bureaus may occur, for example, if a policy recommendation is seen as having a positive impact in one region and a negative impact in another.

The third intradepartmental rift is produced by the notion held by American Foreign Service Officers (FSOs), as well as military attaches and advisers assigned to U.S. embassies abroad, that Washington-based bureaucrats are out of touch with the local situation on the ground. Washington should defer to the advice of the country experts.[48] Their home offices respond with a globalist-type argument by noting that the country-level vantage point blinds these country experts to the larger regional picture and produces narrow parochial thinking. The country experts are often chided for suffering from acute cases of "clientitis," in which they behave more as host government advocates than representatives of the U.S. government.

The results of these three rivalries over the years highlight two factors that have affected American policy toward the Horn. First, shortly after the Africa Bureau became a regional decision-making center at the State Department following its creation in August 1958, it assumed a posture that has provided SOP policy guidance for American policy makers to this day: a recognition of the sanctity of Africa's colonial borders as embodied in the 1963 OAU (Organization of African Unity) Charter, which ipso facto made Somalia one of the "bad guys" of Africa. This status quo policy stance was coupled with an assessment that Ethiopia was the most important country in the Horn of Africa. The policy consequence of these guidelines was the designation of Ethiopia as the preferred site from which the United States should attempt to maintain a political-military presence at the southern end of the Red Sea and that its territorial integrity should be preserved. Nevertheless, the implied policy which followed from these premises—that U.S. military involvement in Somalia should be avoided at all costs, or at least as long as Somalia was viewed as posing a threat to Ethiopia—would be challenged by other units within the national security bureaucracy.

Thus, a second component brought into play by these bureaucratic rivalries is the turf-defending role forced on the Africa Bureau. American globalist thinkers, other regional bureaus at the State Department (most notably the Arabists at the Bureau for Near East and South Asian affairs), and some country experts have shown a willingness to pursue what might be labeled anti-Ethiopia policies. Despite repeated challenges, some of which have been successful in moving U.S. policy in an "undesired" direction, the Africa Bureau has shown remarkable resilience in preserving its established policy tenets. For example, Washington's decision to form an arms relationship with Somalia in 1980 against the wishes of the Africa Bureau was tempered by the condition that the United States would provide only "defensive" arms and not condone Somali aggression against Ethiopia. Thus, the regionalist perspective propounded by the Africa Bureau provides the focal point for the playing out of interdepartmental rivalries as well as internal policy disputes.

In the overall scheme of U.S. foreign policy, the Horn of Africa occupies at best a marginal position. No presidential doctrines have been declared extending the U.S. security blanket over Africa, nor have American defense planners ever expected either Ethiopia or Somalia to make any significant military contribution in the event of a global or localized superpower conflict. Consequently, the Horn of Africa has rarely been the object of high-level attention in Washington. Only for short spurts in times of crisis have top-ranking officials taken an interest in the area. Decision-making authority, therefore, has rested almost exclusively in the hands of lower-ranking foreign policy bureaucrats, whose institutional instinct is to avoid disrupting the status quo and to resist drastic policy reorientations proposed by high-ranking "uninformed" officials.[49]

Disruption avoidance is appealing to American policy makers of both a globalist and a regionalist persuasion, though for different reasons. For the globalist, U.S. relations should not be jeopardized with pro-Western governments in the Third World.[50] Those who approach bilateral relations from the regionalist perspective are more likely to be acting upon State Department SOP policy guidelines, which tend to favor the political status quo. In either case, there is a predilection to minimize risk-taking and to avoid jeopardizing relations. Slow evolution, not fast-paced innovation, is a principal trait of institutionalized foreign policy decision making.[51]

AMERICAN DEPENDENCE AND INFLUENCE

The preceding analysis has identified the potential sources of U.S. dependence and susceptibility to a manipulation of weakness bargaining strategy by its arms clients in the Horn of Africa. It has also isolated the determinants of (and delineated the limits of) Washington's ability and willingness to use the threat of defection vis-à-vis these two states. Three factors would appear to affect the degree to which the United States would be vulnerable to the manipulation of weakness: (1) U.S. perceptions of the Soviet geostrategic threat, and to a lesser extent that posed by regional antagonists; (2) Washington's perceived need for access to military facilities in the vicinity of the Horn; and (3) the organizational interests and procedures of the national security bureaucracy (the State Department's Africa Bureau most particularly) in preserving an American position of influence in the Horn. Three considerations would seem to frame Washington's use of the threat of defection: (1) the nonexistence or dissipation of the Soviet threat, (2) the opening of strategic options in the region from the mid-1970s onward, and (3) the existence of discord within U.S. foreign policy–making circles over the value of the stakes at risk in the Horn.

Given Washington's sensitivity to the Soviet threat and strategic base requirements as well as the predominant role played by the U.S. national security bureaucracy in foreign policy decision making, several observations might be made concerning supplier-recipient bargaining behavior in U.S. relations with Ethiopia and Somalia. First, policy disputes would more likely be instigated by Addis Ababa and Mogadishu rather than by Washington, whose national security bureaucracy maintains an interest in not jeopardizing relations with client states, although the U.S. Congress might also challenge the propriety of U.S. policy and cause a disruption in relations. Second, Ethiopia especially, as well as Somalia, would be able to manipulate Washington's perceived geostrategic weakness and/or desire for stability in bilateral relations with some success. Third, only in times of an immediate, high-risk crisis might one expect sudden, dramatic changes in U.S. policy. Fourth, in resisting the demands of its arms clients in the Horn, the United States would generally refrain from the overt use of a threat of defection, despite the availability of other options.

Washington's primary strategy for exerting influence involved manipulating the weaknesses of Ethiopia and Somalia. The use or threat of harsh sanctions to keep a client in line—such as the termination of military assistance, a halt to all arms transfers, or a threat of defection—would only be likely to occur either before the American bureaucracy established institutional stakes in a country or if the permanent bureaucracy's role in decision making was usurped by other uncommitted domestic actors. Typically, U.S. bargaining strategy in the Horn of Africa seemed to be designed to maintain control over the flow of arms transfers to the Horn by highlighting the advantages that would accrue to these weak states by associating themselves with a great power such as the United States, and on occasion by threatening to impose mild sanctions (that is, reducing aid, prohibiting or delaying certain weapon transfers). The strategy, further, was to avoid disruption in U.S. geostrategic relationships by not resorting to blatant threats of defection.

2

The National Security Calculation of Ethiopia and Somalia

Located in the northeast corner of Africa are two of the continent's poorest countries, Ethiopia and Somalia, which until recently possessed two of sub-Sahara Africa's largest and best-equipped military forces. Ethiopia's armed forces, which throughout the 1960s and into the mid-1970s stood at 40,000–45,000 army, navy, and air force personnel, fielded 250,000–300,000 soldiers before its collapse in the spring of 1991 before the advancing forces of the Ethiopian People's Revolutionary Democratic Front (EPRDF) and Eritrean People's Liberation Front (EPLF).[1] Somalia almost doubled the size of its standing military forces from 16,000 to 31,000 between 1967 and 1976—reaching a peak of 54,000 during the latter half of the 1970s—and, until the fall of Siad Barre in January 1991 maintained some 45,000 military personnel.[2] How these two impoverished African countries were able to create and maintain military forces of this size and scope can be explained by their (1) devoting inordinate amounts of internal resources to the military, (2) emphasizing the importation of sophisticated weapons over other goods, and (3) accepting great-power arms patronage.

Despite a per capita GNP of less than $200 for Ethiopia, and approximately $300 for Somalia, the governments of these two countries diverted a significant portion of government revenues from improving their health and educational systems to building and maintaining their armed forces.[3] Since the latter half of the 1960s Addis Ababa incurred one of the highest military expenditures/central government expenditures (ME/CGE) ratios in the world.[4] Over the past decade and a half, military spending has typically accounted for one-fourth, and as much as one-third of Ethiopian central government expenditures.[5] Mogadishu's defense expenditures were of approximately the same magnitude, ranging between 13.3 and 27.5 percent of the national budget during the period 1967–1984.[6] The priority given to military spending as reflected in government spending highlighted the importance attached by the political and military elites in Addis Ababa and Mogadishu to security concerns.

Further evidence of the predominant role security issues have played in the Horn of Africa is provided by the arms imports/total imports (AI/TI) ratio. During a decade-long period (1977–1986) Ethiopian arms imports, which before 1975 generally were less than one-tenth the total value of nonmilitary imports, totaled 50 percent or more in nine of those years, and on five occasions exceeded their value.[7] Somalia's arms imports, which never surpassed one-seventh the value of nonmilitary imports before 1972, subsequently increased and ranged between 25 and 47 percent of their value.[8] Between 1977 and 1986, Somali arms imports varied between 26.8 and 98.4 percent of the level of nonmilitary imports, exceeding 49 percent in six of those years.[9]

Finally, the military buildup in these two countries was dependent upon the compliance, and to a considerable extent financial underwriting, of outside powers. Addis Ababa imported well over $10 billion worth of arms since the end of the Second World War.[10] The vast majority of these arms transfers (more than 95 percent) have arrived since 1977 from the Soviet Union.[11] Following independence in 1960, Somalia began to acquire, from a variety of sources, weapons calculated to be worth somewhere in the neighborhood of $2 billion, about 90 percent of which have been provided since the mid-1970s.[12] The great tragedy of this situation is that this military buildup, aided and abetted by outside powers, occurred in an area of the world in which hundreds of thousands of people have died as a result of famine and starvation, and millions more have been forced to become political refugees.[13]

While the human tragedy in the Horn of Africa is not the central focus of this study, one reason more has not been done to alleviate this incredible suffering is that Ethiopia's and Somalia's obsessive pursuit of their national objectives and the desire of beleaguered regimes to maintain themselves in power required them to maintain substantial military forces. To achieve their goals, Addis Ababa and Mogadishu looked to outside powers for support. Over the past four decades both the United States and the Soviet Union, in particular, played great-power arms patron, owing to their capability and willingness (though reluctant at times) to provide vast quantities of sophisticated military hardware of all types (jet fighters, tanks, naval vessels, etcetera) and on financial terms (grant aid, loans, barter arrangements) that other suppliers could not match.[14] This latter attribute was especially important for the economically weak states in the Horn of Africa. In attempting to secure the best possible political and economic terms to go with these arms transfers, however, Addis Ababa and Mogadishu resorted to manipulation and even the extreme threat of defection to have their way. Their willingness and ability to influence the arms transfer policies of foreign suppliers, most particularly the United States, has been framed and constrained by (1) threats arising from the Horn's unresolved nationalities question, (2) their perceived arms requirements and need to attract political-military support from outside parties, and (3) the internal nature of the political systems of the Horn countries in which national survival has been equated with the personal political survival of a leader.

THE NATIONALITIES QUESTION AND SECURITY DILEMMAS

The security equation for both Ethiopia and Somalia has revolved around the thorny nationalities question, which has torn apart the Horn of Africa for the past thirty years.[15] Two diametrically opposed interpretations of the Horn's political history are posited by these two governments. Addis Ababa contends that Ethiopia is a sovereign national entity that by escaping the nineteenth-century "scramble for Africa" preserved its national independence and, therefore, was entitled to move into the power vacuums left by the retreating European colonial powers. Consequently, the Ethiopian central government has maintained that it has the right to do whatever is necessary to preserve its unity. Leaders in Mogadishu, along with various subnational ethnic groups inside Ethiopia, claim that the Ethiopian state is a modern-day African imperialist entity that should be dismantled. Because of Addis Ababa's refusal to negotiate the terms of this dismemberment peacefully, they claim the right to seek national self-determination by military force or subversion. In short, the struggles and violence in the Horn of Africa today are the result of apparently irreconcilable objectives between the Ethiopian center and its periphery, which pits the right of self-preservation versus that of self-determination.[16]

Paradoxically, Ethiopia and Somalia represent two extreme case studies of how the ethnic makeup of a country can affect a government's national interests and security objectives. In this era of fervent Third World nationalism, an ethnically diverse and religiously fragmented country such as Ethiopia will be politically and militarily sensitive not only to its external environment, but also to events and forces operating within its borders. The culturally homogenous state of Somalia, on the other hand, has been destabilized by clan-based politics. Until the collapse of the Somali central government in January 1991, there did seem to prevail among these rival clans a consensus that a Somali state (in at least its present configuration, if not in an extended form) should survive. Thus, while both governments must be cognizant of external security threats to their national survival,

Addis Ababa's security calculation is further complicated by ethnonationalist threats from within.

The net result of the geographic proximity and historical development of these two states has been three decades of intermittent war and insurgency in the Horn of Africa, with Ethiopia serving as the focal point for these conflicts. In Ethiopia's northeast province of Eritrea the various factions of the Eritrean Liberation Movement (ELM)—the dominant faction now being the Eritrean People's Liberation Front (EPLF)—began waging a secessionist struggle against the Ethiopian central government in the early 1960s.[17] In 1975 the Tigre People's Liberation Front (TPLF), operating in Ethiopia's Tigre Province, took up arms against Addis Ababa in order to depose the military government.[18] The Oromo Liberation Front (OLF), based in the Oromo-inhabited areas in the southern part of Ethiopia, which comprise approximately half of the country's population, followed suit in 1976.[19] At one point in the mid-1970s ten of the country's fourteen provinces were in armed revolt against the central government.[20] While these insurgencies differed in terms of their political agendas, ideologies, and level of external support, they are all indigenous movements seeking to assert their own particular ethnic interests in opposition to the narrowly based Amharic ethnic minority that historically has dominated the Ethiopian political landscape. The question remains open, however, whether in the aftermath of their victory against the Ethiopian central government in May 1991 these ethnic-based movements will continue to cooperate, go their own separate ways, or find themselves in armed confrontation.

Somali opposition to the Ethiopian central government has been motivated also by a desire to throw off perceived political, economic, and cultural domination by the Amharas. But it differs from the other movements in the sense that a foreign government was directly involved in supporting the insurgency. The government of Somalia had identified itself intimately with the struggle being waged by the Western Somali Liberation Front (WSLF) and for a time the Somali-Abo Liberation Front (SALF) in Ethiopia's Somali-inhabited Ogaden Province.[21] On at least three occasions—in 1964, 1980 and 1982—large-scale fighting broke out between Ethiopian and Somali military forces. Moreover, between June 1977 and March 1978 the two countries fought a full-blown war in which both sides suffered thousands of casualties, and the threat of a superpower clash loomed over the conflict.

Given these contradictory claims, both sides have been willing to use the military instrument of coercion to secure their interests. After the 1977–1978 Ogaden War, Ethiopia began to augment its primarily defensive response by providing support to insurgency movements seeking to oust the government of Siad Barre, including the Somali Salvation Democratic Front (SSDF) and the Somali National Movement (SNM), whose military successes in 1988–1989 placed Somalia in a state of civil war.[22] Ethiopian military operations and occupation of areas inside Somalia during the 1980s clouded somewhat the traditional portrayal of Somalia as the aggressor and Ethiopia as the victim in this conflict. Nonetheless, the proxy war waged between Addis Ababa and Mogadishu throughout most of the 1980s demonstrated that neither side was immune from attack or subversion.

The international relationship between Ethiopia and Somalia for most of the past thirty years presented a classic example of the security dilemma at work. Each side assumed the worst about the other and reacted to every move (weapons acquisition) as though there were some ulterior motive. In the case of the Horn of Africa, however, such an assumption was probably correct in some instances, and produced overreaction at other times. Despite the political rapprochement reached by Siad Barre and Colonel Mengistu in April 1988, which called upon both sides to cease support for insurgents operating inside the other country, the suspicions and antagonisms felt by each side toward the other still remain and may ultimately undermine this unstable peace.[23] Except for the fact that in the spring of 1991 Somalia was in a virtual state of anarchy, after the collapse of the Ethiopian central government at the end of May the Somalis might have been tempted to strike and attempt to seize the Ogaden once again.

Thus, for both Ethiopia and Somalia the security threat has been very real and imminent. Moreover, it is a threat that can easily be manipulated by outside powers wishing to stir up trouble and exploit an opportunity. Although the official U.S. policy line over the years has been that the United States would not exploit the problems of the Horn, the possibility of undertaking such actions either overtly or covertly was raised within some of Washington's policy-making circles following the termination of military relations between the United States and Ethiopia in 1977.[24] Perhaps to a greater extent in the case of Ethiopia, which has been fending off numerous internal and external challenges for decades, arms suppliers have found particularly vulnerable and dependent client states in the Horn of Africa.

The primary national security interests of Ethiopia and Somalia have remained essentially unaltered through the years. Ethiopia's foreign policy has been shaped by a desire to gain and maintain access to the Red Sea, while the prime directive for Mogadishu has been to liberate Somalia from foreign rule, or at a minimum obtain an improvement in the living situation of the Somali-speaking people in the Horn of Africa. In both instances the path they chose for resolving their respective national security dilemmas required the importation of arms.

ETHIOPIA'S GEOPOLITICAL IMPERATIVE

The lands and peoples over which the struggles for self-determination are waged today in the Horn of Africa have been under Ethiopian control for about a century. Although Ethiopia's political leaders trace the origins of the Ethiopian state back more than 2,000 years, the consolidation and centralization of the empire did not begin to occur until the middle of the nineteenth century under the rule of Theodore II and Yohannes IV.[25] While the concept of a centralized nation-state had firmly taken hold in Europe by the eighteenth century, Ethiopia had regressed during the Era of the Princess (1769–1855) into a feudal, decentralized system in which local warlords and traditional nobility competed for supremacy.[26] But it was during the reign of Menelik II (1889–1913), who claimed the emperor's crown after the death of Yohannes IV in 1889, that the present configuration of the Ethiopian state began to take shape.[27] From his Shoa base in the central highlands, Menelik consolidated the core of the Abyssinian empire and moved into the surrounding areas. By 1906, through a combination of conquest and diplomacy, Menelik had added the Ogaden, Bale, Sidamo, Wollamo, Kaffa, and Illubador to the central core of the Ethiopian state. Emperor Haile Selassie completed the task after the Second World War when he gained control over Italy's Red Sea colony of Eritrea.

The internal conflicts in Ethiopia largely reflect the split between the politically dominant Christian Amharic community located in the core and the predominantly Muslim groups that reside in the empire's periphery. Political power has resided almost exclusively in the hands of the Amharas since the mid-nineteenth century. The May 1991 victory by the Tigre-dominated EPRDF, however, threatens Amhara dominance. Nonetheless, over time, the culturally united Christian community in the Ethiopian highlands developed a strong sense of identity based upon its perception of itself as a "Christian island surrounded in a hostile Moslem sea."[28] Because of the political and cultural biases of the Ethiopian central government through the years, a firmly rooted ethnic-based (with a quasi-religious appeal) opposition to the central government has emerged in the Ethiopian periphery. Thus, a century-long foreign policy of territorial expansion lies at the root of Ethiopia's internal problems today.

Addis Ababa has been willing to fight these debilitating internal and external wars for three decades because of its definition of Ethiopia's geopolitical interests, conditioned by a history of foreign invasion and regional threats. Ethiopia's sense of being a state under siege began to develop following the sixteenth-century invasion by Ahmad Gran and the Turks. The siege mentality was imprinted in the Ethiopian psyche as a result of various attempts by the Egyptians, British, and Italians to encroach upon Ethiopia during the nineteenth century and by Italy's military occupation of Ethiopia between 1935 and 1941. In the post–World War II period, a reemergent Islamic threat under the guise of Arab nationalism reappeared and violently manifested itself in the 1960s in the Eritrean rebellion (though the Eritrean community is split between Muslims and Christians) and the Somali claim on the Ogaden Desert. A common thread linking these episodes has been the use of the East African coastline as the staging point for these hostile forces.[29]

Given this history of foreign threats coming from various positions along the Red Sea, Ethiopia's rulers have been haunted by the specter of the Red Sea coastline—Addis Ababa's only link to the outside world—falling under the control of unfriendly powers. Ethiopian leaders, therefore, have come to view maintaining an outlet to the Red Sea as vital to the country's national security.[30] Holding such a position would prevent strangulation of the empire and facilitate the flow of arms into the country for national defense. These forward positions along the Red Sea also would serve as protective buffer zones, insulating the central core of the Ethiopian state from outsiders.[31]

Since the end of the Second World War, Ethiopia's security assessment has produced a rigid foreign (and domestic) policy guided by this geopolitical imperative. In terms of actual policy it has meant the subjugation of those areas contiguous to Djibouti (which includes the Ogaden) that are transversed by the Addis Ababa–Djibouti railway, as well as first acquiring and then maintaining control over Eritrea's Red Sea coastline. The federation of Ethiopia and Eritrea in 1952 and Addis Ababa's annexation of the area ten years later, coupled with Emperor Selassie's ability to gain international recognition for the idea that Africa's colonial borders should remain sacrosanct, were seen as critical diplomatic victories. Whether or not Ethiopia could survive as an independent actor without one or the other of these transit points that link the core of the empire with the Red Sea is a matter Addis Ababa has not been willing to consider, given the heterogeneous and fragmented nature of the state. If the central government were to grant some form of autonomy or independence to one region, so the thinking goes, other areas might expect and demand the same treatment. Concessions or compromise might be interpreted as a sign of weakness and produce a contagion or domino effect throughout the country. The ultimate result of such a perceived policy of appeasement would be the disintegration of the Ethiopian state.

Addis Ababa's regional security perspective, therefore, has been shaped by a strong sense of national survival in a hostile environment. A particularly interesting facet of Ethiopia's geopolitical thinking is that it has transcended time and ideology. In the post–World War II era the Ethiopian monarch Haile Selassie formulated and articulated this security perspective, and it was followed by his Marxist-Leninist military successors. One constant of Ethiopia's external relationships has been the geopolitical imperative of maintaining unhindered access to the Red Sea. Thus it will be interesting to see in the aftermath of Mengistu's fall whether the alliance between the TPLF (whose political agenda calls for a change in the government) and the EPLF (which has fought to secede from the Ethiopian state) will hold together.

THE GREATER SOMALILAND QUEST

While the contemporary conflicts in the Horn of Africa revolve around the internal policies of the Ethiopian government, it is the external policy of Somalia that has precipitated military confrontation between these two states. Mogadishu's regional foreign policy has been shaped by the threat Ethiopia and other regional and external powers pose to its irredentist dream of reuniting all the Somali-speaking people of the Horn of Africa under one flag.[32] Somali claims include parts of Kenya, the ministate of Djibouti, as well as Ethiopia. Somalia's hostility toward its larger and more populous African neighbor arises from the conviction that Ethiopia played, and continues to play, a pivotal role in erecting arbitrary political barriers that divide the Somali nation. Of course, this concern is now secondary, given the threat of fragmentation facing Somalia, and it has held greater attraction for the Somali clans of the south than for those in the north.

For centuries the Somali people who inhabited "Greater Somaliland" were able to move about freely in search of grazing land and fresh water, since no political boundaries existed that would hamper the seasonal migration patterns of these nomadic people.[33] This situation changed abruptly when in the latter half of the nineteenth century four expanding empires—the British, French, Italian, and Ethiopian—dismembered what had been Greater Somaliland. But Menelik's conquest of the Ogaden in 1887 was not formally recognized by the other colonial powers until ten years later, following Ethiopia's stunning victory over the Italians at the battle of Adowa in 1896. London then decided it was time to come to terms with the Ethiopian emperor: in 1897 the British government concluded an agreement with Emperor Menelik II that gave Ethiopia jurisdiction over a large part of the Ogaden, as well as the Haud and Reserved areas, two rich grazing lands located in the northeastern part of the Ogaden.[34]

Although the agreement guaranteed Somali grazing rights in these areas, modern-day Somali nationalists have challenged the legality of Great Britain ceding Somali areas to Ethiopia at this time and do not recognize Addis Ababa's claim to the Ogaden based upon the 1897 Anglo-Ethiopian Treaty.[35]

By the beginning of the First World War, all of Somaliland had been brought under the administrative control of the three European powers and Ethiopia.[36] Great Britain occupied the area around Berbera and along the Gulf of Aden, as well as the Somali-inhabited Northern Frontier District (NFD) of Kenya. Italy's rule extended from the Gulf of Aden coastline west of Berbera to the regions south of Mogadishu that bordered the NFD. France bounded British Somaliland in the northeast in the Territories of the Afars and Issacs (Djibouti). Ethiopia controlled the dagger-shaped interior between British Somaliland and Italian Somaliland. This foreign occupation of Somaliland met fierce resistance, the most famous and celebrated episode of which involved British forces, who fought a nightmarish war against the Dervish forces of Mullah Mohamed ibn Abdullah Hassan for more than two decades (1899–1920).[37] Although the British managed to restore relative peace after the mullah's death in 1920, Somali resentment continued to grow because of continued foreign domination and the occasional harassment Somali nomads were subjected to during their seasonal migrations across the "international borders" dividing their traditional grazing grounds.[38]

The process and outcome of the decolonization of Africa in the postwar period would be bittersweet for the Somalis.[39] During the Second World War, all of the Somali areas had fallen under British military control. But in September 1948 the British had transferred control over the Ogaden back to Ethiopia under the terms of wartime agreements reached with Emperor Haile Selassie in 1942 and 1944. A year later the United Nations decided that beginning in 1950 Great Britain and Italy would administer separate ten-year trusteeships over their prewar Somali territories. Then in 1954 London agreed to return the Haud and Reserved areas to Ethiopia. Britain's decision to allow Kenya to retain the NFD, that became Kenya's northeastern province upon independence in 1963, completed the postwar division of the Somali people. Independence and the subsequent merger of Italian and British Somalilands in 1960 would not be enough to make the Somalis forget just how close they were to reunification.[40] Today, Somalia's citizens are constantly reminded of the pan-Somali quest by the five-pointed star on the Somali national flag on which each of the five points represent one of the "lost Somali territories"—the Ogaden and Haud in Ethiopia, Kenya's northeast province, Djibouti (former French Somaliland), British Somaliland, and Italian Somaliland.

AN INVITATION TO GREAT-POWER INTERVENTION

The influence of patrons in the Horn of Africa has also been the result of their ability to affect the internal and external balance of power. Balance-of-power relationships have been seen as crucial to the resolution of security problems raised by the nationalities question. Arms transfers have played a central role in meeting these internal and external security threats. Uninterrupted access to large quantities of high-quality weapons, preferably with minimum political restrictions, was considered a sine qua non for the attainment of Ethiopia's and Somalia's security objectives. For this reason, outside powers, particularly the superpowers, have been welcomed intruders in the Horn.

An invitation by local powers to outsiders to intervene on their behalf, directly or indirectly, has a long tradition in the Horn of Africa. Ethiopia looked to the Portuguese in the sixteenth century, the British and French in the late nineteenth and early twentieth centuries, and the Americans and the Soviets in the post–World War II era for assistance and protection in the form of weapons or military forces.[41] Though newer to this game, Somalia also has learned the importance of maintaining a military linkage with a great-power benefactor, starting first with the Soviet Union from 1963 to 1977, and since 1980 with the United States. Addis Ababa and Mogadishu, therefore, have both consciously sought to globalize their regional dispute in order to secure weapons. A Somali proverb neatly captures the security perspective of both Somalia and Ethiopia: "Either be a mountain, or lean on one."[42] Both countries, nevertheless, would also discover the dangers of becoming overly reliant upon a single great-power supplier.

ETHIOPIA: GLOBAL DEPENDENCE AND REGIONAL ISOLATION

Ethiopia's military relations with foreign powers have been conditioned by its primarily defensive posture in the Horn. Because of the persistent internal and external threats to the country's territorial integrity, Ethiopian leaders have preferred to maintain a stable arms connection with a single power. The superpowers have been quite cognizant of this preference. Ethiopian threats to defect from one superpower to the other, though somewhat effective as a source of leverage, have often been dismissed by Ethiopia's arms patrons. The precarious security situation the country finds itself in, as well as the short-term dangers Addis Ababa would be exposed to in making the logistical change from one military system to another, weakens Ethiopia's hand in its arms dealings.[43] Consequently, since 1953 Ethiopia's external arms relationships have fallen into two periods, twenty-five years of American military patronage, succeeded in 1977 by Soviet sponsorship, which in 1991 would come to an end.

After levering the British military presence out of Ethiopia in the early 1950s Emperor Haile Selassie placed his country's security needs in the hands of the United States. Although Washington did not hold a complete arms monopoly, an overwhelming majority of the weapons acquired by Addis Ababa were provided by the Americans. Even during the latter phases of the U.S.-Ethiopia military relationship, when Addis Ababa was experiencing trouble in purchasing arms and felt it was not receiving adequate military assistance from Washington, the United States still accounted for over 70 percent ($135 million out of $190 million) of the arms imported by Ethiopia.[44] The U.S. military connection was even more invaluable in that until 1976 almost all of these weapons were acquired by Ethiopia on a grant basis via the U.S. Military Assistance Program (MAP). In real terms, Washington supplemented an estimated $562 million spent by the Ethiopian government on military purchases between 1967 and 1976 with an additional $100 million worth of MAP and IMETP funds.[45] Though the levels of U.S. aid pale in comparison with what the Soviet Union has provided to Ethiopia in recent years, such aid nonetheless allowed Addis Ababa to make purchases and accomplish objectives it otherwise would have had to forego.

As a result of the problems the new Ethiopian military government began to have with Washington after the overthrow of Haile Selassie in 1974, Ethiopia did experiment briefly with cross-bloc diversification. Between 1974 and 1978 its military government concluded arms transactions with the United States, the Soviet Union, France, West Germany, Czechoslovakia, Poland, Italy, and the People's Republic of China. Still, Moscow would account for over 80 percent of the $1.6 billion worth of arms supplied to Ethiopia during this period.[46] But by the end of 1978 the Russians had acquired a virtual monopoly over arms transfers to Ethiopia. American officials estimate that between 1977 and 1990 the Soviet Union provided $11 billion worth of arms to Ethiopia.[47] Over the past four decades Addis Ababa acquired more than 95 percent of its weaponry from Moscow.[48]

Except for (the former) South Yemen, Ethiopia has been estranged politically from the Arab-Islamic states rimming the Red Sea. This isolation has forced Ethiopia to maintain a great-power security connection, since the oil-rich Arab states of the Middle East have eschewed developing close ties with Addis Ababa. Among the Red Sea's regional actors, only Israel, itself dependent upon U.S. military and economic assistance, has cooperated in security matters with Ethiopia.[49] But by the end of 1989, with the Soviet Union announcing its intention to disengage militarily from Ethiopia, Israel emerged as an important source of arms. Until the massive airlift (Operation Solomon) in May 1991 that brought the remaining 14,000 Ethiopian Jews (Falashas) to Israel, the Mengistu government had used the Falashas as a lever to acquire arms from Israel.

Addis Ababa's diversification options, therefore, have been constrained by economic and political realities. The need for a generous donor willing to assume a long-term security responsibility narrowed the field to the United States and the Soviet Union. Ethiopia's response to these circumstances was to globalize the conflict in the Horn in order to draw in a great power: a game that has now come to an end.[50] The cost of this tactic, however, was that Addis Ababa had to be careful not to alienate its global patron; else it risked being left to face its opponents alone.

SOMALIA: PLAYING THE ISLAMIC CARD

In contrast to Ethiopia, Somalia has demonstrated much more flexibility in its dealings with foreign powers than Ethiopia. This is attributable in part to fate, but also to necessity. Mogadishu's fortunate fate is the Islamic bond it shares with oil-rich states such as Saudi Arabia, Iran under the shah, Iraq, as well as the Arab military giant of the Red Sea, Egypt. These governments have rewarded Mogadishu for its stances on global and regional issues, and in some instances have used their influence with the United States on Somalia's behalf.

The Americans, as well as the Soviets, however, have viewed a security relationship with Somalia as an invitation to trouble. Because of the Ogaden issue and the perception that Ethiopia is the strategic prize to be won in the Horn of Africa, both Washington and Moscow prefered Addis Ababa to Mogadishu. So while Somali leaders have sought out a superpower security connection, they realize that neither the United States nor the Soviet Union consciously would take any action or support Somalia in such a way that would permanently burn their bridges to Addis Ababa. In recognition of this post-Ethiopian revolution political reality, Mogadishu has been forced to pursue over the past fifteen years a varied and somewhat complex (some would say opportunistic) arms acquisition policy.

Mogadishu's external military relations with the East and West blocs have been characterized by sharp shifts since independence.[51] In the early 1960s several Western countries—Italy, Great Britain, France, and West Germany as well as the United States—assumed responsibility for providing a relatively small amount of military aid (approximately $3 million) to Somalia, and for training and equipping the Somali police force. But after rejecting what the Somalis felt was an inadequate military aid package offered by the West, Mogadishu concluded an arms agreement with Moscow in 1963 valued at $30 million. Then in 1967 the Somali government looked back to the Western bloc for aid, frustrated by Moscow's decision to reduce arms supplies. There was emerging, further, a Somali political leadership willing to seek peaceful accommodation with Ethiopia. Following the 1969 military coup d'état in Mogadishu, however, the new Somali government ended this brief interlude with the West and came to rely almost exclusively upon Soviet arms transfers over the next seven years. Between 1967 and 1976 Mogadishu imported $185 million worth of arms, of which $181 million arrived from the Soviet Union.[52] When diplomatic relations between Mogadishu and Moscow began to deteriorate in the spring of 1977 as a result of increasing Soviet arms transfers to Ethiopia, Somalia again turned to the West for arms. Although Mogadishu actively sought out, and finally concluded a security assistance agreement with Washington in 1980, since that time Somalia has continued to deal with diverse arms suppliers.

Somalia's seven-year exclusive military relationship with the Soviet Union in retrospect seems to be more of an aberration than an SOP guideline for Mogadishu's arms transfer policy toward the superpowers. Moscow's willingness to support Mogadishu during this period in such a bold manner can be attributed to the absence of any opportunity in Ethiopia for the Soviet Union until after the 1974 revolution. Throughout the late 1950s and 1960s, Soviet diplomats made numerous overtures to Ethiopian officials to throw out the Americans and replace them with Russian advisers and military assistance. When presented with the opportunity, Moscow exploited it to the hilt with little regard for its Somali arms client.[53]

The manner in which Washington and Mogadishu entered into their arms-for-access arrangement in August 1980 also suggests that if given a choice, the Americans would do the same and opt for Ethiopia over Somalia. The U.S. government limited the size and scope of security assistance for Somalia to "defensive arms." Moreover, Washington encouraged Mogadishu to acquire weapons from other friendly Western and Middle Eastern sources.[54] Obviously, the United States did not wish to bear the full responsibility, or sole blame, for Somali actions in the Ogaden. Therefore, during the first half of the 1980s, the United States only supplied about 20 percent of the weapons acquired by Mogadishu.[55]

Because of Ethiopia's perceived geopolitical predominance in the Horn of Africa and the fact that within the Africa policy context Addis Ababa is viewed as being on the "right" side of the Ethiopian-Somali conflict, Somalia has looked to its Islamic-Arab connections in the Red Sea region to guarantee that it would have access to military hardware and supplies. The Islamic card that Somalia has played, however, does not reveal itself so vividly in the arms transfer statistics compiled in the West. Since the end of the 1977–1978 Ogaden War, Mogadishu has acquired arms from the United States, France, the United Kingdom, China, and most notably Italy, as well as from other sources. But when one considers, for example, that Somalia's total government military expenditures during the late 1970s and through the mid-1980s averaged about $120 million per year, it becomes difficult to imagine how Mogadishu could shoulder the noncapital investment and recurring manpower burden of fielding an armed force that varied in size from 43,000 to 54,000 soldiers and still be able to purchase weapons from Western suppliers.[56] American security assistance, which totaled almost $300 million between 1980 and 1986, of which approximately $240 million came in the form of grant aid—MAP, IMETP, and ESF (Economic Support Funds)—certainly provided some important financial relief.[57] The financial support provided by Saudi Arabia, and the willingness of Egypt and the shah of Iran to provide excess defense articles from their military inventories, also was significant.[58] Then, at the end of the 1980s, Libya began to supply arms to Somalia, partially filling the vacuum left by the United States.

The perceived "offensive" nature of Somalia's foreign policy objectives in the Horn of Africa has made the task of maintaining a stable and assured arms connection with the global powers a rather tenuous proposition. Although Mogadishu also participated in globalizing the Ethiopia-Somalia conflict, the Somali cause would be better served, it would seem, if the Horn were removed from the superpower agenda. By keeping the conflict limited to interested powers in the Red Sea region or the Middle East, who possess a more direct stake in the outcome of this conflict, the regional balance of external forces favors Mogadishu.

But like its regional rival, Somalia's policy is also subject to constraints. Because the risk of alienating or losing its superpower arms supplier was so high, arms diversification became a necessity. Consequently, Somalia must also maintain friendly relations with fellow Islamic countries who will help underwrite a Somali military buildup. To ensure itself of this support, Mogadishu will be a follower, not a leader of political change in the region, particularly as it pertains to relations between the primary Red Sea powers (Egypt and Saudi Arabia) and the superpowers.

THE "RULER'S IMPERATIVE" AND FOREIGN RELATIONS

In the Horn of Africa, personalities and elite group ideologies rather than institutions have tended to dominate and determine foreign policy.[59] Except for Somalia during the 1960s, when there existed constitutional checks within the Somali political system and perhaps in the democratic

Ethiopia expected to emerge in the 1990s, domestic politics as well as the external relations of Addis Ababa and Mogadishu have been framed by a "ruler's imperative" in which the leader's primary objectives have not been to improve the living conditions of the people over which they rule, but simply to keep themselves in power.[60] Such leaders adopt a Machiavellian view of politics in which the survival of the state is seen as an extension of their personal political fortunes.[61] Hence they have a direct stake in the creation, maintenance, and manipulation of a particular political system that provides an ideological justification for subordinating social forces as well as the institutions and power of the state to their control. Given the symbiotic link between the rulers and the political system constructed to legitimize their political authority, prudence and survival would preclude alignment with foreign powers who might attempt to disrupt or subvert their basis of power.

The impact of the ruler-dominated political systems of Ethiopia and Somalia on supplier-recipient relations through the end of the 1980s has been short-term stability and long-term uncertainty in their respective arms partnerships. Leaders in both countries have been quite willing to take or threaten actions that cause tensions; they have destabilized or disrupted an arms relationship in order to secure state objectives and preserve their own power. For Ethiopia the formation of a great-power arms connection has revolved around the issue of system maintenance, first of the Ethiopian monarchy, then of the Ethiopian revolution. Somalia's arms relationships with the superpowers and other suppliers have been framed by the clan politics of the Somali state. In both cases the personal and ideological considerations of political elites have affected the interactions of these two states with their respective great-power arms patrons.

ETHIOPIA: THE PRESERVATION OF MONARCHY AND REVOLUTION

Addis Ababa's perception of the desirability of maintaining an arms connection with foreign powers has been shaped by Ethiopia's political history. Two periods stand out for analysis: (1) the reign of Emperor Haile Selassie that began in 1931 and ended in September 1974; and, (2) the bloody and tumultuous transition period that ultimately resulted in the emergence of the strongman Col. Mengistu Haile-Mariam in February 1977. In both cases, the internal political power and authority of these two leaders had an ideological basis. Consequently, they sought to align Ethiopia politically and militarily with the superpower who would be most supportive of, or present the lesser threat to, what they hoped to achieve internally. So, despite their belief in starkly contrasting ideologies, both shared a common objective: to maintain a particular political system that would ensure their own survival.

Haile Selassie established a constitutional monarchy in Ethiopia on July 16, 1931, a few months after his coronation as emperor. Selassie based his rule upon a dynastic family line that he traced back to the Queen of Sheba and King Solomon. In Haile Selassie's Ethiopia political parties did not exist. The bicameral Parliament that he created, in the revised constitution of 1955, had essentially no teeth to perform a checks and balances function, and the emperor could essentially rule by decree.[62] Selassie not only elected the prime minister and appointed the members of the Senate, but under Article 30 of the 1955 Revised Constitution, the emperor controlled the supreme direction of the empire's foreign affairs, with the exception that certain treaties and international agreements needed to be approved by a majority vote of both chambers of Parliament before becoming legally effective. But because the Ethiopian Senate was chosen by Selassie from among the nobility, the hierarchy of the Ethiopian Orthodox church and other prominent dignitaries, and because the Chamber of Deputies was a very diffuse body as a result of the prohibition against political parties, the emperor held all effective power in his hands.

Haile Selassie based his rule upon a coalition with, and cooptation of the Ethiopian nobility, the Ethiopian Coptic church, and the military.[63] The conservative nature of the monarchy made the emperor particularly sensitive to, and fearful of progressive and radical forces. Despite his frequent flirtations with the Soviet Union and the People's Republic of China, such an external coupling would not only have been an ideological mismatch, but could have proved disruptive internally. Thus, because the democratic countries in the West seemed to present less of an ideological threat to his rule, coupled with Haile Selassie's special personal affinity for the United States, a security relationship with Washington was a safer path to follow than one that would put Ethiopia in the grip of radical forces.[64]

After seizing power in a bloody shoot-out in February 1977, Colonel Mengistu's internal political-ideological objective was to transform Ethiopia into a Marxist-Leninist state.[65] The Provisional Military Administrative Council (PMAC), also known as the Dergue, which assumed control in September 1974, had begun to drift to the left in 1975 in order to legitimize itself ideologically among civilian forces, particularly the Ethiopian People's Revolutionary party (EPRP).[66] In April 1976 the PMAC proclaimed a National Democratic Revolutionary Program and declared Ethiopia to be a People's Republic. Still, there were factions within the Dergue who favored a more moderate course, including continued friendship and alignment with the United States. The execution of a number of these moderates and finally Mengistu's ascension to power, not only sealed the continued radical direction of the revolution, but also established Washington as a threat to the revolutionary government.[67]

Until his outster in May 1991, Mengistu held supreme power in Ethiopia. He was chief of state, commander-in-chief of the armed forces and general secretary of the Workers' Party of Ethiopia (WPE)—the sole political party and most powerful institution in the People's Democratic Republic of Ethiopia (PDRE).[68] For this pre-perestroika, pre-glasnost Soviet-styled political system, relations with a power (the United States) known for conducting destabilization campaigns against left-wing governments in the Third World were to be treated with great caution. However, beginning in 1989 Mengistu sought to improve relations with Washington and had renounced Marxism-Leninism, though not his authoritarian methods. Two years later the United States pressured Mengistu to leave Ethiopia in order to avoid a bloodbath in Addis Ababa. A democratic Ethiopia might now look to rekindle a security relationship with Washington.

The common theme that linked the Ethiopian monarchy's external policy toward foreign powers with the policy of Mengistu was the search for an arms patron who would not subvert the political system. Although personal power and ideology have been the principal determinants in shaping Ethiopia's foreign relations, the Ethiopian military has exerted considerable, though congruous, influence on Ethiopia's foreign relations under both Selassie and Mengistu. The Ethiopian military perspective has been that in order to fulfill its primary defense mission in the periphery of the state, the government must have access to a steady supply of arms. Nonetheless, the military was subordinated or coopted politically, first by the emperor, then by Mengistu, and probably by his successors.

SOMALIA: CLAN POLITICS

Although domestic politics in postindependence Somalia also breaks down into two periods—that of parliamentarism in the 1960s and authoritarianism from 1969 onward (and one might add a third beginning in 1990–1991—anarchy)—the lines of political cleavage within the state as well as the conditioning ideology of Somali leaders have remained unchanged. Even after constitutionalism gave way to a Somali-styled African socialism backed by Marxist-Leninist rhetoric, the Somali people have remained divided along clan lines.[69] This is likely to continue as the three rebel groups who opposed Siad Barre and other parties attempt to shape the post-Siad Somalia. Somalia's irredentist foreign policy objective concerning the reunification of the Somali peoples of the Horn had apparently been one of the few things the various clans generally agreed upon through the years. An axiom of Somali domestic politics was that no leader could renounce the Somali nationalist claim, on the Ogaden particularly, and hope to survive politically.[70] This political fact of life, which has proved so disruptive in the Horn, is a product and function of Somali clan politics—though it seems to hold a greater potency for the Somali clans of the south than for those in the north. Consequently, internal clan politics and kinship ties go a long way in explaining Somalia's relationships with the superpowers.

Although the Somali Constitution of 1960 established Somalia as an Islamic state, taking into account the Sunni Islamic religious background shared by the Somali people, this document could not eliminate or subterfuge the kinship ties that segment Somalia's population.[71] More than 98 percent of the population is divided into two main clan families.[72] There is the numerically predominant and primarily pastoralist-nomadic Samaale clan of the north, which is composed of four subclans—the Dir, Hawiye, Isaaq, and Daarood—and further subdivides into numerous offshoots. The most important of these offshoots are the Ogadeen, Mareehan, and Majeerteen clans, all of whom are linked by a common Daarood root. Less important in this study is the minority and predominantly agricultural Saab clan, found in the south; it is composed of two subclans—the Digil, and Rahanwayn.

At the risk of oversimplifying very complex inter- and intraclan relationships, suffice it to say that since independence Somalia's top-ranking political leaders have belonged to the pastoralist Samaale clans. Somalia's first president, Abdullah Osman, was of the Hawiye clan. Ali Shermaarke, who served as Osman's prime minister for several years and was elected president in 1967, and whose assassination in October 1969 provided the spark for a military coup d'état, was a Majeerteen. Haaji Hassen, who replaced Shermaarke in 1964, was also a Majeerteen, but of a different subclan. Muhammad Egal, who served as Shermaarke's prime minister, was from the Isaaq clan. Siad Barre, was a Mareehan. Today, all the Somali clans, particularly the Hawiye, Darood, Ogadeen, Isaaq, and Mareehan, are competing to fill the power vacuum created by Siad Barre's abdication.

The political domination of the Somali political scene in the postindependence period by Samaale clans explains much about the conflict in the Ogaden, and generally Mogadishu's quest to reunite all of the Somali-speaking peoples of the Horn under one flag. It has been the nomadic Somali herders living in and adjacent to the Ogaden region—dependent upon free and unencumbered migration for their survival—who have been most victimized by the artificial territorial borders erected in the Horn. The bonds of kinship between Somalia's political leaders and the Somali nomads subject to foreign domination have made this nationalist struggle an intense and politically charged issue throughout the postindependence history of Somalia. When the government of President Shermaarke and Prime Minister Egal seemed to be backing away from the Ogaden issue and striking a deal with Ethiopia by tacitly renouncing Mogadishu's irredentist claim on the region, Shermaarke was assassinated, and a new and perceptually more nationalistic military-led government took control.[73] Siad Barre's April 1988 tactical agreement with Colonel Mengistu regarding the Ogaden alienated members of the Ogadeen clan in particular and produced even greater opposition to his rule.[74] But with Somalia now in chaos and on the verge of partition, the Ogaden issue does not currently figure quite so prominently on Somalia's national agenda.

Although the ideology of Somali reunification has acted, for the most part, as a cohesive force within the Somali political system, it is an issue that varies in strength from clan to clan. A distinguishing characteristic of such a segmented system is the propensity for structural instability caused by interclan rivalries.[75] The dominant clans during the civilian parliamentary era of the 1960s were the Hawiye, Isaaq, and Majeerteen clans, of which both presidents and their three prime ministers were members. Siad Barre came to rely upon what has been referred to as the "MOD connection": the Mareehan, Ogadeen, and Dulbahante clans, which all belong to the root Daarood clan.[76] This fragile alliance, however, began to disintegrate after the April 1988 Somali-Ethiopian deal over the Ogaden and as a result of the increased fighting in the northern part of the country against the SNM.[77] Following the overthrow of Siad Barre in January 1991 by the Hawiye-based United Somali Congress (USC), one of the clan-based groups that were in rebellion in 1990, along with the Ogadeen-based Somali Patriotic Movement (SPM) and the Isaaq-based Somali National Movement (SNM), it remains to be seen whether political stability and democracy will return to Somalia, or whether Somalia will remain whole.[78]

Thus, domestic politics in Somalia have been shaped by these various clans seeking advantage for themselves by attempting to dominate the political and economic structures of the Somali state and by forging temporary alliances with other clans. With regard to foreign affairs, Mogadishu's choice of its external political-military partners has been guided by a personal but, more important, clanwide necessity to maintain the system. The ideology of reunification, which is a function of the interplay of Somali clan politics and kinship ties has been a determining force in Mogadishu's relations with its great-power arms patron. But the intensity of clan rivalry within Somalia has not only destabilized the state, but also diminished the chances for building stable foreign relations. In contrast to the perspective of Ethiopia's leaders, Mogadishu's bottom-line political-military assessment of the desirability of forging and maintaining an arms link with particular foreign powers was influenced more by the opportunity of convenience in the pursuit of Somali reunification than by the ideological orientation of a particular supplier.

DEPENDENCE AND INFLUENCE IN THE HORN OF AFRICA

The bargaining positions, if not the tactics, of Ethiopia and Somalia vis-à-vis the United States have been conditioned by quite different forces. Ethiopia's military relationship with the United States was affected by Addis Ababa's (1) perception of high-level threats to its territorial integrity and desire to maintain access to the Red Sea, (2) dependence upon great-power patronage, and (3) belief that some level of ideological compatibility should exist between itself and its arms patron to avoid inviting in a disruptive foreign influence. Somalia's military dealings with Washington have been determined by (1) Mogadishu's long-term commitment to Somali reunification and the threat posed by foreign powers to the achievement of that objective, (2) its ability to exploit its Islamic ties throughout the Middle East, but need to counterbalance Ethiopia's superpower connection with one of its own, and (3) the constraints imposed by Somali clan politics.

Ethiopia's primarily defensive posture and the perceived offensive nature of Somalia's foreign objectives in the Horn have produced several important distinctions in how Addis Ababa and Mogadishu have viewed the role of foreign powers. Ethiopia has sought to promote stability in its arms relationships with the great powers because of its perpetual sense of encirclement by hostile forces. Addis Ababa's fear of territorial disintegration or becoming landlocked and isolated has created a need for outside military support, which consequently has rendered Ethiopia extremely vulnerable to foreign influence and manipulation. While Somalia has reduced its dependence on any one state by nurturing multiple regional ties, the Somalis nonetheless recognize that the superpowers could tilt the balance of forces dramatically in the Horn. Thus, Mogadishu's security calculation has been profoundly affected by what the superpowers do in Ethiopia.

Although the governments of Ethiopia and Somalia used the threat of defection to force their respective superpower arms suppliers to act, the results were not all that impressive. Until the change of regime in Addis Ababa in 1974, Ethiopian threats to turn to the Soviets for arms carried little weight in Washington. Somalia's willingness to defect from one side to the other was a somewhat hollow threat, since both superpowers would prefer, if given a choice, to be entrenched in Ethiopia. Threats of defection must not only be plausible, but also coupled with perceived threats to U.S. geopolitical, bureaucratic, or domestic political interests in order to produce leverage.

In their dealings with the United States, the governments of Ethiopia and Somalia have been the primary instigators of arms transfer policy conflicts, owing to the predominantly military nature of their internal and external interests. The political elite have imported arms into the Horn to ensure their own survival. Moreover, because of the important role that arms transfers play in their respective security calculations, the top-ranking Ethiopian and Somali political elite devote greater attention and energy to these issues than do their American counterparts. Thus, they sought to allow time and persistent pressure in the form of manipulation and threats to break down American resistance to their arms demands.

II

The United States and Ethiopia, 1953–1977

3

The 1953 Arms-for-Bases Exchange

Between 1947 and 1953 the Imperial Ethiopian Government (IEG) tried without success to conclude a formal military arrangement with the United States. Six years of frustration and rejection by the Americans finally came to an end on May 22, 1953, when the U.S. Acting Secretary of State Walter Bedell Smith and Ethiopia's Minister for Foreign Affairs Ato Abte-Wold Aklilou signed a Mutual Defense Assistance Agreement (MDAA) and a Defense Installations Agreement (DIA).[1] These two treaties would serve as the foundation for U.S.-Ethiopian military relations for a quarter century. However, it required nine months of sometimes acrimonious negotiations to reach a satisfactory agreement on the substantive contents of these two documents. In the end a tacit quid pro quo, arms-for-base-rights exchange, was enacted: in return for guaranteed access to Ethiopian military installations, Washington would grant Addis Ababa military assistance and military training.

The United States began preparing for these negotiations in early 1952 in anticipation of preserving its special position at Radio Marina, a communications facility located in the former Italian colony of Eritrea, then under British control. With the British due to relinquish administrative control of Eritrea to the IEG on September 15, under the terms of the December 1950 UN-sponsored Eritrean-Ethiopian federation plan, the Americans recognized that a base agreement would need to be negotiated with Ethiopia. To create the proper atmosphere, on March 6 the Department of State had requested the Defense Department to declare Ethiopia eligible to receive grant military assistance under section 202 of the Mutual Security Act of 1951 and reimbursable military aid under section 408(e) of the Mutual Defense Assistance Act of 1949.[2] The Defense Department responded on April 22 that the Joint Chiefs of Staff would declare Ethiopia eligible only for reimbursable military assistance since Ethiopia did not meet the eligibility requirements for grant aid.[3] Nonetheless, the Americans felt this would be enough to entice Haile Selassie to sign a formal base rights accord.

In August 1952 the American ambassador to Addis Ababa, J. Rives Childs, submitted a draft proposal to the IEG covering U.S. military rights in Ethiopia. On September 11, four days before the federation plan was to be enacted, Addis Ababa granted a continuation of U.S. military rights and privileges at Radio Marina, leading the Americans to believe that the negotiations for a formal base-rights accord could be speedily concluded.[4] In late October, Ethiopia's Foreign Minister Aklilou, accompanied by his American legal adviser John Spencer, arrived in New York to attend the seventh General Assembly session of the United Nations, scheduled to review the Eritrean-Ethiopian federation. During this visit, Aklilou informed Secretary of State Dean Acheson that while Ethiopia was ready to meet U.S. wishes regarding base rights, "There must of necessity be a suitable *quid pro quo*."[5] If the Ethiopians were to conclude what amounted to a unilateral agreement in which only they made concessions, other powers, according to Aklilou, might also insist upon similar one-sided concessions, as "many Europeans bees will want an equal right to sip the Ethiopian honey."[6] For the IEG, suitable compensation would be the right to procure arms and have the United States provide a formal military training mission.

The Ethiopians stalled the base negotiations until after the UN General Assembly adopted Resolution 617 on December 17, certifying that the conditions of the Eritrean-Ethiopian federation had been fulfilled under the terms of the original UN Resolution 390 of December 2, 1950. Then when the negotiations resumed in late December, Aklilou attempted to up the ante. The foreign minister now complained that Addis Ababa was being rushed into signing an agreement far wider in scope than the IEG had agreed to in 1948 during discussions with former Secretary of State George Marshall, and that the Ethiopians were assuming all the risks of military alliance, without obtaining commensurate benefits.[7] Aklilou again assured the Americans that the IEG had no intention of reneging on the 1948 assurances, but he warned that it would be difficult to sell the agreement to the emperor unless (1) it was limited to facilities at Asmara, or (2) he could provide sufficient indication of U.S. support in defense of the area. The latter requirement involved either a written U.S. defense commitment and agreement to consult with the Ethiopians regarding the defense of the area, as well as the provision of a military mission, or the promise of a military mission large enough to train a large Ethiopian army so that the IEG could defend itself.[8] The emperor preferred that Aklilou acquire a broadly written U.S. commitment in which the Americans would defend the U.S.-operated installations against attack by internal and external forces, agree to keep the IEG "fully informed on all matters directly related to or of interest to the defense of East Africa," and provide a permanent military mission of about fifty members, not one that would come to Ethiopia for a brief period to show the Ethiopians simply "how to insert cartridges in rifles."[9]

However, Washington simply wanted to pay rent for Radio Marina and limit its military involvement in Ethiopia. The Joint Chiefs of Staff would agree only to provide a small military mission of unspecified number, probably in the range of ten to fifteen advisers, to be sent for an unspecified period.[10] Moreover, no written commitment would be given, although Ethiopia was welcome to purchase U.S. arms on a reimbursable basis. Aklilou refused to present the emperor with such an offer, and the negotiations broke down. As far as the Department of Defense was concerned, the next move was up to the Ethiopians.[11]

During the interim, the State Department did keep an informal line of communications open to ascertain the IEG's position with regard to the base agreement, the U.S. military mission, and the purchase of arms by Ethiopia by way of John Spencer, who offered U.S. officials at the State Department's Office of African Affairs a "confidential appraisal" of the thinking in Addis Ababa.[12] Of course, the American attorney had his own agenda acting on behalf of the IEG Foreign Ministry: to influence the Americans to sign a military accord that took into account Ethiopian sensitivities. He apparently succeeded. According to Spencer, there were divisions within the Ethiopian government between those who were partial to the United States and others who favored playing the imperial European powers against each other to maximize Ethiopia's benefits. Moreover, some in the Ethiopian military "would be just as pleased to see a Swedish military mission" in Ethiopia as an American one. The issue of reimbursable military assistance also posed a problem; the IEG felt it deserved better treatment from Washington given its contributions in Korea.

Finally, while the emperor was prepared to give complete authority to the Americans within the U.S.-operated installations, complete freedom of import and export and permission to have the necessary cable and wireless communications, he was not prepared to give priority to the movement of goods and troops between U.S. military installations, which seemed to be too much of an infringement on Ethiopia's sovereignty. Thus, when the U.S.-Ethiopia military discussions resumed again at the end of March 1953, the Ethiopian negotiating team of Aklilou, Spencer and General Mulughetta Bulli of the imperial Ethiopian bodyguard were instructed by the emperor not to return home until they had settled three issues: (1) an agreement governing the U.S. Army communications station at Radio Marina and other military facilities in Eritrea, (2) details regarding an American military training mission, and (3) the difficulties concerning reimbursable military aid.[13]

Aklilou would be in the United States for almost two months until the terms of a satisfactory military assistance agreement were processed and approved by the American bureaucracy. In this latest round of negotiations the United States seemed ready to accommodate the Ethiopians' three concerns. Hostilities were winding down in Korea and, more specifically, the emperor had dropped his demand for an explicit U.S. defense commitment.[14] First, Washington accepted a modified base agreement, though one whose major provisions remained substantively the same, in which (1) American military personnel stationed in Ethiopia would be protected by extraordinary extraterritorial rights; (2) the United States was granted complete freedom of flight over all of Ethiopia; (3) military and other storage facilities, as well as port visiting rights, were granted at Massawa and elsewhere, and (4) the United States was assured of free access to Ethiopian facilities covered by the installation agreement, which included Radio Marina, for a period of twenty-five years.[15] Second, the United States agreed to establish a formal military mission to train three Ethiopian Army divisions of 6,000 soldiers. Finally, to resolve the difficulties of providing reimbursable military assistance to Ethiopia, namely, that congressional legislation prohibited a reduction in the price of weapons or long-term repayments (which was the only way the financially strapped IEG would be able to purchase American arms), on April 6 the State Department requested that the Department of Defense declare Ethiopia eligible for grant military aid.[16] The JCS gave its approval on May 8. At this time State sent a letter to the director for mutual security, who recommended on May 12 that the president should declare Ethiopia eligible to receive up to $5 million of grant military aid under section 202 of the Mutual Security Act of 1951.[17] President Eisenhower did so on May 22. That same day representatives for the United States and Ethiopia signed the Defense Installations Agreement and Mutual Defense Assistance Agreement.

ERITREA AND THE ARAB THREAT

Haile Selassie's persistent pursuit of a military accord with the United States was influenced by the hostile Arab reception that greeted his diplomatic triumph at the United Nations concerning the fate of Eritrea. On December 2, 1950, the UN General Assembly had voted forty-six to ten in favor of a federation between Ethiopia and Eritrea which would officially take effect in December 1952.[18] But the federation solution created considerable animosity toward Ethiopia among the Arab states, who had favored independence for the former Italian colony. A U.S. defense commitment or, at a minimum, U.S. military presence came to be seen by the emperor as necessary to deter the empire's Moslem neighbors from military retaliation or subversion against Ethiopia.[19]

Haile Selassie had set his Eritrea policy in motion almost immediately after his return to Ethiopia in May 1941 after five years of exile. The newly restored emperor felt that the security of the Ethiopian state required exclusive control over the coastal Eritrean colony. Twice within his lifetime, in 1896 and again in 1935, Selassie had witnessed the invasion of his country by a foreign army (Italy in both instances) operating out of Eritrea. Ethiopia's political and economic independence could only be preserved, so he thought, by incorporating Eritrea into the empire and thereby removing a potential staging point for hostile forces, while at the same time providing Addis Ababa with direct access to the Red Sea.

The realities of international politics meant, however, that Ethiopia would have little or no say in the postwar disposition of colonial and enemy-occupied territories. Moreover, not only the Arab states, but Italy, France, and the Soviet Union opposed Selassie's design for Eritrea.[20] For Ethiopia to attain this geopolitical objective, therefore, the emperor would need to enlist the support of an influential great power sympathetic to Ethiopia's landlocked plight. In the past, representatives of the United States government had seemed favorably disposed toward resolving Ethiopia's dilemma. In April 1943 U.S. officials had expressed support for the idea that at least part of Eritrea should be given to Ethiopia.[21] Following a meeting between Franklin Roosevelt and Haile Selassie at Great Bitter Lake in mid-February 1945, at which time the Ethiopian emperor made very clear his position that Ethiopia's long-term interests necessitated a port in Eritrea, the United States government verbally committed itself to the idea of shifting at least southern Eritrea to Ethiopia.[22]

But Haile Selassie's concerns went beyond gaining control over Eritrea. The emperor feared most of all being left standing alone as he had been in 1935. Selassie wished to tie Ethiopia in as visibly as possible to a great power. American support would be needed not only to press successfully Addis Ababa's claim on Eritrea at the United Nations, but also to deter those who might seek to undermine the Eritrean-Ethiopian federation.

AVOIDING ENTANGLING ALLIANCES

At the end of the Second World War, the United States was not particularly interested in deepening its military involvement in the Middle East region. American policy makers instead invested U.S. military resources in Europe and the Far East. In other parts of the world the United States emphasized the economic and technical development components of Harry Truman's 1949 Point IV program. The fear of overextension, coupled with the belief that Europe and the rimland areas of the Eurasian land mass were the primary spots where the cold war would be fought, relegated more distant places like the Horn of Africa to the periphery of U.S. foreign policy concerns.

Ethiopia was viewed at this time primarily through a Middle East policy lens since organizationally it belonged to the State Department's Bureau for Near Eastern Affairs (NEA). During the second half of the 1940s, even after the crises in Iran, Greece, and Turkey, American policy makers saw little reason to become involved in arming or forging security arrangements with Middle Eastern states. A December 1947 forecast by the Joint Chiefs of Staff's Joint Strategic Plans Committee had concluded that war between East and West was unlikely to occur before 1957.[23] Of direct consequence for U.S. policy toward Ethiopia, the JSPC did not foresee communism or the USSR making any inroads in the Arab world, and no war-threatening situation developing in the African colonies.[24] Moreover, a July 1947 CIA report had played down the military significance of Eritrea and Italian Somaliland in any Mediterranean, Middle East, or northwest Africa contingency.[25] In the absence of any imminent threat in the region, there was no vital reason for the United States to commit scarce military resources to Ethiopia.

At the start of the 1950s, Washington still remained reluctant to assume any new overseas responsibilities in the Middle East region. A May 1950 report prepared by the NEA contended that the United States was not in a position to consider any security pacts in the Eastern Mediterranean or Near East, and that Washington should neither encourage nor discourage any spontaneous defensive grouping in the area.[26] The NEA analysts argued, "We are not in a position to consider any security pacts with Greece, Turkey, Iran or other Near Eastern countries at the present time because we cannot tell whether our capabilities at this time are adequate to defend our vital interests in Europe."[27] Only an increase in Europe's own defensive strength resulting from NATO and U.S. military assistance would allow Washington to consider further security arrangements.[28] The Truman administration had turned down an offer by Saudi Arabia in 1948 of access to strategic facilities in exchange for military equipment; then in 1950 it refused to sign a treaty of alliance with the Saudi kingdom, which had been sought out by King 'Abd al-'Aziz.[29] American defense commitments in Europe and the Far East, as well as concern about fueling an

Arab-Israeli arms race, curbed Washington's appetite for building binding security relationships in the Middle East.[30]

Washington began to reconsider the benefits of adopting a higher profile posture in the Middle East following the July 1952 military coup in Egypt. Even before the Arab-nationalist government had seized power, Cairo had opposed and blocked U.S., British, and moderate Arab initiatives in the region.[31] Cairo's anti-Western behavior became more pronounced after the Nasser coup. With the decline of British influence in Egypt, and the growth of America's role in the defense of North and West Africa, the United States would need to create a strategic infrastructure in the region.[32]

However, Ethiopia was not the linchpin of this strategy. As part of a larger effort to secure Western interests in the region Washington had concluded a five-year extension with Riyadh in June 1951 for the Dhahran air facility. In 1952–1953, Washington was also engaged in an economic boycott and destabilization campaign against the National Front government in Iran following the nationalization of the British-controlled Anglo-Iranian Oil Company in 1951. That would lead to the August 1953 CIA-supported coup against Prime Minister Muhammad Musaddiq, which returned the shah of Iran to power and restored Iran to the pro-Western camp.

Because Britain, Italy, and France continued to control the Somalilands, Kenya, Sudan and South Yemen, the Western alliance could use any number of locations to support military operations in the southern Red Sea region. But given this volatile regional environment, and with the globalist-oriented Eisenhower administration assuming power in January 1953, America's traditional resistance to the creation of binding alliances in the Middle East had weakened.

THE CZECH THREAT

Following the liberation of Ethiopia in 1941, Addis Ababa had first looked to the Western powers for weapons and military supplies. This experience, however, proved to be quite disillusioning and unsatisfying for the Ethiopians, especially in their dealings with Great Britain. After forcing the surrender of Italian forces in East Africa, Britain was determined to assume the role of predominant great power not only in the occupied Italian colonies, but in Ethiopia as well. London feared that if the Ethiopians were allowed to assist in the war effort, Addis Ababa would demand territorial or other concessions after the war as a reward and would pose a challenge to Britain's paramount position in northeast Africa.[33] So throughout the war British colonial authorities opposed the transfer of military supplies to Ethiopia. To that end, after liberating Ethiopia from fascist rule, the British and South African forces proceeded to remove everything they could that the Italians had brought into the country, including all weapons and military equipment, under the pretense of using it for the war effort. Much of it was thrown into the sea or burned.[34]

The United States initially refused to provide military assistance to Ethiopia because it was reluctant to upset its British ally. Throughout most of the war, the Americans would defer to London when it came to political and security issues in East Africa.[35] Even if the Americans did want to help Ethiopia, their hands were tied by the fact that after London had recognized Ethiopia's independent status through the January 31, 1942, Anglo-Ethiopian agreement, the British continued to exert substantial control over Addis Ababa's internal and military affairs.[36] Although President Roosevelt had declared Ethiopia eligible to receive U.S. Lend-Lease assistance in December 1942, American policy makers had no interest in preparing Ethiopia for war. As explained in a memorandum to President Roosevelt by Secretary of State Cordell Hull in 1944, U.S. actions, including Lend-Lease aid, were simply designed "to maintain a position of equality of opportunity in Ethiopia so that the future development of American interests would not be prevented by exclusive or preferential rights obtained by third parties," such as those enjoyed by the British.[37]

Haile Selassie's task, therefore, was to open a direct line to the Americans to discuss military matters without outside interference. The Ethiopians used the occasion of the World Food Conference held at Hot Springs, Virginia, in May 1943 to present the U.S. War Department with a request for weapons and equipment, including trucks and light tanks for three divisions of 12,000 soldiers.[38] As an added inducement the emperor offered to send one of the divisions to fight in the Middle East theater or elsewhere in support of the Allied cause. Officials at the War Department put together an alternative internal security arms package, which included 5,000 rifles, five armored cars, twelve 37MM field guns, four 75MM field guns, fifty 30-caliber Browning machine guns, fifty 45-caliber submachine guns, and ammunition.[39] British officials, however, stalled the proposed arms transfer for almost a year by raising political and security objections. But the State Department eventually found it "difficult to see how British security in northeastern Africa could be vitally affected by the Emperor's possession of such a small amount of equipment."[40] But, as a sign of things to come, the weapons did not arrive in Ethiopia until April 1945.

Although by the end of the Second World War Great Britain no longer opposed the sale of U.S. arms to Ethiopia for internal security purposes (as long as Washington kept London informed of developments), the U.S. Department of State discouraged requests by the Ethiopian government for weapons and supplies.[41] Immediately after the war, the State Department refused to support an Ethiopian request for equipment for a motorized division on the grounds that Ethiopia's economy would be unable to stand the initial purchase price, let alone the cost of maintaining the unit.[42] Washington also failed to fulfill other more general arms requests because of the unavailability of the type and quantity of weapons desired by the Ethiopians.[43] America's recalcitrance toward turning Ethiopia into a military asset was highlighted when the State Department's Arms Policy Committee approved the sale of a modest amount of weapons to Ethiopia in mid-1947, but on a "nonpriority" basis.[44]

In 1947 Ethiopia began to acquire weapons from Czechoslovakia. Even after the Czechoslovakian communist coup d'état in early 1948, Addis Ababa continued the Czech arms connection. The emperor went ahead and concluded an $8 million arms deal with Prague that included mostly submachine guns, machine guns, and ammunition.[45] According to the American legation in Addis Ababa, the arrangement stemmed from a "lack of success in obtaining arms in the U.S. and U.K. on Ethiopian terms."[46]

At the end of the 1940s, the Soviet Union also began to show an interest in Ethiopia. The American attorney John Spencer, who had been serving as a legal adviser to the imperial government since the mid-1940s, reported that on repeated occasions the Soviet ambassador assured the Ethiopian foreign minister that Russian military aid could be had for the asking.[47] American diplomats in the field, however, did not really expect Haile Selassie to turn to the Soviets for arms. Selassie's diplomatic relations and discussions with Moscow were seen as part of a calculated design to "string them along in order to have someone to play off, later, if he deems it advantageous, against all the Western powers, including the United States."[48] American diplomats in Ethiopia also seemed to think that despite Russian overtures to Addis Ababa the Ethiopian emperor could be expected to block serious penetrations by the Soviet Union.[49] Thus Haile Selassie's attempt to pressure Washington into greater responsiveness to Ethiopian arms requests by fomenting uncertainty about Ethiopia's relationship with the communist bloc was a very transparent bluff.

Selassie abandoned all pretense of playing up to the East bloc following the outbreak of the war in Korea in June 1950. This event jolted the emperor into recognizing that his country too was vulnerable to invasion and that antagonizing the Americans at this time might not be such a good idea. It seemed to be a time for small and weak countries to choose sides.

In August 1950, Emperor Selassie declared Ethiopia to be a loyal ally of the West and offered to send 1,000 Ethiopian troops to fight alongside other UN forces in Korea.

Thus, when the U.S.-Ethiopia military discussions began at the end of 1952, Haile Selassie had given up all pretense of defecting to the East bloc for arms and had declared his loyalty to the West. During the March 1953 military discussions in Washington, Foreign Minister Aklilou pointed out to the Americans that the arms being given to the Arab states might not be used to support the West in a war, but that "the United States can count on Ethiopia more than it can count on the Arabs."[50] Moreover, Ethiopia had demonstrated its loyalty by voting against a Czechoslovakian resolution in the UN General Assembly that spring (stating that the U.S. Mutual Security Act of 1951 constituted aggression and interference in the affairs of other states), while the Arab states had abstained.[51] The emperor was also expressing a desire to join a Middle East defense organization tied to NATO.[52] Ethiopian negotiators utilized the "Northern Tier" concept, being developed by U.S. Secretary of State John Foster Dulles, to argue that Ethiopia should form part of a "Southern Tier"—a secondary line of defense against communism in the Middle East—which could act as a safety valve should the Northern Tier fall.[53] While the Americans never formally implemented the "Southern Tier" portion of this plan, Haile Selassie's clear desire to align Ethiopia in such an overt manner with the United States tended to strengthen Washington's negotiating hand.

"PROJECT 19" AND KAGNEW STATION

Haile Selassie's enthusiasm for establishing a political-military link between Ethiopia and the United States was not initially reciprocated in Washington. With the brief exception of the U.S. arms embargo directed against Italy in the late 1930s following the invasion of Ethiopia, Selassie's empire had warranted no special attention from Washington. After the conclusion in June 1914 of the Treaty of Commerce between the United States and Ethiopia, which contained a "most favored nation" clause, American business never developed more than a limited commercial interest in Ethiopia. Years later, a Treaty of Amity and Economic Relations that had been signed on September 7, 1951, was held up in the U.S. Congress for over two years by private U.S. interests.[54] Strategically, Ethiopia's control over the headwaters of the Blue Nile drew attention only from Cairo, Khartoum, and outside powers such as Great Britain who held a stake in Egypt and Sudan. From a military vantage point, Ethiopia's armed forces were viewed as inconsequential. Diplomatically and culturally isolated in the Middle East, Addis Ababa perhaps could assume a position of political leadership in an independent Africa, but that was years away. Consequently, there was little reason for the United States to respond to Haile Selassie's appeals for U.S. military support.

Whereas Ethiopia itself was of little value to the United States, during the Second World War American defense planners had begun to take an interest in Eritrea after it had fallen under British military occupation as a liberated enemy territory in early 1941. At a secret meeting held at the U.S. War Department on November 19, 1941, the United States government implemented a highly classified operation (Project 19) aimed at aiding the allied war effort in Africa.[55] Under the aegis of the Lend-Lease Act, the United States established a naval repair base at the Eritrean port of Massawa to support the British Mediterranean fleet. U.S. civilians under the management of the Douglas Aircraft Corporation also operated an air base at Gura, Eritrea, to maintain Britain's Royal Air Force (RAF) conducting operations against Rommel's Afrika Korps. Although Rommel's defeat and departure from North Africa in March 1943 marked the end of Project 19, American interest and involvement in Eritrea continued into the postwar years.

As the war in North Africa drew to a close, the United States shifted its primary regional objective from a tactical military to the long-term strategic mission of establishing a fixed radio station site in Africa. At the end of January 1943, the War Department proposed that a communications facility should be established at the former site of an Italian naval radio station (Radio Marina) located outside the Eritrean town of Asmara.[56] In late April a U.S. survey team arrived at Asmara to conduct a feasibility study. Refurbishing the station began the following month. By September the first communications and receiver sets were completed, and a staff of four officers and fifty enlisted men from the U.S. Army Signal Corps were assigned to the facility.

The extraordinary location of what would be renamed Kagnew Station made this communications facility invaluable for years to come. Radio frequency changes were less frequent and operations facilitated because the station was situated in the tropics several thousand feet above sea level, far from the North and South magnetic poles, the Aurora Borealis, and magnetic storms, and in a zone where there was limited seasonal variation between sunrise and sunset.[57] The station possessed an inherent ability to transmit radio signals back to Washington from the Middle East, Europe, North Africa, and the Pacific theater, as well as listen in on transmissions in the Middle East and Africa.[58] Technically, the site was located in an ideal spot to fit into Washington's worldwide defense communications network and serve as an intelligence-gathering outpost in the region.

Washington's objective in the Horn of Africa, therefore, became quite simple—to operate and maintain unimpeded access to this strategic communications facility. During the last years of the war, the problem of access did not arise because final authority over the occupied colony's internal affairs had been in the hands of the British since Eritrea was placed under a British Occupied Enemy Territory Administration in 1941. After the war, American officials apparently felt more comfortable with Great Britain, and thus initially favored ceding only southern Eritrea to Ethiopia and keeping the northern part of the territory, where Radio Marina was located, under British dominion.[59] But London's decision to relinquish control of the entire territory forced a change in Washington's position.

American attitudes toward Ethiopia began to change around the middle of 1948. The Truman administration had now decided that U.S. security interests would be best served if the Italian colony of Eritrea fell under the political domination of Addis Ababa.[60] During the summer and fall of 1948, the U.S. national security bureaucracy began formulating a plan to resolve the dilemma of maintaining access to the communications site without antagonizing other powers. The National Security Council argued against an independent Eritrea on the grounds that it would be a "weak state . . . exposed to Soviet aggression or infiltration."[61] State Department officials recommended against an Italian trusteeship in Eritrea for fear that the unstable Italian government might fall to the communists; given Italy's recent fascist past, the UN General Assembly might decide to restrict the use of the territory for military purposes.[62] So the State Department concluded in early August 1948 that all of Eritrea should be given to Ethiopia. By the end of the year, after a report prepared by the Joint Chiefs of Staff argued that it would be inadvisable to remove the radio facility from Asmara because there was no other suitable location available in the Middle East, the Defense Department also favored Ethiopian control over Eritrea.[63]

The U.S. foreign policy–making community was now in agreement that the communications operation had to be maintained and that some form of Ethiopian control over Eritrea and the radio facility was desirable. Secretary of Defense James Forrestal proposed that the United States obtain written guarantees from Ethiopia so that in the event Eritrea was ceded to Ethiopia there would be no political or technical interference in the operation of the station.[64] Although Addis Ababa offered to supply such a written guarantee, Washington elected to settle for a purely verbal commitment.[65] Consequently, in November 1948 Secretary of State George Marshall offered American diplomatic support for Ethiopia's claim to most of Eritrea, in return for retaining "unhampered use of the radio station in Asmara and possibly other military facilities such as airfields and ports in the Asmara-Massawa area."[66]

When the UN General Assembly turned its attention to the Eritrean question in 1949 the United States' UN delegation, having been formally debriefed about the verbal arrangements made with Addis Ababa concerning U.S. defense requirements in the Horn, began pushing for some form of Ethiopian control over most of Eritrea.[67] By the latter half of 1950, in what was justified publicly as compensation for Ethiopia's offer to contribute troops to the UN police action in Korea, the United States began advocating federation between Ethiopia and all of Eritrea. The American UN Mission presented the federation plan to the United Nations' Ad Hoc Political Committee during the latter half of November, and the plan was adopted in early December. Under the U.S.-sponsored proposal, after a brief transitional period that would take effect in September 1952, Eritrea would "constitute an autonomous unit federated with Ethiopia under the sovereignty of the Ethiopian Crown" beginning December 2, 1952.[68]

THE EMPEROR'S AMERICAN OBSESSION

Haile Selassie's determination to link Ethiopia with the United States was an outgrowth in part of his experience with Great Britain in the 1940s. Selassie wanted a patron who could be trusted not to interfere in Ethiopia's internal affairs, contrary to British behavior. Given the fall of the European states from the great-power ranks, the emperor was essentially left with two choices. He could either conclude a security arrangement with the United States or with the Soviet Union.

Moscow's credentials to act in this capacity were as solid as those of Washington. Like the United States, the Soviet Union possessed an unblemished anticolonial, anti-imperialist record in Africa. It too was distant enough and distracted by other global matters to assure that Ethiopia would be buffered from constant interference. An arms relationship with Moscow, now recognized as one of the world's two superpowers, also could act as a deterrent against hostile regional forces.

Yet, despite this favorable comparison and continuing Soviet offers of assistance, Haile Selassie always looked to the United States. John Spencer observed, "Throughout his reign, as automatically as a compass needle drawn towards the magnetic pole, His Majesty turned towards the United States."[69] Haile Selassie's particular fascination with the United States could be explained in part by Washington's having carefully avoided involvement in the intrigues of the European colonial powers in Africa.[70] Moreover, unlike Paris and London, Washington had refused to recognize the Italian conquest of Ethiopia in 1935.[71] Despite criticisms of Washington's determination to remain aloof from diplomatic efforts in late 1934 and 1935 to resolve the Italo-Abyssinian dispute, two days after war broke out between Ethiopia and Italy, the United States unilaterally imposed an arms embargo—an action that may have been seen as hurting Italy more than Ethiopia.[72] U.S. actions suggested that among the great powers, the United States had no designs upon Ethiopia.

Tactical political-military concerns also weighed in favor of forging an arms connection with the United States.[73] During Haile Selassie's exile in London, he had approached the Americans for arms to use in his efforts to oust the Italians from his homeland. After Ethiopia's liberation the emperor then attempted to draw the Americans into Ethiopia to pry out the intrusive British. As the 1940s came to a close, Selassie hoped to keep the Arabs at bay through a U.S. presence in Ethiopia. The Ethiopian emperor developed a penchant for turning to the United States when in trouble. Selassie felt he could use and manipulate American power to counterbalance the activities of other external powers in Ethiopia and within the region. To this end, the emperor wanted to see Americans working on the ground inside Ethiopia by drawing the United States into a more direct and visible role in building and maintaining his country's military forces.

Ethiopia's arms options were also constrained by logistical and economic considerations. Lend-Lease aid during the war and subsequent aircraft purchases had accustomed the Ethiopian military to U.S. standards, calibers, and equipment types.[74] The construction of an Ethiopian army of the size and sophistication the emperor desired could be accomplished more quickly and efficiently by staying with the Americans, since a large-scale military commitment by another country was not in the offing. Moreover, the State Department had indicated its willingness to provide arms and military training on a grant basis; this made an American military connection all the more attractive and valuable for the financially strapped Ethiopian government. In May 1949, Washington had demonstrated the potential economic benefits of association with the United States by reducing Ethiopia's Lend-Lease debt of more than $5 million to $200,000.[75]

Although the Soviet Union perhaps could have done as much for Ethiopia, given the perceived vulnerability and nature of Haile Selassie's empire, the emperor preferred to keep Moscow at a safe distance. Ethiopia's history had taught Selassie to be wary of great powers. Subversion of his semifeudal empire seemed more likely to be perpetrated by a revolutionary-minded Soviet government than by the status quo–oriented policies of the United States.[76] In his pursuit of a great-power arms connection, Haile Selassie did not want to plant the seeds for his own political destruction.

One alternative Ethiopian negotiators hinted that the emperor might pursue to resolve Ethiopia's security problems would be to reach a political accommodation with the empire's Arab neighbors.[77] Although most hostile Arab pressure had subsided once the Eritrean-Ethiopian federation had been sanctioned by the United Nations in December 1952, Addis Ababa then came under increasing pressure to align itself with the Arab-Asiatic bloc. The emperor could have elected to reduce Ethiopia's perceived military vulnerability and head off future problems caused by the Eritrean issue by throwing in his lot completely with the Arab states. But given Ethiopia's historical troubles with its Moslem neighbors, military alignment with the United States appeared to offer a surer solution to the problem of maintaining control over Eritrea.

The fact that Haile Selassie had staked his personal prestige on concluding a military agreement with the United States further reduced his leverage vis-à-vis Washington. Given Ethiopia's extremely long military traditions, and with the British military mission departed from the scene in 1953, U.S. military assistance was viewed as essential.[78] Concluding a military agreement with the United States had assumed such high importance for the emperor that Ethiopia's Foreign Minister Aklilou was told in the spring of 1953 that he "could not return home without it."[79] Thus, the United States needed to give Ethiopia only enough to keep Selassie interested in light of the emperor's known obsession for things American.

WASHINGTON'S "LOW-PRIORITY" ALLY

Haile Selassie's efforts to draw the United States into a close-knit security relationship met considerable resistance from the U.S. foreign policy bureaucracy. State Department and Pentagon officials held little interest in financing an Ethiopian military buildup. If the cold war erupted into a hot war between East and West, the Ethiopian military was not expected to have any effect upon the outcome. Even by the end of 1948, when Washington had come to recognize Ethiopia's future strategic importance with regard to its acquisition of Eritrea and Kagnew, Ethiopia continued to be viewed as a low-priority ally.

Washington's light regard for Ethiopia's military was aptly demonstrated in mid-1950. Addis Ababa had inquired about the extent to which the United States would assist in equipping and arming a unit of approximately 1,000 officers and enlisted men, and provide formal military assistance to strengthen the IEG's armed forces.[80] U.S. guidelines required that in order to be declared eligible for military aid Ethiopia would have to demonstrate clearly that its ability to defend itself, or to participate in regional defense would contribute to U.S. security. The State Department informed the U.S. embassy in Addis Ababa that a determination in Ethiopia's favor would be "extremely unlikely."[81] Even if Ethiopia were declared eligible, U.S. defense requirements and prior commitments would likely prevent the United States from furnishing the quantities of equipment desired by the IEG in the foreseeable future.[82]

Despite this setback, Addis Ababa continued to press its case through the U.S. embassy. But even among the embassy staff in the field, the emperor won few converts. The concerns Selassie voiced about Ethiopia being forgotten and falling prey to an aggressor in the event of a general war fell on deaf ears.[83] U.S. officials could find no imminent outside threat to Ethiopian security and were generally puzzled as to why the emperor felt he needed aid.[84]

Despite their skepticism regarding Ethiopia's supposed vulnerability, the U.S. embassy staff was troubled by the potential for negative political repercussions undermining not only U.S.-Ethiopian relations, but also the emperor's own position within Ethiopia if Washington kept rejecting Addis Ababa's requests.[85] Rather than becoming more responsive to Selassie's pleas, however, the State Department instead instructed the U.S. embassy to discourage the emperor from requesting arms in the first place. But embassy officials felt that in order to dissuade Haile Selassie from making military expenditures beyond his country's means and constantly pressing Washington for military assistance, some sort of stopgap political-military gesture would be necessary to reassure the emperor of the U.S. commitment to Ethiopia's independence. Thus in mid-November 1950 the U.S. ambassador suggested that Washington send to Ethiopia a high-ranking, well-known American general, perhaps accompanied by some small show of force such as two or three medium bombers, to discuss political-military matters with the emperor.[86]

More than six months passed before Washington acted on the ambassador's advice. During this interval, Defense Department officials debated just what this American military representative should say to the emperor. Because its defense commitments in Western Europe and the Far East had been stretched to the limit since the outbreak of war in Korea the previous June, there was not much Washington could offer Ethiopia.[87] Proponents of this diplomatic venture argued that given the pro-Western slant in Ethiopia's foreign policy over the previous fifty years, coupled with the need to counter any Soviet attempt to intervene in the Red Sea-Indian Ocean region, sending a military mission to discuss mutual interests with Ethiopian officials would at least dramatize symbolically the country's importance and would counter potential Soviet attempts at subversion.[88]

Mindful of the soon to be implemented Ethiopia-Eritrea federation scheme, Washington elected to play to the symbols that appealed to the emperor by dispatching a highly visible military mission to Ethiopia in June 1951 led by Lt. Gen. Charles Lawrence Bolte, deputy chief of staff for the army. General Bolte had been informed by the director of the Joint Staff before his departure that the United States would not be able in the near future to provide either military assistance or a military mission to Ethiopia.[89] The general informed the emperor that because U.S. global priorities placed Africa last, an American military training mission in Ethiopia, though a good idea, was quite low on Washington's priority list.[90] Addis Ababa would have to settle for assurances that the United States took seriously its obligations to support the United Nations in collective security action in the event of aggression and would "always take with great concern any danger to Ethiopia."[91] In essence, the emperor was treated to a symbolic political-military show of support, but little else of substance to go with it.

Bolte returned from his mission concurring with the majority opinion within the JCS that a formal aid program and military mission to Ethiopia was inadvisable.[92] From a military vantage point, a U.S. military training mission would serve no useful purpose. Moreover, at a time when the U.S. embassy was seeking to encourage the emperor to direct his country's resources toward economic development projects, if granted a military mission, the the Ethiopian government would make further military requests that would be beyond justification for a low-priority country. Despite these reservations, Bolte felt that Ethiopia warranted some consideration and recommended that the United States provide a modest amount of weapons such as bazookas and recoilless rifles, as well as communications equipment. The general further suggested that Washington should furnish a small training detachment, as opposed to a formal mission, to train replacements for the Ethiopian contingent in Korea. In addition to rewarding, however minimally, Ethiopia's longstanding orientation toward the West and contribution of forces to the UN Command in Korea, it would serve a worthwhile, though limited, military purpose and represent a gesture of goodwill. It would at least indicate to the emperor that the United States had "not completely shut the door" on his military requests.[93]

General Bolte's limited and qualified military assistance recommendations reflected the dominant perception of the Department of Defense that Ethiopia could play only a very minor role in U.S. global policy. Moreover, the State Department as well as the Pentagon sought to limit the level of U.S. military involvement in Ethiopia. The Joint Chiefs of Staff fought to keep the U.S. training mission proposed by Bolte small and temporary.[94] When the Ethiopian government transmitted a note requesting a complete program of military assistance in October 1951, the State Department did not begin to process this request until the following

March. Ethiopia was declared eligible to receive only grant and reimbursable military aid in June 1952.[95] The low regard in which Ethiopia was held by American policy makers resulted in a tactic of putting off the Ethiopians for as long as possible and then only partially meeting their requests so as to limit the U.S. investment in Ethiopia.

The State Department's decision to request grant military aid for Ethiopia in the spring of 1953 was not the result of an altered view of Ethiopia's value, but of State's having succumbed to the argument that U.S. credibility was now at stake and the diplomatic stalemate could be broken and U.S. base rights protected only by a show of tangible U.S. support.[96] Haile Selassie had fostered close relations with the United States for ten years despite criticism of his policy within Ethiopia and from Arab states. According to the Ethiopians, it was time the United States demonstrated reciprocity toward a country in which American influence and prestige was greater than anywhere else in the Near East. Thus, in early April the State Department transmitted a letter to the Department of Defense citing five reasons why Ethiopia should be declared eligible to receive grant military aid.

1. Ethiopia should be repaid for its contribution to the UN contingent in Korea, which proved that they were on "our side" and strong supporters of collective security. Further, the presence of "colored troops from an independent African country [was] of great value to us in the propaganda war as well as in the Korean War."

2. The effectiveness of Ethiopia's internal security forces needed to be improved particularly in light of the fact that the previous September the IEG assumed responsibility for the defense and security of Eritrea, where U.S. military installations were located.

3. The emperor's pro-American policy had been coming under increasing attack in recent months. Unless that policy showed obvious benefits, particularly in the field of military assistance, Ethiopia might turn to other countries, resulting in the loss of U.S. influence and prestige in a key country in that region.

4. "Arms assistance to Ethiopia could be cited to the states in the Near East area as evidence that genuine cooperation with the United States and the United Nations, as in Korea, leads to mutual benefits."

5. The emperor had recently expressed an interest in joining any alliance or grouping of nations opposed to communism, especially any Middle East Defense Organization, in which the Department of State believed Ethiopia could become an effective member when, or after, MEDO was formed.

CONCLUSION: THE OPENING BID

The outcome of the 1953 arms-for-base-rights negotiations certainly provided benefits for both the United States and Ethiopia. The Americans received a written guarantee granting them long-term access to the strategic Kagnew communications facility. Haile Selassie acquired the much-sought-after great-power arms connection. Still, neither side was completely satisfied with the terms of the exchange.

Washington and Addis Ababa both accepted certain conditions that under ideal circumstances they would have rejected or at least modified. The United States would have preferred to avoid hidden costs and pay straight cash rent for Kagnew. Instead, the United States was required to get involved on the ground in Ethiopia and achieve specified force goal objectives. Haile Selassie desired an outright U.S. security guarantee. But he had to settle for informal promises that the United States would protect Ethiopia's security in international forums, promises that were not particularly reassuring, given the record of the United Nations' predecessor (the League of Nations) in coming to Ethiopia's aid in the 1930s.

Haile Selassie's decision to enter into a military relationship with the United States on less than optimal terms was the product of Ethiopia's military vulnerability coupled with the unavailability of suitable alternative suppliers. The emperor's obsession with security threats had created a perception of dependence upon the United States. Selassie and his associates were at once motivated and constrained by the fact that if they wanted the political, military, and economic benefits flowing from maintaining a great-power arms connection, and if they desired to survive politically themselves, they had no real choice but to go to the Americans. The Soviet Union was a bargaining chip to be used vis-à-vis the United States and kept at a safe distance—as were the Arab states. While an Ethiopian threat to defect to the East bloc or Arab bloc was viable, as far as the Americans were concerned it was not credible.

Washington's bargaining weakness and inability to make a viable or credible threat of defection had to do with Radio Marina (Kagnew). In contrast to Ethiopia's security predicament, during the period leading up to the conclusion of the MDAA and DIA there were no high-level or immediate political-military threats to U.S. interests in the Horn of Africa. The primary concern of the U.S. foreign policy bureaucracy was how to acquire guaranteed access to Kagnew Station while making a minimum investment and having as few strings attached as possible. Though the Defense Department tried to maintain a low profile by waiting out the Ethiopians following the breakdown of U.S.-Ethiopia negotiations in December 1952, Washington's strategic vulnerability was too great. Kagnew's operational uniqueness meant that the Americans could not threaten to go elsewhere or forego a deal without suffering a significant strategic loss. To break the stalemate in negotiations and insure the type of access to Eritrean military facilities the Americans desired, Washington would have to provide arms on a grant basis and a military training mission.

In the short term, the 1953 U.S.-Ethiopia arms-for-base-rights exchange was somewhat disappointing for Haile Selassie. But the emperor took some comfort in recognizing that this was only round one. These two treaties represented a first step in creating a security bond with the United States. The Ethiopians had gotten their foot in the door, and other opportunities would arise to get more from the United States. The 1953 arms-for-base-rights exchange was simply the opening bid made by the Americans for Kagnew.

4

The 1957 Expanded Base Rights Negotiations

Less than nine months after the Mutual Defense Assistance Agreement and Defense Installations Agreement were signed the Imperial Ethiopian Government (IEG) again raised the issue of military aid with Washington. At the end of January 1954, the IEG presented an aide-mémoire to the U.S. embassy requesting further assistance, including help in establishing a coast guard service and a military air-training program.[1] Then in early May, several weeks before Emperor Haile Selassie was to arrive in the United States on a good-will tour, the Ethiopian ambassador to the United States, Yilma Deressa, met with Assistant Secretary of State for Near Eastern Affairs Henry Byroade and the director of the Office of African Affairs, John Utter, to express concern over the delay in the arrival of U.S. military equipment and to press for a reply to Ethiopia's January request. Secretary Byroade informed Deressa that while Addis Ababa was welcome to purchase equipment and services on a reimbursable basis, "Worldwide demands on the United States made it imperative that we give priority to those countries most vulnerable to communist subversion, and Ethiopia did not fall in this category."[2]

However, Ethiopia was unwilling to let the matter rest. Because no specified amount or time period had been stipulated in the MDAA, Washington's commitment to fulfill future military requirements beyond the initial $5 million seemed suspect. The State Department contended that the presence of the U.S. Military Assistance Advisory Group (MAAG) in Ethiopia provided evidence of Washington's continuing interest in the military needs of Ethiopia and that American "friendship should not be measured by the amount of money [given] to any particular country."[3] If the IEG wished to obtain aid, it could transmit any requests to the chief of MAAG in Addis Ababa who would then forward the requests to the Department of Defense where they would be assessed. Mindful that it had taken the U.S. bureacracy two months to approve grant military aid for Ethiopia in the spring of 1953, the IEG was not mollified by this suggestion.

The Ethiopians used the emperor's seven-week visit to the United States (May 26–July 14) to initiate what they hoped would be a new round of military negotiations. During a meeting with Secretary Byroade on June 15, Ethiopia's Foreign Minister Aklilou offered the Americans, on behalf of the IEG, what amounted to a new quid pro quo.[4] Ethiopia would grant the United States additional military facilities, including air and naval bases, in return for enough military equipment to equip completely one division of the Ethiopian Army. This offer provided the background for two days of what Secretary Byroade insisted were military "discussions," not negotiations, at the State Department on June 29–30.[5]

Although a variety of issues were discussed at these meetings, particularly Ethiopia's desire for U.S. support to construct new ports at Assab and Massawa in Eritrea, Aklilou stated very clearly that the military question differed from the other investment and development issues raised by the Ethiopians because the basis for such aid had been established in the MDAA and DIA of 1953 which they viewed as interdependent.[6] The IEG was troubled that while the DIA was in force for twenty-five years, the MDAA seemed to be good for only one year. Addis Ababa feared that the Joint Chiefs of Staff had downgraded Ethiopia's strategic importance to the detriment of the U.S. military aid program. This conclusion was supported by Washington's claim that there were no MAP funds available to provide training aircraft or training for Ethiopian pilots and refused to provide a specific commitment to address the IEG's naval requests. The State Department's retort that it was willing to discuss the subject of military aid further and would give IEG requests serious consideration appeared to be nothing but another brush-off.[7]

The emperor and his entourage left the United States empty-handed. Even the quid pro quo offer was rejected. While the Americans appreciated the Ethiopian offer, the Joint Chiefs of Staff, noting Ethiopia's strategic position, had no immediate need for military facilities in Ethiopia.[8] Though the United States would "consider their generous offer if such need should arise in the future,"[9] Ethiopia's offer was considered a ploy to acquire increased U.S. military assistance and perhaps get the Americans to develop Eritrean ports and airfields for the IEG on military grounds.

It was not until mid-1956, when Western relations with Egyptian President Gamal Nasser were rapidly deteriorating over the funding of the Aswan High Dam, control over the Suez Canal, and East bloc arms shipments to Egypt, that Washington began to reexamine its military aid program and defense posture in Ethiopia.[10] As the Suez crisis built toward its October 29–November 7 climax, the Eisenhower administration was already considering the political and strategic implications of implementing a new American doctrine for the Middle East. It was obvious that British and French predominance in the region was coming to an ignominious end. The United States began planning for the possibility of direct U.S. intervention in the Middle East in order to safeguard Western interests. This would necessitate the establishment of military facilities in the region. U.S. defense planners, who had began considering the possibility of requesting additional base rights in Ethiopia the previous June, now recommended that Washington acquire expanded base rights to Ethiopian military facilities.[11]

On February 15, 1957, the United States submitted a request to the IEG requesting additional base facilities in Ethiopia. In March 1957 Vice President Richard Nixon was dispatched to the Middle East in order to sell the recently announced Eisenhower Doctrine. In Ethiopia Nixon was to raise the issue of acquiring expanded U.S. base rights directly with Emperor Selassie, since the IEG had failed to respond to the U.S. request.[12] Not to exacerbate an already tense political situation in the region, Washington tried to keep the negotiations under wraps. When confronted with a question at a March 13 news conference about American plans to seek a Red Sea base along the Ethiopian coast, President Eisenhower equivocated: "We have no plans at the moment for any base; . . . we do have arrangements with Ethiopia for communications facilities and things of that kind . . . and negotiations are going on, [but] we have no plans further than that at this moment."[13] When asked if the vice president was in Ethiopia to inquire about bases, Eisenhower responded, "I think there is some mistake, because we have no immediate plans for a base; . . . as of now the subject of the base itself or of a base is not in our consideration. . . . It is facilities that we would like to keep there, communications facilities, largely."[14] Despite what the president was trying to feed the American public and foreign audiences, the nature of the Nixon mission was a poorly kept secret in Washington as well as in Ethiopia.[15]

In this instance, Addis Ababa was not so quick to jump on the U.S. strategic bandwagon. Haile Selassie felt that Ethiopia already had granted the United States extraordinary basing privileges, more favorable in fact than those anywhere else in the Middle East, yet had been left hanging by the Americans after the first year of military assistance.[16] The emperor wondered how the Americans could expect him to agree to additional long-term privileges when Ethiopia was still without the means to defend these installations. Already the target for criticism by other Middle Eastern states because of the U.S. presence at Kagnew, Ethiopia, in granting these new American demands would no doubt raise considerably more political problems. Only recently Egypt had objected to the presence of U.S. naval units in the Red Sea. If Ethiopia were to give privileges to the U.S. fleet at Massawa, according to the emperor, "serious political repercussions may be expected at this time, both as regards other countries in the Middle East and public opinion in Ethiopia."[17]

Haile Selassie apparently had made his point. The Nixon delegation left Ethiopia somewhat shaken by what they had heard. In a report submitted to the White House detailing the vice president's conversations with Ethiopian officials and the staff at the U.S. embassy, Nixon recommended, "In order to reassure Ethiopia of our good intentions and our desire to assist them, we [should] increase moderately the size of our military and economic programs; . . . this will be necessary in any event if we are to secure the additional base facilities we are now seeking [and] should be done this year, if possible, but in any event next year."[18] At the end of March the vice president also sent a letter to the secretary of defense asking for a moderate expansion of the military program in Ethiopia.[19] Then in mid-April a second U.S. diplomatic mission arrived in Addis Ababa, led by Eisenhower's special ambassador, James P. Richards, to continue the negotiations. But the stalemate continued. By now it had become very apparent to the National Security Council that while Ethiopia would allow the United States continued use of existing military facilities, Washington's request for additional military facilities (the air force communications installations and certain naval requirements in Eritrea, such as anchorage rights) would "be considered in light of the magnitude of U.S. aid to [Ethiopia's] armed forces."[20]

Haile Selassie clearly intented "to use pending U.S. requests for additional military facilities as a means of obtaining more military aid."[21] The emperor was of a mind that it was time for the Americans to pay up. According to the U.S. embassy, the figure the Ethiopians had in mind was at least $10 million in military assistance for the coming fiscal year and help in establishing an Ethiopian Air Force.[22] Anything less than this would be unacceptable to the IEG.

Washington refused to budge. Both the State Department and Defense Department opposed the idea of allowing Ethiopia to link the question of additional military facilities to the request for air force aid, especially since Washington had recently agreed to conduct a survey of Ethiopian Air Force requirements.[23] The Department of Defense, in particular, which had agreed in the fall of 1956 with a State Department request to provide Ethiopia with approximately $5 million in military assistance for FY 1957 and to stabilize MAP aid for Ethiopia at that level over the next four years (FY 1957–FY 1960), felt the asking price was too high.[24] Moreover, the

Pentagon had now determined that U.S. requests for additional facilities were not "of such urgency as to warrent their use by [the] IEG as [the] basis for increased military assistance."[25] On the evening of April 11, the State Department sent a telegram to the U.S. embassy and the Richards mission instructing them not to give any indication to the Ethiopians that U.S. action on the air force request and increased aid would be conditioned upon any quid pro quo.[26] By the end of the year, the negotiations for expanded U.S. base rights in Ethiopia had been terminated.[27]

THE GREATER SOMALILAND THREAT

Haile Selassie's attempt to blackmail the Americans into upping the ante in this latest round of negotiations was motivated by the crisis he anticipated would erupt once the British and Italian Somaliland territories received their independence in 1960. Already in the mid-1950s an open propaganda campaign for the dismemberment of Ethiopia was under way in the Horn. Tribal attacks and raids by foreign military planes had exposed the vulnerability of Addis Ababa. The IEG did not possess any antiaircraft units, antitank units, mines, minesweeping equipment, or fighter squadrons, and only enough rifles for one army division.[28] Thus, according to a March 1957 U.S. embassy report, Ethiopia could not defend itself against external aggression or maintain internal security in the face of "deliberately subversive campaigns supported from nearby territories with funds and agents."[29]

Haile Selassie had studiously followed the Somaliland issue since the Allied liberation of East Africa in 1941. During the subsequent period of British administrative and political predominance in the area, London's colonial office had developed the idea of incorporating the Somali-inhabited parts of Ethiopia, Italian Somaliland, and British Somaliland into a Greater Somaliland.[30] The movement favoring the creation of a Greater Somaliland had been restrained temporarily after the United Nations decided to allow Italy to administer a UN trusteeship over its Somaliland territory beginning in 1950. But as Italy's and Great Britain's ten-year trusteeships over the Somalilands drew to a close, the Greater Somaliland issue reappeared and became a source of tension that pitted Addis Ababa against West European colonial powers, the Somalis, and Arab states.

With the Somaliland issue assuming a position at the top of Addis Ababa's national security agenda, as he had done in the case of Eritrean federation, the emperor once again looked to the United States for support. Selassie did not trust the British, especially in the wake of London's offer in the spring of 1956 to purchase the Haud and Reserved areas from Ethiopia.[31] The Ethiopians were not enamored of the French, who controlled Ethiopia's access to the sea through Djibouti and charged high freight rates on the French-owned railway.[32] Addis Ababa viewed Gamal Nasser's "Unity of the Valley of the Nile" concept as a guise for an Egyptian version of Greater Somaliland that would subordinate Ethiopia to Egypt. Moreover, the Islamic content of Egyptian propaganda broadcasts seemed designed to stimulate Somali nationalism and that of other Moslem minorities inside Ethiopia.[33] Given Addis Ababa's sense of isolation on this issue, the primary objective of the Ethiopian foreign ministry during the latter half of the 1950s was to prevent Washington from aligning with London on the Somaliland issue.[34]

Washington was quite aware of the potential for crisis presented by Somali independence. The State Department had received reports from the field at the end of 1955 indicating that the Ethiopian government had been having problems with Somali tribesmen. A January 1956 Department of State intelligence report had explored the economic, political, and social weaknesses of an independent Somalia and the effect such a state would have upon the Horn. The report concluded that Somali leaders would likely encourage militant irredentism on behalf of creating a Greater Somaliland in order to divert attention from internal problems.[35] When the National Security Council adopted NSC 5615/1 as the U.S. government's official policy guideline toward Ethiopia in mid-November 1956, one of the general considerations highlighted by this document was that the Somali problem likely would create instability in the Horn over the next few years.[36] It would therefore be crucial for the United States to ease Selassie's fears concerning the Somali threat; the emperor was becoming so overly preoccupied by the Somali issue that he lacked adequate appreciation for the communist subversive threat in the region.[37]

Selassie's obsession with the potential threat posed by an independent Somali state was brought to the attention of officials at the highest levels of the U.S. government. At the London Suez Canal Users Association conferences held in August and September 1956, Ethiopia's Foreign Minister Ato Aklilou spent considerable time explaining the Somali threat to Secretary of State John Foster Dulles. President Eisenhower also was aware of this problem and during the Suez crisis expressed privately to Secretary Dulles his grave misgivings over London's handling of the Ethiopian-Somali situation, believing the British would "make a mess of it."[38] Then in March 1957 Vice President Richard Nixon was treated to a firsthand account in Addis Ababa by Haile Selassie of Ethiopia's defense problems and the Somali threat.[39] Thus, the dangers posed by Somali nationalism to Ethiopia were well known in Washington.

The American embassy in Addis Ababa played a critical role in advocating the IEG's position. According to the U.S. mission, a subversive campaign was being waged against the Ethiopian government by agents in the

Ogaden who were "Moslems, and for the most part, at the same time, communist sympathisers."[40] As outlined in an embassy document detailing the defense problems of Ethiopia, antigovernment agents operating in the interior were advancing the argument that by remaining faithful to the West and in granting base facilities to the United States, Ethiopia was "showing her unfaithfulness to the Arab world and, to Moslems in Ethiopia, in particular" and "that the attachment of the central government to the Western Colonial powers [was] evidence that the government [did] not have the interests of the Moslems at heart."[41] The propagandists concluded, "So long as Ethiopia continues with the West the only salvation for the Moslem inhabitants of the Ogaden territory is to seek to unite in order to form in 1960, the great and independent state of Greater Somaliland."[42]

In early 1957, the Ethiopian Ministry of Foreign Affairs presented the Nixon delegation with an alarming memorandum in which Ethiopia was described as confronting "a studied campaign pursued by certain colonial interests as well as by anti-Ethiopian elements in the Middle East, for her dismemberment."[43] Selassie used the occasion of the Nixon visit to express vehemently his great dissatisfaction with the level of U.S. military assistance, as well as Washington's perceived lack of support on the Somali issue.[44] The imperial government had come to believe that "a thoroughgoing re-examination of Ethiopian-American relations in the light of the situation existing in the Middle East" was in order.[45] Of course, such a reassessment would not be necessary if Washington were to increase the level of U.S. military aid.

NASSER, SUEZ, AND THE EISENHOWER DOCTRINE

During the mid-1950s, the Eisenhower administration began to expand U.S. involvement in the Middle East, incurring the wrath of Egypt's President Gamal Nasser. In the spring of 1954 Washington had established bilateral military aid programs with the pro-Western governments in Iraq and Pakistan. By the fall of 1955, the United States had drawn together Iraq, Pakistan, Iran, Turkey, and the United Kingdom into the Baghdad Pact—the culmination of Secretary Dulles's Northern Tier concept.[46] But the conclusion of the Baghdad Pact, which included an Iraqi government at odds with Cairo, coupled with the ongoing tensions between Egypt and Israel and Washington's refusal to provide Cairo with arms on Gamal Nasser's terms, led to a deterioration of U.S. relations with the Egypt, as well as with other Arab governments who had fallen under the sway of Nasser.[47]

Top-ranking American officials, Secretary of State Dulles in particular, would come to view Nasser as a communist stooge especially after Cairo signed an arms agreement with Prague in the fall of 1955. Nasser's method of retaliation against "union busters"—threatening any state that broke ranks with him—seemed to further Soviet interests and undermine those of the West.[48] Because of his alignment with the United States, Haile Selassie was one of the targeted union busters. As a result the United States needed to support Ethiopia so that the emperor would not be intimidated by Nasser and feel compelled to expel the U.S. military presence.

The Eisenhower administration's concept of promoting regional self-defense, as embodied in the Baghdad Pact, was to all intents and purposes a dead letter by the end of 1956. In recognition of this fact, during the fall of 1956 the Pentagon had begun working on a new plan for the defense of the Middle East. The result of this effort was the announcement of the Eisenhower Doctrine in January 1957, which was passed by a joint resolution in the U.S. Congress in early March. The new defense doctrine contained three features: (1) increased U.S. economic cooperation with nations in the Middle East, (2) greater flexibility for the president to use funds already allocated to assist any nations desiring military assistance and cooperation; and (3) a willingness to use the "armed forces of the United States to secure and protect the territorial integrity and political independence of such nations, requesting such aid, against overt armed aggression from any nation controlled by International Communism."[49]

Egyptian, not to mention Soviet, opposition to Washington's call for an enhanced U.S. presence in the Middle East made the Ethiopian connection, at least in the short term, seem quite valuable to the United States in light of the political-military ramifications of the Eisenhower Doctrine. Politically, this policy was extremely provocative to the Arab nationalist governments in the region. Addis Ababa's willingness to support this doctrine would lend it some legitimacy. Militarily, U.S. operational plans required the development and maintenance of a strategic infrastructure. Kagnew Station, as well as a pending request for expanded U.S. base rights at Massawa, would form part of this base network. Vice President Nixon's March 1957 trip to Africa and the Richards mission sent to the Middle East the following month were designed to prepare the way politically and militarily for the implementation of the Eisenhower Doctrine.

The military assistance component of the Eisenhower Doctrine was premised upon three primary U.S. objectives: (1) to keep nations of the Middle East independent of communist domination; (2) to secure strategic positions, resources, and transit rights in the area; and 3) to deny resources and strategic positions to the communist bloc.[50] Eisenhower's authorization for the use of U.S. forces in the area was expected to increase the will of pro-Western governments to resist communist aggression and decrease their susceptibility to overtures from those states not aligned with the West. Moreover, U.S. plans for military operations were based on a concept of cooperation using combined forces, including U.S. forces possessing an atomic capability. To support U.S. forces deployed to the area in a given contingency, the Defense Department needed to acquire base and transit rights in the area for greater flexibility. Thus, U.S. military assistance would be used to reward those governments who helped to facilitate the execution of this policy, and who would undoubtedly wish to receive maximum aid.[51]

Haile Selassie felt that Ethiopia, in particular, deserved special consideration when it came time for Washington to hand out military aid. Selassie's embrace of the Eisenhower Doctrine had provoked increased Arab nationalist propaganda attacks against his government. In this tense atmosphere, the emperor might opt for the easy way out by giving in to Egyptian pressures and expelling the Americans from Ethiopia. The Eisenhower administration believed that in order to prevent further Soviet penetration in the Middle East, Egyptian influence had to be checked as well and U.S. support had to be extended to leaders such as Haile Selassie who would resist Nasser's call for regional unity.[52]

More than ever before the American foreign policy–making community appreciated the need to keep Ethiopia out of the neutralist camp. Some U.S. diplomats feared that powers hostile to the West had already beaten Washington to the punch in consolidating a position behind the Northern Tier.[53] Although American influence and prestige in Ethiopia was viewed as still being quite high, affording Washington a chance to salvage the situation, the Ethiopians could no longer be taken for granted. Moreover, the possible political decline of the besieged Ethiopian emperor was cause for great concern in Washington: Selassie was seen as the key to stability in Ethiopia, and his demise would adversely affect U.S. interests.[54] In order to counteract internal and external forces threatening the emperor, strenghten Addis Ababa's political-military alignment with Washington, and secure the U.S. strategic position in the Middle East from hostile interlopers, the United States would need to provide tangible evidence of a long-term interest in a strong Ethiopia.

However, Ethiopia was somewhat remote from the central Middle East arena where the communists seemed to be threatening. Because of the lack of a present danger to Ethiopia it would be difficult to justify a major increase in military aid for the IEG under the Eisenhower Doctrine.[55] The State Department believed that African countries on the periphery of the Middle East such as Ethiopia, Libya, Tunisia, and Morocco could be protected by increased aid to those states most directly threatened and that they should as far as possible not be offered amounts of aid that "would invite invidious comparisons."[56] In seeking access to Ethiopian facilities to help implement the new U.S. regional defense doctrine, the United States refused to invoke the Eisenhower Doctrine to justify additional benefits to Ethiopia.

FEAST OR FAMINE

For Haile Selassie, American interest in Ethiopia could best be expressed in the form of military assistance. Judged on this basis, U.S. support seemed dubious, given the way the Americans had extended military aid and training to the Ethiopians after the conclusion of the 1953 Mutual Defense Assistance Agreement. During FY 1953–FY 1957, Ethiopia was allocated approximately $17 million worth of aid, considerably less than the $25 million Addis Ababa would have received if Washington had adhered to the first year's $5 million figure.[57] Moreover, the IEG claimed that as of the beginning of 1957 less than $8 million worth of arms had actually been delivered.[58] Thus, the new situation in the Middle East was seen as an opportunity for Addis Ababa to exploit its strategic location and press the Eisenhower administration to increase MAP funding and expand U.S. military programs in Ethiopia.

Following the June 1954 military discussions, U.S.-Ethiopia relations entered a very rocky period. Addis Ababa was particularly frustrated by the United States' refusal to make a long-term military commitment to Ethiopia. Washington would only approve MAP funding on a yearly basis, as opposed to guaranteeing aid levels for a longer period. The net result was an Ethiopian military assistance program that was described by a high-ranking member of the JCS's Joint Staff in mid-1956 as "feast or famine"—$5 million one year, $1 million the next.[59] In fact, the Department of Defense was planning in the spring of 1956 to request only $554,000 in MAP funding for Ethiopia in FY 1957.[60]

The Ethiopians were also upset by how the MAP program was being implemented. Besides erratic deliveries and delays in the program approval process, it seemed that the Americans were deliberately concealing information regarding the price of equipment delivered and that the actual value of the weapons and equipment received was less than the amount of military assistance allocated by Washington.[61] Particularly disappointing to the emperor was that most of the equipment the Ethiopian military received was used and required extensive repairs to be made serviceable.[62] The IEG claimed that it had been supplied with used and recharged ammunition—a charge the DoD denied.[63] This all added up to an insult to the IEG, which was proud of its long military tradition and now was being treated in such a second-rate manner by the Americans.

The American military training mission also was plagued by problems that disturbed the IEG. In 1954 the chief of the U.S. Military Assistance and Advisory Group had informed Emperor Selassie that the "MAAG would train personnel and assist in any way the Ethiopian government desired, including the foundation at Harrar, of a military academy."[64] Twenty-one months later, Washington declared the promise of the MAAG chief to have been "completely unauthorized."[65] Moreover, because about 10 percent of U.S. military assistance was used to train Ethiopian officers in the United States, there was less available to purchase weapons and supplies.[66] These problems, plus the "frequent and unfortunate experiences of the Ethiopian officers with [racial] segregation in the United States," began to alarm the U.S. embassy in Addis Ababa that the United States was failing to achieve the originally "designed purpose of fostering closer and more friendly relations as well as improving the technical standards of the Ethiopian army."[67]

Perhaps the one event that most strengtened Haile Selassie's bargaining leverage vis-à-vis the United States at this time occurred in September 1955, when Egypt concluded an arms agreement with Czechoslovakia. The Czech-Egyptian arms deal established the East bloc as a viable arms alternative to the Western powers in the region. Ethiopian overtures and threats to turn to the Soviet Union for aid if the Americans did not satisfy their military requests now had to be taken more seriously than in the past. Although Emperor Selassie feared the communists, the Soviets could still be used to bluff the Americans.

Haile Selassie's ability to use a threat of defection to the Soviets against the Americans was made all the more plausible by Gamal Nasser's already having done so. American defense planners were particularly sensitive to the possibility that a repeat of the Egyptian defection to the East bloc for arms could be replayed in Ethiopia and jeopardize U.S. base rights. Admiral Radford, chairman of the Joint Chiefs of Staff, had received a memo from his staff at the end of June 1956 in which the emperor indicated he wanted American military and economic assistance on an "urgent basis," or else Ethiopia would turn to the Soviets.[68] During the fall of 1956 President Eisenhower had been made aware of an implied Ethiopian threat to get arms elsewhere if they could not get them from the United States.[69] Because the Pentagon and the NSC were exploring the possibility of obtaining additional base rights in Ethiopia at this time, the president felt that Ethiopia's friendship had to be assured even if it meant establishing new military programs; however, he hoped they could be kept as small as possible.[70]

The IEG had nurtured this threat of defection from the Western bloc by implying that Ethiopia might go the neutralist course by a series of diplomatic initiatives. Between December 1955 and June 1956, Selassie played host to Marshal Tito for two weeks, signed a general trade agreement with Czechoslovakia, welcomed the head of a touring Chinese communist cultural delegation, and allowed the Soviet Union to raise its legation in Addis Ababa to the embassy level. Moreover, throughout the first half of 1956 the IEG had begun to seek out a political rapprochement with Gamal Nasser, who still hoped to gain Ethiopia's adherence to Cairo's Unity of the Valley of the Nile concept and planned to receive the emperor on a state visit to Egypt at the end of the year. Although the emperor aligned Ethiopia with the U.S. position during the Suez crisis, he would subsequently decrease his backing and his support for the U.S. position in the United Nations as well as delay responding to the U.S. base request.[71]

EXPANDING BASE RIGHTS

Although Kagnew Station represented Washington's core interest in Ethiopia, U.S. strategic interests in Ethiopia kept expanding during the mid-1950s. Not only had the scope of U.S. operations at Kagnew grown over the years, but also requests for further expansion were being submitted almost continuously to the Ethiopian government. American officials, of course, were quite cognizant of the explicit linkage between U.S. military assistance and base rights in Ethiopia. Thus, when the Joint Chiefs of Staff began contemplating in mid-1956 the idea of asking the IEG for additional base rights privileges, they realized that the emperor would use the request to up the ante.

During October 1956, a draft statement for U.S. policy guidance toward Ethiopia (NSC 5615/1) was being circulated throughout the U.S. national security bureaucracy; the statement examined the base-rights question in Ethiopia in light of U.S. defense requirements. On November 19, 1956, President Eisenhower approved a slightly edited version of NSC 5615/1.[72] Two days later, the Joint Logistics Plans Committee for the JCS submitted its base requirements for U.S. forces in the Middle East in support of CINCSPECOMME (Commander-in-Chief, Special Command Middle East) Operations Plan 215–56.[73] Although recognizing that in the aftermath of the Suez Crisis, with tensions and anti-Western sentiments still inflamed, it might be inadvisable to seek basing rights outside the NATO structure, the JLPC considered it appropriate to inform the Joint Chiefs of Staff about "the nature of and type of additional requirements necessary to implement plans in the Arab-Israeli dispute . . . so negotiations may be effected."[74]

NSC 5615/1 essentially defined those U.S. strategic requirements in Ethiopia that prompted the United States to enter into the base-rights negotiations with the IEG in 1957. In this policy guidance the U.S. Air Force indicated the need to establish a signal communications base in Eritrea, in lieu of Aden, and the Joint Chiefs of Staff "established requirements for post-D-Day facilities" in Ethiopia.[75] Along with Aden and Port Sudan in the Red Sea area, the U.S. Navy requested that an agreement be reached with Ethiopia to permit continued procurement of petroleum products, the maintenance of petroleum, oil, and lubricants (POL) and ammunition storage sites, and access to anchorage and harbor facilities for replenishment and repair operations at Massawa. This access would support shipping lanes to the Far East, Europe, and the Middle East.[76] Thus, NSC 5615/1 defined U.S. strategic objectives in Ethiopia at the end of 1956 to include assuring "continued use of existing military facilities and to obtain additional military rights as required."[77]

The Eisenhower administration knew it would have some difficulties in these negotiations, given the recent and frequent expressions of dissatisfaction by the IEG with the American effort in Ethiopia. After Selassie's 1954 visit to the United States, the president had directed that annual funding for U.S. MAP assistance to Ethiopia be maintained at its original $5 million level. When this did not happen, Eisenhower received a disturbing note from the Ethiopian emperor in 1956 which implied that the United States had violated the 1953 MDA agreement with Ethiopia. The Joint Chiefs of Staff also had been warned at the end of June 1956 that the breakdown in U.S. military aid, as perceived by the Ethiopians, "would not only make negotiations for new bases impossible, but could also result in cancellation of our present base rights."[78] While the latter threat seemed extreme, the former was taken very seriously.

However, in negotiating with the IEG over these expanded base rights, the Eisenhower administration did not have to give away the shop, especially since by April 1957 the Pentagon no longer saw any urgent need to acquire access to Ethiopian facilities. NATO facilities in Greece and Turkey would be available for a Middle East contingency. Through 1957 the Arab governments in Iraq, Jordan, and Saudi Arabia still maintained a pro-Western posture in crises outside the realm of the Arab-Israeli conflict. Moreover, the port facilities in Eritrea were not in the best condition, as the Ethiopians had been trying for years to get the Americans to finance the improvement of them.[79] While these facilities could prove valuable for backup support it would require a substantial U.S. financial investment to improve their handling capacities, and given the time lag involved in construction and dredging the harbors they would be of little value in the short term. If in 1962 the Eritrean Parliament chose to dissolve the federation, then soon after the improvements were made at Massawa, Eritrea might not even be a part of the Ethiopian empire. Washington's strategic cost-benefit analysis simply weighed against investing more than the $4.1 million in MAP funding approved for FY 1957—an amount that represented a more than $3 million increase over what had originally been proposed by the Defense Department for Ethiopia.

THE NEUTRALIST DEBATE IN ADDIS ABABA

While Ethiopia's sense of threat made it almost inevitable that the IEG would use a threat of defection to the Soviets for arms in order to pressure Washington to meet its security needs, and the 1955 Egyptian-Czech arms deal suggested that this threat was viable, it was questionable whether the emperor would actually implement such a threat. According to the U.S. embassy and the IEG, he would.[80] The possibility of Ethiopia going the neutralist course and seeking aid from both East and West seemed more credible because the Soviet example in Egypt had created a crediblity problem for the United States in Ethiopia. As a result, neutralist elements in Addis Ababa were gaining support for their argument that Ethiopian interests would best be served by going the neutralist course and terminating the military relationship with Washington.

Ethiopian critics of the IEG's pro-West policy began their argument by noting the greater benefits received by neutralist states. During 1956 Moscow had provided Egypt with $450 million worth of arms, while Syria and Yemen, states much smaller in population and size than Ethiopia, had received armaments valued at $60 million and $7.5 million, respectively, from the Soviet Union.[81] Moreover, these arms transfers had apparently occurred without an exchange of bases. In contrast, Ethiopia had supported the United States during the entire Suez Canal episode and had endorsed almost immediately the Eisenhower Doctrine for the Middle East, yet had received little material support in return. It made little sense to antagonize Egypt by supporting the Americans if Ethiopia's security needs continued to be ignored.

Moreover, as reported by the U.S. embassy and the IEG, a propaganda campaign that exhibited a distinct anti-Western theme was being waged in Addis Ababa and elsewhere. Ethiopia was accused of betraying its geography and tradition as a Middle Eastern state in working with the Western colonial powers and the United States and "playing the stooge of the Colonial Powers, in sending her sons to die in Korea and in being the stalking horse for the imperialist designs of those same powers [seeking to limit] freedom of national development, of which the two Suez Canal Conferences [were] but the most recent examples."[82] The Western powers were using Ethiopia to further their own imperialistic designs as evidenced by the fact that "the Communist Powers fully support with arms, the struggle of Middle Eastern peoples towards freedom and independence," while "the West has never intended seriously to support Ethiopia's defense efforts, on the contrary, the arms received by Ethiopia are pitiful in comparison with those being received elsewhere in the Middle East."[83] Although the United States wished to use Ethiopian territory for bases, the Americans "refused to defend the territory or the bases and [had] sent no arms that would permit Ethiopia to defend them herself."[84] If Ethiopia would "refuse to act as a stooge of the West, the problem of Greater Somaliland could be immediately solved, and at the same time, the problem of national defense."[85]

This seemed like a lot of shrill talk back in Washington. Besides voicing his doubts about the seriousness of the dangers facing Ethiopia, Eisenhower's special envoy James Richards told Ethiopia's Foreign Minister Aklilou during the April 1957 round of negotiations that the benefits of U.S. friendship were "worth more than [the] dangers involved in the presence of [U.S.] bases."[86] International communism was the main threat the IEG should be worried about and how to stop its advances. If the Ethiopians did not think this was so, remember that "some countries behind [the] Iron Curtain once felt [the] same way."[87]

While attempting to throw the communist scare into the Ethiopians, American officials were mainly concerned that the emperor might cast his lot with the neutralists rather than fall in with the communist bloc. Although the communists were seen as building up nationalism in Africa to undermine Western influence, the State Department felt that the threat of communist penetration was not particularly great or imminent in Ethiopia. Even given the feeling in Ethiopia that the benefits of Addis Ababa's pro-Western alignment had been small, the communists had made few inroads in Ethiopia.[88] On the other hand, pro-U.S. groups in Ethiopia had been weakened while the influence of the xenophobic clique that favored isolationist or neutralist policies had increased, particularly in the aftermath of the Suez crisis, owing to Washington's perceived indifference.[89] Since the Eisenhower administration was determined to check and reduce communist as well as Egyptian influence in Ethiopia and the rest of Africa, the Americans would have to give the emperor something to keep him on their side.[90]

THE STRUGGLE OVER MAP STABILIZATION

Perhaps the most serious difficulty the IEG faced in dealing with the Americans was that the U.S. military assistance and training programs in

Ethiopia were shaped and implemented by a defense establishment that first and foremost assessed Ethiopia's military requirements in terms of its ability to contribute to global or regional defense. Unfortunately for the IEG, the Pentagon did not take the Ethiopian military very seriously. In a February 1957 review of U.S. military assistance programs in the Middle East, the Joint Chiefs of Staff had observed that Ethiopia's armed forces were, and would continue to be, "too small to be of any consequence in global war."[91] Addis Ababa's military forces—then composed of three commands totaling 24,000 soldiers and 4,000 support troops—were deemed to be capable only of maintaining internal security and offering limited resistance to local aggression; they were considered unable to provide "effective defense against invasion by an army with modern weapons."[92] Thus, the Pentagon saw its military mission in Ethiopia as very limited—to provide equipment and training so the Ethiopians could maintain internal security and resist local aggression.

The Defense Department seemed determined to resist bureaucratic pressures from outside as well as inside the department to enhance the scope of the U.S. military mission in Ethiopia. In November 1955 the Joint Chiefs of Staff had received a report from General Orvall R. Cook who, "while not much impressed with the needs of Ethiopia," recommended that the JCS not only reassess the Ethiopia program, based upon a number of geopolitical considerations, but also undertake a number of new tasks within the country.[93] The following March the Joint Chiefs reported, "Present conditions do not justify a change in MDAP (Military Defense Assistance Program) objectives."[94] At the end of 1956, in putting together the FY 1957 Program Guidance for Ethiopia, the JCS recommended "only such minimum military assistance . . . as will insure utilization of the U.S. base rights."[95] Even after President Eisenhower directed the NSC in the fall of 1956 to stabilize the U.S. MAP in Ethiopia, the Pentagon persisted in its belief that no sound military rationale existed for extending military aid to Ethiopia and that the United States was wasting time, energy and resources on a client state that could be better spent in other places.

The Defense Department's inherent hostility toward the Ethiopian MAP program was counterbalanced by a State Department that favored extending U.S. military and economic assistance to as many countries as possible in order to score political points in the battle to contain communism and radicalism. Secretary Dulles felt that increased military aid to Ethiopia would serve a propaganda purpose in the area, especially in light of the Egyptian challenge to U.S. policy in the Middle East.[96] Even though the emperor seemed more interested in strengthening Ethiopia's armed forces than in undertaking political, economic, and social reforms, the

State Department favored stabilizing the U.S. military assistance program in Ethiopia on political grounds.[97] It was well known at State that Haile Selassie devoted an inordinate amount of attention to military affairs, so failure to follow through with some kind of military program would have a negative impact on the IEG's pro-West orientation.[98]

The Department of State typically found itself in the hot seat with regard to Ethiopia when it came time to justify U.S. foreign military and economic assistance programs before Congress, thanks to the IEG's low-priority rating among U.S. aid recipients. In years in which U.S. foreign aid programs were subject to reductions, as in FY 1955, Ethiopia was a likely candidate to be cut out altogether.[99] Since the beginning of the U.S.-Ethiopia military relationship, "It was only the strong pressure of the State Department for political considerations that led to any money at all being allocated to Ethiopia."[100] Thus, if the State Department was not on Ethiopia's side the game would be lost.

In July 1956 the deputy undersecretary of state for political affairs sent a letter to the assistant secretary of defense requesting that the Pentagon scrap its original half-million dollar proposal and instead submit a MAP program for Ethiopia in the range of $5 million for FY 1957.[101] State based this request on the grounds that "neutralist or outright hostile elements" were making it difficult for the United States to cooperate with certain Arab governments. Given Ethiopia's political stability, desirable geographical location, and friendly attitude, the United States could use Ethiopia to "build a position of strength in the area."[102] Washington hoped to establish "a crescent of friendly countries south and west of Egypt" which, if successful, would reinforce the American position in the Middle East and obstruct the further penetration of Africa by "inimical forces."[103] Basing its action almost exclusively upon political considerations, the National Security Council decided in October 1956 to provide the IEG with $20 million in MAP aid over a four-year period (FY 1957–FY 1960) and to increase the size of the Ethiopian Army to 28,000 troops by FY 1962.[104] To maximize the political impact of this decision Secretary Dulles sent a personal message to Ethiopia's foreign minister informing him that for FY 1957 the United States would provide $5 million for the Ethiopian Army, a naval patrol craft, up to $5 million in economic aid and conduct a survey of Ethiopia's air force capabilities. Aklilou's immediate response to what amounted to a total aid package in excess of $13 million was that "the military aid figures were too low."[105]

Aklilou's curt response was predictable; the four-year $20 million MAP package had the effect of setting an upper limit on the level of military assistance that the United States would provide to the IEG through the end of the decade. There was no doubt that the United States hoped to use this decision to achieve political objectives in Ethiopia while avoiding "a military build-up which would seriously strain the Ethiopian economy or lead to commitments for indefinite U.S. support."[106] Washington's strategic interest in acquiring expanded base rights in Ethiopia was counterbalanced by a desire to avoid a costly military buildup that would do little to enhance the global or regional defense posture of the United States. Besides, the State Department had stretched the political line of argumentation to the extreme to get $5 million annually for Ethiopia; it could not turn around only months later to ask for double that amount in military aid for such a low-priority ally. Moreover, if the United States did not give in to the emperor's $10 million arms demand this time around, Selassie might learn that whenever the IEG wanted something from the United States he could not simply exploit Washington's strategic vulnerability by using Ethiopian facilities to blackmail the Americans.

CONCLUSION: WASHINGTON PASSES

The 1957 expanded base rights negotiations ended in a stalemate because of the refusal of either side to adjust its original demand. Washington, which had initiated the negotiations, finally terminated them because the emperor's $10 million asking price was deemed too high, especially in light of the fact that the administration had just committed itself to give Ethiopia approximately $5 million annually in military aid through the next four fiscal years. Addis Ababa, on the other hand, did not view Washington's decision in the fall of 1956 to stabilize the U.S. MAP program in Ethiopia as compensation for expanded base rights. It was merely a fulfillment of what the Americans should have been doing in the first place as part of the original 1953 MDAA-DIA quid pro quo. Granting the United States expanded base rights in appreciation for this decision would be like giving the Americans something for nothing.

Ethiopia was under no great pressure to knuckle under to the United States in this newest round of negotiations. While Addis Ababa was concerned about the Somali threat, there was no need to panic. Somalia would not receive its independence until mid-1960, and the emperor could play the neutralist game to stall the opposition. Although Washington still seemed to be the place to go to receive military, economic, and technical aid on generous terms, the Soviet Union was proving to be a very viable alternative—an option that if not exploited at the moment could be later when Ethiopia's needs became more pressing. The emperor of course had no real desire to realign Ethiopia with either the communists or the neutralists. But to placate those who felt that he had been deceived and taken advantage of by the Americans in the past, out of political necessity

Selassie had to set a high price on Washington's request for additional facilities.

Washington, too, felt no compelling reason to enter into a new and expended quid pro quo with the Ethiopians. In contrast to Ethiopia's position, Washington's perception of threat had reached the point of panic. But it would be other more centrally located Middle Eastern states such as Jordan, Lebanon, Turkey, and Iraq that would receive increased aid and emergency U.S. arms shipments under the rubric of the Eisenhower Doctrine during the latter half of 1957 rather than Ethiopia.[107] The Americans appeared vulnerable to manipulation because of their desire to acquire expanded base rights in Ethiopia. This perceived vulnerability, however, was offset by the marginality of these facilities, at least in the short term, in supporting U.S. intervention in a Middle East contingency. Moreover, the Department of State could only go so far in justifying increased U.S. military assistance to a low-priority ally, and one that could add little to U.S. defense capabilities. Because the Pentagon was willing to forego these expanded base privileges there was nothing more for State to do for Ethiopia; it had already made a good-faith effort in acquiring the NSC's consent to stabilize MAP aid to Ethiopia. Thus, if the Ethiopians wanted to up the ante on them, the Americans could simply back out of the negotiations without undercutting the U.S. military defense posture in the region.

Washington's decision to terminate the 1957 base rights negotiations simply meant that Addis Ababa would have to try again. Persistent IEG pressure had resulted in a four-year commitment from the United States to provide military assistance at the original $5 million level. While the $13 million military, economic, and technical grant aid package Ethiopia received for FY 1957 was nothing for the IEG to snub, in the military realm it fell far short of what the emperor desired. Despite his avowed friendship with the United States, Haile Selassie had no qualms about playing hardball to acquire support for the Ethiopian Air Force, higher levels of guaranteed grant military aid, and a U.S. security commitment.

5

The 1960 "Secret" Commitment

The Middle East crisis of 1956–1957 left unresolved a number of issues in the U.S.-Ethiopia military relationship. Although the United States agreed to stabilize MAP assistance to Ethiopia at higher levels, this commitment fell far short of the amount required to accomplish two high-priority IEG force goal objectives: establishing a fourth Ethiopian Army division and creating a modern Imperial Air Force. Moreover, with Somali independence drawing near and the IEG seeing itself isolated internationally on this issue, an American security commitment would provide the necessary guarantee Haile Selassie felt he needed to combat this threat.

For its part, the United States was uncomfortable with the idea of paying "rent" for Kagnew Station in the form of military assistance. It seemed that U.S. arms transfers and MAP aid had the effect of creating new Ethiopian demands and placing Washington in the uncomfortable position of having to reject IEG requests. Washington's decision to stabilize MAP aid to Ethiopia in 1956 at least ensured continued U.S. access to Kagnew for another four years, although at the end of this time a new arrangement would doubtless be required in which the emperor would attempt to up the ante.

Despite American efforts to play down the military side of U.S.-Ethiopia relations, events conspired in the late 1950s to bring the Eisenhower administration around to Haile Selassie's way of thinking that a new understanding between the two arms partners was in order to solidify the original arms-for-base-rights agreement. A first indication that American resistance was wearing down occurred in 1958 when the Eisenhower administration agreed to provide aid to the Imperial Air Force. Then, in mid-July 1960 Ambassador Arthur Richards presented an aid package to the IEG worth almost $25 million, including $14.7 million in military assistance.[1] Richards's presentation was favorably received by the emperor.[2] What followed from this American offer was the conclusion on August 29, 1960, of a secret executive agreement between the United States and Ethiopia that laid out an enhanced security framework for cooperation.[3]

The military component of this agreement was rather straightforward. In exchange for continued access to Ethiopian military facilities, the United States agreed to train and equip an imperial army of 40,000 soldiers. Washington also pledged to continue providing military assistance to Addis Ababa. As a result of this "secret" commitment, U.S. military aid (including MAP and IMETP funds) to Ethiopia averaged more than $10 million annually over the next fifteen years (FY 1961–FY 1975), a marked contrast to the previous eight-year period (FY 1953–FY 1960) during which U.S. military assistance averaged about $5 million per year.[4]

Perhaps the most significant and controversial aspect of the 1960 agreement involved a clause in which Washington reaffirmed its "continued interest in the security of Ethiopia and its opposition to any activities threatening the territorial integrity of Ethiopia."[5] Ten years later when this military commitment was revealed before the U.S. Senate Committee on U.S. Security Agreements and Commitments Abroad, State Department officials would contend that the executive branch gave only a minimal interpretation to this particular clause. In their eyes it simply meant that in the event of any attack against Ethiopia, the United States would "use all our good offices in the United Nations and elsewhere to insure the maintenance of Ethiopia's integrity."[6] However, the Ethiopian government as well as several distinquished U.S. senators felt that it implied more. At a minimum it suggested that the United States would come to Ethiopia's defense if attacked.[7] A maximalist interpretation suggested that the United States had committed itself to intervene, if necessary, with military forces and to defend the Ethiopian state from external as well as internal attack, and to preserve the political status quo in the Horn of Africa.

The ambiguity of the 1960 secret military commitment allowed both sides to apply their own favored interpretation to the meaning of this agreement. Haile Selassie viewed it as marking a new starting point in political-military cooperation between the United States and Ethiopia.[8] Washington claimed that it merely represented a programmatic, standard arrangement that ensured continued access to Kagnew without committing the United States to a fixed timetable or deadline in the completion of its military mission in Ethiopia.[9] While Selassie had upped the ante on the Americans, the United States could use the agreement to put a cap on increasing Ethiopian military requests. So, although the 1960 secret agreement was not the product of a formal negotiation, Washington's offer of a new long-term security understanding would perhaps avoid a future showdown with the IEG over the American presence at Kagnew.

SOMALI INDEPENDENCE AND IRREDENTISM

It was no mere coincidence that the U.S.-Ethiopia secret military agreement was concluded less than two months after the formation of the Republic of Somalia. During the two years leading up to Somali independence, Ethiopia had been placed on the diplomatic defensive internationally. Discussions in certain Afro-Asian diplomatic circles and events occurring in the Somaliland Trust Territories pointed to the conclusion that Addis Ababa's continued control over the Ogaden would be severely challenged after independence. Haile Selassie needed the United States to enhance its security commitment to Ethiopia in order to meet this challenge.

The unresolved question concerning the delineation of the Ethiopian-Somali border provided the Somalis with legal grounds on which to challenge Addis Ababa's control over the Ogaden. Somali leaders had never accepted the validity of the Anglo-Ethiopian Treaty of 1897, which ceded sovereignty to Ethiopia over Somali-inhabited territories.[10] After Great Britain had backed away from the idea of creating a Greater Somaliland (the Bevin Plan) from the territories it had administered in the Horn after defeating the Italians and liberating Ethiopia in 1942, London and Addis Ababa concluded another agreement in 1954 that reaffirmed the 1897 treaty and handed the Ogaden as well as the Haud and Reserved grazing areas over to Ethiopia. However, at the time no de jure borders had been established between Ethiopia and the Somaliland Trust Territories, only a "provisional administrative line."[11] Moreover, the Somalis would justify their efforts to redraw the borders in the Horn on the basis of the UN Charter and various resolutions and declarations that recognized the right of self-determination for colonial people.[12]

As the date for Somali independence drew near, Haile Selassie sought to defuse the potentially destabilizing effects of a movement that threatened one-fifth of Ethiopia's territory and that, if successful, would bring a large expanse of the Addis Ababa–Djibouti railway under foreign control. As one solution to this problem, the IEG proposed in 1957 a federation with Somalia as had been done with Eritrea.[13] In 1958 the emperor asked the United States to support an association of Ethiopia, Somalia, and Sudan under Ethiopian leadership.[14] Washington tabled this idea since it would require additional U.S. military and economic aid.[15] While the emperor claimed not to be against Somali independence, it was obvious that any words or actions that might stimulate irredentist elements within his empire were deemed threatening and to be opposed.

Haile Selassie would ultimately triumph on the diplomatic front with regard to the Somali problem following the creation of the Organization of African Unity (OAU) in 1963. The OAU enshrined the principle of respect for the colonial-drawn borders of Africa in its charter. Throughout the 1950s, however, the Somali cause was supported by various African leaders and regional conferences. The idea of adjusting or abolishing the imperialist-constructed frontiers of Africa was given indirect support by the first Afro-Asian solidarity conference held in Cairo in 1957, which accepted a Somali resolution condemning all forms of colonialism, an oblique reference to Ethiopian rule in the Ogaden.[16] At the December 1958 All-Africa Peoples Conference in Accra, a resolution was passed denouncing the artificial frontiers drawn by the imperialist powers "to divide the peoples of the same stocks" and called for the abolishment or adjustment of such frontiers "founded upon the wishes of the people."[17] The second All-Africa Peoples Conference held in Tunis in January 1960 also gave its support to the struggle of the people of Somaliland for independence and unity.[18] Although these resolutions might have been seen as simply supporting the idea of merger between Italian Somaliland and British Somaliland, the IEG put a worst-case interpretation on these words, fearing they would lend momentum to forces seeking to dismember Ethiopia. The fact that Ghana's President Nkrumah, one of Selassie's rivals for influence in Africa, was drawn to the Somali case, further exacerbated Addis Ababa's sense of threat.

Haile Selassie was also alarmed by political developments in the Somalilands. The Somali Youth League (SYL), whose primary objective since its founding in 1943 as the Somali Youth Club was to prevent the repartition of Somaliland, was very active in pressing the unity issue at international conferences and was becoming increasingly influential in the politics of Italian Somaliland.[19] In 1959 the SYL, the Greater Somaliland League, and other allied parties issued the Mogadisico Manifesto calling for the union of Italian Somaliland (Somalia) with Kenya's Northern Frontier District, British Somaliland, French Somaliland and Ethiopia's Ogaden region. Thus, Haile Selassie had every reason to be concerned about Somali designs on Ethiopia, especially when the SYL emerged as the most powerful political party in the Republic of Somalia after the merger between Somalia and British Somaliland on July 1, 1960.[20]

Moreover, additional evidence that Ethiopia would be subjected to constant pressure by the newly independent Somali Republic was provided by Somalia's new constitution. The Somali constitution, which was ratified in June 1961, but most of which had been drafted in the final months of the colonial period, referred in the preamble to the "sacred right of self-determination of peoples enshrined in the Charter of the United Nations" and an obligation "to consolidate and protect the independence of the Somali nation."[21] Subsequent articles described the Somali people as "an indivisible unit" and declared that "the Somali Republic [would] promote, with legal and peaceful means, the union of the Somali territories."[22]

Now that the Somali threat was at Ethiopia's front door, Haile Selassie was in immediate need of solidifying the security relationship with Washington. Because the emperor had little in common politically with the forces controlling the Afro-Asian bloc in international forums, coupled with their disapproval of Addis Ababa's already close relationship with Washington, Selassie felt compelled to look to the United States for support. But given Washington's reluctance to make more than minimal gestures in the past, he would have to use Kagnew once again to blackmail the United States to increase military aid and, as a psychological crutch, insist upon an explicit security commitment aimed at the Somali threat—a commitment that subsequently would be directed at the Eritreans as well.

THE COLD WAR SHIFTS TO AFRICA

Washington's perception of threat underwent a rather abrupt shift in 1960. Africa replaced the Middle East, at least temporarily, as the primary cold war arena. In 1960, sixteen states on the African continent gained independence. While the transition was for the most part peaceful, in the Congo destabilizing political strife prompted the new Congolese government to seek assistance from the Soviet Union to help it through its troubles, much to Washington's displeasure. In this new regional context, Ethiopia came to be valued as an African state with no political ax to grind against the West and willing to cooperate with the United States and the United Nations in bringing order to the Congo, thereby keeping the Russians out of Africa.

The crisis in the Congo came at a time when the situation in the Middle East semed to be settling down following the July 1958 revolution in Iraq, which overthrew the pro-West monarchy and prompted the dispatch of 5,000 U.S. Marines to Lebanon. By the end of 1958, the Soviet-Egyptian threat, which had been cited as justification for seeking additional U.S. base rights in Ethiopia the previous year, had apparently dissipated. Although Iraq would leave the Baghdad Pact in March 1959, Egypt's recent behavior calmed Western anxieties somewhat. In January 1959 London and Cairo had reached an agreement resolving their outstanding differences arising from the 1956 Suez crisis concerning frozen Egyptian assets and compensation for nationalized British properties. Nasser had also become publicly critical of Soviet attempts to penetrate the new Iraqi regime and interfere in Arab affairs. While some problems would arise in early 1960 between Egypt and Israel, from Washington's perspective, all was relatively quiet in the Middle East.

The Eisenhower administration, in fact, had come to the conclusion during the fall of 1958 that the United States should adopt a less confrontational approach toward Nasser and seek to normalize relations with the Egyptian-led United Arab Republic (UAR).[23] While the United States did not want to see newly emergent African states such as Sudan, or Ethiopia, fall under Cairo's domination, American policy makers on the National Security Council recognized that Egypt would maintain an interest in the policies and actions of the Nile riparian states, and that those interests should not be threatened.[24] Washington's newfound willingness to view Nasser in this light was based on the premise that Cairo's political objective of displacing—or blocking—foreign influence in the region was aimed at the communist bloc as well as the West.[25] He was not playing favorites. While the core interests of Cairo would conflict at times with those of Washington, and Egypt's expanding influence in the Middle East and Africa would continue to pose problems and dilemmas for the United States and the West, there was now less inclination to view Nasser simply as a Soviet stooge.[26] The change in Washington's outlook could also be attributed to the fact that John Foster Dulles had become less active in policy making at the end of 1958 due to illness, and would resign in April 1959 for health reasons.

While the situation in the Middle East had become more stable, in the summer of 1960 the cold war shifted to Africa. The trouble began on June 30, 1960, when the Republic of Congo received its independence after seventy-five years of colonial rule by Belgium. Almost immediately an army mutiny occurred, followed by general civil unrest and attacks against Westerners, which Belgium cited as justification to delay its troop withdrawal, and the secession of the province of Katanga.[27] Although the United States and Egypt would support opposing factions during this crisis, the primary culprit in Washington's eyes was Moscow, which at the beginning of August was threatening to intervene with military forces to help the government of Prime Minister Patrice Lumumba resolve its internal problems. Lumumba, who had appealed to the Soviet Union for bilateral aid in mid-July, was described by CIA director Allen Dulles as "a person who was a Castro or worse . . . [and had] been bought by the communists."[28]

Ethiopia proved to be a staunch supporter of UN policy, which during the early phases of this crisis converged with U.S. policy objectives.[29] In mid-July, UN Secretary-General Dag Hammarskjold had dispatched an all-African peacekeeping force to the Congo, which included Ethiopian forces. By the end of the month, over 11,000 United Nations peacekeeping forces were in the Congo drawn from the armed forces of Ghana, Morocco, Tunisia, and Ethiopia, as well as Sweden and Ireland. General Iyassu Mengesha of the Ethiopian Imperial Army served on the UN military staff in Leopoldville and later commanded UN troops in the rebellious Stanleyville area. Subsequently in September 1961, with Washington's blessing, Ethiopia sent four U.S.-supplied F-86 jet fighters to the Congo to support the UN operation.

While the Congo crisis in central Africa did not have a direct bearing on U.S.-Ethiopia military relations, it created an atmosphere in which the United States wished to reward its friends. Ethiopia's support for the UN operation in the Congo not only kept the Russians out of central Africa, but also allowed Washington to find a balance between appeasing its NATO ally (Belgium) and maintaining an anti-imperialist stance in Africa. There was also the hope that the many new African states would look toward Ethiopia, as the oldest independent state in Africa, rather than to radical leaders such as Nasser, Sekou Toure of Guinea, or Ghana's President Nkrumah for foreign policy guidance.[30] Thus, Washington sought to use, and would reward, conservative African states such as Ethiopia to keep the cold war out of Africa.

PLAYING THE SOVIET CARD

The new beginning that Haile Selassie sought in the U.S.-Ethiopia military relationship necessitated that once again the IEG use the threat of defection to the Soviet Union against the United States. In contrast to previous episodes, this time the threat was taken quite seriously by top-ranking officials within the Eisenhower administration. One reason for this was that Moscow's position of influence in the Middle East seemed to be growing as the Soviets had established relations with the new Iraqi leader, Brig. Gen. Karim Kassim, who seemed to exhibit procommunist sympathies. Moreover, owing to his obsessive concern with the Somali threat, Haile Selassie began playing hardball with the Americans by going to Moscow in 1959 seeking aid.

The threat of communist penetration in the Horn of Africa had begun to receive more studied attention in early 1958, when the Office of Naval Intelligence prepared a study on the opportunities for communist penetration of Ethiopia and the Horn of Africa.[31] Soviet penetration opportunities had thus far been few because of the emperor's fear of communism as a threat to his throne. However, Somali independence in 1960 and political disaffection in Eritrea might be exploited in the future as sites for penetration by the communists. Although Ethiopia's expressed dissatisfaction with the level of U.S. assistance probably was exaggerated to obtain increased aid, according to the naval intelligence analysis, there was a genuine feeling that the United States had not been as generous to Ethiopia as to other states.

At the time, it seemed unlikely that Ethiopia would align with the Soviet bloc. Ethiopia itself did not present favorable grounds for communism. But Addis Ababa might elect to go the neutralist path, accepting aid from East and West, thereby diminishing U.S. influence. Any communist advance or Western loss in the Horn had to be taken seriously, for it would offer the Russians the opportunity to encamp themselves on alternative sea and air routes to the Far East and South Africa; threaten communications in the Atlantic, the Red Sea, and the Indian Ocean; and provide a position to gain control of Egypt and expand into East and Central Africa, thereby threatening the strategic mineral resources of the Belgian Congo.[32] Thus, Washington's penchant for employing a domino theory in the region could be exploited by Addis Ababa.

The U.S. Navy's March 1958 assesment of the communist threat, though highlighting the strategic implications of a hostile takeover in the Horn, nonetheless essentially dismissed the likelihood that the Ethiopians would follow through with their threat to defect to the Soviets. In mid-1958 the NSC progress report on U.S. policy toward Ethiopia (NSC 5615/1) observed that the Soviets would not make much headway in Ethiopia as long as Haile Selassie remained in power.[33] Communism had made no significant gains among Ethiopia's small educated elite, and had minimal impact, if any, among the vast majority of the country's peoples. The NSC's Operations Coodinating Board thus concluded, "It is unlikely that bloc offers of aircraft and training facilities will be accepted, although Ethiopia may use these offers to seek more aid."[34]

However, Haile Selassie apparently believed that he could shock the Americans into action by bluntly playing the Soviet card. At the end of June 1959 the emperor went to the Soviet Union on an official state visit. During his stay Selassie signed a long-term, low-interest credit agreement worth $100 million with Moscow. On a more disturbing note, the Ethiopian prime minister had issued a public statement praising the Soviet Union. It appeared to the White House that after visiting the Soviet Union the Ethiopians, including the emperor, had completely reversed their opinion of that country.[35] By according Moscow greater respectability, it was feared that future Soviet operations in Ethiopia would be facilitated and that disgruntled individuals within the imperial government, as well as politically active elements in Addis Ababa, could push for the emperor to follow a neutralist policy.[36]

Despite the emperor's dramatic action, the State Department believed that the U.S. position in Ethiopia was still quite secure.[37] The Soviet-Ethiopian credit agreement was simply a way for Addis Ababa to gain implied East bloc diplomatic support on the Somaliland issue.[38] No doubt the Ethiopians would also use the Soviet credits to blackmail Washington. But it was expected that several key government officials would both "covertly" and by "traditional means effective in the past" prevent or impede the use of these credits in sensitive political areas that might undermine U.S. influence.[39] Their success, however, would depend upon Washington's responsiveness to Ethiopia's military and security requirements.

SPUTNIK, POLARIS, AND KAGNEW STATION

Despite the failure to acquire expanded base rights in 1957, the American strategic stake in Ethiopia continued to increase. Kagnew Station still remained the driving force behind U.S. security policy toward Ethiopia. Not only were U.S. officials within the executive branch in agreement about the strategic value of this communications facility, but also members of the legislative branch who knew of Kagnew were impressed by its capabilities. After returning from a tour of the station in 1955, Congresswoman Frances P. Bolton exclaimed before an executive session of the Foreign Relations Committee in February 1956 that the United States in possessing Kagnew had "[one of] the most important radio facilities in the world."[40] She went on to describe the communications site as "the greatest factor in security in the whole area."[41]

Even U.S. diplomats were impressed by Kagnew. Upon visiting Kagnew for the first time following his appointment as U.S. ambassador to Ethiopia in 1959, Arthur Richards was awed by the instantaneous hookup that permitted him to speak with his family back in the United States.[42] Kagnew's capabilities were beyond anything else the United States had in the region, if not the world. Maintaining unencumbered access to Kagnew, therefore, constituted the principal mission of the U.S. diplomatic mission in Addis Ababa.

As a consequence of Kagnew Station's recognized strategic value, during the 1950s American requests for expansion were submitted almost continuously to the IEG.[43] In each instance, Haile Selassie had personally given orders to grant Washington's requests.[44] The U.S. Army, in particular, had a major stake in Kagnew, since it formed a major link in the army's worldwide communications system. Washington's diplomatic corps in Africa also used Kagnew extensively to send and receive messages. Presumably, the National Security Agency (NSA) and the CIA had an interest in intelligence intercepts picked up at the station.

However, by the end of the decade U.S. strategic interest in Kagnew Station had expanded beyond diplomatic and army communications and intelligence-gathering operations. Kagnew's strategic value was now being assessed in the context of U.S. nuclear strategy vis-à-vis the Soviet Union. The launching of Sputnik I by the Russians in October 1957 had created a new strategic environment. As a consequence of the success of the Russian ICBM (intercontinental ballistic missile) program, American cities and strategic forces were now vulnerable to a Soviet nuclear attack.

In response the Eisenhower administration accelerated the ICBM program as well as the Polaris SLBM (submarine-launched ballistic missile) program.[45] The Polaris program, in particular, offered a new type of technology to counter this new threat. Submarine-based Polaris missiles would increase the survival capacity of U.S. strategic forces because of their mobility and would put Soviet assets (cities and other "soft" targets) at risk. The main drawback to the Polaris program was one of "command-and-control"—how to maintain communications with a mobile underwater system.[46] Kagnew would help solve this problem by acting as a communications link for Polaris nuclear submarines operating in the Indian Ocean.

As a result of these strategic developments, the U.S. embassy's diplomatic mission in Ethiopia continued to build momentum. To fulfill its future nuclear mission, the U.S. Navy now acquired an institutional stake in Kagnew Station. Shortly before Ambassador Richards presented the U.S. aid package to the IEG in 1960, President Eisenhower also noted "the importance of maintaining an atmosphere in Ethiopia which would assure continued unimpaired use of the key facilities at Kagnew."[47] Thus, when the United States entered into the secret military agreement with the IEG in August 1960, U.S. strategic nuclear considerations constituted part of the policy backdrop.

THE AIR POWER COMMITMENT

Although Haile Selassie kicked the Americans rather hard in playing the Soviet card in 1959, the likelihood that Ethiopia would actually defect to the Russians was diminished by the fact that the IEG was about to receive a squadron of F-86 Sabre jet fighters from the United States. The emperor was finally going to receive a tangible prestige item to show for his years of close association with the United States. Few Third World nations possessed such sophisticated weapons, and Selassie was not going to jeopardize U.S. Air Force support, for which he had fought so long to acquire, by getting too close to Moscow. He also knew that in order to support the imperial army and air force, the United States would have to increase military assistance to Ethiopia.

During the first half of the 1950s, Haile Selassie had focused his energies on acquiring U.S. support to equip and expand the Ethiopian Army. By the second half of the decade, however, the idea of creating a modern Ethiopian Air Force had assumed a certain psychological importance for the emperor.[48] The centralized decision-making style of the Ethiopian monarchy led Selassie to believe in the importance of things that people could see as an expression of personal as well as national prestige.[49] President Eisenhower appreciated the imperial mindset, noting to one of his cabinet members, "You have your 'best drag' in that country when you do something for the Emperor."[50] Thus the Americans came under a persistent and expected diplomatic assault to provide combat aircraft and pilot training for the Ethiopian Air Force.

Addis Ababa first broached the air power issue with Washington in 1956 by means of a subtle, but not very well disguised request for the United States to conduct a survey of Ethiopia's air force capabilities. Until this time the United States had not set or accomplished any air force objectives, owing to Ethiopia's "limited capacity to use and maintain additional or modern equipment."[51] But in October, the National Security Council agreed to grant this request with the understanding that the United States was not committing itself to a future air force program in Ethiopia by undertaking this survey.[52] Because the Americans did not think anything constructive would result from this survey, as a stopgap measure President Eisenhower had ordered the U.S. Air Force in January 1957 to supply the IEG with a Constellation 749 aircraft drawn from Washington's special mission squadron.[53] The plane arrived in June and crashed two weeks later.

The creation of a modern Ethiopian Air Force was one issue on which the emperor refused to allow the Americans to sidetrack him. Selassie remembered the devastation caused by the Italian Air Force in the 1935–1936 war, which had dropped poison gas on his troops and broken the morale of his army.[54] Twenty years later the Swedish-trained Ethiopian Air Force was equipped with fifty-eight "unmodern aircrafts" and no modern bombers or fighter units.[55] Addis Ababa's most urgent need, according to the U.S. embassy's March 1957 report on the defense problems of Ethiopia, was to get started "training activity on modern airplanes at the Attack Wing." This training activity would require the United States to deliver during FY 1957, or as soon as possible, ten dual-seater jet trainers, twelve Dakota C-47s, one Cessna L-19A or Cessna EO-1, and PBY Catalinas.[56] These aircraft were expected to be fully equipped and provided with spare parts and repair instruments necessary to keep the planes in service for five years. A detailed list for other equipment also was submitted by the Ethiopians through the U.S. embassy; the Ethiopians were leaving nothing to chance.

By the end of 1957, Selassie's expectations regarding American air force support and Washington's reluctance to commit to this specific force goal objective had created major operating problems for U.S. policy in Ethiopia.[57] The emperor had made known to the Americans that he attached great importance to this issue and was anticipating the receipt of U.S. aid following the air force survey.[58] American diplomats in the field argued that Haile Selassie's obsession with the development of a modern Ethiopian Air Force, underwritten and trained by the United States, provided a perfect opportunity for Washington to demonstrate a long-term interest in Ethiopia.[59] Achieving this force goal objective would take a number of years and require continued American financial support to offset increased recurring costs. Thus, both the U.S. embassy and MAAG supported Ethiopia's request for air force assistance.

The USAF survey team that visited Ethiopia in April 1957 "favored extending assistance over a period of years starting with a modest jet training program."[60] Although the CINCEUR (Commander-in-Chief, Europe) recommended support for an Ethiopian Air Force, EURCOM (European Command) and the Joint Chiefs of Staff opposed the idea. Because Ethiopia belonged neither to NATO nor the Baghdad Pact, "no valid military requirement for jet aircraft or for an Ethiopian Air Force to support current U.S. or NATO war plans was perceived."[61] On August 27 the JCS informed the secretary of defense that they saw "no valid military requirement" for providing such a program.[62] The Department of Defense concurred with the JCS decision on October 9, also finding "no valid military requirement at this time for the establishment of force goals for the Ethiopian Air Force and . . . [that] none should be established."[63]

Though it was considered an unsound military concept by the Pentagon, Ethiopia's air force demands were kept alive by political rationales. During the previous year the U.S. embassy had advocated that aid to the Ethiopian Air Force was necessary in order to maintain "a strong U.S. position in Ethiopia."[64] In order to reverse the rapid erosion of American influence in the country that supposedly occurred during 1957 and to reach a "political accommodation that would secure current and future base rights," the Eisenhower administration had agreed to initiate a small air force program in 1958 and provide three T-33 jet trainers, one C-47 aircraft, and training for pilots in the United States.[65] Finally in June 1958 the U.S. ambassador informed the IEG that the United States would program funds to provide a total of twelve F-86 jet fighters. Delivery of the F-86 Sabre jets, however, was conditioned on the grounds that proper preparation was made for their maintenance and operations, which pushed the delivery date back into 1960. Nonetheless, the decision to furnish Ethiopia with a modern weapon system few other Third World countries possessed reinforced Haile Selassie's belief that the key to enhancing Ethiopia's security and his own personal authority resided in the hands of the United States.

THE AFRICA BUREAU

As a consequence of the June 1958 U.S. air power commitment, MAP assistance to Ethiopia was increased in FY 1959 and again in FY 1960, totaling $5.8 million and $7.7 million, respectively.[66] However, the IEG made little headway in persuading Washington to train and equip a fourth Ethiopian Army division. The Department of Defense continued to oppose this idea as long as it required an increased budgetary commitment.[67] As it was, Pentagon officials already held a low opinion of the Ethiopian military, feeling that the Ethiopians were partially to blame for problems in the MAP program because of their "low maintenance aptitude . . . to operate motor vehicles successfully."[68]

After being rebuffed by the Americans in the spring of 1957, Haile Selassie again raised the army issue with U.S. Ambassador Don Bliss in late October.[69] The emperor asserted his view that the Ethiopian armed forces should be increased and MAAG training extended to the imperial bodyguard without reducing aid to the army. On November 5, the State Department notified the U.S. embassy that "no justification was seen for increasing the number of commands."[70] While the United States was willing to provide supplies for two bodyguard brigades, there would have to be a corresponding reduction of MAP assistance for the army. This was unacceptable to the IEG, which refused to accept the U.S. force goal proposal to confine the Ethiopian armed forces to seven intact brigades.[71]

If the IEG was to make any headway on this issue, either something dramatic would have to happen in the region or a change in attitude would have to occur in Washington. While the U.S. embassy and MAAG team in the field were willing to support IEG military requests, Ethiopia had no full-time advocate in Washington. The Joint Chiefs of Staff and the Department of Defense, preoccupied with U.S. defense requirements in Europe, the Northern Tier of the Middle East, and the Far East, were generally unsympathetic to the idea of increasing the U.S. military commitment to Ethiopia. Organizationally, Ethiopia fell under the Bureau for Near Eastern Affairs (NEA) at the Department of State. The bureau was dominated by Arab specialists who were not particularly sympathetic to the sometimes anti-Arab, anti-Islamic content of Addis Ababa's security arguments. While occasionally President Eisenhower or Secretary Dulles might intervene for political reasons on the emperor's behalf, U.S. policy toward Ethiopia was formulated for the most part on an ad hoc basis. Except for a small and relatively impotent Office of African Affairs located within NEA, there was no agency in the American bureaucratic machinery whose institutional mission was advanced by advocating Ethiopia's cause.

Thus, until the very end of the 1950s the only full-time advocates for IEG military requests were the U.S. embassy and MAAG in Addis Ababa, located far from the corridors of power and influence in Washington. It was only around 1956–1957 that even they began to support Ethiopian military requests on a regular basis. Moreover, Ethiopia was a poor second cousin in the eyes of NEA, which formulated U.S. policy primarily within a Middle Eastern context. The drawn-out 1952–1953 and aborted 1957 base-rights negotiations, as well as the inconclusive military discussions of 1954, had all been conducted under the auspices of NEA. It was not until late 1956, in anticipation of the massive decolonization process about to occur in Africa, that the State Department began to expand its facilities and program for training specialists in African affairs.[72]

Momentum for creating a separate Bureau for African Affairs continued to build in the spring of 1957. Upon returning from his March 1957 trip to Africa, Richard Nixon had recommended that an Africa Bureau be created.[73] One argument given for expediting this reorganization was that it would reorient states such as Ethiopia and Sudan away from Arab affairs and more toward Africa.[74] This would presumably enhance Washington's influence, because in the late 1950s the United States' position in Africa was less tenuous and susceptible to regional challenges than its position in the Middle East.[75] Thus, Ethiopia and Sudan were placed in the Africa Bureau when it was formally established in August 1958.

This bureaucratic restructuring at the Department of State would have a significant long-term impact on U.S. policy toward Ethiopia and enhance Addis Ababa's leverage vis-à-vis the United States. Instead of being "a little fish in a big pond," Ethiopia now became "a big fish in a little pond." While the Africa Bureau was a "weak sister" at the State Department, the positions adopted by Ethiopia on various international and regional issues now carried greater weight and received more studied attention than they had at NEA. The Eisenhower administration hoped that Ethiopia's continuous support for the U.S. position at the United Nations in preventing the seating of Communist China, Selassie's backing of the Canadian-U.S. proposal for narrow territorial limits at the 1960 Geneva Law of the Sea conference, and participation in the UN military operation in the Congo would positively influence the positions of other Afro-Asian states.[76]

Thus, the Africa Bureau looked for Ethiopia to lead by example in orienting the newly independent African states toward the West.

The Eisenhower administration also hoped that Ethiopia could influence African states to support the general concept of keeping the cold war out of Africa.[77] At the start of the new decade, Africa seemed to be breaking down into antagonistic blocs that held different perceptions of the Soviet threat in Africa. On the one hand there existed a group of twelve formerly French African states, which came to be known as the Brazzaville bloc, who chose to maintain their links to Paris, opposed Sovet policy, and rejected any communist influence in Africa. These states were more particularistic and less pan-Africanist in their orientation by advocating cooperation not political union among independent African states; they generally aligned themselves with the West, particularly in favoring compromise solutions to the Congo crisis and the French-Algerian War.[78] They were opposed by a more radical nationalist group of five states—Ghana, Guinea, Mali, Morocco, and the United Arab Republic—known as the Casablanca bloc, which favored pan-Africanist schemes, maintained friendly relations with the Soviet Union, were not opposed to accepting aid from the communist bloc and harshly attacked Western "neocolonialism" in Africa.[79] Although not formally aligned with either bloc, Ethiopia's foreign policy clearly fell in line with the more conservative Brazzaville group. Together, they could act to blunt what Washington perceived as the destabilizing policies of the Casablanca bloc.[80]

Thus, the conclusion of the 1960 secret agreement between the United States and Ethiopia occurred in a vastly different regional and organizational setting than previous negotiations. The cold war had shifted to Africa, and it seemed likely that the United States would come under increasing pressure to provide arms to Africa as decolonization progressed. Washington was determined to deny the strategic location, resources, manpower, and influence of Africa as well as the Middle East to the communist bloc. In a 1960 Future Developments in Africa projection, the National Security Council observed, "In instances where the Bloc offers to furnish arms, as is currently the case in Ethiopia, the United States may have to face the difficult decision whether to run the risk of allowing African states to turn to Bloc sources of supply or pursue a distasteful policy of preclusive arming."[81] With the Africa Bureau adopting Ethiopia as the focal state for U.S. policy in Africa, it was more likely that Washington would opt for the latter course in its dealings with Addis Ababa.

CONCLUSION: UPPING THE ANTE

The 1960 U.S.-Ethiopia military agreement was more than simply a reaffirmation of the 1953 MDAA and DIA treaties. While the underlying quid pro quo of the relationship remained intact, the IEG had upped the ante on Washington. Annual U.S. MAP funds for Ethiopia more than doubled as a result. Haile Selassie had finally achieved the three political-military objectives he had sought from the United States since the early 1950s: training and equipment for a four-division Ethiopian Army, support for a modern Imperial Air Force, and what he considered to be an explicit U.S. security guarantee.

However, the 1960 secret agreement carried a potentially disruptive political cost for the IEG and for Haile Selassie personally. As U.S. operations at Kagnew continued to expand, the radical nationalist governments in the region, who were already critical of Ethiopia's close association with the United States, increased their activities to destabalize the IEG. Moreover, if the Americans did not follow through with a good-faith effort in implementing their side of the agreement, the emperor's throne itself could be in jeopardy. Selassie accepted these risks because he felt vulnerable to the threat posed by an independent Somali state and believed that only the United States could provide the appropriate level of political and material support to keep the Somalis at bay; the Americans proved this belief through the 1958 air power commitment and the delivery of the F-86 Sabre jets. While the emperor thought he had an ace in the hole in threatening to turn to the Soviet Union for assistance, Addis Ababa was in an extremely vulnerable position as Somali independence drew near. Selassie could not risk exposing Ethiopia or his own position by defecting to the Russians at such a precarious time. Besides, the Americans might decide to counter an Ethiopian threat of defection to the Russians by threatening to arm Somalia.

Washington's decision to make this new political-military commitment to Ethiopia was primarily related to the value attached to Kagnew Station, which after more than fifteen years of operation and expansion had become indispensable. But the United States had also become increasingly sensitive to the changes taking place in Africa and the threat of the cold war spilling over into the African continent. Moreover, with the creation of the Africa Bureau in 1958, there was a more favorable bureaucratic climate in which to justify arms transfers to Ethiopia, which became the centerpiece for the new regional bureau's policy. Given these concerns the United States found itself in a very vulnerable position vis-à-vis Ethiopia, becoming more susceptible to manipulation. Although when compared with the amounts of military aid the United States was providing to other states in the Middle East, the expanded U.S. military commitment to Ethiopia still seemed to be a bargain. Moreover, given the imprecise language of the agreement, there was considerable latitude in how the United States could interpret and implement its terms.

Subsequent events would prove that the 1960 U.S.-Ethiopia military agreement caused more complications than it resolved. It was not quite the new beginning in U.S.-Ethiopia military relations that Haile Selassie had expected, or the simple programmatic arrangement envisioned by Washington. Whereas the IEG became suspect of Washington's commitment to enhance the fighting capabilities of the Ethiopian military, the emperor continued to use Kagnew to blackmail the United States. Because of the imprecision in the language and varying expectations with regard to the 1960 agreement, new problems and conflicts would soon emerge in U.S.-Ethiopia military relations.

6

The 1966 F-5 Freedom Fighter Transfer

Although the 1960 U.S. military commitment was a step in the right direction, Haile Selassie wanted more than simply supplies and training for a fourth Ethiopian Army division. Notably absent from the secret agreement was an American commitment to increase the strength or upgrade the quality of the Ethiopian Air Force. Though the Americans had begun to supply Ethiopia with a squadron of F-86 Sabre jets, they were outdated, Korean War–vintage aircraft. Selassie wished to acquire state-of-the-art military items for the Imperial Air Force. Personal and national prestige demanded that Ethiopia possess a modern military equipped with the latest hardware, not outdated or secondhand equipment.

But the Kennedy administration, which assumed from its predecessor responsibility for implementing the 1960 commitment, had no interest in underwriting a technological arms race in Africa to satisfy the personal whims of the Ethiopian emperor. John Kennedy had brought to the White House a notion that the cold war in the Third World could be won by emphasizing social, economic and political reforms.[1] Excessive and unnecessary arms transfers would only divert scarce resouces away from programs designed to help these governments improve the living conditions of their people and thereby promote stability. However, if this effort failed, counterinsurgency warfare and paramilitary police training provided a fallback position for securing U.S. interests.

A year after the Kennedy administration took office, the IEG began an unremitting campaign to acquire more air force hardware. Initially the emperor simply wanted to acquire a second squadron of F-86 Sabre jet fighters. During a January 1962 meeting at the Pentagon, General Assefa Ayene, a top-ranking commander in the Imperial Air Force, had requested four F-86 fighters to replace the four the Ethiopian government had temporarily assigned to the Congo.[2] Pentagon officials not only agreed to replace the four aircraft on loan, but urged Assefa to press the administration for a full second squadron. By mid-February Washington was under heavy pressure to provide a second squadron of F-86s to Ethiopia for what was termed an "ill-disguised" payment for Kagnew.[3]

The Kennedy administration responded to this pressure by concluding another, though more limited, agreement with the imperial government in 1962. As a follow-up to the secret U.S.-Ethiopia executive agreement, Secretary of Defense Robert McNamara and Ethiopian Defense Minister Mengesha Merid signed a memorandum in which the Americans promised to speed up delivery of army items (such as ammunition, armored personnel carriers) promised in the 1960 commitment, to provide the navy with one LCM; and to provide T-28D, F-86, and T-33 aircraft as well as "to continue support of the T-28A and F-86 squadrons."[4] Although the United States had now added an explicit air power commitment not contained in the 1960 agreement, it too was rather vaguely worded; it did not establish a timetable for delivery or force goal objectives. The Ethiopians would come to view the 1962 McNamara-Merid memorandum and a subsequent agreement signed in 1963, which among other things required Washington to discuss the organization of the Ethiopian Air Force and Navy, as having been made at the expense of the original commitment.[5] Haile Selassie would use this argument to force Washington to reevaluate Ethiopia's air power requirements.

Ultimately the emperor requested a squadron of F-5 Freedom Fighter supersonic jets. The genesis of the F-5 episode in U.S.-Ethiopia military relations remains somewhat murky. Apparently, sometime in 1962 U.S. officials had informally promised to provide Addis Ababa with the new supersonic F-5 fighters that were about to become available for export to the Third World.[6] Recognizing they had blundered by promising something that threatened to provoke an unnecessary arms race in the region, the Americans would spend the next two years attempting to dissuade the imperial government from acquiring these weapons. But once it had become known that these supersonic jets would be exported to the Third World, there would be no dissuading Selassie from acquiring them. Without F-5s in the imperial arsenal, it would appear that Ethiopia possessed only a second-rate air force.

Because there seemed no way to turn back from this commitment without negatively affecting U.S.-Ethiopian relations, the United States played a game of delay. It was not until mid-June 1964 that the U.S. ambassador to Ethiopia, Edward Korry, delivered a message informing the IEG that the United States would provide a squadron of 12 F-5 aircraft to the Ethiopian Air Force.[7] Still feeling uneasy about a decision that might escalate the arms race in the Horn, Washington attempted to push back the delivery date. The first F-5s would not arrive in Ethiopia until the latter half of 1966. But in following through with this arms transfer, the United States had broken a qualitative arms barrier by making Ethiopia the first black-ruled state in sub-Sahara Africa to possess supersonic jet fighters.

THE 1964 BORDER WAR

Following its declaration of independence in July 1960, Somalia seemed to pose no real threat to Ethiopian security. Mogadishu possessed an internal security force of only 4,000 troops, compared to some 30,000 soldiers in the imperial army. Moreover, the United States offered to become Somalia's arms supplier—a move that would allow Washington to regulate the flow of weapons into the Horn. Thus the Somali security threat to Ethiopia could be kept in check, as well as the emperor's ability to raise the ante on the United States any further. But in 1960 and again in 1962, Addis Ababa vetoed Somali requests for military assistance from the United States.[8]

In 1962, shortly after Washington had been pressured to reject Mogadishu's second arms request, Czechoslovakia had offered Somalia a modest arms package. To avoid a replay in the Horn of the Czech-Egyptian arms deal, Washington encouraged its NATO allies to make an arms offer to Somalia. But a joint British-Italian military program valued at $8.4 million came unraveled at the end of 1962 as a result of the rapid deterioration in relations between London and Mogadishu over the disposition of the Northern Frontier District, which the British government decided would remain part of an independent Kenya.[9] In its place the United States, Italy, and West Germany agreed to furnish Somalia with roughly $10 million worth of equipment and training for an army of 5,000–6,000 soldiers.[10] But once again Washington's attempt to act as the "balancer" in the Horn failed.

Mogadishu viewed the Western arms initiative as a thinly disguised plot to perpetuate Ethiopia's military predominance, thereby bringing to an end the Somali irredentist quest in the Horn. In light of Washington's commitment to support an Ethiopian Army of some 40,000, along with the provision of two squadrons of F-86 Sabre jets during the preceding three years, Mogadishu certainly had reason to feel that the Western aid package was not only inadequate, but anti-Somali in nature. Given such a military imbalance, Addis Ababa would have little motivation to negotiate with Mogadishu over the fate of the Somalis in the Ogaden. Thus, in October 1963 Somalia accepted an unconditional offer from the Soviet

Union for $30 million in military aid to expand the Somali Army from 4,000 to 20,000 soldiers, and to assist in the development of an air force.[11]

Mogadishu's acquisition of a superpower arms supplier did not necessarily mean that Somalia would be able to challenge Ethiopia militarily, certainly not in the near future. The Soviet Union seemed to have little to gain by encouraging Somali aggression in the Horn. Politically, it would put Moscow on the wrong side of the many newly emergent African nations that faced similar threats from ethnic-based national movements. Moreover, on the military balance sheet Somalia would lose a war against its bigger and stronger neighbor. Arming Somalia might, however, be used as leverage to force Ethiopia to distance itself from the United States.

The newly acquired Soviet arms connection, however, had ramifications that went beyond Moscow's intentions. It seemed to provide a psychological boost to the Somalis to challenge their Ethiopian adversary militarily. At the end of 1963 the U.S. embassy reported an increase in the frequency of small-scale Somali military intrusions in the disputed Haud grazing area, a problem that had begun less than six months after Somalia's independence, resulting in military clashes between Ethiopian and Somali forces.[12] Even more disturbing for Haile Selassie, and a source of encouragement for Somalia, was the poor showing of the Ethiopian Army in these clashes. Mounting casualties and demoralization within the Ethiopian Army prompted calls for Selassie to give the army a green light to take the offensive against Somalia, or witness the disintegration not only of the Ethiopian empire, but of his own political authority.[13]

By February 1964 the fighting in the Ogaden had escalated into a full-scale border war. Pressures began mounting on the United States to react strongly in support of its Ethiopian client. The State Department was bombarded with cables from the U.S. embassy in Addis Ababa warning of the serious implications of the Ogaden crisis for Haile Selassie's tenure as emperor as well as for the U.S. tenure at Kagnew.[14] Frustration and anger in Addis Ababa were being directed at the United States, which was seen as having refused to take sides on the Ogaden issue over the previous six months, and now failed to respond adequately and in a timely fashion to Ethiopian military requests.[15] In this crisis atmosphere, sensitive and potentially embarrassing questions were being raised by the Ethiopians about just what the U.S. military connection had done for them.

Washington's refusal to do more to help Ethiopia during the early stages of the Ethiopian-Somali crisis had created an opportunity for the Soviet Union to go "fishing in troubled waters."[16] According to the U.S. embassy, Soviet embassy officials had reportedly told the IEG in early January that the Soviet Union would provide Ethiopia with as many arms as it desired.[17] Haile Selassie had felt compelled to write a personal letter to Nikita

Khrushchev asking him to explain the nature and purpose of Soviet arms transfers to Somalia. While it did not seem time to take any dramatic action, the IEG "might be inclined to do buiness with [the] Russians in a few months hence."[18]

The IEG's war of nerves with the United States was designed to force the Americans to make a strong commitment to Ethiopia. Throughout the crisis Washington had attempted to remain impartial, urging both sides to show restraint (in particular for Ethiopia not to invade Somalia), to implement a cease-fire, and resolve the issue bilaterally or through the services of the OAU.[19] Washington prohibited U.S. Military Training Teams (MTT) from conducting training in the Ogaden and banned the airlift of ammunition to the IEG.[20] In maintaining this public posture of neutrality in the dispute, the United States on one occasion issued a sharply worded diplomatic rebuke to the emperor for an Ethiopian Air Force raid inside Somalia against the town of Hargeisa in late March shortly before the Khartoum cease-fire agreement was to go into effect.[21] The attack, supposedly intented to destroy an airfield in order to prevent the Somalis from using it as a base for MiG fighters soon to arrive from the Soviet Union, was a failure: the Ethiopian Air Force instead destroyed a locust control center. Though prefacing his remarks with a reiteration of U.S. support for Ethiopia's territorial integrity and independence, Ambassador Korry warned Selassie that U.S. MAP aid was conditioned on the understanding that the equipment was to be used solely for defensive purposes and that Washington's ability to respond to Ethiopian military requests was not "helped by such actions as the Hargeisa attack."[22]

Washington's supposed posture of impartiality in the dispute, however, came under attack after the cease-fire had gone into effect, when U.S. Air Force units transported construction equipment to the Callafo airfield, which the Ethiopians were reinforcing in a forward position in the Ogaden. This action, coupled with Washington's decision in mid-March to lift the ban on emergency airlifts of ammunition and the deployment of U.S. army combat training teams with Ethiopian forces, was viewed as inappropriate by the U.S. embassy in Mogadishu because it did not seem to be "consistent with the United States' desire to confine the dispute to the African context."[23] Washington's military intervention in the unresolved Ethiopian-Somali dispute, according to the U.S. ambassador in Mogadishu, would be equated to British military actions in the Northern Frontier District; as a result, the United States might pay a heavy political price in Somalia if all of these U.S. actions were to be exposed.[24] American support for Ethiopia appeared to be motivated less by a desire to help the Ethiopians avoid construction delays at Callafo than by the exigency "to gain acceptance of the IEG of the 1966 delivery date for the F-5s," which were not even scheduled for delivery to the U.S. Air Force until mid-1964.[25] Ethiopia's "legitimate self-defense" needs seemed to keep expanding. The U.S. embassy in Mogadishu warned that in not drawing a line on its involvement in Ethiopia, the United States would find it more difficult to refuse each new step—a fact probably not lost on the imperial government.[26] In contrast, Somalia was building an army more or less from scratch, which would be one-fourth the size of Ethiopia's forces (10,000 men), and equipped with a squadron of subsonic jets; in light of this, the U.S. diplomatic mission in Mogadishu concluded, "The introduction of F-5As, mobile training teams, and the kind of direct support to Ethiopian forces involved in C-130 flights (to Callafo) in themselves constitute escalation uncalled for by the actual threat."[27]

The Mogadishu embassy's appeal for the United States to slow down, if not cancel, certain military programs in Ethiopia received a somewhat sympathetic hearing at the Department of State, but it did not alter U.S. plans.[28] In mid-March 1964, the State Department had prepared an internal research memorandum assessing the implications of the war in the Horn of Africa. The thrust of the paper, as interpreted by the U.S. embassy in Addis Ababa, placed the blame for tensions in the Horn solely on the shoulders of Somalia. According to Ambassador Korry, (1) Somali irredentism lay at the core of Ethiopian-Somali difficulties; (2) Mogadishu was the principal arms supplier for, and benefactor of, the Ogaden insurgents; (3) convinced that time was on its side, the Somali government would continue to apply steady pressure on Ethiopia and Kenya, hoping they would crumble; (4) Mogadishu would continue to provide covert support for the dissidents, so they could act as an irritant to Addis Ababa; and (5) continued fighting would eventually wear Ethiopia down and lead to the dismemberment of the empire.[29] To preserve the emperor's influence and U.S. interests in Ethiopia, the United States would have to make its military assistance program more effective in response to Addis Ababa's growing disillusionment with MAP. While some of the imperial government's requests were deemed "extreme and patently ridiculous," providing the F-5 Freedom Fighters would be necessary to reverse the decline of U.S. influence brought on by the Ogaden War.[30]

KENNEDY, JOHNSON, AND CONTAINMENT

U.S. policy toward the Third World regained a globalist rigidity in the mid-1960s that prompted a heightened sense of threat and willingness to rely on a military response. Although the doctrine of containment remained firmly in place during the early 1960s, the Kennedy administration had removed some of its sharper edges with regard to neutralism in the Third World.[31] Under the Johnson administration, however, the United States reverted to a stricter zero-sum assessment of political trends and alignments in the newly developing areas of the world.[32] As a result, Washington became more susceptible to the argument that the communist bloc, to advance its geopolitical interests, was actively campaigning to dislodge the United States from the Horn of Africa. Delivering the F-5 Freedom Fighters would thus ensure Ethiopia's fidelity to the American cause.

Though committed to the cold war policy of containment, the Kennedy administration distinguished itself from its Republican predecessor's general orientation by a greater receptiveness to the idea that the major foreign policy interests of neutralist states were local or regional.[33] Nonalignment would achieve those interests. Politically, it was not an inherently procommunist or necessarily anti-Western movement. Rather than adopting a confrontationist stance, Washington could deal with these leaders and movements in other ways. In Africa, this meant identifying with African freedom, independence, and decolonization.[34]

At the same time, the Kennedy administration hoped to avoid fueling regional arms races by limiting military assistance to levels deemed necessary for internal security and border control. But U.S. security interests required denying the Sino-Soviet bloc the strategic resources and geographic flanking position of the African continent.[35] While the United States should not "yield to blackmail," State Department and Pentagon policy guidelines called for the United States to be prepared to supply military aid to preclude or limit arms transfers from communist governments.[36] Moreover, when it came time to distribute military and economic assistance, the United States would be justified in granting "preferential treatment to more pro-West countries."[37] Thus, the U.S. national security bureaucracy under John Kennedy sought to strike a balance between identifying with nationalist forces in Africa and containing communist penetration of the politically unstable continent.

Chester Bowles, Kennedy's special assistant for Third World affairs, promoted the idea of playing down the U.S. military role in African affairs. Ethiopia, in particular, was a favored target for Bowles's criticisms of U.S. military aid programs. After a fact-finding trip to Africa in 1962, Bowles argued against the United States' transfer of the second squadron of F-86 Sabre jets to Addis Ababa: Sudan possessed only a modest military strength, Uganda and Kenya were still under British protection and posed no threat, while Somalia maintained a national police force of only 2,000–3,000. As the Sudanese foreign minister put it to Bowles, "Who was the Ethiopian Army supposed to fight?"[38] Chester Bowles concluded, "If in the face of these facts we increase U.S. military aid to Ethiopia the result sooner or later will be an arms race with Ethiopia's neighbors [which would] allow the U.S.S.R. to do precisely what it has been doing in Egypt and Afghanistan."[39]

The argument that U.S. MAP policy was effectively pushing the neighbors of those states provided with American weaponry into the Soviet embrace received a less sympathetic hearing after Kennedy's assassination in November 1963. Under Lyndon Johnson, U.S. policy toward the Third World became reminiscent of the Eisenhower-Dulles years. The Johnson White House was less willing to tolerate the neutralist proclivities of Nasser and others. Johnson and his advisers felt that the United States needed to choose sides, and to do so forcefully, in combating communist expansionism and insurgencies in the Third World. This belief contributed to U.S. military escalation in Southeast Asia, the president's decision to embrace Israel in the Middle East conflict, and a demonstration of U.S. support for Ethiopia in the Horn of Africa through the delivery of the F-5 Freedom Fighters.

The Johnson administration's willingness to choose sides in regional disputes opened the way for advocates of the F-5 arms transfer, such as Edward Korry, to state their case by playing upon possible threats to U.S. interests. At the end of Korry's first year as U.S. ambassador to Ethiopia, he began to see a plot developing in which the communist bloc would use Somalia to lever the United States out of Ethiopia.[40] Having concluded the arms agreement with Mogadishu at the end of 1963, Moscow would then offer to diminish aid to Somalia if the imperial government adopted a pro-East policy and forced the Americans to leave Kagnew. At a minimum, Ethiopia could end up in the neutralist, nonaligned camp, toward which Ethiopia seemed to be headed anyway in furthering the emperor's aspiration to play a pivotal role in African affairs. But perhaps this pace could be moderated or even reversed if Washington took the right steps.

Ambassador Korry, among the first Americans to feel that the United States should provide Ethiopia with the Freedon Fighters, argued for a speeded-up delivery of the F-5s. Although the U.S. strategic stake at Kagnew Station formed the core of his argument, Korry also felt that Ethiopia's geographic location alone warranted Washington's interest.[41] In 1964 and again in 1966 Korry argued before the Joint Chiefs of Staff that because the British were "out of the game" in the region, the United States would have to fill the void if the Russians, who had been moving in this direction for some 200 years, were not to displace the West. As an indication of Russian intent, the ambassador pointed out that in 1964 Moscow had offered Haile Selassie anything he wanted if he kicked out the Americans; in 1965 the USSR had given Ethiopia a transport aircraft and two helicopters from a relatively new line of production, and in 1966 the commander of the Red Fleet had visited both Cairo and Massawa, and attended the graduation ceremony of the Ethiopian Naval Academy. Korry envisioned a scenario in which the Soviet Union, in trying to break out of the Eastern Mediterranean from the Black Sea, would seek to penetrate the Red Sea by gaining a foothold in Somalia and then attempt to dislodge the Americans from Ethiopia using the cause of pan-Arabism. Washington could not afford to sit idly by and allow Moscow to gain control over a country lying along the Red Sea oil route and whose government potentially could exert some influence over Egypt, using Sudan and the Nile River as pressure points. Moreover, in advocating so strongly the timely delivery of the F-5s, Ambassador Korry wished to avoid the inevitable negative repercussions if the United States got "caught in the lie" of promising to modernize the Ethiopian armed forces while deliberately dragging its feet.

Although Edward Korry's line of reasoning was not widely accepted at first in Washington, over the long term it gave momentum to the argument that in placing its credibility on the line by providing military assistance to Third World governments, Washington could not allow itself to be dislodged by anti-Western forces. The notion of preparing for American disengagement from potential political hot spots, which was being considered during Kennedy's presidency, came to be viewed as an unacceptable option under Lyndon Johnson. Threats to U.S. interests and clients should and could be faced down. The Johnson administration's thinking with regard to Ethiopia and elsewhere in the Third World was premised on the notion that American political, economic, and military interests could be safeguarded by a better effort and greater investment of resources.

"MANEUVER-WITHOUT-COMMITMENT"

During 1964, Addis Ababa's foreign policy had been paralyzed by unanticipated external events. Haile Selassie had expected the many newly emergent African states to look to him for political leadership and guidance. Instead, an independent Africa was turning out to be a rather hostile place for the Ethiopian monarch. Selassie could seek to reach a political accommodation with these vibrant regional forces. But opting for the neutralist course might endanger the F-5 deal and leave the empire open to external attack or subversion.

Selassie might also choose to embrace the United States and openly align with the West. But this would jeopardize the emperor's leadership role in sub-Sahara Africa. The benefits of such a move did not seem to be worth the price, given Washington's spotty record of support for the Ethiopian military. It would simply incite increased anti-Ethiopian activity. Until Washington was prepared to provide greater tangible evidence of its commitment to Ethiopian security, Selassie would need to placate neutralist and radical forces.

While Haile Selassie sought to promote his image as the leader of a new Africa, he was also becoming more and more preoccupied with ensuring his own survival in this vastly changed regional environment. The emperor had won an important diplomatic victory in 1963 when the Organization of African Unity had been established and had located its headquarters in Addis Ababa. The OAU Charter, which had been crafted by one of the emperor's American legal advisers, essentially placed a stamp of legitimacy upon Ethiopia's de jure borders by espousing the concept of respect for Africa's colonial-drawn borders.[42] Since then, however, he had been on the defensive.

Addis Ababa was having to contend with not only Somali dissidents in the Ogaden, but also a growing insurgency in the recently annexed territory of Eritrea. The dissolution of the Ethiopia-Eritrea federation in 1962, which resulted in the incorporation of Eritrea into the Ethiopian empire, had led the Eritrean National Movement to resort to guerrilla warfare against the central government. Though the emperor dismissed the Eritreans as *shiftas* (bandits), he would bring in Israeli and American counterinsurgency experts to help the Ethiopian military cope with this problem. In 1964 the Johnson administration initiated a civic action program, led by fifty-five American Green Berets.[43] Thus, as Haile Selassie sought to resolve the Eritrean and Ogaden problems by military means, the need to maintain the U.S. connection increased in importance.

Ethiopia's external environment, however, seemed far more troubling and less prone to a military solution, or even a political compromise that would not ultimately endanger the viability of the empire. Since the conclusion of the 1964 border war, Ethiopia's security situation seemingly had deteriorated.[44] Incoming Soviet military hardware was strengthening Somalia's armed forces. In support of the antimonarchical nationalist forces in Yemen, 40,000 Egyptian troops were stationed across the Red Sea from Ethiopia. The OAU office in Addis Ababa had turned out to be something of a Trojan horse, allowing foreign governments to orchestrate anti-Ethiopian schemes from the Ethiopian capital. In September 1964, leftist rebels had established a "Peoples' Republic" at Stanleyville in the Congo, and Addis Ababa was under pressure to recognize this government. To the north in Khartoum, a civilian government had assumed power in November; this government enthusiastically embraced radical African and Arab nationalist causes and became involved in supporting the Congolese rebels as well as dissident groups operating inside Ethiopia.[45]

The imperial government appeared confused over what path to follow in meeting these perceived threats. Appeasement might plant the seeds for the destruction of the Ethiopian monarchy. Confrontation would require overextending the responsibilities of an ill-prepared military establishment.[46] Something had to be done. According to the U.S. embassy, these forces were sending the emperor an ominous message: "Play our game or we will take steps to see that you do, even if it means remaking your government structure and possibly slicing off Eritrea and the Ogaden."[47]

Addis Ababa's traditional response when under the shadow of threats and where the consequences of options were unclear had been to "maneuver-without-commitment."[48] The Ethiopians would say what the radicals and neutralists wanted to hear while avoiding concrete actions to match their words. At the same time, the imperial government would privately voice its support for the West. Although Selassie was still anxious to receive the Freedom Fighters, caution dictated that this was not a time to draw attention to Ethiopia's arms connection with the United States. The Americans meanwhile remained unwilling to commit themselves fully in Ethiopia. Thus, unless open alignment with the United States would provide requisite benefits for Ethiopia, the emperor would hedge his bets by playing the neutralist game.

THE STONEHOUSE PROJECT

At the start of the Kennedy administration's second year in office, the State Department began to explore the question of strategic disengagement from the African continent. Such an option, in effect, would enhance Washington's policy flexibility and leverage vis-à-vis those governments with whom the United States had concluded arms-for-base-rights arrangements. This idea first appeared in the Department of State's March 1962 policy guidelines for Africa, which defined as one short-term (two years) American objective in Africa the need to assure continued use of U.S. military facilities "while planning for the possibility that we may be obliged for overriding political reasons to do without them even though a high priority military requirement for them still exists."[49] To that end, the State Department recommended that the United States "develop, as soon as possible, alternatives to communications and satellite tracking facilities in the African continent when the location of such facilities in certain African countries involves substantial political liabilities."[50] Although officials were thinking specifically of the situations in Madagascar and South Africa at the time, the concept of planning for the removal of U.S. bases in Africa also would allow Washington to avoid making defense commitments on a continent with highly arbitrary state borders that were exceedingly likely to be challenged in the future.[51]

But in the early 1960s U.S. defense requirements included space and missile research projects. The Department of State's March 1962 secret guidelines had also observed that because of new space research and development activities and military contingency operations, "U.S. requirements for installations, rights and facilities in Africa [were] becoming increasingly important to further U.S. national security interest."[52] North Africa and the Horn of Africa were of particular military value to the United States "because of their strategic location and influence in securing NATO's southern flank."[53]

For the Defense Department, the communications station at Kagnew already was "of critical importance to a variety of communication and intelligence objectives."[54] Then in 1963 Defense had begun drawing up plans to implement a new secret operation at Kagnew Station that would become known as the Stonehouse project.[55] The initial impetus behind this project was to offset the USSR's perceived lead in space research in the early 1960s. As part of this effort, two huge parabolic antennas would be installed at Kagnew. The official cover story was that the United States was simply planning to conduct research in satellite communications.[56] In fact, the new equipment would be used to intercept Soviet space telemetry and aid in the development of U.S. ballistic missiles.[57]

The Stonehouse project, however, posed a political problem for Washington as well as for Addis Ababa. Though a highly secret project, it was also highly visible. The two structures, twelve to fifteen stories high, would require special arrangements to be brought to the port at Massawa, transported to Kagnew, and erected on a site within viewing distance of Asmara. This would expose Addis Ababa to charges of collusion with the United States. Although the Ethiopians had heard this before, they were becoming more sensitive to such accusations, given the nationalist and neutralist feelings sweeping through Africa. If Washington could not prevent a general deterioration in U.S.-Ethiopian relations, there could be mounting pressures against Kagnew resulting in the cancellation of the Stonehouse project.

Immediately after the February–March 1964 Ethiopian-Somali conflict in the Ogaden, the American embassy in Addis Ababa began calling for a review of the U.S. National Policy Paper on Ethiopia, issued the previous December. Among other things, the embassy felt that the issue of Kagnew needed to be thoroughly explored in light of the forthcoming installations.[58] Kagnew unquestionably represented the single most important U.S. interest in the Horn of Africa, but it was also the source of complications for U.S. policy objectives in the area. Much to the embassy's chagrin, Washington's attitude appeared to be that Kagnew was a "vital installation whose use is assured indefinitely and into which [the United States] can continue to pour additional investment with impunity."[59]

But political trends in Africa were starting to overtake U.S. defense policy. Washington had lost access to the Zanzibar tracking station, U.S. base rights at Wheelus in Libya were in jeopardy, and the Moroccan naval communications facility was seemingly on the way out. This would mean that Kagnew might soon be the only remaining U.S. military installation in Africa.[60] Moreover, the OAU Head of State Assembly to be held in Cairo that July, as well as the upcoming Bandung II and Belgrade II nonaligned conferences, were all expected to turn their attention to foreign bases in Africa.[61] To the U.S. mission in Addis Ababa, there appeared to be a stepped-up campaign, instigated by the Soviet Union, China, the United Arab Republic, and Ghana, to sow doubts about Kagnew. Given these building pressures against the imperial government—likely to increase with the addition of the new, highly visible structures at Kagnew and coupled with the lack of compensation or rent in the form of additional military and economic aid—negotiations with the Ethiopian Foreign Office over new land needed for the new installation could become complicated.[62] Some reciprocal gesture of friendship was needed to placate foreign and domestic critics, thus clearing the way politically within Addis Ababa for the Stonehouse project.

The quid pro quo connection between the Stonehouse project at Kagnew and the F-5 Freedom Fighters was very explicit. In May 1964, the two parabolic antennas arrived at Kagnew. The following month, Ambassador Korry delivered Washington's message to the imperial government promising that the United States would give Ethiopia a squadron of F-5 jet fighters. Kagnew was no longer a free bonus thrown in by the Ethiopians. Any attempt by the United States to affect or limit future deliveries of MAP equipment, or to recover unused equipment, could "jeopardize continued effective U.S. use of the vital communications facility at Kagnew."[63] Though the U.S. embassy and Addis Ababa considered the F-5s proper compensation, this arms transfer might also have been viewed as blackmail.

THE EMPEROR'S PATH OF PRUDENCE

Haile Selassie was in no position to be complacent about the stability of his tenure as emperor of Ethiopia. In December 1960, less than four months after the United States had pledged a continuation of military assistance to Addis Ababa and reaffirmed its support in helping to maintain the regional political status quo, the Ethiopian imperial bodyguard staged a coup against the emperor.[64] To the government's consternation, the United States remained neutral on the first day while the outcome was in doubt. Then on the morning of the second day, when the outcome seemed clear to U.S. military advisers, the Americans moved to meet their MDAP obligations and provided "advice" to government forces. Although the rebels were ultimately crushed on the third day, allowing Selassie to return safely to the capital, this event highlighted the vulnerability of the Ethiopian monarchy.

Washington responded to the December 1960 coup attempt by pressing harder than before for internal Ethiopian reforms.[65] Western-based liberal ideas, however, contradicted almost everything the emperor and his government stood for.[66] Given its strategic stake in Ethiopia, the United States could only push so hard. But to keep American aid flowing, Haile Selassie put on a face of reform while underneath the Ethiopian state remained fundamentally unchanged.[67]

The State Department recognized that the emperor had no intention of drastically altering Ethiopia's political system. Instead, the U.S. embassy in Addis Ababa pressed for economic and administrative reforms in the country throughout the 1960s.[68] Ethiopian reformers and progressives, however, would continue to challenge the imperial system. How much longer the aging emperor could play this Byzantine game was unknown. Thus, in the early 1960s the State Department began planning for the contingency that Haile Selassie might soon be overthrown.[69]

State Department analysts were a bit premature in writing the emperor's political epitaph. Selassie knew how to survive politically by using foreign policy to divert attention from domestic issues. Instead of undertaking real political reforms, he used Kagnew to kick the Americans hard until they paid up, and in the meantime assumed an apparently neutralist posture in international affairs to appease Ethiopia's radicals.[70] The emperor could thus claim that he was neither a lackey of the Americans nor did he allow the United States to exploit Ethiopia.

Manipulating Ethiopia's internal political situation in this way, however, had its dangers. Despite what American officials might interpret as anti-U.S. actions by the imperial government, Ethiopian leaders had "no great interest in casting their lot with the radicals."[71] More often than not, according to the U.S. embassy, Addis Ababa found itself "reluctantly on the fringe area of doing so in order to preserve Ethiopia's and the Emperor's necks."[72] But if this repeated tactic of anti-American, neutralist diversion were to become a long-term strategy, Ethiopia's radicals might soon gain influence in the government. Then, by aligning Addis Ababa with radical external forces, they could create the conditions conducive to establishing a new Ethiopia, minus the emperor.

The prudent path for the emperor not only necessitated mollifying or undercutting internal opponents by manipulating Ethiopia's external policy, but also required that he avoid antagonizing foreign governments. Although diplomatic relations between the Soviet Union and Ethiopia became somewhat strained in early 1964 when heavy fighting broke out in the Ogaden, the moderate Soviet presence in Ethiopia was not affected by Moscow's military assistance to Mogadishu.[73] According to the U.S. embassy, the Soviets were seeking to create a favorable image by not inciting rebellion and remaining on good terms with Haile Selassie.[74] Moreover, compared with the activities of the Chinese communists in Africa, the Soviet Union appeared less militant and threatening.[75] Nonetheless, Haile Selassie must have realized that the Soviets were simply waiting for his demise, when they could usurp the U.S. position in Ethiopia.

Despite his dissatisfaction with U.S. military assistance, Haile Selassie had no desire to burn his bridges with the United States. A turn to the communist bloc for arms could prove politically fatal for him. The game of diversion Selassie was playing with his internal critics would be exposed, and the Soviets would probably abandon him to his fate if these domestic foes rose against him. The U.S. military connection gave the emperor a sense of security that he did not wish to jeopardize.

Haile Selassie's willingness to wait until 1966 for the delivery of the F-5s was due also to imperial prestige and personal ego. In acquiring supersonic combat jets, Ethiopia would be the only country in sub-Sahara Africa to possess such weaponry and to have crossed the "sophisticated arms barrier," thereby enhancing the emperor's status within the Ethiopian military establishment as well as in the region. Even given the delay in the delivery of the F-5s, only a handful of Third World states—Israel, Egypt, South Africa, Morocco, Saudi Arabia, Syria, and Ethiopia—would possess such sophisticated weaponry.[76] While both superpowers had transferred sophisticated arms to North Africa and the Middle East, the Soviet MiG-17 combat fighters were of a lesser quality than the F-5s. So in spite of the time lag between the 1964 commitment and 1966 delivery date, the emperor would not have settled for anything less than the F-5 Freedom Fighters.

THE GREAT STALL

The diplomatic controversy surrounding the F-5s arose partly because of the vagueness of the June 1964 commitment to provide the Freedom Fighters and disputes as to when the United States was obliged to deliver them. No delivery date was mentioned in the diplomatic note presented by Ambassador Korry to the imperial government except that the "deliveries of the aircraft were conditioned upon the preparedness of the Ethiopian Air Force to receive them."[77] Less than a month later, Drew Pearson wrote a series of articles extremely critical of the U.S. military assistance program in Ethiopia, suggesting its government had been conned into choosing the F-5s without being given delivery dates.[78] The U.S. embassy immediately refuted this charge, stating that the imperial government had opted for the F-5s "in the full knowledge that the delivery dates would be in 1966" and sought to disparage Pearson's analysis by noting that the journalist's trip had been paid for and sponsored by the Ethiopian government.[79]

By mid-September 1964, however, Ambassador Korry was recommending that the Pentagon "start biting away at the large accumulating backlog in promised army equipment" by increasing American MAP funding for Ethiopia and "expedite delivery of the first F-5As."[80] Korry's transformation from a critic to the leading American advocate for the F-5 transfer owed much to the metamorphosis in the ambassador's views after spending a year in Ethiopia. When Korry first arrived, he had been unimpressed by the emperor's military requests. In a mid-December 1963 telegram to the State Department regarding U.S. force goal objectives in Ethiopia, he noted that Ethiopia could not support effectively the 28,000-man army, which the United States had promised to increase to 40,000, and the nation was experiencing budgetary problems as well as difficulty in absorbing U.S. military assistance.[81] Solving these troubles would mean deemphasizing long-range threats and focusing on Ethiopia's ability to absorb military aid and the immediate Ogaden situation.[82] Although Korry was unsettled by the fact that the United States seemed to be getting "into increasingly hot water" over its inability to meet existing MAP commitments, including its commitment to equip a 40,000-man army (supposedly within five years), he felt that Washington should push back or find substitutes for some of the air force items, such as the multimillion-dollar F-5A jets, clearly meant to address long-range threats.[83]

Soon after this, the ambassador reversed his position. Over the next two years Korry advanced in no uncertain terms the political and strategic need for the United States to deliver the F-5s in a timely fashion. During the flare-up in the Ogaden, he had assailed Washington's MAP policy toward Ethiopia as "trying to get by with 'stretch-outs' and words instead of actions."[84] His telegrams to Washington between February and May 1964 stressed that the United States should do more than simply point to the $80 million worth of MAP delivered to Ethiopia. Given the U.S. record of delay, delivering defective equipment and equipment with shortages, and dropping this programmed equipment on an unprepared recipient, something tangible and effective needed to be done.

Although Korry's presentations of the Somali threat in the Ogaden, the U.S. stake at Kagnew, and Ethiopia's geopolitical importance helped to bring about the F-5 commitment, he was less successful in persuading Washington to speed up the delivery of the jets. Korry had recommended in September 1964 that the United States reallocate funds for producing the Freedom Fighters to permit delivery of the first F-5s in 1965, with the remainder to follow shortly.[85] The State Department was at the time in the process of revising the National Policy Paper for Ethiopia and avoided making such a commitment. Although the importance of Ethiopia was reflected in the revised NPP edition, and the U.S. role in Ethiopia was given thorough scrutiny, with respect to the F-5s the State Department wanted Korry to delay the Ethiopians: "We would hope the Ethiopians would be encouraged to begin preparation of necessary facilities and select candidates for training in order to be prepared to receive the aircraft when delivery becomes possible."[86] A three-part telegram fired off by the ambassador to the Department of State at the end of the year highlighting the external threats to Ethiopian security, internal threats to the emperor, and the precariousness of the U.S. position in Ethiopia, had little perceptible effect.[87]

The State Department's indifference to Ethiopia's alleged security plight was in part a backlash against, or aversion to the anti-Arab nature of Korry's arguments.[88] Even after the creation of a separate Africa Bureau in 1958, Arabists continued to exert considerable influence over U.S. policy toward Ethiopia. This intra-departmental reorganization had left Ethiopia grouped with a number of Islamic, Arab-oriented African states such as Morocco, Libya, Tunisia and Sudan. When the Africa Bureau was further subdivided, Ethiopia remained grouped with Sudan and Somalia in the East African Affairs division.

The ambassador angered Arabists as well as Kremlinologists by suggesting that the Soviet Union would attempt to use pan-Arabism (via Somalia) to lever the United States out of Ethiopia.[89] While Moscow might try to undermine the U.S. position by using Kagnew to embarrass Washington, the State Department felt there was no strategic value for the Soviet presence in Somalia, which was not even a member of the Arab League and so unlikely to gain Arab support. Moreover, during this period of relative calm in the Middle East, when Washington was trying to initiate an arms limitation program for the region, the United States did not want to give Nasser or other radical Arab leaders any reason to acquire even more arms from the Soviet Union. Korry was deemed to be suffering from a severe case of clientitis.

The Defense Department was no more sympathetic to the ambassador's arguments. Pentagon officials still looked upon the Ethiopian military as a ragtag army that would be able neither to make any contribution to free world defense, nor prevent or deter local war.[90] Ethiopia fell into the Pentagon's third and least important category of MAP recipients—those for whom assistance was aimed at maintaining internal security against subversion, guerrilla warfare, or infiltration. The CINCMEAFSA (Commander-in-Chief, Middle East, Africa, and South Asia), in whose area of command Ethiopia fell, opposed a speeded-up delivery schedule for the F-5s.[91]

Moreover, the Pentagon apparently gave little thought to what the U.S. MAAG mission in Ethiopia should accomplish. When Edward Korry received his briefing at the Department of Defense shortly before assuming his new post in Addis Ababa the briefing officer had told him that the United States would give the emperor his $10 million in military aid in "solid gold Cadillacs" if he wanted it that way.[92] Following a visit to Ethiopia in early 1962, John Kenneth Galbraith, U.S. ambassador to India, reported that the U.S. MAAG in Addis Ababa tended "to look on the Ethiopian forces much as its private army without regard to its impact on our regional and national policies."[93] The idea that the United States need provide only enough military aid to maintain access to Kagnew Station, without regard for its impact or effectiveness, dominated Pentagon thinking.

Thus, Korry's geopolitical warnings, which were linked to the need to upgrade the Ethiopian armed forces, fell largely upon deaf ears even at the Department of Defense. The idea that Soviet activities in the Horn of Africa were related to the strategic situation at the eastern end of the Mediterranean struck a responsive nerve only within the navy, which, because of its predisposition to think in Mahanist terms and foreseeing the worldwide mission of nuclear submarines and the need for forward basing, supported Korry's line of argument.[94] As for the rest of the Joint Chiefs of Staff, they felt the ambassador was reading too much into it. Washington's strategic position in the Horn of Africa was not being threatened, so there was no urgent need to alter the F-5 delivery schedule for Ethiopia.

Washington's attitude toward the F-5 delivery began to change during 1966. Although the aircraft were due to be delivered anyway, two premises upon which the United States had based its stalling policy were no longer operable.[95] First, the notion that the Soviets would not acquire bases in Somalia became suspect; construction at the port of Berbera begun by the Soviets in 1964 was nearing completion, suggesting that Moscow might strike a base deal with Mogadishu. Second, the idea that Moscow would not put any heavy armament into Somalia began to crumble in 1965–1966, as Moscow executed a rapid buildup of the Somali Air Force, including delivery of six MiG-15s, twenty Yak-IIs, and twelve MiG-17s.[96] Although none of these Soviet-supplied aircraft fell into the category of "sophisticated" (supersonic jet fighter) weapons, delivery of the F-5 squadron assumed a heretofore unappreciated diplomatic-military urgency.

The State Department now felt that the F-5s had to be delivered in 1966 as promised, in order to preserve American credibility.[97] If Washington failed to respond visibly to the Soviet-Somali MiG deal, it would create a negative perception of the United States within Ethiopia, and possibly throughout the rest of the region. Moreover, Washington had run out of stalling tactics as the Ethiopian Air Force was ready to receive the jets. Thus, the Johnson administration proceeded with the delivery of the F-5 Freedom Fighter squadron during the latter half of 1966 and completed the transaction in 1967.

CONCLUSION: CROSSING A THRESHOLD

The F-5 arms transfer broke new ground, not only militarily but also politically, in the U.S.-Ethiopia arms relationship. Washington's decision to provide Addis Ababa with the F-5 Freedom Fighters meant crossing a military threshold in sub-Sahara Africa, bringing Ethiopia into a select group of Third World states possessing sophisticated weaponry. But for Haile Selassie, the arms transfer meant crossing a political threshold as well. By giving Ethiopia the F-5s, the United States had proved that it had a long-term interest in maintaining Ethiopia's security. U.S. officials also recognized the political implications of the F-5 deal, which was why sending the Freedom Fighters aroused such resistance in the first place, and their delivery was stalled.

The F-5 episode was a classic example of a weak client state manipulating the weakness and vulnerability of its arms patron. Although Ethiopia's vague threat of defection hung over this episode, first the Soviet and then the neutralist threat, owing to Washington's lack of responsiveness, it was U.S. plans to expand intelligence-gathering, research, and communications operations at Kagnew that allowed the Ethiopians to blackmail the United States. Moreover, with the Johnson administration reverting to a mid-1950s stance of viewing the Third World through a zero-sum lens, and since Somalia had brought the Soviets into the Horn, Ethiopia's pro-Western alignment had to be rewarded to prevent Moscow from scoring a geopolitical victory in the Horn of Africa. The fact that from early 1964 the U.S. embassy vehemently advocated the F-5 transfer also aided the emperor's cause.

The United States was in a no-win situation; the best it could hope to do was control the damage caused by its blunder in first offering the F-5s to Ethiopia. Damage control in this instance meant delaying the transfer.

Following the 1964 border war with Somalia, which had exposed Ethiopia's military vulnerability, Selassie could not afford to lose the American military connection. Whereas accommodation with the neutralist camp might mean losing the Ogaden and Eritrea, or lead to the emperor's own political demise, the United States could give Haile Selassie what he needed to keep his empire intact. Still, the American decision to cross the sophisticated arms export threshold in Ethiopia and end its game of delay exposed the fact that the United States had no option but to deal with Addis Ababa because of Kagnew. Despite the negative attitudes held toward the role of the U.S. military mission in Addis Ababa, the State Department viewed Ethiopia as an important actor in the African arena whose friendship should be retained.

Again a tangible exchange had taken place between the United States and Ethiopia. In this case, however, Addis Ababa seemed to get the better of the deal, while Washington absorbed the greater risk. Certainly Haile Selassie gave the Americans greater privileges at Kagnew. But there was no additional risk for Selassie, because he was already seen as being in league with the Americans. Washington, on the other hand, was forced to up the ante again by crossing a qualitative threshold. Moreover, in the long term, the F-5 arms transfer exacerbated the arms race in the Horn and forced the Americans to pour even more arms into Ethiopia in order to protect their investment at Kagnew and credibility with the IEG.

7

The 1973 Arms Package Controversy

Throughout the latter half of the 1960s and into the 1970s, U.S.-Ethiopia military relations were relatively uneventful. The delivery of the F-5 Freedom Fighters in 1966–1967 had satisfied Haile Selassie's political concerns by signaling in a very tangible fashion Washington's commitment to Ethiopia and the special place that Addis Ababa held in Africa. Subsequently, Washington introduced a second squadron of F-5s into Ethiopia and supported the buildup of a small Ethiopian navy.[1] In 1971 the Pentagon began to implement a five-year plan for "across-the-board equipment" modernization of the entire Ethiopian Army, replacing the outmoded M-10 rifles with M-16 machine guns.[2] But, for the most part, IEG military requests were of a modest nature.

The idea that the United States, by the F-5 transfers and other military modernization programs, had put its best foot forward in Ethiopia was only partially true. In the mid-1960s the F-5s did represent Washington's top-of-the-line air force export item to the Third World. But even before the Freedom Fighters had been delivered to Ethiopia, the United States had put into production another line of jet aircraft that eclipsed the combat capabilities of the F-5s—the F-4 Phantom jet.[3] Only a very select group of U.S. arms clients would receive this new generation of combat jet fighter before the mid-1970s, and Ethiopia was not one of them.[4] Washington sought to satisfy the air force requirements of the vast majority of its Third World military recipients by pressing on them the less expensive and less advanced F-5 Freedom Fighters.[5] Still, the IEG had to be impressed by what the United States was doing in the way of arming its military. Ethiopia was among a select group of sub-Sahara African states armed with supersonic jet fighters.[6] Addis Ababa had received over 80 percent of all U.S. MAP funds programmed for Africa.[7] Washington was also providing Special Forces counterinsurgency training to help the IEG deal with the rebellion in Eritrea.

The tenor and tempo of the U.S. military assistance program seemed to be perfectly suited to Ethiopia's relatively relaxed security environment. After the June 1967 Arab-Israeli War, Cairo and other Middle East antagonists focused their attention on regaining their lost territories from Israel, not harassing Ethiopia. About the same time, a new government had been elected in Somalia that expressed a desire for political rapprochement with its African neighbors, including Ethiopia. Addis Ababa seemed to have enough breathing space, and the Americans were doing enough that U.S.-Ethiopia military relations ran rather smoothly.

However, this serene atmosphere became one of high intensity in 1972–1973. Not only was the insurgency in Eritrea heating up, but also Somalia had adopted a more militaristic approach in pursuing its claim on the Ogaden. Near the end of 1972 a small probing force of Somali soldiers had crossed into the Ogaden near an area where oil and natural gas deposits had been discovered the previous April by the U.S.-based Tenneco Oil Company.[8] Addis Ababa dispatched to the area a sizable military force which clashed with Somali troops in 1973.

But even more alarming was the growth of Soviet military activities in Somalia. Haile Selassie was becoming concerned that Mogadishu was on the verge of a large-scale military buildup that, in combination with the growing military burden of Eritrea, would alter the balance of power in the Horn. In February 1972 Soviet Defense Minister Marshal Grechko had signed a $60 million military aid agreement with Mogadishu.[9] The emperor was "appalled at the concentration of Soviet arms in Somalia" and sought to "counteract the mounting concern among [IEG] ministers and the military."[10] In an effort to head off this shifting balance, which potentially might threaten Ethiopia's security and the emperor himself, Haile Selassie used the occasion of an official state visit to the United States in early May 1973 to meet with President Richard Nixon and present a $450 million shopping list for modern military equipment, including Phantom Jets, M-60 tanks, surface-to-air missiles, and air-to-ground missiles.[11]

Before leaving for the United States, Haile Selassie had boasted that "everything would be solved" after he met with the president.[12] Instead, the emperor's trip turned out to be "an unqualified disaster."[13] His case for vastly increased U.S. arms transfers was hampered by factions at the U.S. embassy in Addis Ababa over the extent of the Somali threat and whether American credibility really was at stake in the Horn. Ambassador E. Ross Adair and his senior political advisers had endorsed the Ethiopian arms request over the objections of several junior embassy officials who did not take the Somali threat so seriously.[14] However, the State Department overruled the embassy and advised the White House against providing any of the heavy arms on the emperor's shopping list.[15] The State Department considered the idea that the Somali Army held "strategic superiority" in the Horn of Africa to be a myth, as Somalia appeared incapable of making a large-scale attack on Ethiopia or even using much of the Soviet weaponry in their arsenal.[16]

Thus, the Nixon administration politely rebuffed the emperor, offering instead a moderate increase in credit and cash sales, but no grant military aid.[17] Although the Americans agreed to support a new armored vehicle brigade with defensive weapons and ground-to-air missiles, they refused to underwrite the transfer of M-60 tanks or Phantom jets.[18] While Haile Selassie did not leave the United States empty-handed, he received only a small fraction of his original request, with a promise that it would be studied further.[19] If the emperor wanted more, he would have to go to the Pentagon's cash-and-carry department.[20]

INSURGENCY IN ERITREA

Although Addis Ababa's perception of the growing Somali threat served as the primary catalyst for Haile Selassie's ill-fated mission to Washington, the IEG was also concerned about antigovernment military operations in Ethiopia's northeast province of Eritrea. The Eritrean insurgency, once derisively dismissed by the IEG as the activities of *shiftas* (bandits), had gained strength in the early 1970s as a result of increased Arab financial assistance to the rebels and the movement's own internal political dynamism. Increased guerrilla activities now threatened to cut off Addis Ababa and Ethiopia's central highlands from the two deep-water ports at Massawa and Assab. Moreover, if the IEG did not snuff out this insurgency, the United States, having just disengaged itself from direct military involvement in Vietnam, might decide to abandon Ethiopia too.

When Haile Selassie annexed Eritrea in 1962, he realized that such an action would provoke Arab governments who took a special interest in Eritrea; this interest was based on a feeling of kinship for the large portion of the Eritrean population who were Muslims as well as for the potential strategic benefits that might be derived vis-à-vis Israel in bringing this coastal Red Sea area under their influence. The emperor had expected some isolated instances of internal disorder that could be easily controlled by the Ethiopian military. Once he showed the capacity to control the province, Selassie assumed that Arab propaganda attacks would cease. What the emperor apparently miscalculated was the intense passions that his actions would arouse within Eritrea and how Ethiopia's association with Israel would be exploited by the insurgents to acquire Arab assistance.

The emperor's decision to annex Eritrea was hardly a surprise to anyone, given IEG actions in the years preceding the dissolution of the Eritrean parliament on November 14, 1962.[21] Having observed Addis Ababa's policies in the federated territory at close range, the U.S. consul in Asmara had warned the State Department in May 1962 that Selassie would try to force the union issue in September.[22] The Eritreans also sensed what was coming and in 1958 had founded the Eritrean Liberation Movement (ELM) with a platform calling for the creation of an independent Eritrean state. Although the ELM was established as a political organization, the group turned to direct action in September 1961 as it became apparent that the federation would fail and Ethiopia would take control of Eritrea.

The Eritrean insurgency had only limited success in the 1960s. Because of the relatively small-scale nature of rebel operations, Addis Ababa as well as the U.S. embassy dismissed the danger posed by the *shiftas*. By 1968 the insurgency appeared to be on the verge of dying out altogether, as Arab support for the Eritrean cause dwindled after Israel's decisive victory in the 1967 war.[23] The Eritrean insurgency was now at perhaps its most vulnerable stage: ammunition was in short supply owing to the disarray among its Arab supporters, and thus antigovernment activities in the province diminished considerably.

Sensing a perfect opportunity to destroy the rebels once and for all, the IEG intensified its counterinsurgency operations. By the end of 1969, Addis Ababa had committed 8,000 imperial troops, backed by a squadron of T-28 aircraft and a squadron of F-86 Sabre jets, to Eritrea.[24] Despite being completely overmatched, the Eritreans continued to resist and frustrate Ethiopia's attempt to seal off the Sudanese border.[25] After absorbing the IEG's military offensive, the Eritreans stepped up the pressure, staging an ambush in November 1970 that killed the commander of the Ethiopian Second Division on the road between Asmara and Keren. In the wake of this attack, 90 percent of the province was placed under martial law.

Clearly, the IEG was not simply dealing with a *shifta* problem in Eritrea. In January 1971 rebel strength was estimated to number between 1,700 and 2,000 insurgents.[26] The Eritreans were also beginning to benefit again from increased financial support from the Arabs. Moreover, the ELF's ability to attract support and gain political recognition in Damascus, Aden, Baghdad, Beirut, Khartoum, and Mogadishu had turned Ethiopia's internal problem into an affair with international ramifications.[27]

Haile Selassie did score two diplomatic successes that took some of the pressure off the government in Eritrea.[28] In 1971 he recognized the People's Republic of China, in exchange for which Peking severed its ties with the Eritrean insurgents and pledged $100 million in economic aid. The following year, as a result of Selassie's mediation in negotiating an end to Sudan's seventeen-year civil war, the Sudanese government began to reduce assistance to the Eritrean insurgents who used Sudan as a safe haven and conduit for acquiring arms. Although the IEG began to regain the upper hand, the war continued unabated.

Therefore, when Haile Selassie arrived in Washington in May 1973, he had not only the Soviet and Cuban-backed Somali threat to be concerned about, but also a full-blown insurgency in Eritrea supported by the Arabs and Soviet bloc.[29] Addis Ababa had committed almost one-fourth of its army and a substantial portion of the Ethiopian Air Force to Eritrea, leaving Ethiopia extremely vulnerable to an external attack. A thrust by a strengthened Somali military force into the Ogaden at this time would overextend the capabilities of the Ethiopian military, given its present level of armament. Addis Ababa's security calculation now necessitated having the capacity to wage simultaneously a prolonged counterinsurgency operation and full-scale desert war.

SUPERPOWER DETENTE AND EGYPT'S DEFECTION

Given the international climate, Haile Selassie's May 1973 arms request came at a very inopportune time. Since the beginning of the decade, U.S. perceptions of threat had been undergoing a considerable transformation in some policy-making circles. At the working level of the State Department, among moderate and liberal members of the U.S. Congress and all the way to the White House, there was a growing belief that global and regional threats to U.S. interests were on the decline. Consequently, these changes in perception gave the United States greater latitude in its dealings with Ethiopia and limited the IEG's ability to manipulate and exploit Washington's fear of radical usurpers.

At the end of the 1960s, the relationship between the United States and the Soviet Union began moving away from zero-sum confrontation to détente and limited cooperation.[30] Concurrently, President Nixon and National Security Adviser Henry Kissinger were exploring and exploiting the China option vis-à-vis the Soviet Union to enhance U.S. maneuverability on the world stage. On a bilateral level, Washington and Moscow reached limited accords on trade issues, limiting strategic nuclear weapon systems and bringing about U.S. disengagement from Vietnam. After the India-Pakistani crisis of 1971 there also seemed to be a genuine desire to avoid being drawn into conflictual situations in the Third World that might result in direct superpower confrontation. Whether this was due to the new climate surrounding U.S.-Soviet relations or, as Henry Kissinger argued, because U.S. demonstrations of firmness on India-Pakistan and

Vietnam "must have convinced the Kremlin that one more crisis would overload the circuit," it seemed unlikely that Moscow would encourage Somalia to go to war against Ethiopia even if Mogadishu acquired a military advantage.[31]

In sub-Sahara Africa, the potential flash point for conflict and East-West confrontation was in southern Africa. However, the administration believed the situation would remain stable as the white minority government in South Africa, Ian Smith's outlaw government in Rhodesia, and the Portuguese colonial authorities in Angola and Mozambique seemed to be there to stay.[32] In the Horn of Africa, Soviet involvement in Somalia and the insurgency in Eritrea were given little thought by high-ranking members of the Nixon adminstration.[33] Africa as a whole was apparently a low-priority item on the administration's national security agenda.

Besides the breakthrough in U.S.-Soviet relations in the early 1970s, a dramatic though more covert and latent transformation was occurring in the Middle East that further mitigated Washington's sense of threat. In September 1970 Washington's longtime nemesis, Gamal Nasser, died and was succeeded by Anwar Sadat. At first it appeared that Egypt's close political-military association with the Soviet Union would remain unchanged. In May 1971 Sadat signed the Treaty of Friendship and Cooperation with Moscow. The following February, and again in April, the Egyptian leader visited the Soviet Union hoping to acquire a blank check for diplomatic support and military assistance, as had been extended by Moscow to India during its conflict with Pakistan in 1971.[34]

Despite these surface appearances, things were not going so smoothly between Cairo and Moscow. In early April 1972 the Egyptian government opened a secret diplomatic channel to the White House. Because of the administration's preoccupation with a Vietnamese offensive and Henry Kissinger's forthcoming trip to Moscow, as well as for tactical negotiating purposes designed to create "maximun restlessness with the [Middle East] status quo" in Egypt, the White House delayed in responding to Egypt's request for a secret high-level meeting.[35] Nonetheless, Kissinger now "felt confident enough to advise Nixon that the Soviet-Egyptian relationship was clearly more reserved than in Nasser's time."[36] Although the U.S.-Egyptian contacts were primarily concerned with finding a workable Middle East peace scheme between the Arab states and Israel, these discussions marked the beginning of a dramatic shift in Egyptian policy. The diplomatic bombshell that served notice that Soviet influence was on the wane in Egypt came on July 18, 1972, when President Sadat expelled more than 15,000 Russian military advisers and experts.

Thus, Haile Selassie arrived in Washington with a poor negotiating hand because of external events that had diminished his capacity for, and U.S.

vulnerability to, the manipulation of foreign threats. Although threats to U.S. interests had not completely disappeared, the United States had not been in such a favorable position in the Middle East and Africa since the early 1950s. Nasser was gone, and the Soviet Union did not seem to be willing to challenge U.S. interests in the Third World. The main two villains that the emperor had used in the past to prod Washington into action were gone or apparently changing their ways.

THE MOGADISHU COUP

Since the latter half of the 1950s, the Somali irredentist threat had been the primary rationale for Ethiopia's military requests. But until 1973 it was a threat that had no real teeth. The military cooperation between the Soviet Union and Somalia came nowhere near matching that between the United States and Ethiopia. U.S. military assistance to the IEG dwarfed by comparison the amount of aid Moscow provided Mogadishu. The absence during this time of any formal political-military arrangement or exchange between the two nations suggested that the Soviets might just be biding their time in Somalia until they could lever the Americans out of Ethiopia. To that end, Moscow would want to avoid doing anything in Somalia that might ruin that opportunity, should it present itself.

Soviet military activity in Somalia remained fairly limited throughout the 1960s. Following the conclusion of the $30 million Soviet-Somali arms agreement in 1963, no other major weapons accord materialized. Moscow did provide training and a dose of Marxist-Leninist indoctrination for some 500 Somali pilots, officers, and technicians in the Soviet Union; Russian military advisers stationed in Somalia also trained army and air force personnel.[37] But in terms of affecting the balance of power in the Horn, even with the introduction of combat fighters and bombers into Somalia in the mid-1960s, the Soviet effort had minimum impact.

Somalia was having considerable difficulty absorbing Soviet military assistance. Reports of arms and equipment shipments left rotting in Somali ports suggested that much of Moscow's effort was being wasted in Somalia and that perhaps the Russians were proving to be as ineffective in executing their military mission, as the Americans allegedly were in Ethiopia.[38] From 1966 to 1969, Soviet arms deliveries to Somalia had virtually ceased. So at the start of the 1970s Mogadishu's military threat amounted to a force of 20,000 soldiers equipped with outmoded World War II and Korean War–vintage weapons, enough to make trouble but not enough to win a war against the U.S.-supplied Ethiopian military.[39]

The slowdown in Soviet arms transfers to Somalia in the latter half of the 1960s was partly the result of a decision made in Mogadishu in 1967 to seek political accommodation with its neighbors and to increase cooperation with the West.[40] In October 1967, Somalia's Prime Minister Muhammad Ibrahim Egal and President Jomo Kenyatta of Kenya signed the Arusha Memorandum of Understanding in which the Somali government expressed its desire to resolve their border dispute peacefully. Mogadishu later resumed diplomatic relations with London and Nairobi, which had been severed in 1963 over the Northern Frontier District (Northeast Province of Kenya) problem. In January 1968 Vice President Hubert Humphrey had been warmly received in Mogadishu. The following September Prime Minister Egal met with President Charles de Gaulle in Paris and promised that Somalia would not disrupt French efforts to negotiate the terms of independence for France's Territories of the Afars and Issas (French Somaliland). Then, after Egal met with Haile Selassie in September 1969, emergency regulations were lifted along the Ethiopian-Somali border.

Somalia's drift toward the West came to a sudden end following the October 1969 military coup d'état in Mogadishu.[41] The new Supreme Revolutionary Council, headed by Maj. Gen. Mohammed Siad Barre, undertook a number of policy initiatives that were clearly anti-American—openly trading with North Vietnam, expelling American Peace Corps volunteers from the country, declaring several U.S. diplomats persona non grata for allegedly interfering in Somali internal affairs, and at the end of June 1970 seizing an American ship on suspicion of spying.[42] Mogadishu not only began strengthening ties with Arab states that were seeking confrontation with Israel; it actively solicited aid from the Soviet Union.[43] Despite Somalia's deteriorating relationship with the United States, Mogadishu reiterated its intention of continuing to foster good relations with Ethiopia.[44]

Somalia's continuing political confrontation with the United States, coupled with the Marxist-Leninist pronouncements of the Supreme Revolutionary Command, offered Moscow an opportunity to negotiate an ideologically based political-military alignment with Mogadishu. However, if the Soviets seized the initiative in Somalia, they would close the door in Ethiopia which they had maneuvered to keep open for so long. Somali irredentism already had forced Kenya and Ethiopia into close alignment with the West.[45] Meeting Mogadishu's requests for increased military assistance would push Ethiopia and Kenya even further into the Western camp at a time when Moscow still hoped to cultivate relations with Addis Ababa and Nairobi.[46] In looking at the broader African regional context, Moscow, which had endorsed the 1963 OAU declaration concerning the maintenance of postcolonial borders in Africa, would lose much goodwill on the continent by supporting a country broadly perceived as an aggressor.

Two years would pass before the Soviet Union warmed to the idea of moving into a closer political-military alignment with Somalia. Moscow's decision was based partly on the assessment that expanding Soviet naval activities in the Indian Ocean required support facilities, coupled with a desire to preempt the possible formation of a Sino-Somali alignment.[47] But Soviet frustrations in dealing with Ethiopia also influenced this decision. Moscow too had been manipulated over the years by Haile Selassie. Though the emperor and his advisers always hinted at accepting arms from the Soviet Union, in the end the IEG always came down on the side of the Americans. Unless some drastic political change occurred in Addis Ababa, the Ethiopian option would remain closed to Moscow.

Thus, the stage was set for a quid pro quo arrangement between the Soviet Union and Somalia. In February 1972 Soviet Defense Minister Marshal Andrei Grechko signed a military cooperation agreement with the government of Siad Barre. Moscow agreed to provide Mogadishu with $60 million worth of Soviet military aid over a two-year period to upgrade and expand the Somali armed forces. In return, Somalia granted the Soviet Union access rights to Somali military facilities.

Although the strategic implications of the Soviet-Somali arms-for-access arrangement had a chilling effect in Washington as well as in Addis Ababa, in terms of the U.S.-Ethiopia relationship, it actually enhanced the United States' leverage in dealing with the IEG. Moscow's decision to stake its claim in Somalia effectively ended Addis Ababa's game—or charade—of threatening to defect to the Soviets whenever the Americans were not adequately responsive to Ethiopian demands. The drawback for the United States was that Addis Ababa would use the Soviet-Somali agreement to press for increased levels of U.S. military assistance. But, then again, Addis Ababa always exaggerated the Somali threat. At least now Washington could assess the Ethiopian-Somali military balance on the more objective basis of what Moscow was doing in Somalia, not what Haile Selassie said the Russians would do for Ethiopia.

KAGNEW'S DIMINISHING RETURNS

The primary rationale for giving military assistance to Ethiopia, which made all other issues concerning U.S. policy toward the Horn of Africa superfluous, was Kagnew Station. Into the 1970s a variety of defense-related communications functions were performed at Kagnew. The State Department used the facility to relay and receive messages from the

U.S. embassy in Addis Ababa and to communicate with the diplomatic community in East Africa. However, Kagnew's uniqueness as a strategic asset was related to its functions performed under Department of Defense auspices. Kagnew served as a relay station for the United States' worldwide strategic communications network (STRATCOM) and as an earth terminal for the Defense Satellite Command System (DSC). These two functions consumed almost all of the station's operating time.[48]

Kagnew's strategic value was made further evident by the secrecy surrounding U.S. operations at the station. Information concerning activities at Kagnew and even the specific location of the facility were, until the 1970 Symington hearings on U.S. overseas military agreements and commitments, discussed in executive session and deleted from the public record. Administration officials referred to Ethiopia as a "MAP country with an important U.S. military installation." Of course, it was recognized that there was a direct link between the level of U.S. MAP assistance for Ethiopia and the American operation at Kagnew. Assistant Secretary of State for African Affairs David Newsom acknowledged before the Symington committee that, "If it were not for Kagnew, I would hope that our military involvement would be substantially reduced."[49]

In fact, in the early 1970s U.S. strategic dependence upon Kagnew Station was already on the decline. Satellite technology had progressed to the point that it could perform many of the station's DSC and STRATCOM functions, including intelligence gathering. By May 1973, Kagnew's primary strategic mission was to serve as a communications link-up for U.S. Polaris submarines operating in the Indian Ocean—a function that space satellites could not yet adequately perform.[50] The future utility of the station, therefore, was contingent upon advances made in the realm of satellite technology or how quickly the United States moved toward turning the sparsely populated Indian Ocean island of Diego Garcia into a radio communications center that could then perform the Polaris communications mission.[51]

The United States, with the approval of Congress, was acquiring the capacity to move American strategic operations entirely offshore. Consequently, U.S. strategic interests would be less vulnerable to political instability in host countries and Washington would be less prone to blackmail in having valued operations held hostage as points of leverage. In the case of Ethiopia, it had become quite evident by 1973 that the United States was phasing out Kagnew and would not renew the twenty-five-year lease when it expired in 1978. The U.S. diplomatic, military, and intelligence-communities were relying more and more upon satellites for information.[52] In March 1972 when the Army Security Agency (ASA), the original host unit for the facility, began closing down its operations, no other agency was willing to assume control. After STRATCOM declined the invitation, the navy "inherited" Kagnew by default.[53]

At the same time, the primary mission of the U.S. embassy in Addis Ababa and the State Department's longtime rationale for U.S. arms transfers to Ethiopia were affected by these changes. Foreign service officers stationed in Ethiopia now admitted that Kagnew was a "convenient but dispensable" facility.[54] Once the radio communications center on Diego Garcia opened in March 1973, Kagnew's mission as a ship-to-shore communications link-up in the Indian Ocean's western quadrant would become largely redundant. American technicians at the station already were "listening mostly to garbage."[55] Kagnew was no longer an irreplaceable strategic asset.

However, the State Department found itself in a diplomatic quandary. In 1970 department officials had espoused the principle that as the strategic value of Kagnew declined so would the levels of U.S. military assistance to Ethiopia. But now, with Kagnew's strategic importance rapidly declining, such an opportunistic withdrawal and diminution of MAP funds for Ethiopia would send an unfavorable message about the United States and its treatment of a longtime friend and ally. The executive branch sought to reconcile this dilemma by keeping aid at a stable level and insisting that Kagnew still served a strategic purpose.

Thus, the Kagnew rationale for U.S. arms transfers to Ethiopia died a slow death as the Pentagon and State Department continued to use it as the primary MAP justification. In June 1971 Gen. Robert H. Warren, the deputy assistant secretary of defense for military assistance and sales, described the communications facility as "one of the most important the United States has anywhere in the world" and noted that as a practical matter the Ethiopian military assistance program related explicitly and exclusively to Kagnew.[56] Congress seemed to know better, but nonetheless only marginally reduced MAP and IMETP funds for Ethiopia from $11.75 million to $10.6 million for FY 1972.[57] In the FY 1973 budget, another $1.25 million was slashed, leaving Ethiopia with $9.35 million worth of military assistance—the lowest level since FY 1960.[58]

Whatever bargaining leverage Kagnew had given the Ethiopians had diminished significantly when the emperor arrived in Washington in May 1973. The huge depreciation in Kagnew's strategic value meant that the emperor had no valued asset to offer the United States in exchange for arms. Moreover, the Ethiopian arms request came just as high-level U.S. decisions were being made concerning further reductions at Kagnew.[59] Less than two months after Haile Selassie met with Richard Nixon, the DSC Stonehouse space communications project was shut down. Then in August 1973 Nixon approved a Defense Department recommendation that Kagnew be phased out.[60] The days of Addis Ababa using Kagnew to coerce or blackmail the United States were over.

THE NIXON DOCTRINE AND PRESIDENTIAL RELATIONS

Of his own doing, Haile Selassie found himself in a very precarious political situation in the spring of 1973. Selassie's boast that he would succeed in his mission to Washington created expectations that if not met would negatively affect his ability to rule. However, perhaps the emperor had cause for confidence. First, the Nixon Doctrine suggested that the United States would be amenable to meeting Ethiopia's security needs. Second, if that was not enough, Selassie expected his longtime personal relationship with Richard Nixon to pay big dividends.

Since the Nixon administration's first year in office, the declared policy of the United States had been to use arms transfers to secure U.S. interests overseas. The central thesis of the Nixon Doctrine, first enunciated at Guam Island at the end of July 1969, called for the United States to reduce its need to act as world policeman by looking to "the nation directly threatened to assume the primary responsibility of providing the manpower for its defense."[61] Secretary of Defense Melvin Laird subsequently elaborated on this theme, stating that the United States would be willing to "participate in the defense and development of allies and friends, but that America cannot—and will not—conceive all the plans, design all the programs, execute all the decisions, and undertake all the defense of the free nations of the world."[62] The Nixon Doctrine was designed to project a low profile overseas and to limit U.S. military commitments by promoting self-help. Washington would supply "the fire extinguisher, but not fight the fire."[63]

The implications of the Nixon administration's formula for maintaining international peace and stability were apparently not considered very carefully in Addis Ababa. First, it repudiated the Ethiopian interpretation of Washington's 1960 political-military commitment to Addis Ababa because the United States would not commit American forces to defend the Kagnew facility or Ethiopia. Second, the administration continued to place Africa at the bottom of Washington's list of foreign policy priorities.[64] Secretary of State William Rogers outlined the administration's four-point policy for Africa while in Addis Ababa in early February 1970, recognizing the United States' "special obligation" to provide aid to Africa, although African leaders would have to remember that "[U.S.] resources and capacity are not unlimited."[65] Moreover, the types and quantities of arms the emperor was seeking in May 1973 were more on a scale of what the United States would give to special clients like Israel or Iran, not a low-priority arms client in a low-priority region. Given Washington's low-profile policy for Africa and the diminishing threats to U.S. interests, the Nixon administration was not about to grant such a request and turn Ethiopia into the regional policeman of Africa.[66]

Selassie apparently also believed that his personal relationship with Richard Nixon would open the door to the U.S. arsenal. But he was staking his political fortune on a president who was coming under partisan attack in the United States and whose ability to conduct foreign policy was being eroded daily.[67] With the Watergate scandal beginning to blow up in Nixon's face and the United States still indirectly involved in supporting the South Vietnamese government, the president was reluctant to undertake any action that might draw additional fire. Selassie did not appreciate the implications of the political storm that had gathered over Nixon's head.

Selassie's belief that he could persuade President Nixon to override political or bureaucratic resistance to the IEG arms request perhaps could be attributed to his last meeting with Nixon in July 1969. In greeting the emperor at the White House, the president spoke of a relationship between the two countries that would be "further broadened, not to the exclusive advantage of one party, but with a view toward bringing forth mutual benefits and advantage."[68] Nixon later recalled that evening, in a lengthy toast to the emperor, full of accolades, how the emperor had treated him so royally when he had visited Ethiopia in 1967 as a supposedly washed-up politician and remarked, "This is a man with an understanding heart."[69] Perhaps in a debt of personal and political gratitude Richard Nixon might repay Selassie with some kindness of his own.

Thus, in May 1973 the emperor used the occasion of the White House state dinner in his honor to make Ethiopia's case before the president and invited guests. Replying to President Nixon's toast in Amharic, Selassie began by noting "the mutually beneficial cooperation of long-standing that has existed between our two countries."[70] He then proceeded to suggest that a review of these matters was in order and that "these relations, covering a wide part of our mutual interest, [needed to] be sustained at increasing levels."[71] Obviously, this was a thinly veiled reference to the IEG military shopping list. Selassie concluded his remarks by attempting to box the administration into a corner by observing that "Ethiopia is gratified to know that she can always count on the continuation of this assistance."[72]

Emperor Selassie's last-ditch plea for the United States not to abandon Ethiopia in its hour of need had only a marginal effect, if any. There was nowhere else he could go for arms on such favorable terms (grant aid). Now Selassie would have to deal with the political consequences of not getting what he had promised. A quick trip to Moscow shortly thereafter failed to restore his prestige, as he again returned home empty-handed.[73] In overestimating the value of his personal relationship with Nixon (and perhaps the Somali threat as well), and misinterpreting what the Nixon Doctrine meant for Ethiopia, he set himself up for a largely unnecessary personal political failure.

NO MORE VIETNAMS

If the Nixon administration had been operating in a political vacuum, perhaps it may have been more receptive to Haile Selassie's May 1973 arms request. But it was not. The battle between the U.S. executive branch and Congress over control of U.S. foreign policy was at its peak.[74] Stung by what it viewed as presidential deceit, manipulation, and arrogance in waging and expanding the war in Southeast Asia, the legislative branch sought to assert its constitutional authority to avoid a replay of Vietnam in other Third World countries. Although the balance of power ultimately still favored the executive branch in the planning and execution of American foreign policy, the White House would have to exhibit greater political sensitivity to the concerns of Congress. Such awareness would be required particularly with regard to U.S. arms transfers to the Third World, because these transactions in the form of military assistance were viewed by many as lying at the root of Washington's escalating involvement in Vietnam.[75]

In the post–World War II period, the legislative branch had virtually ignored or viewed with great skepticism and paternalism the effect of U.S. arms transfers to the Third World. This was especially true in the case of Africa. In the late 1960s Congress had imposed a ceiling of $25 million on grant military assistance and a $40 million limit on all arms transfers (including MAP and FMS sales) to Africa.[76] Some justified this action on the grounds that providing military equipment "to primitive nations all over the world" was not the way Washington should be running its overseas security program.[77] Others voiced the concern that by diverting the scarce resources of an impoverished country like Ethiopia away from its enormous development needs American policy would in time lead to serious internal upheaval.[78]

Despite these reservations, the levels of U.S. military assistance proposed by the executive branch for Ethiopia and other arms clients passed through Congress virtually untouched year after year.[79] In the case of Ethiopia, this constancy was due to the U.S. communications operation at Kagnew. But as a result of the increasing scrutiny that U.S. military involvement in Vietnam came under at the end of the 1960s and early 1970s, however, controversy arose on Capitol Hill as to whether the U.S.

tenure at Kagnew threatened to draw the United States into another Vietnam-type situation in Eritrea. While the executive branch dismissed this idea, some influential members of Congress saw a very disturbing analogy between the two situations.

When the IEG annexed Eritrea in 1962, the United States had remained silent, so as not to risk its tenure at Kagnew.[80] State Department officials realized, however, that Washington had inherited a problem which would keep the United States on the "hot seat" in Ethiopia for some time. The U.S. embassy's standard operating policy toward the problem in Eritrea was to stay clear of any involvement in the civil war.[81] Americans were to avoid intermingling with Ethiopian forces in Eritrea, or showing any signs of support for IEG actions in the province. Despite the intentions of the State Department directive, the United States could not totally dissociate itself from local actions taken by Addis Ababa.[82]

The State Department's disclaimer of noninvolvement in Eritrea did not match reality, however, in spite of the embassy's efforts to enforce such a policy. Edward Korry recalled that in 1965 he felt obliged to dismiss an army colonel attached to the Army Security Agency (ASA).[83] The colonel, who had already been reprimanded by Korry for disobeying the embassy's standard operating procedure, sent twelve to sixteen U.S. soldiers in full battle gear parading around Asmara in jeeps as a "show of force." According to a Peace Corps volunteer, in the spring of 1965 politically inspired strikes in Eritrean schools started a rumor that Eritrean insurgents were ready to invade Asmara.[84] The commander of Kagnew, fearing for the security of his base, ordered all military personnel to wear battle dress and arm themselves. Military jeeps patrolled the city with U.S. soldiers alert behind machine guns. Although U.S. officials later claimed that the guns were not loaded, many Eritreans resented this parade of strength, which had the effect of supporting the IEG.[85]

Despite State's disclaimers, the U.S. approach to getting the United States off the "hot seat" was to help Addis Ababa put an end to the rebellion by political-military means. The civic action training program implemented by the United States in 1964 constituted part of the general approach to counterinsurgency warfare. Finding water and drilling wells, among other things, were intended to decrease Eritrean hostility toward Addis Ababa. But the presence of U.S. Green Berets in Ethiopia highlighted Washington's indirect support for the emperor's attempt to impose a military solution in Eritrea.[86]

In the fall of 1966, a 164-man advisory team operating under the code name "Plan Delta" was sent to Ethiopia for two to three years to "try to increase the professional skills in the Ethiopian army."[87] Another team of twelve advisers spent twenty-six weeks in Ethiopia during 1968 training the armed forces in civic action.[88] During the 1960s, the U.S. AID Office of Public Safety also provided approximately $3 million to train the Ethiopian police on routine matters as well as in paramilitary and counterinsurgency techniques.[89] If not in fact, then at least symbolically and certainly indirectly, these actions implicated the United States in the IEG's attempt to suppress by force the insurgency in Eritrea.

Washington's role in Ethiopia did not go unnoticed by the Eritreans. During the latter part of 1969 the ELF kidnapped for several hours the American consul general in Asmara, Murrey Jackson.[90] They gave Jackson a full briefing on the Eritrean struggle and had him sign a statement acknowledging that he had spoken with ELF representatives and observed their troops. Following Jackson's release, houses in a nearby town were destroyed by Ethiopian troops, prompting one U.S. official to comment, "It did not seem to me to be too good an idea; . . . it puts us too closely in league with everything the army does."[91] At the time of the Jackson kidnapping, the U.S. Senate was conducting hearings to review U.S. defense commitments around the world; to avoid drawing attention to the hidden war in Eritrea, the State Department classified the incident as highly confidential and kept it under wraps for several months.[92]

The kidnapping of the U.S. consul general was evidence of the increasing vulnerability of the 1,500 U.S. military personnel and the more than 3,200 Americans (including dependents) stationed at Asmara. There was a growing perception among Eritreans of U.S. complicity with the IEG's policies in the area.[93] Washington could no longer deny a connection between the potential threat to those Americans living in Eritrea, U.S. security at Kagnew, and internal instability in Ethiopia. These issues became matters of public record on June 1, 1970, when for five hours members of the Symington committee, which for the past eighteen months had been examining U.S. security commitments worldwide, scrutinized the political-military relationship between the United States and Ethiopia.[94] As a result of these hearings, the 1960 executive agreement, the series of other military agreements concluded between Washington and Addis Ababa in the early 1960s, as well as the counterinsurgency nature of U.S. civic action programs instituted during the second half of the decade, were revealed.

During the hearings, the State Department and Pentagon attempted to draw a distinction between the policies of the IEG in Eritrea and the role played by Washington, and to minimize the threat posed by the ELF to Americans and the internal stability of Ethiopia. Committee members pictured instead the makings of another Vietnam. Ethiopian colonialism and Eritrean nationalism (an echo of French colonialism and Vietnamese nationalism), mixed with Washington's desire to maintain access to a communications facility located in the midst of this caldron, would only lead to deepening U.S. involvement. The United States was walking a fine line in trying to separate U.S. military support for Ethiopia from Addis Ababa's policies of repression in Eritrea.

The Symington hearings had no immediate effect on U.S. policy toward Ethiopia. Military assistance continued at approximately the same levels over the next several years. Despite the increasingly anti-American statements made by ELF leaders, Washington equipped three Ethiopian battalions operating in Eritrea with new automatic M-16 rifles in 1971.[95] The executive branch appeared to have calculated correctly. Except for a few isolated and largely accidental incidents, the ELF refrained from direct attacks on U.S. personnel.[96]

However, the Symington hearings would have a more subtle, latent impact upon American policy. Whether members of Congress truly believed that the situation in Eritrea could develop into another Vietnam was not so important. Rather, the secrecy that appeared to surround U.S. dealings with foreign governments had been broken.[97] Presidents could not expect to increase U.S. military commitments to countries like Ethiopia and not have their policy challenged. Since the stakes (Kagnew) and the risks (the Eritrean insurgency) had been spelled out, administration officials would experience more trouble convincing Congress of the need to maintain the level of military assistance to Addis Ababa, especially as the value of Kagnew diminished and the problem in Eritrea deepened.

Thus, by the time Haile Selassie arrived in Washington with his military shopping list, the U.S. Congress had established itself as a counterbalance to an executive branch prone to making unbridled, or deepening, U.S. military commitments to Third World governments. Vietnam had destroyed the American foreign policy consensus in Congress. To avoid another such débacle, Congress was now willing to challenge or force the executive branch to be more accountable for U.S. policy in a far-off, little-known place like Ethiopia. But by placing this political-constitutional constraint on the executive branch, the U.S. Congress gave the administration a built-in excuse for denying, trimming, or putting off Ethiopian military requests.

PLAYING A WEAK HAND

Whatever the emperor's illusions about a special political-military relationship with the United States, they were shattered by his May 1973 visit. The rebuff not only severely damaged the emperor's personal prestige; it also signaled declining U.S. interest in Ethiopia.[98] This change was particularly dangerous for Addis Ababa: IEG military requirements were on the upswing, while U.S. strategic requirements in Ethiopia were moving in the opposite direction. The State Department was now forced to invoke the credibility argument to justify MAP aid to Ethiopia.[99] In using this rationale, the Nixon administration managed to win a $1.3 million increase in military assistance to Ethiopia for FY 1974.[100] But maintaining U.S. credibility in Ethiopia was not going to be worth much more than $11 million per year because Kagnew, a tangible asset, had never been valued at much more than that during the peak of U.S. operations at the station.[101]

Thus, Haile Selassie arrived in Washington with a very weak hand to play. By May 1973 the quid pro quo arrangement underlying the U.S.-Ethiopia relationship was for all intents and purposes dead. Threatening the U.S. tenure at Kagnew was no longer a viable bargaining tactic. Moreover, because of deepening Soviet military involvement in Somalia, the emperor could not use the traditional Ethiopian bluff of threatening to defect to the Soviet Union for arms. Addis Ababa really had little choice but to accept whatever Washington provided, since its military depended upon U.S. arms. The emperor had no interest in jeopardizing the U.S.-Ethiopia relationship: despite Washington's diplomatic rebuff, Selassie's personal relationship with Richard Nixon might pay some dividend in the near future.

The American bargaining position vis-à-vis Ethiopia was never stronger. External threats to U.S. interests had receded in recent years and Kagnew was almost worthless, so there was no compelling reason to do anything extraordinary for Ethiopia. Further, as a result of the new political climate that had taken hold in Washington during the early 1970s in response to the war in Southeast Asia, the possibility of U.S. military disengagement from Ethiopia was very real. Addis Ababa had no lever with which to force Washington's hand.

The diplomatic rebuff of Selassie's 1973 arms request marked the beginning of a new period in U.S.-Ethiopia military relations. It was evidence of a trend already emerging in Washington's relations with other arms recipients: increasing client reliance upon FMS financing (loans) and FMS sales. Given this worldwide MAP phase-out, the IEG could take satisfaction in the fact that the United States continued to give Ethiopia some grant military funds. But if Ethiopia wished to respond to the Soviet-supported arms buildup in Somalia and suppress the insurrection in Eritrea, it would have to pay its own way if it wished to acquire increased levels of arms from the United States.

8

The 1977 Collapse of U.S.-Ethiopian Military Relations

Following Washington's rebuff of Haile Selassie's May 1973 military request, U.S.-Ethiopia relations were a continuing series of crises. These problems emerged as the old imperial regime slowly disintegrated during 1974. The overthrow of Haile Selassie on September 12, 1974, was the culmination of the so-called creeping coup that over an eight-month period stripped away the powers of the emperor.[1] What began in early 1974 as an isolated mutiny at a small army garrison over food and water shortages soon spread throughout the military and sparked civilian actions against the government. Selassie's feeble attempt to salvage the situation by appointing a new cabinet and promising constitutional changes and broad reforms was ultimately met by the seizure of power by the armed forces. The Armed Forces Coordinating Committee (later known as the Dergue), established in the spring of 1974, snipped away at the powers of the emperor so that by early summer Selassie had been reduced to nothing more than a figurehead. On September 15, three days after Emperor Selassie had been deposed and imprisoned, the Dergue created a Provisional Military Administrative Council (PMAC) to rule over Ethiopia.

The first of many controversial arms decisions to arise over the next three years occurred in May 1974, when Haile Selassie was still clinging to power. At a meeting of the Washington Special Action Group, Secretary of State Henry Kissinger ordered a moderate step-up in U.S. arms deliveries to Ethiopia, including thirty-six M-60 tanks. Kissinger felt that the United States could not risk compromising its credibility by seemingly turning its back on a longstanding MAP partner.[2] In ordering this action, he had overruled the advice of State Department and Pentagon officials who felt that Addis Ababa was again exaggerating the Somali threat. But by the end of the summer, the Africa Bureau was in agreement with Kissinger that more had to be done for the Ethiopian military.

Earlier that summer the United States had agreed to increase arms transfers to Ethiopia, extending $11 million in FMS credits on concessionary terms and increasing MAP aid to $11.5 million for FY 1974 as well as allowing large-scale cash purchases. A Department of State issue paper prepared on August 29 argued, "As long as there exists a distinct possibility that the present situation will result in a strengthened, more moderate state, and in a continuation of the traditional Ethiopian ties with the West, we should continue to carry out our program of military aid and sales as agreed."[3] It was hoped that this action "would bolster Ethiopia's confidence in its ability to defend itself and in the United States as a reliable associate" as well as strengthen more moderate elements within the military.[4] Because the administration was "severely limited" in the amount of military assistance it could provide owing to congressional restraints, the State Department also recommended that the United States "should continue to encourage appropriate third countries, namely Iran and Saudi Arabia, to provide any assistance they can to Ethiopia in acquiring the arms it considers necessary to face the Somali threat."[5] As Washington's longtime friend slipped from power, the United States still sought to maintain influence with the emperor's eventual successors. However, what the Americans considered a generous arms offer was not well received in Addis Ababa, whose military rulers were dissatisfied with the slow delivery time for some items and the high proportion (over 50 percent) of cash purchases compared to the level of credits and grant aid.[6]

Two months after Haile Selassie was removed from power, the United States, now led by Gerald Ford who had replaced Richard Nixon as president on August 9, confronted an even more perplexing situation in Ethiopia. In November, Gen. Aman Adom, a moderate and leader of the PMAC, was killed and fifty-nine former officials of the IEG were summarily executed. Then in December the PMAC declared its intention to turn Ethiopia into a one-party state and at the beginning of 1975 announced plans to nationalize the enterprises and properties owned by aristocrats—an action extended late in 1975 to U.S. businesses and properties. At the same time, the war in Eritrea had intensified, prompting an urgent request from the PMAC on February 12, 1975, for an emergency U.S. airlift of $30 million worth of small arms and ammunition. A month went by before the administration agreed to sell Ethiopia up to $7 million worth of ammunition. What was seen in Washington as a compromise solution to a controversial problem involving Arab and Ethiopian interests angered the PMAC, which interpreted the delay and small quantities offered as "an unambiguous sign that Washington was opposed to the revolution and was backing out of a long-term commitment to supply Ethiopia with arms."[7]

In mid-1975, the United States confronted a new problem regarding the transfer of two squadrons of F5-E fighter bombers to Ethiopia. Early that summer the PMAC had indicated a desire to purchase one or two squadrons of F-5E aircraft as well as M-60 tanks. The State Department favored increasing FMS credits for Ethiopia from $5 million (the amount justified before Congress) to $25 million and to provide these credits on concessionary terms to help finance these purchases, which were expected to total between $100 million and $135 million.[8] Because of mounting concern in Congress about the administration's lack of a coordinated policy regarding arms sales worldwide, President Ford considered delaying any response to Ethiopian approaches in order to await the outcome of a National Security Council review to be concluded by the end of the summer.[9] Arguing that the NSC review was general, not specific to Ethiopia, and that the credit terms for FY 1975 had to be signed before July 1, Henry Kissinger and the State Department pressured Ford into signing a presidential determination (PD) granting the credit request.[10] This allowed for the transfer of ten F-5 jets on the basis that "it is important to [U.S.] national security."[11] This authorization was done despite Ethiopia being one of the countries falling under section 502B of the Foreign Assistance Act, stating a sense of Congress that except in extraordinary situations the president should "substantially reduce or terminate security assistance to governments which engage in a consistent pattern of gross violations of human rights."[12]

However, in October the question was raised, in light of events that had transpired in Ethiopia, whether the United States should go ahead with the delivery of the jets. Although the F-5E delivery was part of a comprehensive modernization plan for the Ethiopian armed forces drawn up by the U.S. MAAG in Addis Ababa a few years before, and although it was Ethiopia's turn on the waiting list to receive delivery of these aircraft, the United States was becoming more involved in government military actions in Eritrea.[13] At the time, four Americans were being held hostage by Eritrean insurgents. Due to "larger policy considerations," namely, that the "acquisition of these aircraft at an early date is a matter of great importance to the Ethiopian government and has become a touchstone of our bilateral relations," the United States proceeded with the delivery of eight F-5Es which arrived in Addis Ababa on April 15, 1976.[14]

By the end of 1975, however, global rather than regional considerations began dominating U.S. policy calculations.[15] As a result of the victory in Angola by the MPLA (Popular Movement for the Liberation of Angola), and following the final defeat of the South Vietnamese army in spring 1975, top-ranking administration officials, including the president, felt that other nations would view these communist-backed victories as symbols of

U.S. helplessness.[16] They believed U.S. credibility was at risk following reports of Cuban troop movements into Somalia in early 1976—joining an estimated 2,500 Soviet military advisers already there. In February 1976 the Dergue had published a thirty-nine-page memorandum entitled "War Clouds in the Horn of Africa" warning that Somalia was preparing for war.[17] The United States eventually agreed in early July 1976 to provide approximately $175–$200 million worth of arms to Addis Ababa on a cash and credit basis.[18] The proposed arms package—to include the transfer of two squadrons of F-5E and a squadron of F-5G jet fighters, several dozen M-60 heavy tanks, three to six C-130 transports, an early warning radar system, a number of armored personnel carriers (APCs), and several thousand antitank weapons—was designed to counter what the administration viewed as a post-Angola trend of expanding Soviet influence throughout Africa.[19]

Although U.S. arms transfers to Ethiopia reached an all-time high in 1976, including more than $100 million in cash sales, hard-line and radical factions within the PMAC, whose informal memberships overlapped, were still unhappy with the United States. The hard-liners, who favored continuing the war in Eritrea, were dissatisfied by Ethiopia's increasing reliance upon cash purchases and reductions in MAP assistance from the United States at this critical time. Radicals felt uncomfortable being in league with an imperialist power whom they did not trust. In late December 1976 Colonel Mengistu Haile Mariam, the leader of the radical faction (and a hard-liner as well) within the Dergue and first vice-chairman of the PMAC, visited Moscow and signed a secret military agreement worth at least $100 million.[20]

Before the revelation of this secret Ethiopian-Soviet military agreement several months later, the State Department still hoped to salvage the situation in Ethiopia by doing more of the same in supplying arms to the PMAC. But there was growing discontent on Capitol Hill. In November 1976 the U.S. Congress had designated Ethiopia as one of nineteen countries whose government engaged in such a persistent pattern of gross violations of human rights that it should be declared ineligible to receive U.S. military assistance. That same month, the American people elected Jimmy Carter president, a man who campaigned for the promotion of human rights overseas and reductions in U.S. arms sales abroad.

On 3 February 1977 a shoot-out occurred in the old Menelik Palace that left Gen. Teferi Banti, the PMAC chairman, and several of his principal supporters dead, and elevated Colonel Mengistu to the top spot as undisputed leader of Ethiopia. This event, coupled with the government's continuing repression of the civilian population, resulted in Secretary of State Cyrus Vance's informing the Senate Appropriations Committee on

Foreign Operations that grant military assistance to Ethiopia was being suspended because of human rights violations.[21] For all practical purposes, the Carter administration's human rights-based aid suspension was largely symbolic, since Ethiopia was being phased out of the military assistance program anyway on budgetary grounds as part of the Pentagon's worldwide MAP reductions.[22] However, this action was cited by the PMAC as evidence of Washington's hostile attitude toward the revolutionary developments in Ethiopia, and further justification for drawing closer to Moscow.

The U.S.-Ethiopia military relationship came to a swift end several months into the Carter presidency in a series of retaliatory actions. On April 22, 1977, Washington informed Addis Ababa that the United States would close down Kagnew Station before the end of September—eight months before the twenty-five-year lease expired—and because of congressionally mandated cuts, the number of U.S. MAAG advisers in Ethiopia would be reduced from forty-six to twenty-four by the end of the summer. The next day Ethiopia ordered the closure of the U.S. MAAG, Kagnew Station, the Naval Medical Research Unit, the U.S. Information Agency (USIA) office and the consulate general's office in Asmara, and subsequently unilaterally abrogated the 1953 MDAA treaty. On April 28 the United States suspended the remaining $10 million FMS credit program and $6 million in outstanding MAP funds for FY 1977 and halted the delivery of some $100 million worth of arms still in the pipeline. A month later Mengistu ordered a 50 percent reduction in the U.S. embassy staff. Then in June, Congress passed the International Security Assistance and Arms Export Control Act of 1977, which stated that military assistance, training, and FMS credits for Ethiopia as well as FMS cash sales and deliveries of military equipment financed by military assistance, credits, or guarantees, were prohibited unless the president declared that U.S. national security interests were at stake.[23] No such recommendation was forthcoming; in a calculated move to irritate the Ethiopian government, the Carter White House made a public issue of the horrendous human rights crimes in Ethiopia and declared its intention not to consider future arms requests from Addis Ababa. According to Carter's assistant secretary of state for African affairs, Richard Moose, in using the human rights issue to justify the U.S. position on arms transfers to Ethiopia, the Carter administration "slammed the door on the way out for emphasis."[24]

THE ESCALATING WAR IN ERITREA

The collapse of the U.S.-Ethiopia military partnership had its origins in Ethiopia's increased demand for arms resulting from its desire to impose a military solution in Eritrea. On the one hand Washington wished to demonstrate that the United States was not inherently hostile to the Ethiopian revolution, whose ideology of "Ethiopian socialism" seemed to be another version of African socialism rather than a companion of Marxism-Leninism or Maoism.[25] On the other hand, after the 1973 Arab-Israeli War, which heightened Washington's sensitivity to the concerns of moderate Arab states such as Egypt and Saudi Arabia, supporting the Ethiopian war effort in Eritrea might be construed as an anti-Arab action. Apparently taking a page from the 1973 war, the American design was to bring about a stalemate by giving Addis Ababa enough arms to turn back any Eritrean offensive but not enough to win the war outright. By continuing to supply a moderate level of arms to Ethiopia, the United States hoped to open the way to negotiations between the two sides.[26] Unfortunately, the Ethiopian military government was not interested in a political compromise in Eritrea.

The formation of the Provisional Military Administrative Council (PMAC) in mid-September 1974 held out some promise that the civil war in Eritrea might be resolved peacefully. General Aman Michael Adom, an Eritrean and a known quantity to U.S. embassy officials and the State Department, had been appointed head of the new government council.[27] Aman had chaired an armed forces group established the previous August to conduct an investigation into the Eritrean rebellion. Although the Eritrean guerrilla organizations declared that they would negotiate only if Addis Ababa acceded to their demands for full independence, Aman apparently believed that with a free hand he could solve the Eritrean problem short of granting full independence.[28]

While General Aman's political solution—believed to be a return to federation status for most of Eritrea—found favor among the Americans, it set him at odds with the majority of the PMAC.[29] Ethiopian nationalism, embodying the idea that it was the Ethiopians' patriotic duty to preserve the unity of the empire, was one of the few ideological positions on which members of the military government could find common ground.[30] Aman's initiative ran counter to the predominant PMAC belief in an indivisible Ethiopia. In favoring a dictated political settlement or imposed military solution, both of which would mean continued war in Eritrea, this majority ensured that Ethiopia would continue to place heavy emphasis on acquiring arms from foreign sources.

Any hope of achieving a quick political settlement in Eritrea vanished in mid-November when the split between the moderate accommodationists and hard-line militarists within the Dergue was settled in a bloody manner, giving the upper hand to the latter faction. General Aman had resigned as PMAC chairman to protest three of the council's policy decisions: (1) the summary execution of former government officials, (2) the establishment of a new penal code to legalize the arrests, forthcoming trials of former officials, and seizure of property, and (3) the order sending another 5,000 troops to Eritrea.[31] Aman was later killed in a firefight at his home on November 22. That same night the PMAC decided by a simple majority vote to execute without trial fifty-nine political detainees, including two former prime ministers and seventeen generals.[32] "Bloody Saturday," as it became known, marked the ascendance of a hard-line policy faction within the PMAC which selected Brig. Gen. Teferi Banti as the new chairman and Major Mengistu Haile Mariam as its first vice chairman.

In late January 1975, the PMAC announced its intention to achieve a military settlement in Eritrea, ending what it called Addis Ababa's policy of restraint in the province. However, Ethiopia's military offensive would confront rebel forces that over the previous six months had substantially increased their armed strength, reinforced positions around Asmara, and ended the self-destructive infighting between the Eritrean Liberation Front (ELF) and Eritrean People's Liberation Front (EPLF) by forming a united Revolutionary Council.[33] By early February, a full-scale battle was being waged in and around Asmara between rebel and government forces. Reports filed from Ethiopia gave the nation's military little chance of sustaining this vastly increased level of conflict much longer without more aid and supplies.[34]

In contrast to Ethiopian presentations made to Washington in the past, now the insurgency in Eritrea, not the Somali threat, was cited as the primary rationale behind Addis Ababa's newest arms request. Secretary of State Henry Kissinger had discussed the arms issue with the Ethiopian foreign minister, Kifle Woduju, in early February. A week later the U.S. military mission forwarded an Ethiopian shopping list requesting some $30 million worth of light weapons and ammunition.[35] Framing an appropriate reply to this request proved difficult, given the events that had taken place in Ethiopia over the past several months, including the Dergue's deliberate escalation of the civil war in Eritrea.

Following the "Bloody Saturday" executions the Ford administration had postponed all major decisions regarding new arms shipments to Ethiopia in order to allow the State Department time to evaluate the political situation in the country.[36] As a result, U.S. responses to Ethiopian arms requests were now being formulated on an ad hoc "wait-and-see" basis. Decision making was further burdened by increasing congressional attention to the Eritrea problem. Moreover, in the wake of the reorientation of foreign policy in the region following the 1973 Arab-Israeli War, Ethiopia's security requirements were being viewed in light of Washington's Middle East policy, which produced a clash between Arabists and Africanists at the State Department over the PMAC's February 1975 arms request. Arabists opposed Addis Ababa's request because of growing Arab concern over Ethiopia's military policy in Eritrea. The Africa Bureau countered that (1) the breadth of Arab support for the Eritrean cause was not so great; (2) Washington, in acting as Ethiopia's sole arms supplier for over twenty years, had created a heavy dependence upon the United States for spare parts and ammunition, and could not now be totally unresponsive to their request; and (3) by turning down the Dergue it might create the perception in Africa that Washington was unwilling to help reform-minded, or leftist-leaning governments.[37]

A compromise solution was finally reached in mid-March designed to appease all parties—Africanists and Arabists at the State Department as well as the Ethiopians and Arabs—except the Eritreans. The United States agreed to provide $7 million worth of ammunition to the Dergue, far less than the original request, but enough to demonstrate continued U.S. interest in Ethiopia. It was hoped that the five-week delay in responding to Addis Ababa, as a result of keeping the request under review, would lend credence to Washington's claim that it was not taking sides in the conflict.[38] To reinforce this impression of neutrality, in announcing its decision on the arms package, the administration expressed the "hope that the two sides in the Eritrean conflict would soon enter into negotiations in order to end the fighting in the province and find an acceptable solution."[39]

This episode and subsequent events illustrated that the security calculations of Washington and Addis Ababa were fundamentally at odds. American policy was being influenced by the desire to maintain U.S. credibility in Ethiopia and, at the same time, not to antagonize any of the Arab governments being courted by Washington. On the other hand, it was quite clear by the end of the Dergue's first six months in power that the new government was determined to pursue the military option in Eritrea. Consequently, if not the United States, then some other power would have to be found who would be willing to underwrite Ethiopia's hard-line policy in Eritrea.

OIL LANES AND THE SOVIET NAVAL THREAT

During the mid-1970s, a new security environment was developing for the United States that had the somewhat paradoxical effect of decreasing the U.S. strategic stake in Ethiopia. Détente between the two superpowers did not put an end to the expansion of military capabilities on both sides. Of particular concern to the United States was increased Soviet naval activity in the Indian Ocean region. The 1973 Arab-Israeli War and the 1973–1974 Arab oil embargo had heightened U.S. sensitivity to potentially threatening activities that might disrupt the flow of oil to the West. However, U.S. defense planners ultimately made no strategic connection between the growing Soviet naval threat, and securing sea lanes in the Indian Ocean region, with providing military assistance to Ethiopia.

The demise of Kagnew's strategic value in the 1970s did not spell the end of U.S. interest in Ethiopia. A past, present, and future U.S. strategic objective in the Red Sea and northwest quadrant of the Indian Ocean concerned the protection of the sea lines of communication (SLOCs) connecting the Middle East and South Asia with the Western world. Access to the Eritrean ports of Massawa and Assab, coupled with control over Ethiopia's Dahlak Island chain, could prove useful in countering any threat to shipping in the southern Red Sea and northwest quadrant of the Indian Ocean. Questions concerning U.S. security assistance to Ethiopia, therefore, could be linked to a broader regional objective of maintaining Western access to Middle Eastern oil.

The Soviet naval threat in the Indian Ocean began to materialize during the latter part of 1973. Before the perceived emergence of this strategic threat, the United States had been content to assume a "low-key, low-profile" position in the region.[40] This policy was based on the apparent absence of any grand Soviet scheme to control the oil faucets.[41] A successful naval interdiction along the sea lanes leading from the Middle East and Persian Gulf oil fields to Western markets seemed to lie beyond the Soviets' capability. In 1972 James H. Noyes, deputy assistant secretary of defense for Near Eastern, African, and South Asian Affairs, described the Soviet naval threat in the Indian Ocean as "moderate."[42]

Moscow's naval weakness stemmed in part from the lack of a regional strategic infrastructure. The Soviet navy had to rely primarily upon its own bases for logistical support and had only limited access to onshore facilities. As Secretary Noyes explained to the U.S. House of Representatives Subcommittee on the Near East, "This lack of Indian Ocean shore bases for repair, maintenance, and the long supply lines from the Far East place practical limits on the size and length of Soviet naval deployments to the Indian Ocean."[43] However, as Noyes warned, "These limitations could be alleviated by gaining access to shore facilities in the Indian Ocean, or by the reopening of the Suez Canal, or both."[44]

Thus it was with keen interest that the Pentagon observed Soviet military construction activities, which got under way at Somalia's port of Berbera in the fall of 1972.[45] The Soviets began constructing an army barracks at Berbera and assigned a Soviet naval repair vessel to operate from the port. In December a long-range communications facility became operative. The following year, the Soviet Union started constructing missile-holding and storage facilities. Given enhanced Soviet naval support capabilities in the area, as Moscow was also cultivating political-military relations with South Yemen, defense analysts were prone to envision a worst-case scenario in which the Soviet Union could interdict Western SLOCs.

Confronted with a growing Soviet naval threat in the Indian Ocean region, executive branch officials attempted to make a strategic connection between the Horn of Africa and the United States' interest in securing access to Middle Eastern oil. Testifying before Congress in June 1974, Adm. Thomas H. Moorer, chairman of the Joint Chiefs of Staff, cited Ethiopia's "strategic location in the Horn of Africa" along with the residual communications operations still being performed at Kagnew Station as grounds for continuing U.S. military assistance to Ethiopia.[46] Secretary of Defense James Schlesinger declared in 1974, "The Horn of Africa is of particular strategic importance due to its geographical proximity to the troubled Middle East."[47] During the FY 1975 congressional appropriations hearings, the director of politico-military affairs and acting undersecretary of state for security assistance, George Vest, described Ethiopia as occupying a "geographical place right at the hub of northeast Africa" and as a "major center of moderation in a geographically vital area sitting astride oil lanes . . . [and] the Soviet supported base in Somalia."[48] Even after the overthrow of Haile Selassie, the argument was made that the termination of U.S. arms transfers to the Dergue would allow an uncontested Soviet "takeover" of the Horn that would seriously threaten Western SLOCs running through the Red Sea and along Africa's northeast littoral.[49]

However, by 1975 the Soviet naval presence in Somalia was viewed by the Department of Defense as a way to justify the construction of a large U.S. naval base at Diego Garcia, rather than as an argument to preserve the U.S. position of influence in Ethiopia. In early 1975 Defense Secretary Schlesinger had presented evidence of a "significant new facility" at Berbera and a Soviet missile buildup in Somalia to justify an additional $108 million to expand the U.S. base at Diego Garcia.[50] Even if Diego Garcia were not in the picture, the case for Ethiopia's geostrategic importance was tenuous at best. Any advantage the Soviet navy would gain following the reopening of the Suez Canal in 1975 could be effectively negated in wartime by Western military technology.[51] Moreover, Ethiopian bases would not be required to perform sea control operations at the Suez Canal and Bab al-Mandab.[52] Besides, if war closed the Suez Canal, the strategic importance of the southern Red Sea, at least for the Western powers, would be greatly diminished. Therefore Washington could disengage from Ethiopia without diminishing its ability to protect the Indian Ocean sea lanes and the oil traffic.

Moreover, by early 1975 indigenous political forces were conspiring with technological developments to encourage a rapid U.S. disengagement from Ethiopia. Following the outbreak of heavy fighting in the Asmara area in early 1975, Washington ordered an emergency evacuation of more than 100 American dependents and nonessential personnel from the province, leaving only a residual staff of forty-four military and civilian technicians at Kagnew and nine members of the consulate general's staff in Eritrea. Despite increased safeguards, in 1975 several Americans were kidnapped by Eritrean rebels, and Kagnew Station itself came under attack. Moreover, given the Pentagon's desire to locate transmitting and receiving facilities at a single site (Diego Garcia) and the fact that satellites were already on order in early 1975 that would be able to take over Kagnew's remaining naval communications functions, an early U.S. withdrawal from Ethiopia was feasible. Although administration officials would continue to argue into the latter part of 1976 that Kagnew Station was required to perform a residual ship-to-shore communications service in the Indian Ocean region, in private conversations high-ranking State Department officials admitted that Kagnew was essentially a backup facility whose loss would mean only minor reductions in U.S. military communications capabilities in the region.[53] Given the deteriorating political-military situation in Eritrea and a congressional go-ahead for construction at Diego Garcia, it seemed a safer bet to counter Soviet activities in Somalia and elsewhere in the Indian Ocean region from a more secure location.

SOVIET GEOPOLITICAL MOMENTUM

By the end of 1975, the Soviet arms option, which had been considered largely a bluff in the past, became a very real possibility. Since the 1973 Arab-Israeli War, the Soviet Union had been more willing to undertake high-risk operations in the Third World. Policy makers in the Kremlin who favored restraint had apparently lost out to other top-level officials willing to commit Moscow more deeply in providing military support for Third World clients.[54] The forceful manner in which the Soviet Union had seized the initiative and consolidated its position in Angola during 1975–1976 contrasted with Washington's perceived timidity following the collapse of South Vietnam in April 1975. Soviet geopolitical momentum in the Third World seemed to be growing, sending a potent message that, unlike the United States, the Soviet Union would use all military resources at its disposal to meet its commitments to client states—an important consideration for the hard-liners as well as radicals within the Dergue.

Even before its intervention in Angola, the Soviet Union had demonstrated in the Horn of Africa what it could do for an arms client. In the latter part of 1973, Moscow had started delivery to Somalia of 100 T-54 heavy tanks to add to the estimated 150 T-34 tanks already in the Somali arsenal. In February 1974 the Soviets began supplying to the Somali Air Force, which had been equipped with some twenty-one outmoded MiG-15 and MiG-17 jet fighters and bombers, the more modern MiG-19 aircraft and a squadron of advanced MiG-21 jet fighters, along with SA-2 surface-to-air missiles. This compared quite favorably with the Ethiopian arsenal, which included approximately fifty M-41 medium tanks and twenty M-24 light tanks and 37 aircraft, the best of which—the F-86 Sabre jets and F-5 Freedom Fighters—would be outclassed by the MiG-21 fighters.[55] The Soviet-sponsored arms buildup in Somalia demonstrated Moscow's ability to alter the balance of forces in the Horn if it so desired. Combined with its military activities in Angola and the Middle East, the buildup drew Addis Ababa's attention to the possibility of defecting to Moscow.

However, the USSR viewed events in Ethiopia with caution. During the first year of the revolution, the Soviet Union had expressed a sympathetic interest in the Dergue's radical rhetoric and revolutionary program. Although the Soviets renewed their offer to replace the United States as Ethiopia's arms supplier, it was not until early 1976 that they agreed to supply Ethiopia with nonlethal equipment.[56] Like Washington, Moscow was not sure what to make of Ethiopia's new military leaders.[57] The Soviets also had to consider whether it was worth risking the political-military investment it had already made in Somalia to pursue the Ethiopian option, given the uncertainty of the PMAC's pro-Soviet credentials.[58]

During this time, key political decisions were being made within the PMAC that laid the groundwork for Ethiopia's later political-military realignment. At the end of 1974 and again in 1975, the PMAC reportedly made approaches to the Soviet Union for arms. In 1975 the PMAC sent some of its members to Eastern Europe for political training. These military cadres would eventually become the nucleus of the Marxist-Leninist political organization, Abyot Seded (Revolutionary Flame), established by the Dergue in the latter part of 1976.[59] At the end of 1975 Mengistu established ties with the Marxist-Leninist student group, the All Ethiopia Socialist Movement (known as MEISON), and made its leader Haile Fida his ideological adviser.[60] In summer 1976, Ethiopia's government-controlled press, already quite critical of U.S. policy, launched a series of anti-American attacks. Every insurrectionary act was attributed to the "paid agents of the EPRP, EDU, ELF and CIA."[61] The Dergue attempted to discredit opposition from the civilian Marxist-oriented Ethiopian People's Revolutionary party (EPRP) by claiming it was in league with the CIA.[62] This all seemed to be part of a carefully orchestrated plan to establish the Dergue's ideological credentials and credibility with Moscow. It also had the short-term effect of making Washington more responsive to Ethiopia's arms requests to prove it was not hostile to the revolution.

By early 1975, Ethiopian as well as American policy makers held mirror images of each other, neither side considering the other much of an ally. Given Ethiopia's vast security requirements resulting from the situation in Eritrea and the Somali threat, the PMAC now actively explored the Soviet arms option. While there were fewer constraints on Moscow's behavior than on Washington's, several things had to be set in order to open the way for a realignment: (1) moderates within the PMAC, who favored the continuation of the U.S. arms connection, would have to be eliminated; (2) Moscow would have to offer an arms package more attractive than the terms offered by Washington; and (3) the Soviet Union would have to feel confident about risking its strategic investment in Somalia to acquire a larger, more powerful, and ideologically compatible, though unstable, arms client.

THE ISRAELI SECURITY ARGUMENT

By 1975 the rationalization of U.S. policy toward Ethiopia had little to do with strategic interests. Instead, international political considerations and a rather subtle manipulation of Congress by the executive branch created an atmosphere in which the United States avoided forcing a decisive confrontation with the PMAC over its military policy in Eritrea and increasing human rights abuses. In the first instance, U.S. policy was based on (1) the Africa Bureau's desire to maintain American political credibility in the region by demonstrating a willingness to work with left-of-center progressive governments, and (2) Henry Kissinger's obsession with enhancing U.S. global credibility in the face of Soviet intrusions into unstable regions of the Third World. Since such rationales found few adherents on Capitol Hill, especially given their role in prolonging U.S. military involvement in Vietnam, the executive branch began to invoke more frequently and publicly the Israeli security argument to distract congressional critics of U.S. arms transfers to Ethiopia.

Throughout the 1960s and into the 1970s, the Israeli security argument was rarely evoked by the executive branch to justify military assistance to Ethiopia. It was unnecessary, since Kagnew made all other rationales largely superfluous. But the State Department occasionally reminded Congress that the Ethiopian military was engaged in operations against a radical Arab-supported insurgency. This was a backhanded way of justifying the Ethiopian military assistance program, and Addis Ababa's counterinsurgency operations in Eritrea, on the grounds of Israeli security.

Although this rationale would strike a political nerve in Congress, U.S. officials did not elaborate on this point or speak of the Israeli-Ethiopian military aid connection publicly in order to avoid placing Addis Ababa in an even more precarious position vis-à-vis its Arab neighbors.[63]

Israel's interest in Ethiopia, like that of the United States, revolved around Eritrea. Israeli defense analysts feared that an independent Eritrean state would adopt a pro-Arab, anti-Israel foreign policy orientation. Arab pressures applied against the Ethiopian empire were seen as part of Israel's own battle with Egypt and Islam, and Eritrea was a part of this confrontation.[64] Thus, Tel Aviv viewed the Eritrean civil war as a southerly extension of the Arab-Israeli conflict—a perception reinforced by allegations that surfaced after the June 1967 war of a PLO-ELF link.[65]

Israel's strategic objective in Ethiopia, therefore, was quite simple and dovetailed with U.S. and Ethiopian interests—to prevent the emergence of an independent Eritrean state. To this end, Israel established an elaborate intelligence network inside Ethiopia, trained Ethiopian police and counterinsurgency units, and maintained extensive trade links with Addis Ababa.[66] According to Edward Korry, the Israelis had established a better exchange system with Ethiopian security than the CIA, which seemed to have no interest in what was going on in Ethiopia and sent few informative reports back to Washington.[67] However, Ethiopia's Israeli connection did have its costs: Arab states used it to justify their intervention in the Horn on the pretext of fighting Israel, even though Arab actions were also motivated by a desire to counter leftist forces.[68] Although as the result of Arab pressure Haile Selassie severed diplomatic relations with Tel Aviv after the 1973 Arab-Israeli War, trade relations as well as covert military assistance continued unabated.[69]

The Israeli security argument, as presented in Washington, was based upon a worst-case analysis constructed by Israeli defense officials. It envisioned the Red Sea being converted into an Arab lake in the event of an Eritrean victory in the civil war. Consequently, the Arab states would be able to bring pressure to bear on Israeli commerce at Bab al-Mandab, and off the Eritrean coast in the two-mile strait between the islands of Zugar and Abuail, which formed part of Ethiopia's Dahlak Archipelago. Israeli as well as Western shipping would have to travel through a waterway completely engulfed by Arab, or Arab-oriented states—a prospect that on the surface would appear to present a strategic problem for the United States as well.[70]

The Israeli security argument became public in Washington at about the same time that the Eritrean forces were repelling the Ethiopian military offensive in early 1975. During the debate on Capitol Hill about the Dergue's $30 million arms request, the Africa Bureau had attempted to play down the Arab-Eritrean connection. However, while Addis Ababa's request was under review, Israeli military analysts were publicly expressing concern over the future of Israel's shipping in and out of the Red Sea if the Eritreans were to gain control of Ethiopia's coastal province.[71] In August 1976 the political impact of an independent Eritrean state upon Israel's security was discussed by several leading experts on the Horn of Africa before a U.S. Senate committee.[72] Although no consensus was reached during this hearing, the fact that the subject received such scrutiny demonstrated the seriousness with which the U.S. Congress approached any question that might affect Israel's security.

Despite its power of persuasion on Capitol Hill, the reasoning underlying the Israeli security argument was seen by some as flawed.[73] An Arab position in Eritrea would be largely redundant. Egypt had successfully blockaded the Bab al-Mandab during the 1973 war with existing facilities. Moreover, an independent Eritrea would be economically dependent upon foreign commerce and have a common interest in preserving regional stability and the free flow of trade in the Red Sea. Besides, Israel's proven military capabilities would be enough to deter or retaliate against any aggression. The Israeli security argument seemed to be a diversion used to buy time on Capitol Hill while the administration attempted to make sense of events in Ethiopia.

The Ethiopia-Eritrea-Israel triangle highlighted a domestic political reality that constrained U.S. policy in the Horn of Africa as well as the Middle East. Before Washington would pursue any Arab-Islamic option, whether it entailed support for a government or an insurgency movement, it would first have to apply the Israeli litmus test. Were the security interests of a particular government (Somalia) or nongovernmental (Eritrean movement) actor compatible with those of Tel Aviv? Because Ethiopia had already passed this test, it was less risky domestically for the Ford administration to maintain relations with the Dergue than to pursue politically provocative options.

By the time Jimmy Carter entered the White House in January 1977, the political-strategic situation in northeast Africa had changed dramatically. While the Israeli security argument was still potent, it was now bending under the pressure of change and the emergence of forces in certain Arab capitals favoring accommodation with the West. In July 1976, Anwar Sadat had expelled the few remaining Soviet military advisers from Egypt and quickly invited the United States to replace the USSR as Cairo's arms patron. Then at the end of 1976, several months after a Libyan-sponsored coup failed to overthrow Sudan's President Jaafar Nimeiri, the United States declared Khartoum eligible to buy U.S. military equipment. At about the same time, the Somalis were sending signals to Washington that they too were dissatisfied with their Soviet military connection and would consider a U.S. security connection. So, as the Carter administration assumed control over U.S. foreign policy, Ethiopia not only became expendable from a strategic vantage point, but also because the United States had acquired increased political flexibility in the region.

THE DERGUE DRIFTS TO THE LEFT

Since the early 1960s the Department of State had pondered the question, "After Haile Selassie, what?" The working assumption at the State Department was that the emperor would not survive in power to the end of the decade.[74] Haile Selassie's age was starting to catch up with him; he was showing signs of senility and inability to keep up with the affairs of state.[75] While the State Department believed it was time for a change, few foresaw that pressure from Somalia and Eritrea, discontent among those seeing an opportunity to establish a limited form of democracy or a more radial socialist experiment, together with the IEG's attempted coverup of the Wollo famine that killed tens of thousands, and the declining physical condition of the emperor, would produce a "creeping revolution" that would bring down the monarchy and subsequently take a bloody, leftward turn.[76] All that could be predicted was that a change in leadership would occur as the result of a coup d'état or the death of the aging monarch.[77] In either case, U.S. diplomats were confident that the U.S.-Ethiopia relationship would survive.

Twenty years of U.S. political-military penetration of Ethiopia had created bonds that Washington believed could withstand a change in Ethiopia's government. If the Ethiopian military took control, the leaders of such a government would likely be familiar figures with close ties to the U.S. military establishment. In the event of an orderly transition upon the emperor's death, Crown Prince Asfa Wossen, considered the probable successor to the throne and part of the Western-educated political establishment, was expected maintain close ties with the United States. Whatever the outcome, it seemed probable that any new Ethiopian government would desire stability in its foreign relations while it adjusted to life without the emperor.

Through the years, however, the U.S.-Ethiopia military relationship had been steadied by the wide ideological gulf that separated Addis Ababa and Moscow. This chasm had effectively ruled out any serious bid on the part of the Soviet Union to develop a partnership with Ethiopia. The United States represented a more politically compatible and safer source for arms for the conservative, feudal-based imperial government. But the ideological gulf between Ethiopia and the Soviet Union began to close after the Dergue seized power in 1974. The dismemberment of the old imperial institutions throughout 1974, culminating in the emperor's overthrow, had left a vacuum that would be filled by a militant, Marxist faction led by Colonel Mengistu.

The secrecy in which the Dergue shrouded itself upon assuming power made it virtually impossible for any outsider to gauge what was going on inside the Ethiopian government.[78] The political and economic contradictions of the military government's domestic policies contributed to the confusion. Sweeping social and economic reforms implemented during the first half of 1975 suggested that the Dergue might be a leftist-leaning reformist government that would eventually return power to the people. But the Dergue's forceful repression of the radical intelligentsia and labor activists in the fall of 1975 pointed to the emergence instead of a military dictatorship. The unfolding political program of the Ethiopian revolution was difficult to decipher as "the contradiction between social advance and political regression spread a pall of confusion on the scene which obscured the real trend of events."[79]

The Dergue's leftward drift was accelerated by civilian pressures for reforms which the military government attempted to deflate by "outlefting" the left. As a response to pressure from students, the labor unions, and the civilian left, the Dergue issued a land reform decree in March 1975 and in July nationalized all urban land and extra housing. However, these economic reforms only partially met the objectives of civilian political activists, who began demanding the removal of the military from power. Resisting these demands to surrender power, the Dergue responded to strikes, demonstrations, and work actions with a sweeping crackdown on all forms of political dissidence, using Ethiopian security forces to stamp out opposition.

The repression of the civilian left, most particularly the Ethiopian People's Revolutionary Party (EPRP)—MEISON's rival—during the fall of 1975 produced a deep rift within the PMAC.[80] Leading moderates, such as Air Force Maj. Sisay Habte, chairman of the PMAC's Political and Foreign Affairs Committee, favored reconciliation with the civilian opposition and negotiations with the Eritreans. A hard-liner/radical coalition led by General Banti (PMAC chairman) and Colonel Mengistu (first vice chairman) wished to continue with the repression of the civilian opposition—especially of the EPRP—and to escalate the war in Eritrea. The outcome of this internal schism would have a profound effect not only on Ethiopian domestic policies, but also on relations between Addis Ababa and Washington.

Briefly in the spring of 1976 the moderates held the upper hand in influencing PMAC policy.[81] On April 20 Addis Ababa had announced the

Programme of the National Democratic Revolution, which recognized the right of self-determination for all nationalities within Ethiopia. Four weeks later the government issued a Nine-Point Policy on Eritrea, which further elaborated upon the theme of regional autonomy for the province. An apparent attempt to subvert this peace initiative by organizing a "peasant march" was halted in May after Secretary of State Kissinger sent an ultimatum that if the plan went forward it would jeopardize U.S. military assistance, including the delivery of the F-5Es still in the arms pipeline.[82] Although the "peasant march" was resumed in June on a smaller scale, it ended in a military rout and decreased the influence of the hard-liners and radicals within the Dergue.[83] Thus, through the summer and fall of 1976 the moderates had an opportunity to consolidate their position, resolve some of the political-security dilemmas confronting Addis Ababa, and ease Washington's diplomatic predicament as well.

However, the PMAC's move toward moderation met another setback that summer. Upon his return from the annual OAU summit meeting in July 1976, Major Sisay was arrested, tried, and executed on five counts of counterrevolutionary activity. One charge in particular—that Sisay had made contact with "imperialist agents" (presumed to be the CIA) in an attempt to destabilize the government—was a forewarning of things to come in relations between Addis Ababa and Washington. Despite the anti-American attacks appearing in the Ethiopian press, there were still moderate and even hard-line members on the military council who favored continuing close ties with the United States.

Although the coalition of military hard-liners and radical ideologues were united in their approach toward Eritrea and the repression of the civilian opposition, they differed over whether Ethiopia should turn to the Soviet Union for arms. A December 1976 reorganization of the Dergue had removed a number of Colonel Mengistu's main supporters and elevated to power less radical members who seemed ready to improve relations with the United States and to block Mengistu's pro-Russian policy.[84] The division within the PMAC now found some of the so-called military hard-liners (such as PMAC chairman Banti) aligned with ideological moderates in desiring to maintain cordial relations with Washington. This pro-U.S. versus pro-Soviet schism within the Dergue was resolved by the February 1977 shoot-out that left Colonel Mengistu in control of the PMAC.

The now dominant radical faction within the Dergue, led by Mengistu, believed that the best way to ensure the integrity of the Ethiopian revolution and their own political survival was to defect to the Soviet Union. They could thus forge an arms partnership based on compatible ideological beliefs. While an examination of U.S. policies toward Ethiopia between 1974 and 1976 might suggest that the United States was willing to work with the new government, the perception in Addis Ababa was that the United States would eventually act to prevent the emergence of a truly leftist-oriented revolutionary government. Thus, after coming to power Mengistu quickly moved to align Ethiopia with the socialist bloc and pressed the Soviets to implement the secret arms agreement he had signed with Moscow in December. Soviet weapons, supplies, and military advisers began to arrive in Ethiopia from South Yemen in March 1977, rendering the U.S. military connection expendable. Interestingly, unlike Haile Selassie, Mengistu never got into the cold war game of playing the United States and the Soviet Union off against each other.[85] Mengistu appeared to be firmly committed to the Eastern bloc, at least until international conditions changed in the late 1980s.[86]

GLOBALISM AND HUMAN RIGHTS

Military relations between the United States and Ethiopia might well have moved along an entirely different track had effective control over U.S. policy remained in the hands of the Africa Bureau. The institutionalized decision making at the State Department would have been less prone to, or perceived as less engaged in, ideologically motivated behavior of a hostile intent.[87] Though deemed a bit radical, the Dergue's 1975 land reform and nationalization programs suggested to the State Department that the new government was attempting to improve the lot of the masses at the lower end of the socioeconomic scale and thereby to create a more stable political environment for the conduct of U.S.-Ethiopia relations.[88] As late as spring 1977, as the "red terror" spread throughout Ethiopia, State Department officials continued to favor providing some form of security assistance to the Dergue in order to maintain a long-run relationship with Ethiopia.[89] State feared that severing the military connection would mean the end of the U.S. position in Ethiopia.[90] Moreover, an American presence was deemed desirable to contain Soviet penetration in the region, maintain Western access to Middle East oil, and provide for freedom of passage for Israeli shipping in the Red Sea.[91] Thus, before Ethiopia ran afoul of Washington on human rights grounds, the Carter administration was prepared to request $10 million in FMS credits, $1 million in IMETP funds, and an additional $1.1 million in MAP aid for the delivery of equipment for FY 1978.[92]

By the fall of 1976, there was little interest outside of the Africa Bureau in salvaging U.S.-Ethiopia relations. After his July 1976 order to allow massive FMS credit and cash sales to Addis Ababa, Henry Kissinger seemed to lose interest in the situation. The White House's only stake in Ethiopia was to ensure that the Republican right wing would not attack

President Ford for "losing" another African state to the Soviet Union (Angola being the first).[93] Later Ethiopia became a showpiece for Jimmy Carter's arms sales and human rights policies, being one of only three states singled out for U.S.-imposed military sanctions.

Although the formal break with the United States came several months into the Carter presidency, the PMAC's belief that to survive it would have to switch arms partners was generated during the last few months of the Ford administration and concerned the chief architect of U.S. policy, Henry Kissinger. At first glance Kissinger appeared to be the ideal policy maker to take charge of U.S. policy toward Ethiopia during such a tumultuous period. His willingness to continue relations with the military government in Chile after the bloody September 1973 coup against President Allende was based on the notion that not to do so would run the risk of driving the junta toward "anti-American nationalism or collapsing it in favor of the totalitarian left."[94] Kissinger's reflections about the situation in Chile appear relevant to the Ethiopian situation: "I do not mean to condone all the actions of the junta . . . but it did inherit a revolutionary situation in which government-sponsored violence played an important role."[95] Particularly maddening to Kissinger was the "exceptional severity" with which American and foreign critics attacked the junta, eventually resulting in the termination of U.S. military assistance in 1976 "while it faced near–civil war conditions."[96] Ethiopia seemed to be confronting a similar situation.

Ironically, Kissinger's reputation for realpolitik contributed to the belief that the United States, as an enemy of progressive revolutionary movements, would attempt to subvert the Ethiopian revolution. A significant difference between the Chilean and Ethiopian situations had to be factored into Addis Ababa's calculations: the military coup-makers in Santiago were right-wing; those in Addis Ababa were leftists. Although the United States provided Ethiopia with some $15 million in MAP and IMETP funds, $25 million in FMS credits, and had delivered almost $130 million worth of arms through FMS cash sales in 1975 and 1976, these transactions occurred at a time when the Dergue was suppressing the leftist civilian opposition and moderates, and pro-American hard-liners still held sway within the PMAC. After the execution of Major Sisay, the Ford administration seemed to write off Washington's chances of preventing the further leftward drift of the Dergue. Kissinger's attitude toward the PMAC may have been hardened by his annoyance at what he saw as the double standard of Democrats in Congress who singled out right-wing governments (for example, Chile) for harassment while continuing to support many radical left-wing states.[97] Thus, when Congress condemned Ethiopia for human rights violations in the fall of 1976, the administration made no special plea on behalf of the Dergue.

The Collapse of U.S.-Ethiopian Military Relations

The Ford administration handed Jimmy Carter a rapidly deteriorating situation that may have had as much to do with Secretary Kissinger's reputation as with Washington's slow, reactive policy. Accurate or not, a perception abounded that the Nixon administration, under Kissinger's guidance, had conspired to bring down the Allende government in Chile only three years before.[98] Given the administration's known preference for a moderate leader to emerge from within the Dergue, radical ideologues might logically assume that Washington would prevent them from coming to power.[99] Thus, the Carter administration began dealing with a government of which some members may have felt that a U.S. campaign was under way to bring about their political demise.

The problem was compounded by the new administration's international agenda. Jimmy Carter brought to the White House a vastly different global outlook from that of his predecessors. The U.S.-Soviet rivalry was no longer perceived as the dominant issue in a highly interdependent and pluralistic world system.[100] Instead, the Carter administration would attempt "to promote a new system of world order based upon international stability, peace and justice."[101] Mutual cooperation rather than competition would form the core value for interaction in this new world order. Human rights, normalizing East-West and North-South relations, arms control, and resolving conflicts in the Middle East and Africa headed the administration's global agenda.[102]

Given Carter's view of the new era into which U.S.-Soviet relations had moved, the new administration would be less likely to respond in a knee-jerk manner to Soviet activities around the globe. Coupled with the theme of normalization, the implication seemed to be that the United States would be willing to work with and not subvert left-wing governments in the Third World. Moreover, Jimmy Carter's expressed intention to return primary responsibility for crafting U.S. foreign policy to the State Department should have provided an opening for getting U.S.-Ethiopia relations back on track.[103] However, the administration's new policy direction was also geared toward reducing U.S. arms transfers overseas. During the 1976 presidential campaign, Carter had declared that he "would not hesitate as president to assess unilateral reductions in arms sales overseas."[104] Moreover, on a number of occasions including his inaugural address, Carter had expressed a general concern for human rights abroad and a willingness to link U.S. arms transfers to human rights conditions in recipient countries. Thus, the administration's initial approach regarding the conduct of global and bilateral affairs did not fit the militaristic thinking in Addis Ababa.

Carter's willingness to make an example of Ethiopia following the PMAC's February 1977 internal purge was made easier in that, in terms of general principles, it was reflective of the mood in Congress to reduce the level of U.S. arms sales as well as to place greater emphasis upon human rights abroad.[105] Since he had pledged in his campaign to reduce arms sales and to affirm human rights, Carter needed to demonstrate his willingness to bring U.S. pressure to bear in linking these two issues to preserve his own political credibility on Capitol Hill. The fact that the administration hoped to play down issues of East-West confrontation also mitigated the potentially adverse impact of Moscow's introduction of arms into Ethiopia in March 1977. Thus, with his own human rights agenda added for color, Jimmy Carter merely put the finishing touches on an arms relationship that had already decayed beyond repair.

By the spring of 1977, voices favoring U.S. disengagement from Ethiopia completely drowned out all others. Conservatives had no sympathy for the plight of the leftist government. Moderates and liberals were put off by the human rights violations of the Dergue. Although the professional bureaucrats at the State Department had regained control of U.S. policy, they had a weak political basis from which to argue that the United States could or should recapture its position of dominant influence in Ethiopia.

SWITCHING PARTNERS

The collapse of the U.S.-Ethiopia military relationship in April 1977 was indicative of the emerging shared belief that the tangible rewards of the partnership were marginal at best. Top-ranking American and Ethiopian decision makers now believed that the rising political and military costs of maintaining the arms linkage outweighed the benefits. Moreover, the assets being offered by each side were considered expendable or replaceable. Continued cooperation between Washington and Addis Ababa might, in fact, hinder the attainment of their primary local and regional objectives. Thus, the security calculation of both supplier and recipient pointed to the conclusion that termination of the arms linkage was the best cure for this illness.

By 1977 the PMAC saw itself under siege and on the verge of being overwhelmed by the protracted war in Eritrea, the Soviet-supported arms buildup in Somalia, and domestic strife in Addis Ababa. The amount of grant military aid the United States was willing to provide to Ethiopia—the primary American economic payoff in fulfillment of the original 1953 quid pro quo—was no longer enough, given the PMAC's determination to resolve the Eritrean problem by force, suppress the civilian opposition in Addis Ababa (as well as violently resolve its own internal disputes), and respond to Somalia's growing military power. While Washington appeared committed at least to upholding Ethiopia's territorial integrity in the Ogaden, even in that instance the Americans still required Addis Ababa to rely heavily on making huge cash arms purchases. In addition, the United States was perceived as eminently hostile toward the Ethiopian revolution. U.S. economic, political and military support seemed to be ultimately designed to subvert rather than promote the revolution and the dominant radical faction within the PMAC. Throughout the last months of the U.S.-Ethiopia arms partnership, Addis Ababa neither made use of the $10 million in FMS credits provided by Washington for FY 1976, nor drew on the $6 million in MAP funds or $10 million worth of FMS credits allocated for Ethiopia in the FY 1977 security assistance budget. Several months into 1977, Ethiopia had purchased only a few items on a cash basis. Given the growing ideological divergence between the two arms partners, coupled with increasing Soviet interest in Ethiopia's revolutionary government, the PMAC's threat of defection to Moscow not only was a viable and credible scenario; it had to be carried out.

By the end of 1976, Washington apparently had little to gain, but much to lose, by continuing its support for the PMAC. Kagnew Station was obsolete and at best a redundant strategic facility. Ethiopia was nonessential to protect oil routes. Israel had the proven military capability to protect its Red Sea interests. With human rights abuses being committed by the military government on such a level that Ethiopia was cited by Amnesty International and the U.S. Congress for gross violations, coupled with what were viewed as extremist economic reforms, the executive branch could not justify aid to Addis Ababa on any grounds. Furthermore, improving U.S. relations with a number of Arab states in the region had increased Washington's policy options, so a continued presence in Ethiopia and association with Addis Ababa's "anti-Arab" war in Eritrea did more harm than good.

By the spring of 1977, neither the United States nor Ethiopia exhibited much interest in salvaging a relationship that had been allowed to atrophy. Ideology had an important effect on both sides. Mengistu and his radical colleagues perceived the United States much as Haile Selassie had viewed the Soviet Union: as a threat to his political survival. The contradiction of a Marxist-oriented government tied to the leading world imperialist entity had to be resolved. Perhaps out of fear that such talk might provoke Washington into taking some preemptive action against them, Mengistu waited until he had consolidated his position before publicly defecting to Moscow and terminating the U.S. arms connection. While the initiative for the termination resided in the hands of the PMAC, for the United

States it reconciled the dilemma posed by espousing human rights while providing U.S. weapons to a brutal military government. Thus, in the end, Washington and Addis Ababa, somewhat noisily and bitterly, but with an almost audible sigh of relief, called an end to their quarter-century-long military relationship.

III

The United States and Somalia, 1977–1990

9

The 1977–78 Ogaden War and U.S. Arms Rebuff

As U.S.-Ethiopia relations continued to decay in the spring of 1977, the Carter administration began to consider offsetting Washington's impending loss of position in Ethiopia by moving into Somalia. Mogadishu had already begun exploring the possibility of having the United States replace Moscow as its main arms supplier. Somalia's approach had captured the attention of Jimmy Carter, who had taken a special interest in the Horn of Africa. During his first few weeks in office, Carter spent hours in government briefings and diplomatic discussions with Anwar Sadat, Prince Fahd of Saudi Arabia, and various European leaders about the maneuverings in the region, and read voluminous studies that he had ordered about the area.[1] Thus he certainly understood the political and strategic implications of what was happening in the Horn as well as the potential for conflict between Ethiopia and Somalia.

In March 1977 a memorandum sent by Vice President Walter Mondale to President Carter advocating a U.S.-Somali rapprochement was rebutted by the NSC's Horn specialist, Paul Henze, who warned of the dangers of becoming involved in Somalia.[2] Nonetheless, in early April, in the presence of a news correspondent for *Time* magazine, Carter instructed Vice President Mondale, "Tell Cy [Vance] and Zbig [Brzezinsky] that I want them to move in every possible way to get Somalia to be our friend."[3] Little happened until after Ethiopia had signed a second arms agreement with Moscow in May. The resulting fallout from this accord was that Mogadishu recognized a shift was occurring in Soviet policy and the White House became more interested in levering the Soviets out of Somalia. In June, a private back channel was established between Jimmy Carter and Somalia's President Siad Barre.[4]

On June 16, a few days after a secret White House message had been delivered through this private channel to Siad Barre, the Somali ambassador met with President Carter and presented an urgent request for U.S. military assistance. The president informed the ambassador that although it would be difficult at the time to provide military aid, Washington would encourage its allies to help Somalia maintain its defensive strength.[5] Apparently interpreting this response as a "forthcoming attitude," Mogadishu made a specific request for arms on July 9.[6] Six days later, President Carter approved a decision "in principle" to cooperate with other countries in helping Somalia meet its defense requirements.[7] On July 25 the Somali ambassador was informed that the United States had agreed in principle to supply Somalia with defensive arms. The next day Secretary of State Cyrus Vance announced the decision.

It appeared briefly that the Carter administration had executed a bold diplomatic coup by at once establishing a foothold in Somalia and countering the Soviet position in Ethiopia without endangering broader, long-term U.S. interests in Africa. A week after Secretary Vance's announcement, however, it became apparent that Washington had miscalculated Somalia's ultimate intent when Somali regular forces were positively identified in the Ogaden. Several days before Vance's arms announcement, and unknown to U.S. officials, Somali government forces had entered the Ogaden and were fighting alongside Western Somali Liberation Front (WSLF) guerrillas to help liberate the territory from Ethiopian control.[8] Because of travel restrictions on American officials in Somalia, the U.S. embassy did not know what was going on.[9] Besides the usual tensions along the border, there was no sign that something out the ordinary might occur; Siad Barre cleverly hid his attack by personally delivering the invasion orders to Somali units, traveling at night to remain undetected.[10] Although U.S. intelligence analysts already suspected before Vance's announcement that regular Somali forces were in the Ogaden with the WSLF, once the extent of Somalia's attack was confirmed in early August, White House enthusiasm for helping Somalia abruptly ended.[11]

Washington's reaction was swift and, from Modagishu's perspective, ultimately quite damaging to the Somali war effort in the Ogaden. At the State Department it was assumed that because it had been made clear from the start that the United States would not give Somalia weapons to attack or destabilize its neighbors, in accepting the U.S. aid offer Mogadishu had understood and would abide by Washington's terms. By their action the Somalis showed that they could not be trusted. On August 4, Assistant Secretary of State for African Affairs Richard Moose told Somalia's ambassador that while the U.S. agreement in principle still stood, it could not be implemented under the circumstances. The Somali military delegation, which was in Washington August 5–9 to discuss U.S. military assistance, was informed that no American weapons would be forthcoming as long as Somali soldiers continued to fight in the area.[12] To further emphasize its opposition to Somalia's military adventure, the administration relayed a message to the Somali ambassador on August 18 that the United States also would not approve of third-party transfers of U.S. weapons as long as Somali forces were in the Ogaden.[13]

Despite Washington's refusal to implement its arms offer, Somalia continued to press ahead in the Ogaden. In fact, Somali forces met with considerable success in the early going and by mid-September were occupying nearly 80 percent of the Ogaden.[14] The political upheaval in Addis Ababa, along with the insurrections in surrounding provinces and the escalating civil war in Eritrea, gave Somalia an opportunity to exploit Ethiopia's momentary weakness and seize the Ogaden.[15] So long as the Somalis continued their invasion and military triumphs, arms discussions between Washington and Mogadishu were moot.

Despite Somalia's early battlefield successes, it was evident by mid-October that Mogadishu would not achieve the quick, decisive victory Siad Barre had sought in the Ogaden. Soviet military aid, which had made the Somali invasion possible in the first place, had been reduced and then completely cut off in mid-October. The Somali offensive also faced logistical problems: the Somali National Army (SNA) and WSLF forces were operating along overextended supply lines and were beginning to run out of ammunition and spare parts.[16] A stalemate ensued as the combined Somali forces were unable to seize the key Dire Dawa air base or the strategically important town of Harar. Then in November, with the appearance of several hundred Cuban military advisers alongside Ethiopian forces and increased Soviet aid to the PMAC, the tide of war turned against Somalia. At the end of November, Moscow began a massive military airlift that within several months brought an estimated $1 billion worth of Soviet arms supplies and some 17,000 Cuban troops to Ethiopia.[17] Although the situation was now becoming desperate for the Somalis, Siad Barre refused to order his army's withdrawal from the Ogaden, apparently believing he could now persuade the United States and other Western powers to intervene on his behalf. However, the Western powers had reached a consensus at a meeting in London on November 10 not to help Somalia, nor to mediate or take the matter to the UN Security Council, even though it then seemed likely that the Somalis would be expelled from the Ogaden as a result of the increasing level of Soviet-Cuban military support for the Ethiopian war effort.[18]

Despite frequent and urgent pleas by Mogadishu and several of Somalia's Middle Eastern friends for the United States to provide weapons after Somalia had ended its Treaty of Friendship and Cooperation with the Soviet Union and broken diplomatic relations with Cuba in mid-November

1977, Washington refused to become involved except to urge Somalia to withdraw from the Ogaden and seek a negotiated settlement. Perhaps the greatest temptation for the Carter administration to reverse its position arose in February 1978 as Ethiopian and Cuban forces were driving toward the Somali border, raising the specter that they might take the offensive into Somalia. While some top-ranking officials, most notably National Security Adviser Zbigniew Brzezinski, considered various military options, the administration refrained from intervening beyond seeking assurances from the Ethiopian government that it would not send its forces across the border and keeping the pressure on Moscow to hold them back.[19]

Despite Soviet-Cuban involvement in the war, the Carter administration refused to budge from its original position that Somalia had to disengage from the Ogaden and promise not to invade again before the United States would consider any request for military assistance. Repeated and desperate Somali requests for help were refused by Washington, as Barre continued to resist withdrawing his forces. On March 7, Ambassador John Loughran delivered a very strong and blunt message from the White House to Siad Barre. Jimmy Carter told the Somali president, "Leave Ethiopia now, or take responsibility for further pointless bloodshed, face certain military defeat and sacrifice all hope of later American aid."[20] By this time 8,000 Somali troops had been killed, three-fourths of the tank force destroyed, half of the Somali Air Force was out of commission, and no help was on the horizon.[21] Following a phone conversation with President Carter on March 8 in which Siad Barre was forced to confront "the coldest kind of reality," the Somali Army was ordered to withdraw from the Ogaden.[22] By March 14 the Somali withdrawal was virtually complete, although WSLF guerrilla activity continued in the area.

THE SOVIET DEFECTION TO ETHIOPIA

Mogadishu's decision to invade Ethiopia in the summer of 1977 was the product of a rational calculation based upon erroneous assumptions. Ethiopian forces were stretched thin at the time, combating insurgents in Eritrea and the Ogaden. Political upheaval in other provinces and in Addis Ababa itself, as the Dergue directed the "red terror" campaign against civilian opposition groups, provided a further cover by diverting the attention and resources of the Ethiopian military government from Somalia's preparation for war.[23] The instability resulting from Ethiopia's revolutionary transition appeared to present a unique opportunity for Somalia to annex the Ogaden. Given the deteriorating political and military situation in Ethiopia during the late summer of 1977, the liberation of the Ogaden as well as the emergence of an independent Eritrea were likely scenarios.[24]

But Somalia's assessment was also premised on the belief that the Soviet Union would not take sides, or intervene in such a manner as to upset this scenario. Because Soviet influence in Somalia was so pervasive, it seemed unlikely that Moscow would risk its predominant political position and strategic assets for an unsure situation in Ethiopia. Moscow had provided Mogadishu with several hundred million dollars' worth of arms over the previous five years and was involved in training the Somali armed forces and internal National Security Service.[25] East bloc diplomats and advisers had easy access to senior members of the Somali government and were well informed on what was going on in Mogadishu.[26] To give one measure of the intrusive Soviet presence, there were 3,000 Russians in Somalia—one for every 1,000 Somalis.[27] Moreover, given the Soviet stake in the military base facility at Berbera, which gave Moscow the ability to control access to the Red Sea and to conduct surveillance of U.S. naval operations in the Arabian Sea, the Kremlin would refrain from taking any drastic action that might risk this investment.[28] It also seemed unlikely that the Soviet Union would turn against a government with a pronounced commitment to Marxist-Leninist ideology.[29] Thus, even after Moscow had decided to arm both Ethiopia and Somalia, if forced to choose sides, the Soviets were expected to choose the safe course and remain neutral or to side with its traditional Somali ally.[30]

When the Somali invasion of the Ogaden began in late July, it was imperative that the Soviet Union maintain at least a neutral policy in the Ethiopian-Somali conflict, especially once the Carter administration made clear its unwillingness to supply U.S. weapons. The refusal of other Western states to supply arms meant that in the short term the Ethiopian-Somali War would be fought between Somalia's Soviet-built military and Ethiopia's U.S.-supplied and partially Soviet-armed military. Under the circumstances, the military balance seemed to favor Somalia. However, while Mogadishu seemed able to make an independent political decision to initiate war, its ability to sustain and wage war successfully depended heavily on Soviet support and cooperation.[31] The Somali Aeronautical Corps (SAC), in particular, were extremely dependent upon the continued supply of spare parts, ammunition, and maintanence mechanics from the Soviet Union to keep in operation the sixty-six combat aircraft in the Somali Air Force, which included forty-four MiG-15s and MiG-17s and twelve MiG-21s.[32] Moreover, in defecting to the Ethiopian side, the Soviets brought with them intimate knowledge of Somalia's armed forces, order of battle, capabilities, and deficiencies.[33]

As the primary arms supplier for both combatants, and with the United

States on the sidelines, the Soviet Union could act as the sole arbiter of the conflict in the Ogaden. Unfortunately for the Somalis, Moscow elected to support only Ethiopia, and very forcefully, by closing the arms pipeline to Somalia on October 19 and by implementing an emergency arms airlift to Ethiopia and introducing Cuban ground forces at the end of November. Without Western military intervention, the outcome of the war was now a foregone conclusion. Siad Barre had made an enormous political miscalculation in assuming (1) that the West would come to Somalia's aid, thus supporting Somali aggression in the Ogaden, and (2) that Moscow would remain neutral.

Moscow's decision to defect to Ethiopia was evidently based on several factors.[34] The military government in Addis Ababa seemed to be more committed than Mogadishu to Marxist-Leninist ideology; Ethiopia's population was larger than Somalia's; Moscow could gain an outpost on the Red Sea through continued Ethiopian control over Eritrea, as Soviet facilities at Aden and Socotra Island in South Yemen (PDRY) could replace Berbera. Given the recent defection to the West of Moscow's other Arab clients in the Red Sea—Egypt and Sudan—and Somalia's close ties with Cairo and Riyadh, the isolated and besieged military government in Addis Ababa would make a more dependent, and dependable client than Mogadishu.[35] The fact that the Somali president had attempted to play off Washington against the Soviets openly, as well as behind closed doors, and that Siad continued to nurture close ties with the pro-Western governments in Iran, Saudi Arabia, and Egypt, raised a great deal of suspicion and distrust toward Siad Barre in the Kremlin.[36] A Somali government subjected to the financial banishments and religious pressures of fellow Arab League members would not provide a very solid foundation for securing long-term Soviet interests in the region. Finally, Soviet intervention on behalf of Addis Ababa was in defense of the sacred OAU principle to respect other nations' territorial integrity and might actually enhance Soviet relations in Africa.

Moscow's decisive defection to Ethiopia in the fall of 1977 left Somalia particularly vulnerable and isolated. Mogadishu was being shunned by the Western powers. Even within the Arab League, Somalia's cause was not widely supported; more militant and radical Arab states were inclined to back the revolutionary government in Addis Ababa.[37] Mogadishu's only recourse was to acquire weapons from moderate Arab states, such as Saudi Arabia, Sudan, and Egypt, as well as Iran, who feared Soviet penetration in the Red Sea region. However, they had only a limited capability to meet Somalia's arms requirements, and their support did not provide the crucial political-psychological support that U.S. backing would lend to the Somali war effort. Consequently, the regional military balance that had allowed Mogadishu to gamble on war and then ignore U.S. as well as Soviet calls for withdrawal had shifted back in favor of Addis Ababa and made a U.S. security connection even more critical for the preservation of Somalia.

GLOBAL CONFRONTATION OR LOCAL CONFLICT

When Somalia's army was discovered in the Ogaden in August 1977, there was little question in Washington that this was overt aggression on the part of Mogadishu. Almost immediately a consensus emerged in the Carter administration that the United States would not provide weapons to Somalia as long as Somali regular forces remained inside Ethiopia. The State Department adopted what might be labeled an "interested observer" stance, viewing the situation as purely a local conflict that posed no direct threat to vital U.S. interests.[38] While calling for Mogadishu to withdraw its forces from the Ogaden, Washington maintained a neutral distance by refusing to provide arms to either side.

The Carter administration had little difficulty maintaining a public posture of benign neutrality during the first phase of what was generally viewed as a local war between two Soviet client states. But below the surface there was much uncertainty and division among top-ranking U.S. officials regarding the degree of threat posed to Western interests by the Soviet and Cuban presence in Ethiopia, the region's overall strategic value in light of the Arab-Israeli conflict, the emergence of Africa as the newest East-West ideological battleground, the implications of the Horn's location near the Middle East oil fields, and what course of action to follow.[39] This schism within the administration, festering since late summer 1977, publicly surfaced as Cuban combat operations began to expand in mid-November. Zbigniew Brzezinski, in particular, felt that the Cuban military deployments had to be assessed in the context of U.S.-Soviet relations and that an American response of some magnitude was needed.[40]

At the start of the Ogaden crisis, Brzezinski had remained in the background and supported the State Department's low-key diplomatic approach.[41] But as reports began to filter into Washington in the fall of 1977 of an increase in the number of Cuban military advisers in Ethiopia and as the massive Soviet military airlift got under way, Brzezinski became alarmed.[42] These activities, coupled with the recent expansion of Soviet political-military influence in South Yemen, convinced him that the United States would have to confront the Soviet Union in a strong manner. The situation in the Horn had now become more than a border war.[43]

In Brzezinski's mind there were two critical challenges to U.S. interests at stake in the Horn.[44] Soviet advances in the area represented a serious setback in Washington's attempt to develop with Moscow some "rules of the game" for dealing with turbulence in the Third World. These activities might also serve to give domestic political opponents of SALT II ammunition with which to undercut the Carter administration's arms control efforts. To blunt domestic attacks on SALT II and, at the same time send notice to Moscow of Washington's extreme displeasure, Brzezinski proposed linking Soviet-Cuban activities in the Horn with progress on the arms control treaty and the reopening of U.S.-Soviet negotiations on the demilitarization of the Indian Ocean.[45] The NSC adviser went so far as to argue that the United States should adopt a position of open hostility toward Ethiopia and uncritically support Somalia, possibly even exploiting the situation in Eritrea to tie Moscow down in a "costly and endless struggle."[46] Soviet adventurism had to be made costly, else it would weaken confidence in the United States and damage the administration politically.[47]

Brzezinski's belief that Soviet actions were part of a larger, well-defined strategy requiring an assertive U.S. response was countered by others in the administration who, even after the Soviet-Cuban intervention, saw no grand Soviet design and considered the Soviet Union's actions in the Horn to be simply seizing an opportunity.[48] The Department of State saw the Horn "as a textbook case of Soviet exploitation of a local conflict."[49] Moscow would ultimately fail in Ethiopia and be ousted as it had been from Sudan and Egypt, and more recently Somalia. In the meantime, the United States would work with its European allies and African nations to bring about a negotiated settlement to the dispute and keep the lines of communication open to Ethiopia, and if possible, strenghten U.S. relations with Somalia.[50]

Thus, the State Department believed that a combination of diplomacy, negotiation, Western restraint, and sensitivity to African nationalism could resolve this local conflict.[51] Although it was recognized that Soviet activities would influence domestic U.S. opinions of the Soviet Union, the administration's regionalists, proponents such as Cyrus Vance, UN ambassador Andrew Young, and Richard Moose at the Africa Bureau, as well as the president himself, sought to keep the conflict in the Horn from being viewed in an East-West context.[52] Vance opposed Brzezinski's suggestion of linking Soviet activity in the Horn with the SALT II talks, arms control, U.S.-Soviet economic relations or high-level visits; such links might adversely affect U.S. interests and do little to alter Soviet behavior.[53] The two officials would also come into conflict in late February 1978 over the possible use of U.S. military forces in the region. Despite continuing bureaucratic clashes within an administration now divided over how to view the Soviet Union and conflict in the Third World, in early February the State Department had brought some cohesion back to U.S. policy by formulating a five-point strategy that called for the United States to (1) work with NATO to achieve a negotiated settlement, prevent an invasion of Somalia, and obstruct any increase in Soviet-Cuban influence in the area, (2) ensure that other friends in the area—Egypt, Iran, Saudi Arabia, and Sudan—understand and support these goals and urge them on Siad Barre, (3) obtain a Somali agreement to withdraw, (4) lay the diplomatic and political groundwork to help Somalia defend its territory, including the supply of defensive arms after withdrawal, and (5) keep pressure on the Soviets to stop Ethiopian and Cuban forces at the Somali border and support a negotiated resolution.[54]

There was little incentive for the United States to stick its neck out on behalf of Somalia at this time. The threat to U.S. interests posed by the war in the Horn and Soviet-Cuban intervention was seen by most U.S. officials as indirect and minimal. Vital U.S. interests were not at stake. Washington's main concern was to ensure that the Somali Army was not completely destroyed.[55] To avoid that scenario, Somalia would have to get out of the Ogaden. It was obvious that Siad Barre had failed in his bid to manipulate the threat perceptions of the United States by protraying the struggle in the Horn as a war against Soviet intrusion. Instead, Washington and most of the rest of the world saw it as a local conflict in which Somalia was the aggressor.

MOGADISHU'S BREAK WITH MOSCOW

Perhaps one of the most pivotal events of the Ogaden War, one that would have a long-term impact on U.S.-Somali relations, occurred on November 13, 1977, when Siad Barre renounced the 1974 Treaty of Friendship and Cooperation with the Soviet Union. In one swift stroke Barre terminated Soviet use of the base facilities at Berbera, ordered all Soviet military advisers to leave the country within seven days, reduced the size of the embassy staff, and broke off diplomatic relations with Cuba. Barre apparently hoped that this move would open the way to U.S. support and encourage friendly Middle Eastern states to come to his aid.[56] While he succeeded in acquiring increased Arab and Iranian support, in the short term this action had no perceptible effect upon U.S.-Somali relations.

Siad Barre first began to question the Soviet commitment to Somalia following Cuban President Fidel Castro's March 1977 visit to the region, during which Castro proposed the creation of a Confederation of Socialist Republics to be composed of Ethiopia, South Yemen, and Somalia. However, Castro "underestimated the force of Somali irredentism and Ethiopian imperialism."[57] Mogadishu would only agree to the idea if the Ogaden was returned to Somalia and Eritrea was allowed to enter as a separate state.[58] Addis Ababa immediately rejected the Somali suggestion. But it was Somalia, not Ethiopia, that was viewed by the Russians and Cubans as the obstacle to this plan. As a signal of displeasure, Moscow signed a second arms agreement with Ethiopia in May, and Havana withdrew 400 Cubans from Somalia that summer.

Soon after Siad Barre launched the Somali invasion of the Ogaden, it became apparent that Soviet sympathies would lie with Ethiopia. At the end of August 1977, Barre paid a state visit to the Soviet Union to persuade Moscow to modify its policy in the Horn. He received a cool reception and failed to gain an audience with Premier Leonid Brezhnev. Moreover, the Soviets refused to decrease arms shipments to Ethiopia or increase the flow of armaments to Somalia. As a further indication of Moscow's tilt toward Addis Ababa, the government-controlled Soviet press began showing obvious favor toward the Ethiopian position in the war, referring to the "Somali invasion" of Ethiopia's territory.[59]

While relations were deteriorating with the Soviet Union, the Somalis either deluded themselves or were led to believe that the United States was prepared to step in and take Moscow's place as Mogadishu's principal arms supplier. What would become a source of great misunderstanding and produce bitter feelings of betrayal on both sides was a message sent in June by Jimmy Carter to Siad Barre by means of Dr. Kevin Cahill, a longtime personal friend and physician to the Somali president. The secret back-channel communiqué reportedly stated that because the United States had little reason to be nice to the Ethiopians, "Whatever the Somalis do in the Ogaden is their business."[60] The message purportedly went on to offer Mogadishu a quid pro quo whereby if Somalia dropped its territorial claims to northeast Kenya and Djibouti, Washington would "consider sympathetically Somalia's legitimate defensive needs."[61] Although the State Department countered that U.S. approaches to Somalia had always been cautious, and that the Somalis knew the United States would not incite or condone aggression in the region, not surprisingly Siad Barre read the most into this message.[62] Thus the Somalis argued that the Carter administration had given them the green light to invade the Ogaden and had then abandoned them.[63]

Even if the United States had followed through with the July 25 agreement in principle to supply Somalia with arms, U.S. military analysts felt there were too many variables weighing against the United States' ability to affect the outcome of the war short of massive and immediate arms transfers.[64] Somalia's military dependence upon the Soviet Union for spare parts and supplies was too great to be overcome in a short time. A quick change from Soviet to U.S. arms would not be feasible technically, particularly in the midst of a war.[65] In the view of U.S. diplomats, Mogadishu had lost an opportunity to lessen its dependence on Moscow by invading the Ogaden.[66] Once the tide had turned against Mogadishu, there was little Washington or any other outside power could do to salvage the Somali position.

Siad Barre's explusion of the Soviet military presence from Somalia in November was a desperate gamble designed to gain outside support. Barre reasoned that the continuation of the treaty might inhibit others from coming to Somalia's aid.[67] By breaking with Moscow, he could then present the argument that he was resisting the Soviet attempt to destabilize the Horn; the argument, however, was not very convincing as long as the treaty remained in force.[68] Moreover, Mogadishu's treaty of friendship with the Soviet Union was of little value if Moscow insisted on supplying arms to the enemy camp.[69]

Although the Somali people welcomed the break with Moscow because of the Russians' individual behavior and their association with the less liberal aspects of Barre's regime, it was a high-risk move that could prove very damaging.[70] There was no guarantee that the United States would now alter its policy and replace the Soviets. Any hope of the Soviet Union reversing its policy and swinging its support back to Somalia would be foreclosed. Because only the Soviet Union could impose a regional solution at this point, and one that was acceptable to Somalia, the rupture in military relations made this scenario rather unrealistic. Still, in order to hedge its bet, if only slightly, Somalia refrained from breaking diplomatic relations with the Soviet Union.

If Siad Barre had taken the Americans at their word he might have been less inclined to take such a gamble. In October, the Somalis had approached the United States and offered to abrogate the Soviet treaty and end all military ties with Moscow in return for U.S. cooperation and friendship.[71] The Carter administration responded that while the United States wished to cooperate in meeting Somalia's legitimate defense needs, Washington would be prepared to provide defensive arms only if Somalia's forces withdrew from the Ogaden.[72] Nonetheless, after the Somalis expelled the Soviet military mission and broke relations with Cuba in mid-November, they submitted a new request for arms. The United States again refused, advising Mogadishu to accept OAU mediation, seek a negotiated peace, and to give assurances that Somalia would respect the territorial integrity of its neighbors.[73]

With the United States refusing to fill Moscow's shoes in Somalia, Mogadishu was forced to rely upon weapons acquired from international arms merchants and Arab sources.[74] Although prohibited by the United States from passing on any of its U.S. arms to Somalia, Saudi Arabia reportedly supplied sixty French AMX tanks, and the shah of Iran sent British-made Chieftain tanks.[75] Egypt provided over $30 million in arms aid, which was especially beneficial, as both Mogadishu and Cairo had once been Soviet arms clients.[76] The Somalis did continue to make arms presentations to the United States and asked pro-Western governments in the Middle East to make appeals on their behalf, but to no avail. Barre was so desperate that he even hinted at renewing military ties with Moscow, an unrealistic hope, given the Soviet role in killing thousands of Somalis.[77] Siad was ultimately forced to recognize that the Somali cause had failed to win international support and that victory was unattainable.

THE U.S. ARMS EMBARGO

Somalia's invasion of the Ogaden created a dilemma for the United States. While the Carter administration wanted to help Somalia and counter Soviet penetration of Ethiopia, the State Department placed a high priority on keeping communication lines open to Addis Ababa. American officials believed that the strict preconditions originally placed upon arms transfers to Somalia and the suspension of the offer, coupled with public support for preserving Ethiopia's territorial integrity, would demonstrate to Chairman Mengistu that the United States was not seeking to confront or destabilize his regime. On the other hand, because of rapidly increasing Soviet influence in Ethiopia, the United States had little incentive to help Ethiopia's war effort and needed to hedge its bets by keeping the door open to Somalia. To avoid having to choose publicly between Addis Ababa and Mogadishu, and perhaps permanently alienating one of the two parties, the Carter administration imposed an embargo on arms transfers to both sides for the duration of the war.

Washington's arms embargo, of course, provoked friction with Somalia, which claimed to be adversely and unfairly affected by this action. The Somalis felt that the U.S. embargo hurt Somalia more than Ethiopia because the Soviet Union had been slowing the delivery of weapons to Mogadishu.[78] Moscow's decision to plug the Somali arms pipeline in October resulted in the effective strangulation of Somalia's war-making capacity and destroyed any hope of military success in the absence of U.S. intervention. There was little sympathy in Washington for this argument: if the embargo damaged Mogadishu to a greater extent, so be it; it was the Somalis who had started the war in the first place.

What was more surprising and disconcerting to the Carter administration was the hostile reaction in Addis Ababa to this decision. Following Somalia's invasion of the Ogaden, the State Department recommended that the U.S. position on arms transfers to Somalia be fully explained to

Chairman Mengistu in order to keep open the lines of communication.[79] Mengistu was informed that the United States would refuse to supply even defensive military equipment. Neither would it permit its allies and friends to provide U.S.-made weapons to Somalia until the Ogaden affair was resolved. The State Department believed that this contact with Mengistu might prove fruitful in the short term as well as the long run. There was some evidence that the Ethiopians were unhappy with the Soviets, particularly for continuing to supply arms and technical assistance to Somalia.[80] As a sign of possible reconciliation, the Ethiopian government had ordered the media to stop attacking "American imperialism" and calling the United States the primary enemy.[81] While Mengistu's overtures may have simply been a ploy to acquire greater leverage with the Soviets, the Carter administration felt the situation was worth exploring.[82]

During September 1977, discussions took place between U.S. and Ethiopian officials on a variety of issues ranging from economic relations to military issues, although it was the latter subject in which Addis Ababa was now most interested, as Somali forces continued to advance in the Ogaden.[83] While the State Department claimed in mid-September that there were no plans to resume arms shipments to Ethiopia, a series of meetings had been held earlier that month between high-ranking Ethiopian officials and two U.S. envoys—Paul Henze, a staff member of the NSC, and Richard Post, director for East African affairs at the State Department—concerning the arms question.[84] Mengistu hoped to obtain $40 million worth of U.S. weapons that were on order or in the pipeline when Washington halted deliveries the previous June; these included eight F-5E fighters, fourteen M-60 tanks, forty-five trucks, fifty armored personnel carriers, three swift patrol boats and armament for four others, and antitank missiles.[85] Ethiopia was particularly interested in acquiring the F-5Es (or at least spare parts for them), which had performed well against Somalia's Soviet-made MiG-21s.[86] Because Ethiopia owed the United States $30 million for arms bought on credit, that still left a balance of $10 million they wished to claim.[87]

In pursuing these discussions with Ethiopia, the Carter administration hoped that Addis Ababa would in return strike a more balanced policy between the United States and the Soviet Union.[88] However, while the request was still under review, the Soviet Union began making large-scale arms deliveries, and Cuban troops started to arrive in Ethiopia. With Ethiopia even more firmly in the Soviet fold and given the lingering human rights question, the United States embargoed arms to both sides. The Carter administration now moved to tighten its embargo of arms exports and stop the "trickle of military equipment"—mostly spare parts—going to Ethiopia from the United States.[89] Although Washington permitted the delivery of twenty-three trucks and tractors and $400,000 worth of "nonlethal spare parts," in February 1978 the administration blocked the shipment of two patrol boats and $5 million worth of other military equipment, including jet engines and artillery parts, cleared for delivery in June 1977.[90] The State Department also suspended export licenses for thousands of military items in U.S. warehouses bought by Ethiopia the previous year "to avoid fueling the flames" of war.[91]

However, the embargo was not airtight. Israel reportedly provided cluster bombs, napalm, and spare parts for Ethiopia's F-5 jet fighters and sold Soviet arms presumably captured from Arab forces in 1973.[92] Tel Aviv continued its counterinsurgency training in Eritrea, and Israeli pilots were allegedly flying combat aircraft in Ethiopia.[93] Israel's Prime Minister Menachem Begin had even sent a message, which Jimmy Carter rebuffed, urging the United States to help Ethiopia repel the Somali invasion.[94] While the administration publicly criticized Moscow for fueling the war, little was said about Israel's involvement in the conflict and its illegal circumvention of U.S. arms transfer restrictions. Washington's stance was no doubt affected by domestic political concerns and the belief that as long as Israel continued its support for Ethiopia, the United States might maintain some limited influence with Addis Ababa.

Despite Washington's public stance of neutrality in the conflict, Addis Ababa contended that U.S. policy still had the effect of rewarding the aggressor state. American protestations that the suspension of the aid offer and halt to third-party arms transfers to Somalia were designed to force a Somali withdrawal did not impress Addis Ababa.[95] Washington had done little to control, and seemingly had encouraged, Egypt, Iran, and Saudi Arabia to take advantage of the more liberal policies of other Western states and make third-party arms transfers to Somalia.[96] Reports surfaced that U.S.-made M-48 tanks, originally sold to Iran, had reached Somalia by way of Oman.[97] Washington's refusal to publicly condemn the Somali invasion on the grounds that the Carter administration wished to maintain leverage to persuade Somalia to withdraw seemed a lame excuse.[98] American actions or inaction were cited as evidence by Mengistu as affirming U.S. hostility.

Concerned that Addis Ababa might be on the verge of breaking off diplomatic relations with the United States and was preparing to invade Somalia, in mid-February the administration sent David Aaron, deputy assistant for national security affairs on the NSC, to meet with Mengistu and explain the U.S. position.[99] Mengistu assured Aaron that Ethiopia would not invade Somalia. Carter's envoy convinced Mengistu that the United States was not supplying weapons to Mogadishu; he added that it was doing all it could to discourage third-party arms transfers to Somalia and favored a return to the territorial status quo in the Horn. Consequently, for a short time after Aaron's visit, U.S.-Ethiopia relations took a turn for the better.[100]

The U.S. strategy during the Ogaden crisis was designed to keep the communication lines open to all parties—Western allies, the Soviets, Ethiopians, Somalis, interested Arab states, and even Israel. In implementing the U.S. arms embargo, the Carter administration wished to avoid being accused by either side of playing favorites. It would also play down any cold war or "linkage" aspect of the crisis. The Americans also hoped to placate Egypt's President Anwar Sadat, the shah of Iran, President Nimeiri of Sudan, and Saudi Arabia's King Khalid—who had all expressed similar concern about American passivity in the face of Soviet military successes in the Horn—by winking at third-party transfers of non-U.S.-origin weapons to Somalia.[101] In so doing, and in not pressuring Israel to end its support for Ethiopia, the administration sought to have it both ways by keeping its options open with respect to Ethiopia and Somalia. Meanwhile, as the administration waited to see how the situation in the Horn would unfold, in late 1977 the United States announced a $92 million sale of six C-130 transport planes and a $75 million sale of a squadron of F-5 fighters to Sudan; in early March 1978 it agreed to expedite the delivery of twelve F-5s purchased with U.S. credits to Kenya.[102] Despite Carter's pledge of a year before to decrease foreign military sales, the United States was now using arms transfers to achieve maximum flexibility in the region.

SIAD'S ILLUSIONS

What remains somewhat perplexing is Siad Barre's belief that the United States would supply Somalia with arms, especially after Somali forces invaded Ethiopia. Following Somalia's aggressive intrusion, the Somalis claimed, "[the Americans] let us down badly by misleading us."[103] Assistant Secretary Richard Moose countered that U.S. assurances to provide military aid "were not of such a nature that a prudent man would have mounted an offensive on the basis of them."[104] While U.S. officials denied that the secret White House message delivered to Siad Barre in June 1977 was meant to encourage Mogadishu to mount an offensive, it was admittedly ambiguous enough that the Somalis might have got the impression that if they dropped their territorial claims to parts of northern Kenya and Djibouti, then the United States would not care what they did in the Ogaden.[105] But on what basis did Siad Barre assume that the United States would support Somali aggression in the Ogaden?

Siad Barre may very well have misinterpreted Carter's personal message and misjudged the new administration's commitment to an active policy of containment, assuming that a Somali attack against a Soviet client state would be welcomed in Washington. Certainly the Americans had expressed a willingness to provide arms before the outbreak of hostilities. In early July 1977, Secretary of State Vance had stated that the United States would "consider sympathetically appeals from states which are threatened by a buildup of foreign military equipment and advisers on their borders in the Horn and elsewhere in Africa."[106] While this was not an invitation to invade, Barre may have thought that the United States still would consider Somalia's request for arms under war conditions, since Somali actions could be justified on the basis of global containment, or rollback.

However, the Somali president also seemed to have been struck personally by President Carter's commitment to human rights.[107] In his January 1977 inaugural address, Carter had declared, "Our commitment to human rights must be absolute; . . . the powerful must not persecute the weak, and human dignity must be enhanced."[108] In speech after speech President Carter and administration officials pledged to press the cause of human rights abroad with renewed vigor. Carter viewed human rights not only as a matter of reducing the incidence of summary executions or torture of political prisoners, but as a policy that "involved the promotion of democratic principles such as those expressed in our Bill of Rights, the right to emigrate and reunite families, and protection against discrimination based on race, sex, religion, or ethnic origin."[109] Carter recognized that there would be cases in which oppressed people would be able to obtain their freedom "only by changing their laws or leaders," though the administration did not define what actions it would take in support of revolutionary activities.[110]

Siad Barre may well have deluded himself into believing that Carter's human rights policy spoke to the cause of the Somali peoples.[111] Were not the Somalis of the Ogaden oppressed people? Political boundaries prevented the Somali nomads from moving freely across the Ethiopian-Somali border and separated them from their families. For decades Addis Ababa had implemented laws that either directly or indirectly discriminated against the Somalis, their language, and their religion, making them second-class citizens in Ethiopia. The Somalis believed that their policy to liberate the Ogaden by force was not simply aggression, but support for revolutionary activity to obtain freedom for the Somalis.

Whether or not Siad Barre truly believed that the United States would support Somali military actions in the Ogaden on the basis of Carter's human rights policy, he sought to rationalize Somalia's invasion and acquire U.S. weapons on these grounds. The State Department, which raised no dissenting voice against the president's human rights policy in general, feared that it might be used by Barre to persuade Carter to revoke his August 1977 decision not to provide arms to Somalia.[112] To avoid such an occurrence, especially in the aftermath of the back-channel diplomatic blunder of the previous June, the State Department ensured that all messages between Washington and Mogadishu passed through formal channels.

Thus, when the U.S. ambassador to Somalia, John Loughran, returned to Washington in mid-November and attempted to deliver a personal, emotion-laden message to Jimmy Carter from Siad Barre, the State Department blocked his way.[113] Coming in the wake of the Soviet expulsion from Somalia, the Africa Bureau was concerned that the tone and content of Barre's message might lead the president to make promises he could not keep, or the State Department would not want him to keep. After being in Somalia for almost three years, Ambassador Loughran was somewhat suspect, in State Department eyes, of being too sympathetic to the Somali perspective. Although the situation in Somalia had been difficult for Loughran, given the restrictions placed on U.S. diplomats and the occasional harassment by Somali security forces, the ambassador had developed a mutually respectful relationship with Siad Barre and a deep appreciation of Somali history and culture.[114] For three weeks Loughran tried unsuccessfully to gain a private audience with President Carter. At the end of November, Ambassador Loughran finally returned to Somalia with, in the words of Siad Barre, "no good news."[115]

Siad Barre essentially tried to link Somali aspirations in the Ogaden with the guiding liberal principles of U.S. policy. While Washington was prepared to assume a defensive posture in the Horn based on the containment of Soviet influence, armed rollback premised on human rights was an entirely different matter. However, Barre wanted to believe that the United States would not only welcome Somalia's defection to the Western camp, but also support the achievement of its national objectives in the Ogaden. The Carter administration's containment and human rights themes provided the rationales for Somalia's defection from the Soviet camp and attempted realignment with the West.

THE AFRICA BUREAU'S ETHIOPIA IMPERATIVE

At the beginning of the Carter administration, the primary responsibility for formulating U.S. policy in the Horn was returned to the Africa Bureau. Its reassertion of bureaucratic predominance on African issues was supported by many of Jimmy Carter's top-ranking political appointees, who shared the bureau's general inclination not to view every African crisis in terms of the U.S.-Soviet confrontation.[116] Consequently, the Carter administration moved away from its predecessor's globalist obsession to focus on the regional causes of conflict in the Third World. For Africa, this perspective was summed up by the slogan "African solutions for Africa's problems."[117]

The reemergence of the Africa Bureau as the decision-making center for U.S. policy toward the Horn dealt a serious blow to Siad Barre's efforts to forge a security connection with the United States, owing to the inherently pro-Ethiopia, anti-Somalia biases and assumptions of the State Department's Africanist community. In this line of thinking, Ethiopia was considered the key to the Horn. Even after the Dergue had terminated military relations with the United States, the Africa Bureau continued to premise U.S. policy upon the notion that Ethiopia was the most important country in the region. The best policy path lay in mending old fences with Addis Ababa rather than in constructing new ones with Mogadishu. To keep communication open with the Dergue, and at the same time maintain a common basis with the Ethiopians, the State Department insisted that the United States oppose giving any direct or indirect indication of support for Somali irredentist claims. Although the Carter administration did not expect the United States to regain the position it held in Ethiopia before the revolution, in time Ethiopian nationalism, coupled with Moscow's inability to walk the fine line between Addis Ababa and Mogadishu, would allow the United States to reestablish some measure of influence and presence in Ethiopia.[118]

In striking contrast to the Africa Bureau's favorable view of Ethiopia was the generally negative perception of Somalia. Despite the Dergue's horrible record of human rights abuses and Mengistu's embrace of the Soviet Union, Somalia was seen as the pariah of Africa. The OAU Charter principle calling upon African states to respect the colonial-imposed borders of the continent, in effect, had established the Somalis as the "bad guys" of Africa.[119] A policy mind-set had developed during the early 1960s at the Bureau for East African Affairs that U.S. policy needed to be geared toward deterring Somali aggression in the Ogaden and elsewhere in that corner of Africa.[120] American military assistance to Somalia might be construed by other African nations as U.S. support for territorial dismemberment. The consequence of such a policy would be the collapse of the U.S. position in the Horn, East Africa, and possibly elsewhere in Africa.

Washington's harsh assessment of Somalia was reinforced by the memory that it was Mogadishu that had invited the Soviet Union into the Horn in the early 1960s.[121] Somalia had entered that relationship of its own accord and, for a decade and a half, had served Soviet interests and acted as Moscow's closest friend in sub-Sahara Africa. Now, when Somalia expressed a sudden desire to realign itself with the West, one had to ask what the Somalis were up to. Over the years, Mogadishu had never been able to shake this negative image. In 1975, at the invitation of Somalia a joint congressional-Pentagon-State Department mission visited the newly built Soviet base at Berbera. However, the Americans had come away feeling that the Somalis had not been as forthcoming or open as they should have been; indeed, they had tried to pull the wool over their eyes.[122] Mogadishu's secretly sending its forces into the Ogaden, while at the same time conducting arms negotiations with the United States, only confirmed Washington's initial impression of Somali deceit and reinforced the pro-Ethiopia slant of the Africa Bureau.[123] Rather than winning any converts at the Africa Bureau, this behavior confirmed a perception of Somali cunning. The Somalis simply could not be trusted.

The Africa Bureau's predilection for salvaging relations with Ethiopia and keeping Somalia at arm's length posed the greatest obstacle to the formation of an arms relationship between Washington and Mogadishu. Jimmy Carter had created problems when he decided to circumvent the Africa Bureau in communicating with Siad Barre, by means of Dr. Cahill. At the time, the Africa Bureau showed little interest in pursuing the Somali option, having rejected it once before in 1975 when Saudi Arabia had offered financial inducements to Mogadishu.[124] Somalia's invasion of the Ogaden later that summer gave the Africa Bureau a pretext for closing down Carter's private line to Barre and reestablishing its hands-off policy.

In the latter part of 1977 and into 1978, the Africa Bureau, aided by Secretary of State Vance, defended its hands-off policy from assaults by Zbigniew Brzezinski and some Middle East specialists in the State Department. Throwing the credibility argument back at Brzezinski, State voiced a concern that the more commotion Washington made about Soviet activities in the Horn, the more it would make such activities seem like a Russian success story.[125] Brzezinski's outspokenness on an issue the State Department felt the United States could do little about only damaged U.S. credibility in the region. Moreover, U.S. diplomatic appeals to gain African censure of East bloc activities in the Horn had failed because few African governments were willing to condemn the Soviet-Cuban military role undertaken on behalf of territorial integrity.[126]

Washington's Africa specialists felt that the Ogaden conflict had to be dealt with as a purely local issue in order to minimize American losses in credibility and influence. In pushing for a Somali withdrawal from the Ogaden, the State Department argued that the sooner Ethiopia brought the war to a decisive conclusion and reasserted control over the area, the sooner Washington could get back into the influence game and play a constructive role in the Horn.[127] Supplying arms to Somalia would only gain short-term influence for the United States in a losing situation and result in the burning of diplomatic bridges to Addis Ababa. The long-term political costs not only in Ethiopia, but throughout Africa, of fueling the war in the Ogaden by arming Somalia were simply too great.

The Africa Bureau's influence in this battle was enhanced by the policy consensus that had emerged on Capitol Hill. On February 3, 1978, the House Committee on International Relations published a monograph recommending that the United States, given current conditions, should not provide direct or indirect military assistance to Somalia.[128] Three days later, the House Armed Services Committee issued a report warning of the negative effects of the United States shifting its policy in favor of Somalia.[129] Relations with other African nations, most notably Kenya, would be jeopardized if Washington continued to pursue the Somali option. Thus, no one of influence on Capitol Hill or in the Department of State wished to embrace Somalia's cause.[130]

Despite this general policy agreement between the State Department and Congress, Zbigniew Brzezinski made one final bid in February 1978 to persuade Jimmy Carter to do something more in the way of direct military action in support of Somalia. As the combined Ethiopian-Cuban force began its sweep through the Ogaden toward the Somali border, the administration sent a message and a presidential envoy, David Aaron, warning the Ethiopians not to enter Somalia. The administration also pressured Moscow, through the Soviet ambassador in Washington, to hold the Ethiopians back.[131] Nonetheless, at a February 10 meeting of the Special Coordinating Committee (SCC) and again on February 21 at another meeting of senior foreign policy and national security officials, Brzezinski argued that the United States had to back its verbal message with a tangible show of force.[132] The NSC adviser recommended that the president deploy a U.S. aircraft carrier task force off the coast of the Horn. Such a tangible demonstration of American concern and resolve would ensure that the Somali border would not be transgressed and would enhance U.S. credibility among its skeptical allies.

Brzezinski's demand for a show of force was opposed by Secretary of State Cyrus Vance and Defense Secretary Harold Brown, as well as by the Joint Chiefs of Staff.[133] Vance felt that such an action would draw the United States into a situation where the administration would be forced to put its prestige on the line and to take unnecessary military risks on behalf of a Somali government that had shown itself to be "no great friend of ours."[134] The Somalis had brought this on themselves by invading Ethiopia. Even if the Ethiopians should cross over into Somalia, Vance believed that the United States should refrain from introducing U.S. forces into the area. Secretary Vance reported to the president on February 22 that he felt confident the Ethiopians would show restraint and not cross the border.[135] According to Vance, Addis Ababa had too "many other problems, not the least of which was the growing civil war in Eritrea."[136]

Defense Secretary Brown agreed with Vance that the potential negative consequences of a military show of force outweighed the advantages.[137] Besides, what was the task force supposed to do? There was no clearly defined mission. Moreover, if Somalia were invaded and Siad Barre overthrown, such an eventuality would be viewed as a failure of the U.S. task force to do its job. That failure would impair the credibility of using such a ploy in future crises elsewhere. Unless Washington was prepared to use the task force, its bluff could be called. Brown summarized the dilemma confronting the administration at a February 23 National Security Council meeting: "If we know the situation will come out all right in Somalia . . . then we might deploy the carrier and take credit for success in preventing an invasion. . . . On the other hand, if we do not know [how] the situation will come out, or do not intend to use the aircraft carrier in Somalia, then we should not put it in."[138]

Washington's reluctance to embrace Mogadishu after its defection from the Soviet camp reflected the inherent bureaucratic bias against Somalia in Washington. While Middle Eastern issues constantly intruded and affected U.S. policy in the Horn, U.S.-Somalia relations were also held hostage by the Africa Bureau's Ethiopian imperative. This bias was reinforced by events. The fact that Ethiopia did not invade Somalia was considered a victory for American diplomacy.[139] The lesson to be remembered from this episode was that one could never be too cautious in dealing with the Somalis.

CONCLUSION: UNACCEPTABLE RISKS

The conclusion of a security relationship between the United States and Somalia would be no easy task. Both states had been in league with each other's principal adversary for a number of years and drew assumptions based upon their previous experience. Mogadishu believed that the United States would seize any opportunity to counter the Soviet Union, given the perceived strategic stakes at risk in the Horn. Washington considered Somalia to be the principal cause of the security problems in the region and recognized that Mogadishu merely used outsiders to advance its irredentist interests. Given a different turn of events in Ethiopia, arms discussions between Washington and Mogadishu would not even have taken place.

Siad Barre was playing a losing hand in believing he could draw the United States into a security relationship on his terms, namely, to acquiesce to, if not support, Somalia's seizure of the Ogaden. The dependence of the Somali military offensive on receiving outside superpower support, instead, allowed the United States to dictate the terms of any potential arms relationship between the two sides. By burning his bridges to Moscow, Barre was left with no alternative but to seek American help. The Somali president's great mistake was to believe that on the basis of the U.S. policy of global containment and an ill-defined human rights policy, he could draw the United States into a conflict that fit neither of these criteria. When U.S. aid failed to materialize, Barre was left with no choice but to withdraw from the Ogaden.

Conversely, the United States was dealing from a position of strength in resisting Mogadishu's manipulative maneuvers to acquire U.S. military assistance. Because the conflict in the Ogaden was not viewed as posing a direct threat to vital U.S. interests, Washington was under no pressure to react. In keeping the lines of communication open to Ethiopia and strengthening ties with surrounding states such as Kenya and Sudan, the United States could still retain its influence in the area without running the political risk of maintaining a Somali arms connection. Moreover, except for some members of the NSC and Arab specialists at the State Department, there was minimal support for the Somali option in Washington. Under the circumstances, there were simply too many unacceptable risks associated with entering into an arms arrangement with Somalia.

Through the end of the Ogaden War, the conclusion of a security relationship between Washington and Mogadishu was of greater value to Somalia than to the United States. Washington had little to gain politically or strategically by entering into an arms partnership with Mogadishu at this time. For Somalia, such an arrangement was the key to a long-sought national objective and, for a short time at the end of the Ogaden War, national survival. But for a breakthrough in the U.S.-Somalia diplomatic stalemate to occur, either Somalia would have to alter dramatically its policy toward the Ogaden, or Washington would have to reassess the relative cost-benefit trade-offs stemming from a close political-military association with Mogadishu.

10

The 1980 Arms-for-Base-Access Accord

On March 18, 1978, ten days after Siad Barre had agreed to withdraw the Somali Army from the Ogaden, the U.S. Assistant Secretary of State for African Affairs, Richard Moose, arrived in Mogadishu to explore anew the possibility of the United States providing military assistance to Somalia.[1] Washington now offered to provide "defensive weapons," but only if Mogadishu agreed to (1) honor the existing boundary with Ethiopia, (2) give formal assurances that it would not use force against any other country in the area, and (3) use U.S.-supplied military equipment for defensive purposes, solely within Somali territory.[2] Several late night marathon meetings between Barre and Moose failed to resolve the Ogaden dilemma and break the deadlock on the arms transfer question. Barre refused to provide the kind of assurances the Africa Bureau deemed necessary to give the go-ahead for supplying Mogadishu with defensive weapons.[3] The only tangible reward the U.S. delegation offered Somalia for its break with the Soviet Union at this time was a $7 million economic assistance agreement.[4]

Siad Barre reopened the arms supply question several weeks later, after crushing an April 9 coup attempt. On April 23 the Somali president communicated a weakly worded assurance that U.S. weapons would be used only for internal security or self-defense and not against other countries.[5] But the Africa Bureau lacked confidence in Mogadishu's willingness to play by American rules.[6] State Department officials still did not believe that Somalia had altered the fundamental substance of its policy of aggression toward Ethiopia. In July the implementation of an arms agreement was put on hold once again when it became clear that units of the Somali Army were engaged in operations in the Ogaden in support of the Western Somali Liberation Front (WSLF).[7]

However, this most recent Somali approach provoked increased interest at the White House because of the confluence of a number of domestic and international concerns. Jimmy Carter was coming under intense political pressure at home. Carter had been badly attacked by the conservative right for failing to do something in the Ogaden, and White House advisers now directed the president's attention to opinion polls indicating that he was perceived by the American public as being weak on defense issues.[8] Moreover, Zbigniew Brzezinski had launched a renewed verbal assault against the State Department's regionalist policy posture in frustration over the growing Soviet-Cuban presence in Africa, Washington's losing propaganda battle over the neutron bomb in Europe, a pro-Soviet coup in Afghanistan in April, and the invasion in May of Shaba Province (Zaire) for the second time within a year by Zairian insurgents based in Angola.[9] The Carter administration was also being publicly criticized by Saudi Arabia for not responding more aggressively to Soviet-Cuban intervention in the Horn.[10] Despite State Department and congressional warnings that the Soviet-Cuban rhetoric of the NSC and Riyadh was threatening to distort U.S. policy in Africa, the president felt that under the circumstances the Somali option was still worth exploring.[11]

As a first step in determining Mogadishu's eligibility to receive the proposed $15 million "defensive arms" package, the Carter administration decided to sent a joint State Department-Pentagon survey team to observe the situation on the ground in Somalia. The American mission would be interested not only in assessing Mogadishu's security requirements, but also checking into allegations that Somalia was arming and supporting the WSLF.[12] These reports would have to be disproved before Washington would agree to establish an arms supply relationship. However, Mogadishu put off receiving the U.S. team for several months. Despite the substantial improvement in U.S.-Somalia relations over the previous year, American suspicions about Somalia's real intent were heightened by Mogadishu's foot-dragging on accepting the U.S. survey team and the Somali government's obstruction of the efforts of American diplomats to judge the situation in the Ogaden.[13] Finally on October 20, 1978, Deputy Assistant Secretary of State for Africa William Harrop and Rear Admiral Samuel Packer, commander of U.S. naval forces in the Middle East arrived in Somalia to conduct the political-military review. The Harrop mission returned to Washington at the end of October having found evidence of continuing government support for the Somali insurgents and indications that Somalia itself might intervene directly in the Ogaden.[14] Thus, when Donald Petterson presented his credentials as U.S. ambassador to Siad Barre in November 1978, he reiterated the U.S. position that it would not send Somalia any arms supplies until the Somali government ended its military involvement in the Ogaden.[15]

During 1979, however, several dramatic events occurred in the Middle East that eroded Washington's resistance to taking political risks in Somalia. The abdication of the shah of Iran in January 1979 prompted Zbigniew Brzezinski and Pentagon analysts to press for various alternative military options to replace Washington's fallen guardian of the Persian Gulf: (1) to substitute Pakistan for Iran, (2) to establish a permanent U.S. naval presence in the Indian Ocean, and/or (3) to create a Third World crisis intervention force.[16] As American influence in Iran plummeted, following the fall of the Bakhtiyar government and the return of the Ayatollah Khomeini in February, the Carter administration was transferring $181 million worth of arms to North Yemen in order to neutralize the armed aggression of the Soviet-backed PDRY. At the end of August the Soviet Union conducted a massive military airlift exercise in Ethiopia and South Yemen that purportedly demonstrated Moscow's capability to project its military power into areas situated near the world's major shipping lanes.[17] CIA forecasts that the Soviet Union would become a net importer of oil in the 1980s put an ominous light on Soviet military construction at the islands of Dahlak (Ethiopia) and Perim (PDRY).[18] Then, on November 4 Iranian students seized the U.S. embassy in Teheran and took American diplomats hostage.

Prior to the onset of the hostage crisis in Iran, Soviet activities in the southern Red Sea region were dismissed by regional experts, who claimed, "Nothing has gone on that we know of that changes the balance in the region."[19] While the strategic situation in the Horn of Africa may have remained fundamentally unaltered, U.S. policy in the entire northwest quadrant of the Indian Ocean—northeast Africa, the Arabian Peninsula, the Persian Gulf, and South Asia—now became linked perceptually to the Iranian crisis and the looming Soviet threat. There was a growing willingness within the Carter administration to view Somalia in a broader strategic setting as American policy makers began to plan for the possibility of direct U.S. military intervention in the Persian Gulf.[20] As the hostage crisis entered its second month, and it became obvious that the Nixon Doctrine's twin pillars (Iran and Saudi Arabia) concept for Persian Gulf security could not be resurrected, Somalia began to figure prominently in Washington's short-term political-military response to the deteriorating security situation in the region.

At a December 4 meeting of the National Security Council Jimmy Carter decided to seek access to military facilities in Kenya, Oman, and Somalia. If the president had any doubts about the latest Somalia initiative, they were put to rest at the end of December when the Soviet Union invaded Afghanistan. The risk of encouraging Somali military ventures in the Ogaden by supplying arms was now outweighed by broader strategic considerations. Somalia's cooperation was deemed necessary to implement the Carter Doctrine, announced by the president in his January 23, 1980, State of the Union address: "Any attempt by any outside force to gain control of the Persian Gulf region will be regarded as an assault on the vital interests of the United States of America and such an assault will be repelled by any means necessary, including military force."[21]

Mogadishu, in fact, proved very receptive to the idea of becoming part of U.S. military contingency plans to defend the Persian Gulf. Siad Barre could exploit the administration's desire to use Somalia as a strategic base site to reopen the arms question with the United States and play on Washington's perceived strategic vulnerability to acquire a high "rent" in exchange for granting the United States base privileges at Somali military facilities. Although the United States expected that the prospective host countries would link access and U.S. security assistance, the Carter administration was not prepared to grant the "Israeli-type" $1 billion five-year arms package for advanced military equipment that Mogadishu presented in the early spring of 1980. This package reportedly included a request for long-range missiles and sophisticated air defense weapons.[22] The executive branch was only planning to request $100 million for all three countries for the first year, of which Somalia would receive about 30 percent—less than one-fifth of what Mogadishu expected to receive.[23] Even more disturbing to the Americans, especially the Africa Bureau, was Siad Barre's bid to acquire an accord whereby the United States would recognize Somali claims to the Ogaden and perhaps even provide military support for the liberation of the territory.[24]

Arms negotiations between the United States and Somalia would drag on for more than six months and would be conducted in an atmosphere reminiscent of a Middle Eastern bazaar.[25] Washington had seen a "rug" (that is, Berbera) that it wished to purchase. Mogadishu had set an unreasonably high price for its goods. Now the game would be to see how much the American buyer could bargain down the Somali merchant. Given the circumstances, the American buyer appeared desperate enough to overlook certain commercial improprieties (such as Somali transgressions in the Ogaden) on the part of Somalia. But in this bargaining game Mogadishu was dealing with a customer who could acquire from other merchants (Oman and Kenya) far superior (Masirah Island) and less fragile (Mombasa) goods.[26]

After several months of difficult negotiations, which Washington at one point broke off, the Carter administration presented Mogadishu in mid-July with a five-point, take-it-or-leave-it ultimatum: (1) in exchange for access to the joint port-airfield facilities at Berbera and Mogadishu, the United States would provide $40 million in security assistance over a two-year period; (2) Washington would not recognize Somali claims to the

Ogaden; (3) Mogadishu would agree in writing not to use U.S.-supplied weapons inside Ethiopia; (4) Siad Barre would have to provide firm verbal assurances that the Somali Army would not go back into the Ogaden; and (5) American arms transfers would remain "defensive" in nature.[27] Despite claims that the U.S. policy on the Ogaden did not change even after the Carter administration began seeking access to Somali military facilities, the American position in fact had been softened by events.[28] The American ultimatum, apparently by design, left a political loophole for Siad Barre by no longer requiring Somalia to renounce its claim on the Ogaden, or to desist from supporting indirectly Somali insurgent activities inside Ethiopia.

Mogadishu, on the other hand, realized the futility in pressing for anything more than was contained in this latest American arms offer. In June, the United States had concluded base-access agreements with Oman and Kenya, and questions were being raised in Washington about whether Somali facilities were now really all that vital. It was clear that Somalia was not going to receive a larger arms package than either Oman or Kenya, which were granted $100 million and $60 million, respectively, in security assistance for a two-year period. On August 22, 1980, the United States and Somalia signed a ten-year base rights access–security assistance agreement, which contained the following provisions: (1) the United States was granted discretionary use rights with respect to the facilities, and Washington was required to consult with Mogadishu on major exercises and deployments, (2) Somalia retained sovereign rights over all facilities and ownership of all real property, (3) the United States would pay for all services rendered by the host government, plus a proportionate share of maintenance, and 4) the United States was to be allowed to upgrade the facilities at its own expense.[29]

SOMALIA'S EXTENDED DETERRENT REQUIREMENTS

Somalia's decision to disengage from the Ogaden in March 1978 had put to an end the declared state of war with Ethiopia. However, Somali insurgent activities continued in the Ogaden. A year after the Ogaden War had ended, an estimated 10,000–30,000 Somali insurgents were involved in harassment operations against Ethiopian forces.[30] Mogadishu continued to support these activities with medical supplies, food, clothing, and arms. Moreover, Somali refugee camps were thought to provide safe havens and training grounds for the guerrillas.[31]

But Somalia's continuing support for the insurgents had exposed the country to Ethiopian retaliation. Although Addis Ababa refrained from sending its army en masse across the border, Ethiopia's air force conducted periodic bombing raids inside Somalia. Despite Addis Ababa's relative restraint, Siad Barre had warned the Somali Congress in late January 1979 that the possibility of an Ethiopian invasion was very real because of Mogadishu's support for the WSLF.[32] With Washington's attention in Africa now diverted to the issue of bringing about black-majority rule in Rhodesia (Zimbabwe)—a transition that would represent a great victory for the administration's regionalists—it seemed unlikely that the United States would flex its diplomatic or military muscle to prevent the Ethiopians from marching into Somalia in the future.

The fear of an Ethiopian attack weighed heavily in Somalia's security calculation, given the balance of military forces in the region at the end of the 1977–1978 Ogaden War. Although the war in the Ogaden had exposed the vulnerability of an Ethiopian state confronted by simultaneous threats in Eritrea and the Ogaden, Soviet assistance had allowed Ethiopia to close this window of vulnerability. Consequently, Addis Ababa had quadrupled the size of its armed forces from 65,000 to 250,000 soldiers between 1976 and 1980.[33] During this same period an estimated $2 billion worth of Soviet arms were imported by Ethiopia.[34] By the time the war was over, Addis Ababa possessed one of the largest and best-equipped military forces in sub-Sahara Africa. Although the Ethiopian military buildup was not undertaken with the intent of invading neighboring states, the "offensive-type" weaponry (that is, tanks and jet fighters/bombers) that rolled through the Ogaden could easily move into Somalia.

Mogadishu also increased its military capabilities during the last half of the 1970s. But the Somali military buildup merely placed Somalia at the level Ethiopia had started from prior to the outbreak of hostilities in the Ogaden. In 1980 the Somali armed forces totaled 54,000 soldiers.[35] Between 1976 and 1980 Mogadishu imported $750 million worth of arms.[36] Based on a comparison of the size of the two armies and their arms imports, it seemed clear that Somalia had lost the arms race in the Horn.

Mogadishu hoped that it might eventually exploit two tactical advantages: (1) the division of the Ethiopian Army between Eritrea and the Ogaden, and (2) an intimate knowledge of the battle terrain in the Ogaden. However, the Ethiopian arms buildup had more than compensated for these weaknesses, at least in the short term. There was little doubt that Ethiopia could defeat Somalia in a conventional war. An unsuccessful large-scale probing action undertaken by the Somali Army in the Ogaden at the end of 1979, and which continued through the end of 1980, showed unmistakably that the balance of forces in the area still favored Addis Ababa.

Mogadishu's most viable option would be to wage a low-level, protracted guerrilla war against Ethiopia. Members of the Somali regular army could infiltrate across the border and fight alongside the guerrilla forces. Somalia would act as the safe haven and transit point for arms. Although Addis Ababa could sustain a war of attrition against Somalia, Mogadishu might hope that the Ethiopian state would collapse under the weight of its internal stresses and/or the Ethiopian military would suffer a loss of morale and quit the Ogaden.

However, Mogadishu confronted a potentially dangerous security dilemma in adopting this tactic. Addis Ababa would not likely remain passive in the face of persistent Somali attacks. How far could the Somalis push the Ethiopians without inviting more damaging retaliation? Would the Ethiopians simply be content to slug it out in the Ogaden, or might Addis Ababa decide to take the war into Somalia? Mogadishu could not expect to remain immune forever from an Ethiopian counterattack, especially as Somalia had initiated a "hidden" second war in the Ogaden less than two years after the previous conflict had ended. Of greater uncertainly was whether Moscow might elect to play a different game than the Americans had in Ethiopia and allow the Ethiopian military to invade Somalia.

Given the Ethiopian threat of retaliation, an American security connection would be almost prerequisite to allowing Somalia to continue the struggle in the Ogaden, even by indirect means. The conclusion of a security arrangement between the United States and Somalia would, in the words of one WSLF leader, "make Somalia more secure psychologically" and "enable us to get more aid from Mogadishu."[37] Despite Washington's refusal to arm Somalia during the 1977–1978 Ogaden conflict, the Americans had proven their value in warning Addis Ababa not to invade Somalia, and by using their leverage vis-à-vis the Soviet Union to ensure that Ethiopian-Cuban forces stayed out. An explicit and visible military relationship with the United States would presumably carry with it a tacit U.S. security guarantee and, thereby, ensure American intervention in any future crisis.[38] To obtain that security linkage, however, Mogadishu would have to be prepared to settle for much less than the Israeli-style arms package desired by Siad Barre. But by getting their foot in the door, the Somalis could hope that the U.S. military aid floodgates would open up in the future.[39]

IMMEDIATE DETERRENCE AND THE SOUTHWEST ASIA STRATEGY

The Carter Doctrine represented a continuation and expansion of the post–World War II policy of containment. By explicitly committing the United States to the task of deterring Soviet aggression in the Persian

Gulf, the Carter administration had drawn a line in the sand and dared the Soviet Union to step over it. In this instance, Washington's short-term response to the hostage crisis in Iran and the Soviet invasion of Afghanistan involved increasing U.S. naval deployments in the Indian Ocean and accelerating plans to create a Rapid Deployment Force (RDF).[40] However, these high-profile and provocative initiatives would require the United States to seek the cooperation of regional governments in order to create a strategic military base infrastructure that could support and sustain U.S. military force deployments in the area.

Until the overthrow of the shah of Iran in January 1979, the policy consensus in Washington was that the U.S. strategic posture in the northwestern sector of the Indian Ocean was quite adequate.[41] Although in early 1978 Zbigniew Brzezinski and some Pentagon analysts were considering the possibility of enhancing the U.S. military posture in the region, the United States continued to rely upon the Nixon Doctrine's twin-pillar concept for the region founded upon support for the Pahlavi government in Teheran and the Saudi Arabian monarchy. Consequently, the permanent U.S. naval presence in the area was limited to the three warships assigned to the Middle East Force (MIDEASTFOR) based at Bahrain. As for a U.S. base structure, American planners relied primarily upon Diego Garcia, where significant military construction projects had been funded since the mid-1970s.[42] In exceptional circumstances and given proper notification and authorization, military facilities in Israel, Saudi Arabia, Iran, Oman, and Turkey could also be made available to U.S. forces.[43] But, except for the Soviet-Cuban intervention in the Horn of Africa, the political-military environment in the Indian Ocean arena remained relatively stable through the end of 1978. There seemed to be little reason for the United States to assume anything more than a low-profile military posture.

However, following the abdication of the shah, and as the political situation in Iran became more uncertain, a renewed and vigorous debate concerning U.S. strategic policy in the Indian Ocean region divided the American policy-making community. There were five main objectives framing U.S. policy at this time: (1) protecting Western economic interests in the Persian Gulf, (2) employing or threatening to use force in support of U.S. diplomatic objectives in the Middle East, (3) securing the Indian Ocean air and sea routes against harassment or interdiction, (4) intervening in support of other objectives in the Indian Ocean littoral, and (5) balancing Soviet forces in the region and attaining superiority in a crisis.[44] On Capitol Hill the negative strategic ramifications of recent events tended to be played down.[45] Congressional defense and foreign policy analysts felt that American trade interests in the Indian Ocean basin, which were quite extensive, as well as U.S. political-military objectives could be secured by arms transfers and diplomacy rather than by an increased or more highly visible U.S. military presence in the area.[46] Even with the collapse in February 1978 of the Indian Ocean demilitarization talks between Washington and Moscow—which sought to place restraints on superpower naval bases in the area—because of the developments in the Horn of Africa, and even given the unstable situation in the Persian Gulf, the U.S. military posture was deemed adequate.[47]

Despite far-reaching U.S. objectives in the Indian Ocean, congressional analysts saw little need to establish American bases in Africa. The strategic significance of the Horn of Africa for facilitating these goals was diminished by the limited military and economic value ascribed by congressional defense analysts to the Suez Canal–Red Sea trade route. Because the Suez Canal and the Bab al-Mandab could be sealed off quite easily in a crisis—and Israeli and Western trade had not been seriously impaired when the canal was closed between June 1967 and June 1975—little strategic advantage would accrue to a power in wartime that was encamped along this sea lane.[48] This assessment led to the conclusion that maintaining a military base in the Horn of Africa would have a marginal effect upon broader U.S. military objectives.

However, within other policy–making circles, the United States was seen to be in need of a new security framework for the region in order to reassert U.S. power and influence.[49] The fall of the shah of Iran had demonstrated the risk of relying upon a regional power to protect U.S. interests.[50] Officials on the National Security Council and at the Pentagon expounded the view that the United States must adopt a higher military profile and prepare to go it alone. While Pentagon analysts argued that Washington should increase the U.S. naval presence in the area, Zbigniew Brzezinski renewed his call for the creation of a "quick-strike" force to be used for emergency situations in the Third World.[51]

The situation in Iran also heightened Washington's sensitivity to political constraints that might restrict the use of "friendly" bases in the area, previously taken for granted by American defense planners. Iran, itself, was now off limits. Riyadh's fear of becoming linked too closely with the United States, along with the Saudi kingdom's susceptibility to Arab pressures, meant that Washington could not depend upon access to Saudi Arabia's military facilities in a crisis not directly involving the Saudis.[52] Political constraints would rule out using Israel as a staging area to intervene on behalf of a friendly Arab government. Diego Garcia was too far away to serve as anything but a rear staging area for military intervention in the Persian Gulf; sea-lift operations would require five to six days to travel the 2,500 miles to the Strait of Hormuz.[53] Mombasa in Kenya was fine for conducting sea-control operations along the East African coast, but like Diego Garcia, it was too distant—2,500 miles from the Strait of Hormuz—to support forward military operations in the Persian Gulf area.[54] Although Washington had occasionally used the Masirah Island airfield in Oman, no formal arrangement existed with Sultan Qaboos, and the facilities were badly in need of repair and upgrading.[55] Bahrain, alone, would not be able to support a larger U.S. naval presence. The United States might be prevented from using bases in eastern Turkey in certain contingencies, given the risk to Turkey posed by the Soviet Union, Turkish doubts about U.S. reliability as an ally, and a desire by the Turkish government not to jeopardize its growing economic ties and good diplomatic relations with governments in the Middle East.[56]

Thus, at the end of 1979 American defense planners essentially found the Indian Ocean area devoid of a strategic infrastructure to support U.S. military operations or intervention in the Persian Gulf. These activities could prove extremely difficult to execute if the United States was forced to rely exclusively upon Diego Garcia.[57] Moreover, this single operative base would be the primary target for a focused knockout strike which, if successful, would cripple U.S. military support capabilities. Robert Komer, undersecretary for policy in the Department of Defense, described Washington's predicament in the Indian Ocean as follows:

> In order to support forward deployed forces better and introduce the RDF faster, it is imperative that facilities in the region be made available for U.S. use. Logistic support is critical to the success of military operations. Unfortunately, in the Indian Ocean, the U.S. lacks the logistic facilities to support operations especially during crisis. Access to regional air and port facilities, storage facilities . . . and assured host nation support help to overcome this shortfall.[58]

The Carter administration's newly proposed high-profile policy would depend upon the cooperation of states located close to potential trouble spots. Washington was attempting to make up for years of neglect in having focused its attention on building up military forces and base structures in the Atlantic region and Pacific basin.[59] Constructing a strategic network from scratch would take time. The Carter administration did not feel it had this luxury, given the belief that the United States needed to be able to respond to immediate threats to U.S. interests in the region. In order to deter a Soviet move into Iran, seen as the most likely threat at the time, the United States decided to assume a high profile in the area by increasing the U.S. naval presence and creating the RDF.[60] To support the creation of this immediate deterrent capability, the United States would need to acquire access to existing military facilities.

Thus, Washington's determination to acquire the capability to conduct a forward defense strategy in the Indian Ocean region led the Americans to Somalia. Any doubts raised regarding Somalia's strategic value were overwhelmed by the administration's short-term political and strategic requirements to respond to the events in Iran and Afghanistan. Access to Somali military facilities, especially the much heralded Soviet-built base at Berbera, offered the administration part of a quick-fix solution.[61] By concluding base-access arrangements with regional states, the United States would be able in a short time to fill the void that it had discovered in the U.S. Indian Ocean strategic infrastructure. Washington's perception of an immediate Soviet geopolitical challenge to U.S. interests in Southwest Asia had the effect of raising, at least temporarily, Somalia's strategic value.

MOGADISHU'S ALTERNATIVE ARMS CONNECTIONS

The U.S.-Somalia arms-for-access accord was notable for what was not written into the agreement. On at least three occasions arms discussions between the United States and Somalia had broken down as a result of Washington's insistence on linking U.S. military assistance with securing a promise from Mogadishu to renounce its claim on the Ogaden. Without any direct threat to vital U.S. interests, the United States had no reason to show any flexibility on this issue. However, under the new circumstances, the Americans not only stopped pressing Mogadishu to renounce its irredentist claims, but also now seemed willing to close their eyes to certain Somali indiscretions in the Ogaden. There appeared to be a tacit understanding that so long as Somalia did not intervene directly or provide U.S.-supplied weapons to the WSLF, Mogadishu was free to supply the WSLF with weapons acquired from non-U.S. sources.

While Mogadishu certainly would have welcomed U.S. military support at the level being provided by the Soviet Union to Ethiopia, the primary value of the American security connection was the extended deterrent protection offered from Ethiopian retaliation, not the ability to acquire an offensive capability. Somalia could continue to harass Ethiopia and supply arms to the WSLF even in the absence of a major U.S. military commitment. Somalia was able to lessen the impact of accepting the U.S. security assistance package, which amounted to only a small fraction of what the Somalis originally had demanded, by using its Arab connections to acquire secondhand equipment and to finance arms purchases from European suppliers. Following the termination of the Soviet arms connection at the end of 1977, Somalia had replenished its arsenal without any U.S. assistance. Saudi largesse played a major role in this effort. When the Saudis had first offered Somalia $300 million worth of annual assistance back in 1977, the only condition Riyadh had imposed was that the Somalis kick out the Russians.[62] As long as Somalia stayed out of the Soviet orbit and the radical camp, Saudi Arabia would subsidize the Somali economy and military.[63]

Somalia's security equation was altered during the 1977–1978 Ogaden War by circumstances that forced Mogadishu to adopt a new policy of arms diversification. Mogadishu's break with Moscow in 1977 had ended a ten-year period in which Somalia had developed an exclusive supplier-recipient arms relationship with Moscow. During that time, Mogadishu had acquired more than 95 percent of its arms from the Soviet Union.[64] With financial assistance provided by Saudi Arabia between 1976 and 1980, Somalia began to diversify its sources of supply; it purchased for cash some $600 million worth of arms from nonsuperpower arms suppliers.[65] Italy, in particular, played an extremely important role in this capacity. As far as can be determined, none of Somalia's other suppliers attached any political strings regarding the Ogaden to these arms transactions. Thus, Somalia was in a position to agree to U.S. arms restrictions and still pursue its core interests in the Ogaden.

By pursuing a policy of arms diversification, Somalia had fostered a situation in which certain components of Somalia's policy would be beyond U.S. control. Washington could exert control only by imposing the condition that Somalia not acquire weapons from other sources. In March 1978, the U.S. Congress had suggested that the United States discourage third parties from providing Somalia with other than defensive arms.[66] However, such a policy was bound to fail, given the circumstances of the time. A number of Washington's Arab and West European allies who held a political, military, and economic stake in supplying arms to Mogadishu would oppose the congressional restriction. Somalia would reject the former condition. If the Americans desired access to Somali military facilities, there were some things they would have to live with.

REGIONAL OPTIONS AND A DIVIDED ADMINISTRATION

The Soviet invasion of Afghanistan was a landmark event for the Carter administration. An administration that had set out to create a global community based upon common interests and world justice now sought to establish global stability in an increasingly turbulent international system.[67] In the Horn of Africa, U.S. officials who had previously opposed sending any military equipment to Somalia unless Mogadishu renounced its claim on the Ogaden became resigned to the idea of an arms relationship with Somalia.[68] Washington's global objective of countering the Soviet Union now outweighed U.S. regional objectives in Africa. In order to correct a situation in which U.S. strategic vulnerability had been exposed, the United States needed Somalia. This willingness to take the risk of possibly alienating Ethiopia by embracing Somalia was symptomatic of the Carter administration's "revival of the old U.S. policy of containment with an emphasis on a global political-military response to the Soviet threat in Southwest Asia."[69]

Washington's decision to reopen arms negotiations with Somalia in 1980 was based on a logical assumption: "Once a decision is made that you need greater access for ship and aircraft in that part of the world, Somalia becomes a logical candidate [because] if you look at the map you find that you don't have a lot of choices as to where to go."[70] Advocates of the U.S.-Somalia arms-for-access agreement justified the political risks that Washington would run in taking on Mogadishu as an arms client by highlighting the strategic flexibility offered to U.S. forces by Somali military facilities in the event of a military emergency. Berbera's location—1,350 miles from the Strait of Hormuz—would save two to three days in sea-lift time over Diego Garcia and Mombasa.[71] It would also put American B-52s, which could use Berbera's 15,000-foot concrete runway, within striking range of almost any trouble spot in the region.[72] Moreover, Somalia could act as a rear-staging area in a Suez Canal, Persian Gulf, or Arabian Peninsula military contingency, and as a forward-staging area for crises in and around the Bab al-Mandab.

In more peaceful times, Berbera would be of value in supporting air reconnaissance of the southern Red Sea and Gulf of Aden.[73] Facilities at Mogadishu could facilitate sea-control and reconnaissance operations along the East African coastline.[74] Somalia would fill the gap between Kenya and Oman, and between Kenya and Egypt, making it easier for the U.S. Navy to defend sea lanes.[75] Although some of Berbera's envisioned functions were redundant, given the shifting political winds in the region, anything that increased military flexibility was welcomed by the Pentagon.[76]

The belief that Somalia was a necessary and vital part of any U.S. strategic base network was unfounded, given the security relationships Washington had nurtured over the past several years in the vicinity of the Red Sea. American military relations with Kenya and Sudan, in particular, had enabled the United States to maintain a hands-off approach toward Somalia since the termination of the U.S.-Ethiopia security relationship in the spring of 1977. The attractiveness of Mombasa for the U.S. Navy and the absence of perceived political liabilities in helping a stable, pro-Western state almost surrounded by neighbors heavily armed by the Soviet Union formed the political-military backdrop for American security assistance to Kenya. This assistance totaled just under $90 million between FY 1975 and FY 1979, along with the transfer of an additional $118 million worth of U.S. military equipment through the FMS cash sales program.[77] Moreover, some nine months before the base access idea had even surfaced in Washington, the State Department had proposed a $26 million FY 1980 SAP for Kenya, which represented more than half the total amount ($45.4 million) requested for all of sub-Sahara Africa.[78]

In the Red Sea, Sudan offered the United States another alternative site from which to counter Soviet influence in Ethiopia. Khartoum had established its credentials in Washington by aligning with Saudi Arabia's anticommunist-antiradical front in the Red Sea region, maintaining close ties with Egypt, supporting the Camp David peace process, and exerting moderate influence in the Horn. During the last several years of the 1970s Sudan had been rewarded with token U.S. security assistance—$5 million in FMS financing and some $600,000 for an IMETP.[79] Khartoum had also been permitted to purchase more than $320 million worth of arms from the United States between 1977 and 1979, through FMS cash sales financed by Saudi Arabia.[80] During FY 1980, the Carter administration moved to seal the geopolitical orientation of the Nimeiri government by programming $65.4 million worth of security assistance (IMETP, ESF, and FMS financing) funds for Sudan.[81]

U.S. political influence in northeast Africa and the Red Sea region as a whole was pervasive at the beginning of 1980, even without the inclusion of Somalia. Besides Kenya and Sudan, the United States had cultivated modest ties with Djibouti and the Yemen Arab Republic (YAR) by implementing minimal security assistance programs.[82] In the case of the YAR, ties also involved large-scale FMS cash arms transfers in 1976 ($130 million) and 1979 ($181 million) financed through the courtesy of Riyadh.[83] Egypt, Israel, Saudi Arabia, and Jordan also were aligned to various degrees with the United States on global and regional issues. Thus, Washington could turn in many directions to contain perceived Soviet expansionism.

If American policy makers had continued to see these relationships simply in terms of Red Sea security, the Somali base access option might have been deemed unnecessary and inflammatory. Already U.S. policy gave the appearance of political-military encirclement of Ethiopia.[84] Bringing Somalia into this U.S. network of influence would only increase Ethiopia's dependence upon the Soviet Union, thereby provoking an Ethiopian response that might close the line of communication between Washington and Addis Ababa and require the United States to provide even more security assistance to its regional allies.[85] However, following the Soviet invasion of Afghanistan, the less alarmist regionalist assessment found little favor in Washington outside of the Africa Bureau.

There was little reason at this time for the United States to be sensitive to Ethiopian security concerns. Although Ethiopia continued to receive aid from the European Community and international institutions, and conducted most of its trade with the West, relations were cool with the United States.[86] Addis Ababa opposed the United States on most international issues, and the Ethiopian press and radio denounced the United States as the world's leading imperialist state.[87] Ethiopia was one of the few countries to vote against the 1980 General Assembly resolution calling for the withdrawal of Soviet forces from Afghanistan.[88] In July 1980 the United States invoked the Hickenlooper amendment—requiring the president to suspend foreign aid to any country that nationalizes or expropriates U.S. properties without adequate compensation—and suspended all U.S. aid to Ethiopia except for humanitarian aid.[89] At the end of the month, the Ethiopian government, though not breaking diplomatic relations, asked U.S. Ambassador Frederic Chapin to leave the country.

Given the growing chill in U.S.-Ethiopia relations throughout the first half of 1980, it created a climate for top-ranking administration officials, including the president, to focus upon the broader geopolitical picture in response to the crises in Iran and Afghanistan. When the globalist-Africanist debate resurfaced this time, Zbigniew Brzezinski and his supporters found a more receptive president. Jimmy Carter was in need of a foreign policy success to reverse his own declining political fortunes at home as he headed into the 1980 presidential campaign.[90] As he had done during the 1977–1978 Ogaden crisis, Brzezinski took the lead in challenging State Department policy. Brzezinski's challenge in this instance was facilitated by a number of key personnel changes within the Carter administration that had diluted the ranks of the regionalist advocates. During the first half of 1979, the National Security Adviser eased out the chief of the NSC's Africa policy sector (Henry Richardson, who had espoused the hands-off, regionalist policy favored by the Africa Bureau) and had brought onto his staff a number of individuals who shared his tough-minded approach.[91] In August 1979 Andrew Young, one of the administration's leading proponents of the "African solutions for African problems" policy and a vocal critic of Brzezinski's globalist orientation, was forced to resign as UN ambassador.[92] Thus, by the end of 1979, many top-ranking officials in the Carter administration who had resisted Brzezinski's policy recommendations with regard to the Horn of Africa (including the president) had left or had been converted to his way of thinking.

The Soviet invasion of Afghanistan, in particular, neutralized most opposition to the proposed arms-for-access arrangement with Somalia.[93] Virtually no one outside of the Africa Bureau wanted to examine the pros and cons of a Somali base deal.[94] Instead, the discussion in Washington focused almost exclusively on how to go about getting the designated base agreements.[95] The negotiations with Somalia were turned over to Reginald Bartholemew, director of politico-military affairs at the State Department, who was judged to be attuned to and capable of presenting the big picture to other governments.[96] It was deemed especially important to get Kenya to drop its resistance to the Somali base deal.[97]

The Carter administration certainly was not jumping into Somalia without weighing the consequences. Brzezinski, Robert Komer, and other civilian officials at the Pentagon who favored going into Somalia considered the Ogaden element carefully.[98] They realized it was not a risk-free proposition. But they now assumed that the United States could control the risk that the Somali government would interpret Washington's newfound willingness to provide arms to Somalia as a signal to continue its efforts in the Ogaden.[99] Brzezinski and other proponents of the base deal argued that a U.S. presence in Somalia, along with the improved relations that would follow the implementation of an arms-for-access accord, would give the United States enough influence to contain Somali ambitions in the region.[100] The administration further argued that some sort of political gesture was needed to reward Mogadishu for exhibiting a reasonable attitude toward the Camp David accords and for maintaining close ties with Egypt during this perilous time. In the final judgment of Jimmy Carter and most of his closest advisers, the political risk Washington would run in arming Somalia paled in comparison to the strategic stakes.

MOGADISHU'S OGADEN GAMBLE

During the latter half of 1979, Mogadishu seemed on the verge of making a major concession designed to end its regional isolation and, consequently, to break down American resistance to the idea of furnishing Somalia with arms. In September, Saudi Arabia had brought together Kenya's president, Daniel Moi, and Siad Barre at Taif to discuss Kenyan-Somali differences.[101] At the beginning of the month, the Somali people had approved a new constitution recognizing that "large chunks of neighboring countries [were] not legitimate campaigning grounds for [Somali] insurgents."[102] With apparent reference to Kenya's Northeast Province and the Ogaden, the Somali constitution called for the liberation of "Somali territories [by] peaceful and legal means."[103] Washington's subsequent withdrawal of the renunciation demand, perhaps, was influenced by the hope that Siad Barre would pursue the Somali quest through diplomacy.

However, by the end of the year, these articles of Somalia's new constitution had lost all practical meaning. Unknown to American officials, elements of the Somali Army had reappeared in the Ogaden. The liberation of the Ogaden still ranked at the top of Mogadishu's foreign policy agenda. It had not been sacrificed before and would not be now for the benefit of acquiring American arms and protection. Besides, if the Somali reunification claim were to be renounced, then the U.S. security umbrella would be unnecessary.

In April 1978, Adnan Mohammed, Siad's leading political theorist, publicly discussed the political constraints that shaped Mogadishu's approach to the Ogaden.[104] Telling the Somali Army to stay out of the Ogaden and restricting U.S. arms supplies to defensive weapons was one thing. But to ask the Somalis to renounce forever all claims to other states including the Ogaden was "too much."[105] While it may have been true, as Richard Moose and the Africa Bureau believed, that by 1980 the Somalis were willing to give away their whole country in order to acquire a U.S. base and the benefits that would presumably go with it, the liberation of the Ogaden was not negotiable.[106] Although the Somalis were prepared to quibble over the means of liberation in accepting U.S. preconditions prohibiting intervention by the Somali Army and the introduction of U.S. weapons into the disputed territory, the ultimate objective of liberation was not negotiable with foreign parties. The United States had apparently come to understand this fact of political life, which Siad Barre had also made abundantly clear to Richard Moose during their discussions in March 1978.[107] Thus, when American-Somali arms negotiations reopened in 1980, Mogadishu had already scored a small victory of sorts as a result of Washington's apparent consent to Somalia's indirect or diplomatic liberation of the Ogaden.

Washington might even bend farther with regard to the Ogaden issue, given its heightened sense of strategic vulnerability. Mogadishu, in fact, would gamble that the Somali Army could intervene in the Ogaden and provoke only minimal U.S. reaction. Given the new international situation, the United States might accept this inevitable aspect of Somali policy. At worst, Washington would simply hold up military aid until the Somali Army felt compelled to withdraw. Certainly, the United States would not tolerate the invasion of Somalia by a Soviet client state at this time, even if Mogadishu was the provocateur. With the United States now consumed by the need to respond to any Soviet challenge and in apparent need of Somalia's cooperation, it appeared to be an opportune time for Mogadishu to press its cause in the Ogaden and test the limits of Washington's tolerance and support.

Siad Barre's assessment proved quite accurate with respect to Washington's anticipated reaction. Despite the administration's knowledge that at least two Somali Army brigades were operating in the Ogaden during the summer of 1980, Washington continued to negotiate with Mogadishu. When the arms-for-access accord was signed in August, these Somali units were still engaged in combat operations inside Ethiopia and would remain there for several more months.[108] Washington's obsession with the Soviet factor in regional political-military affairs, in effect, granted Mogadishu greater latitude in pursuing an objective the Americans were led to believe Siad Barre could never renounce.

President Barre's willingness to risk another gamble in the Ogaden was made possible by the proclivity of top-ranking U.S. officials to play down Mogadishu's regional pariah status by placing Somalia into a broader strategic setting. By early 1979 Brzezinski, along with some Pentagon and NSC analysts, had come to view the Horn of Africa as part of an "arc of crisis" bounded by the Horn to the west and the Indian subcontinent to the east, with the Middle East lying at the arc's central core. This geographic entity, which transcended the Department of State's traditional fixed regional lines, was a close approximation of the area Washington would designate "Southwest Asia" at the end of 1979. By blurring regional distinctions, Brzezinski and his allies had established a basis on which to challenge the Africa Bureau's hands-off policy guidelines toward Somalia.

The trick for Siad Barre, as well as for American supporters of the Somali option, was to keep the Carter administration looking at the big picture in the area. This would be the only way to avoid having Somali interests held hostage to the Africa Bureau's "Ethiopia imperative." The arms negotiations could not be viewed as simply a bilateral Horn of Africa matter; if it were, the Africa Bureau could claim preeminence and emphasize U.S. objectives in Africa to the exclusion of Middle Eastern or U.S.-Soviet issues. Rather, the negotiations would have to remain focused upon the role Somalia could play in helping the United States establish a base network in the Southwest Asia region, rather than the political risks posed by the Ogaden issue.

Under the pressure of circumstances, a small but significant crack had developed in Washington's stance toward the liberation of the Ogaden. The United States was now willing to consider the WSLF a separate entity pursuing an independent policy, not simply an extension of the Somali government.[109] Siad Barre had played an important role in forcing (manipulating) the Americans to demonstrate a keener awareness of the political constraints that limited his freedom to maneuver. Since U.S.-Somalia arms discussions began back in 1977, he had stood firm and refused to renounce Somalia's claim to the Ogaden. It was clear that Siad Barre would not formally align Somalia with any foreign power that took away that hope of liberation for the Ogaden Somalis. Washington's insurgency loophole was a necessary political concession that was at least as important, if not more so, than the amount of U.S. military assistance to be provided to Somalia in securing U.S. access to Somali military facilities.

THE AFRICA BUREAU'S HOLDING ACTION

Siad Barre's attempt to force open the crack in the U.S. position and turn it into a crevice ran into a familiar bureaucratic obstacle: the Africa Bureau. The freeze in diplomatic relations between Washington and Addis Ababa had begun to thaw at the end of the Ogaden War. Frederic Chapin, who assumed the post of U.S. ambassador to Ethiopia in July 1978, was given a mandate by the Carter administration to improve U.S.-Ethiopia relations.[110] Chapin recommended a $20 million development assistance program to get the United States back into the influence game in Ethiopia.[111] However, because of some $30 million in U.S. compensation claims for nationalized property which the Ethiopian government showed little interest in settling, the Hickenlooper amendment went into effect and resulted in the termination of U.S. development assistance in July 1979.[112]

Despite the souring of U.S.-Ethiopian relations in 1979, the State Department still wanted to keep the lines of communication open to Addis Ababa and to avoid actions that would make Ethiopia even more dependent upon the Soviet Union.[113] Even after Mengistu established a Marxist-Leninist vanguard party—the Commission for the Organization of the Party of the Workers of Ethiopia (COPWE) in December 1979, supported the Soviet Union's invasion of Afghanistan, and expelled Ambassador Chapin at the end of July 1980, Africanists at the State Department felt that an American military relationship with Somalia, if it had to be, should not come at the total expense of U.S.-Ethiopia relations. But with the window of opportunity in Ethiopia closed for at least the short term, Brzezinski was better positioned to push the Somali arms option once again. Now the Africa Bureau simply hoped to hold the newly drawn line and ensure that Washington's longer-term regional interests were not sacrificed for the sake of short-term global concerns.

Following Somalia's March 1978 withdrawal from the Ogaden, the Department of State went to great lengths defining a policy for the Horn geared toward arms restraint and defensive security requirements. Richard Moose had already drawn the line in private with Siad Barre in Mogadishu. In June 1978 Secretary of State Vance publicly stated that the United States would "consider security requests from African nations with legitimate defense needs," but would not simply respond to Soviet and Cuban activities in Africa.[114] Andrew Young buttressed this regionalist perspective by denigrating Washington's past propensity "to view Africa as if it were Europe, where every mile of territory assumes some strategic significance," and offered the conclusion that so long as Somalia posed a threat to Ethiopia, other African countries with concerns about disputed borders would be grateful for all the help Ethiopia received from the

Soviets and Cubans.[115] Moreover, Ethiopia did not appear stable enough to pose a threat to Western interests in Africa. Before that danger would emerge, in the words of Ambassador Young, "inherent African pride and typical Russian blundering probably will have solved the problem for us."[116] In a statement before the House Subcommittee on Africa in February 1979 Richard Moose reaffirmed the administration's desire not to use security assistance "to match the Soviets rifle-for-rifle, tank-for-tank."[117]

Even in the wake of the crises in Iran and Afghanistan, the Africa Bureau and other Africa specialists in the Washington foreign policy–making community were not ready to concede that Somalia's strategic value merited a reassessment of American policy in the Horn. Within the context of the Southwest Asia strategy Berbera would be a backup facility whose loss would have virtually no strategic impact.[118] Most reconnaissance missions that were expected to be performed from Somali facilities at Berbera and Mogadishu could be accomplished from other sites located in Kenya or Djibouti. Moreover, not much was planned for Somalia in the way of prepositioning military equipment for the RDF.[119] Somalia's strategic utility was marginal at best.

Envisioned military contingencies also raised questions in the minds of the critics about Somalia's value.[120] In the event of an intra-Arab conflict in which Washington provided military assistance to one side, Diego Garcia would provide adequate backing or, if circumstances allowed, facilities in Oman could be used. The Somali government could not be expected to permit its facilities to be used in support of Israel if another Arab-Israeli War erupted. Mogadishu likely would hesitate if Washington wished to take action against an Arab state, such as Iraq, which at the time maintained cordial relations with Somalia, but opposed American policy in the Middle East. If the Soviets invaded Iran or threatened Saudi Arabia, Somalia would not be needed; everything in Europe, Turkey, and probably elsewhere in the northwest quadrant of the Indian Ocean region would be open to the United States. Moreover, with South Yemen lying just across the Gulf of Aden, and the Ethiopian border less than 150 miles away, Berbera was one of the most vulnerable of base sites.

The main argument raised against the Somali component of Washington's new base access approach for Southwest Asia was political in nature: what would happen in the Ogaden? Opponents of the U.S.-Somalia arrangement noted that the Soviets had provided Somalia with hundreds of millions of dollars' worth of weapons, had stationed thousands of advisers in the country, and maintained control of Siad Barre's security apparatus, yet failed to keep Mogadishu out of the Ogaden in 1977.[121] If Somalia were to go after Ethiopia with American weapons, the United States would be faced with two impossible choices. It could commit itself to Somalia and try to control the level of danger or hostilities—a task Moscow had failed to accomplish. Or it could not support Somalia and give rise to the appearance of failing to back an ally—a situation that Washington had found itself caught in three years before in Ethiopia and more recently in the case of the shah of Iran.[122] Why risk U.S. involvement on the side of an aggressor in a war Somalia was bound to lose? Or, why risk credibility and prestige on a nation viewed by the rest of Africa as an outlaw state? Arming Somalia appeared to be nothing but a losing proposition any way one looked at it.

However, these arguments did not prove potent enough to dissuade the White House from seeking out Somalia as an arms partner. The twin crises in Iran and Afghanistan had allowed Zbigniew Brzezinski to outmaneuver the Africa Bureau and win the strategic debate in Washington concerning the need to acquire access to Somali military facilities. Whereas the Africa specialists at the State Department considered the situation in the Horn too complex to attempt a military balancing act and to predict the outcome, top-ranking administration officials were willing to take that chance.

Although Richard Moose and his staff were unable to win the 1979–1980 strategic debate in Washington, they had won and, for the most part, had held the line in the critical policy battle with the NSC adviser in 1978.[123] At the time, the Africa Bureau had persuaded President Carter not to exploit the Ogaden situation or to stir up problems in Eritrea in order to confront the Russians.[124] Washington would encourage Ethiopia to pursue a truly nonaligned foreign policy through affirmative gestures, not confrontation.[125] The administration conceded to Mogadishu the right to support, indirectly, the Somali struggle—a concession the Africa Bureau believed to be a mistake, assuming that "if you gave the Somalis an inch they would take a mile." This assessment proved prophetic in early 1980 when reports began to surface that Somalia's army was back in the Ogaden. The Africa Bureau, nonetheless, prevented the panicked administration from giving Somalia free rein in the Ogaden by ensuring that none of the other preconditions were rescinded.[126]

CONCLUSION: THE RELUCTANT PARTNER

The superpower supplier–arms client realignment in the Horn of Africa finally became complete in August 1980 with the conclusion of the U.S.-Somalia arms-for-access arrangement. However, the switch in the Horn offered contrasting pictures of the formation of a supplier-client partnership. Whereas there existed at least a surface level of compatibility between Addis Ababa's battle to preserve its territorial integrity and Moscow's desire to expand its influence by defending the political status quo in the Horn, the American foreign policy–making community was divided. Many did not believe that such a reinforcing bond existed between Mogadishu's irredentist imperative and U.S. strategic and political objectives in the region. So, while the Soviet Union gladly seized the initiative in Ethiopia, the United States only reluctantly embraced Somalia. The U.S.-Somalia arms relationship ended up being based on a compromise in which the two sides tried to gloss over their differences. Washington would not require Mogadishu to renounce the Somali claim on the Ogaden, and Somalia agreed to modify its means of liberation.

Mogadishu's accession to Washington's July ultimatum had less to do with Somalia's need to acquire American weapons than its growing fear of Ethiopian retaliation. Siad Barre was willing to take measured risks to liberate the Ogaden. But, given the Soviet-sponsored military buildup in Ethiopia, it seemed unlikely, unless events elsewhere distracted Addis Ababa, that the Somalis could defeat the Ethiopians in a conventional war. While the United States had made clear that it would not be a party to any Somali activity seeking to undermine Ethiopia's territorial integrity, Somalia could probe the Ethiopians and support the WSLF guerrilla struggle, by relying upon its other arms sources. What the Somalis needed from the Americans was the psychological and diplomatic backing to ensure that Ethiopia would not invade. While Washington did not overtly manipulate this point of Somali vulnerability, some U.S. officials believed that this political-psychological dependence would give the United States enough leverage to control Somali activities.

The Carter administration's decision to accept Somalia as an arms partner without requiring a formal renunciation of Somali irredentist claims was not the result of a lack of U.S. options, but to Washington's heightened sense of strategic and political vulnerability in the wake of the twin crises in Iran and Afghanistan. Although the political risks and strategic value of going into Somalia was hotly debated in Washington, the voices of those urging caution (namely, the Africa Bureau) were drowned out by other top-ranking U.S. officials who felt that the U.S. response had to be complete. Failure to bring Somalia in the U.S. strategic network would be perceived as a loss. However, the United States was able to resist Somalia's maximalist demands and enhance its bargaining leverage following the conclusion of the base access agreements with Oman and Kenya by hinting that Somalia was now an expendable asset—a supplier version of threatening defection. Moreover, as the sense of threat receded during the year, the Africa Bureau reasserted itself: it refused to condone Barre's military gamble in the Ogaden and resisted his attempt to press Washington to lift one or more of the preconditions.

This would be an uneasy partnership. Washington's principal objective, to be able to deter a Soviet military move into the Persian Gulf, had nothing to do with Mogadishu's ambition to wrest control of the Ogaden from Ethiopia. By entering into the arms relationship with Somalia, the United States was throwing away the ability to exploit any future opportunity in Ethiopia. Somalia, on the other hand, was making a difficult tactical sacrifice even given the loophole in the agreement. But with the Somali Army back in the Ogaden, and given the ground rules for U.S.-Somalia relations established by Washington's preconditions, the arms-for-access arrangement was temporarily in limbo.

11

The 1982 Emergency Arms Airlift

Almost two years would pass from the time the U.S.-Somalia arms-for access accord was signed until the first shipments of American weapons arrived in Somalia. This delay would not have been unusual given the normal lag in U.S. arms transfers between the date orders are placed and their delivery on a nonpriority basis.[1] Sophisticated weapon systems such as the TVS-1 air surveillance radar and Vulcan antiaircraft weapons, which were originally ordered by Mogadishu, required anywhere from eighteen to thirty months for delivery.[2] U.S. officials had estimated that the first major U.S. arms shipments would not arrive in Somalia until 1983 or perhaps even 1984.[3]

However, even if the ordering process were not so cumbersome, the United States was in no hurry to expedite Somalia's arms requests. Within a week after signing the arms-for-access agreement with Mogadishu, U.S. policy makers were having second thoughts about the arrangement. Several days after the conclusion of the U.S.-Somalia deal, Assistant Secretary of State for African Affairs Richard Moose was called to testify on Capitol Hill. In response to allegations that a large segment of the Somali Army was still in Ethiopia as the result of Siad Barre's latest probing action, Moose asserted before the House Subcommittee on Africa that no "significant body of Somali forces [was] in the Ogaden."[4] Although conceding that some Somali patrols continued to operate inside Ethiopia, Moose maintained that the Somalis were leaving the Ogaden and only a small residual force remained. Such a declaration was necessary to clear the way for Washington to begin processing Mogadishu's arms requests. At the time the administration was planning to request that Congress allow the executive branch to reprogram $20 million in FMS credits for Somalia in the FY 1980 SAP budget.

While Richard Moose felt uneasy testifying in favor of a deal he had grave misgivings about, the assistant secretary was placed in an even more awkward position when, following his appearance before the Africa subcommittee, CIA officials revealed in a closed executive session that three Somali regular battalions were still operating in the Ogaden.[5] Mogadishu tried to control the damage by asserting that whatever Somali forces had been in the Ogaden previously had either been completely withdrawn or were being withdrawn.[6] However, seven of the eight members of the House Subcommittee on Africa and fifteen members of the congressional black caucus now mounted a campaign to block implementation of the agreement.[7] While the Africa Bureau would not have been upset if the deal fell through, Pentagon officials lobbied intensely among members of the House Appropriations Subcommittee on Foreign Operations—which had the authority to block the reprogramming of the $20 million in FMS credits—to prevent the reversal of the agreement.[8]

Still, there was too much at stake politically for the administration to forsake the Somali option and admit less than two months before an election that it had made a mistake and wasted eight months negotiating an unfulfillable strategic accord with Somalia. At the Africa Bureau there was a quiet feeling of vindication for its warnings about dealing with the Somalis. Moreover, the responsible subcommittees on Capitol Hill seemed to be attuned to the Africa Bureau's way of thinking. Although reprogramming of SAP funds for Somalia was approved at the end of September, it was done so only on the condition that no U.S. military equipment would be delivered until the executive branch provided "verified assurances" that no Somali regular army forces remained in the Ogaden.[9] The administration was unable to give these "verified assurances" until early January 1981, just before Jimmy Carter was replaced in the White House by Ronald Reagan.

Surprisingly, given the globalist orientation of the newly installed Reagan administration, the United States did not rush into a full embrace of Somalia. Although the new administration viewed Mengistu "with a very cold eye" and rated the prospects for improved U.S.-Ethiopian relations as "very low," it rejected the tough approach favored by some: imposing economic sanctions against Ethiopia, arming Somalia, and providing aid to the Eritrean insurgents.[10] Because of the Africa Bureau's preoccupation with southern Africa, the traditional policy review for the Horn was not undertaken until spring 1982.[11] The new policy finally agreed to in July called for the United States to provide strong support for Sudan, Somalia, and Kenya, but to go slow on arming Somalia, to coordinate U.S. policy with that of Washington's NATO allies, and to establish a dialogue with Ethiopia that would perhaps lead to improved relations.[12] Until late 1983, the U.S. embassy in Addis Ababa was involved in a circuitous diplomatic dance with the Ethiopian Foreign Ministry to arrange talks between high-ranking U.S. and Ethiopian officials, including possibly a meeting between President Reagan and Chairman Mengistu.[13] Despite the best efforts of Ethiopia's foreign minister, Wolde Goshu, the Ethiopian chargé in the United States, Tesfaye Demeke, and U.S. embassy officials, the talks were postponed. However, in December 1985 the U.S. compensation claims were finally settled for $7 million.[14]

Thus the broad outlines of Reagan's policy toward the Horn of Africa seemed to one displaced official of the Carter administration and to Donald Petterson, U.S. ambassador to Somalia from 1978 to 1982, to be similar to those followed during the previous four years.[15] President Reagan's Africa advisers were willing to take a long-term view; they favored maintaining communication with Addis Ababa. Although global and regional strategic concerns remained important, long-term political rather than immediate East-West ideological considerations were to guide U.S. policy toward the Horn. Thus, Washington continued to declare its support for Ethiopia's territorial integrity and to refrain, at least overtly, from stirring up the Somalis in the Ogaden or exploiting the Eritrean insurgency to put pressure on the Marxist-Leninist government in Addis Ababa.[16]

Despite its globalist proclivities, the Reagan administration also kept the same restrictions on supplying weapons to Somalia as established by its predecessor. However, no attempt was made to establish a linkage between the transfer of U.S. arms and Mogadishu's ending its political and indirect military support for the WSLF insurgents in the Ogaden. Administration officials were optimistic that they could monitor and control the situation in the Horn by proceeding with a modest and cautious "defensive" arming of Mogadishu. By avoiding a quick or large-scale influx of U.S. weapons into Somalia, Washington could see how sincere Mogadishu was about keeping its forces out of Ethiopia. U.S. policy toward Somalia, though for different reasons, was reminiscent of Washington's arms transfer policy toward Ethiopia in the 1950s and the first half of the 1960s—a "great stall."[17]

One year after the arms-for-access accord was signed, U.S. military involvement in Somalia was minimal. Military construction had not even begun at Berbera. At the end of 1981, when the United States conducted the "Bright Star '82" military exercises in the region, the Somali component of this practice logistical operation involved mostly U.S. engineering and medical units. In contrast, mechanized U.S. infantry units were flown into Egypt, U.S. Special Forces were sent to Sudan, and 2,000 U.S. marines conducted an amphibious landing in Oman. There was little inclination to include Somali facilities or forces in U.S. contingency plans.

In March 1982, Siad Barre met with Ronald Reagan in Washington—

the first direct meeting between the Somali president and an American president. His visit had little visible effect on U.S. policy. The United States had already agreed to provide Mogadishu with over $45 million in SAP funding and to allow another $45 million in FMS cash sales during FY 1982.[18] That spring the executive branch was planning to propose a security assistance package for FY 1983 worth over $55.5 million, plus a guarantee of $30 million in FMS cash sales.[19] Still, Somalia had nothing tangible on the ground to show in the way of American military support. While the procurement of U.S. weapons was secondary to the extended deterrent protection Mogadishu believed it had acquired through its security connection with Washington, it was difficult to project the impression that the United States was in Somalia's corner when there was almost no U.S. presence in Somalia.

However, Washington's "great stall" came to an abrupt end in July 1982. At the end of June, a mechanized unit of some 9,000 Ethiopian troops had crossed over into Somalia to support an operation by the Ethiopian-based Somali dissident force, the Somali Salvation Democratic Front (SSDF), to seize control of two Somali towns (Galdogob and Balanballe) in an area north of Mogadishu. When the Ethiopian forces first moved into Somali territory the American response was cautious. Washington was unsure of the magnitude of the threat or whether foreign forces were involved in the fighting. It was not until Mogadishu brought the situation to Washington's direct attention in mid-July, as the fighting intensified, that the administration began to react.

On July 24 the State Department announced that the United States was airlifting weapons into Somalia to confront the Ethiopian-supported incursion.[20] It was first reported that the United States had begun sending the sophisticated weapon systems—including air defense radar and Vulcan antiaircraft rockets—ordered under the 1980 accord.[21] But according to administration officials, emergency military aid was limited to rifles, ammunition, and communications gear. Nonetheless, the circumstances had forced the United States to speed up the delivery of previously ordered equipment caught in the pipeline.

The reaction on Capitol Hill to the U.S. arms airlift and continued fighting in Somalia was to pressure the administration to develop a well-formulated policy toward the Horn—one that ideally would link U.S. military assistance to the total suspension of Somalia's support for the WSLF. In an attempt to prompt the executive branch to reexamine U.S. policy, the House Subcommittee on Africa threatened to block future SAP funding for Somalia if the administration did not undertake such a review.[22] Even with this legislative threat hanging over the administration's head, near the end of August the United States reportedly airlifted another $5.5

million in emergency weapons and supplies into Somalia.[23] Although the U.S. arms deliveries helped to stabilize the situation, the SSDF dissidents were able to maintain a position inside Somalia and sporadic fighting between Ethiopian and Somali forces continued into the spring of 1983. Nonetheless, Washington had responded to Mogadishu's plea for arms in a positive, if somewhat restrained, fashion. U.S. arms were now on the ground in Somalia.

SIAD'S CHAD CRISIS

The threat of direct Ethiopian retaliation against Somalia became reality when Addis Ababa sent military forces across the border into Somalia to support the SSDF insurgents. Politically, the situation was embarrassing for Siad Barre; the main rationale behind acquiring the U.S. security connection in the first place had been that it would act as a deterrent against such a contingency. Moreover, if Washington were to stand idly by and not respond to this Ethiopian aggression, the negative political repercussions in Mogadishu might topple Barre's government.[24] A forceful U.S. response was needed to solidify Siad Barre's tenuous political position and prove his astuteness in forging the U.S.-Somalia security connection.

Besides its potential political and military dangers, the Ethiopian-sponsored attack also proved a blessing in disguise for Mogadishu in that it forced the United States to get involved on the ground in Somalia. Siad Barre had been frustrated by the deliberate slowness of the U.S. arms transfer process, in contrast to his experience with the Russians during the previous decade. It was not as if Washington could not respond quickly and effectively in a crisis. The speed with which the United States had wrapped Sudan in its superpower security blanket, by dispatching two U.S. airborne warning and control aircraft (AWACS) to the region along with $100 million in U.S. military assistance to Khartoum during the October 1981 crisis in Chad, was ample evidence of U.S. capabilities. However, Washington's quick, dramatic response to events in Chad was also a source of irritation for the Somali president, who felt that Somalia deserved greater U.S. attention and support than Sudan, which officially was not part of the U.S.-Southwest Asia strategic defense network.[25]

The perplexing question for Siad Barre was not whether the United States *could* respond, but whether it would respond similarly in a crisis involving Somalia. Mogadishu seemed to need a Chad-like crisis involving Soviet-backed or Libyan-backed aggression to push the Americans into action. But Somalia did not want to provoke such a scenario, or even to be suspected of doing so, given the suspicions in the Washington foreign policy community toward Mogadishu. In fact, when in July the United States began its emergency arms airlift in support of Somalia, Congress tended to see Mogadishu's relationship to the WSLF, rather than Addis Ababa's support for the SSDF, as precipitating the crisis. Siad Barre had good reason to be concerned about the intensity of Washington's commitment to Somalia; many U.S. policy makers at the Africa Bureau and members of key congressional subcommittees still preferred the Ethiopia option in the Horn.

Siad Barre could keep Somalia clear of the Ogaden by allowing the WSLF to wage the liberation struggle against Addis Ababa alone. But there were divisions within the Somali state that Ethiopia could exploit. After the Ogaden War, Siad Barre began to rely increasingly upon his extended family clan to rule the country. This policy alienated members of Somalia's northern clans, who felt slighted by the government to the south.[26] Intraclan division would result in the founding of the Somali Salvation Front (SSF) in 1979. Because of its narrow tribal base and links with Ethiopia, the SSF did not seem much of a threat at first. But the anti-Barre base in Somali society widened over the next two years. In October 1981 the SSF joined forces with the Somali Workers' Party (SWP) and the recently formed Somali Democratic Liberation Front (SDLF) to form the Somali Salvation Democratic Front (SSDF).

The military capability of the newly formed SSDF was increased by the external assistance it received from Ethiopia, Libya, and South Yemen (PDRY). For several years before the 1982 crisis in Somalia, Addis Ababa had provided logistical backing and acted as a conduit for Libyan financial aid to the SSF, while the PDRY had provided a base for operations and training for the SWP. With the formation of the Tripartite Pact on August 19, 1981, Ethiopia, Libya, and the PDRY now had a formal mechanism to coordinate their policies and provide financial assistance, arms, military training, and base sites to support the SSDF's destabilization campaign against Mogadishu.

Despite this outside assistance, the SSDF was hindered in its bid for political credibility in Somalia by its dependence on Ethiopia as a staging point for operations—a link used by Mogadishu to discredit the movement. Unlike the WSLF insurgents operating inside Ethiopia, the various components of the anti-Barre forces had been unable to establish an enclave within Somalia from which to conduct their activities. Addis Ababa, also, was walking a fine line in supporting these activities, as the Reagan administration might decide on a more confrontational approach toward Ethiopia. Still, in supporting the SSDF invasion of Somalia, Addis Ababa would place Mogadishu on the defensive, and consequently the

Somalis would have fewer resources and less time to support the WSLF. It would also punish Mogadishu for its long-running collusion with the WSLF.

Ethiopia's military incursion into Somalia in summer 1982 placed Somalia on the defensive for the first time in their two decades-long struggle. However, Mogadishu needed to win the public relations campaign and convince Washington that this time it was the victim, not the aggressor. Unfortunately, the United States had been more interested in monitoring the situation in the Ogaden than helping Siad Barre deal with his foreign or domestic opponents. To get a response like that seen in Chad, Barre needed to incite globalist opinion in Washington.

THE STRATEGIC CONSENSUS

The Reagan administration's decision to airlift arms into Somalia was based on a belief that there was a radical plot to destabilize pro-Western governments in northeast Africa. When coupled with the actions of Libya's Colonel Qaddafi in Chad and against Sudan, Ethiopia's intrusion into Somalia appeared to be part of a stepping-stone pattern of Soviet-backed expansionism.[27] If this destabilization campaign was not blunted, it might spread throughout the region and ultimately threaten Western interests in north, west, and central Africa.[28] Thus, U.S. policy was being driven by a globalist preoccupation with avoiding a domino effect in northeast Africa.

The Reagan administration assumed power in January 1981 believing it could deal effectively with Soviet threats in the Third World. The Reagan approach was premised on the assumption that "Soviet diplomacy [was] based on tests of will"—tests that since the Vietnam War the United States had largely failed.[29] Moscow was engaged in probing actions to detect and exploit Western vulnerabilities: Angola, Ethiopia, and more recently El Salvador were prime examples.[30] In these situations the Soviet Union's advantage stemmed from its capability and willingness to provide arms quickly and in large amounts to its Third World clients, while the United States was often late and hesitant.[31]

Thus, arms transfers and threats would be crucial to Reagan administration foreign policy. In the mind of Secretary of State Alexander Haig, conflict was not the result of arms, "but more often of an imbalance of arms."[32] Providing arms to threatened smaller friends would send an important signal that the United States was prepared to defend its interests. This signal took on particular importance, as the Soviet Union was seen to be in an expansionist period.[33] To make its intentions clear, immediately after taking office the Reagan administration informed the Soviets "that their time of unresisted adventuring in the Third World was over" and that the United States would not tolerate the mischief of Moscow's proxies, Cuba and Libya.[34] The administration undertook three actions to get this message across: (1) U.S. tanks and aircraft deliveries to Morocco, suspended by the Carter administration in 1980, were resumed to counter Soviet aid to the Polisario insurgents in the Western Sahara; (2) Colonel Qaddafi was warned that the United States would oppose his campaign to destabilize the region; and (3) U.S. aid to Nicaragua was suspended owing to evidence of Soviet, Cuban, and Nicaraguan involvement in subverting the government of El Salvador.[35]

The Reagan administration's thinking with regard to the Horn of Africa was influenced by Egypt's President Anwar Sadat's "two crescents policy."[36] One crescent ran through Iraq, Syria, the Yemens, Somalia, and Ethiopia. The other was in southern Africa. Moscow's alleged strategy was to cut Africa in half, thereby isolating moderate Arab regimes, which would be caught in a vise between radical states under Soviet influence. Muammar Qaddafi and the Palestine Liberation Organization (PLO), acting as Soviet clients, would destabilize the region through terror, thus allowing the Soviet Union either to manipulate the Islamic fundamentalist movement or seize control of Iran or the entire Persian Gulf.[37] Proceeding on the belief that the Soviet Union and its radical proxies posed the primary threat to the moderate Arab states (Egypt, Saudi Arabia, Jordan, Sudan, and the Gulf sheikdoms) and Israel, as well as to the United States, Secretary Haig proposed the creation of a "strategic consensus" in the spring of 1981.[38] The idea was essentially shelved, however, following the assassination of Anwar Sadat on October 6, 1981.

In the Horn of Africa and throughout northeast Africa, Libyan adventurism was seen as presenting the greatest security threat. The Reagan administration believed that Muammar Qaddafi was the driving force behind an anti-Western destabilization campaign in the region. In June 1981, Chester Crocker, assistant secretary of state for African affairs–designate, pledged U.S. support to African nations that wanted to resist "intervention" from Libya.[39] The intervention of several thousand Libyan troops in the Chadian civil war earlier in the year had prompted the administration to request major increases in military assistance to Tunisia and Sudan. As relations between the United States and Libya continued to deteriorate amid charges at the end of 1981 that a Libyan hit squad had been sent to assassinate top-ranking U.S. officials, including the president, Washington's primary preoccupation in northeast Africa was the containment of Libya.

A response to a Libyan-backed or Soviet-backed threat to Somalia seemed all the more likely, given the administration's new willingness to use arms transfers vigorously and without apology as an instrument of diplomacy. Under Ronald Reagan, arms transfers would not be restrained for the sake of restraint.[40] Chester Crocker had argued that the Carter administration's active but disarmed diplomacy, because of its reluctance to commit resources at a time when African security issues had come to the fore, had resulted in missed opportunities to gain friends in Africa and win the respect of adversaries.[41] Unaffected by the so-called Vietnam syndrome—reluctance to pledge American aid or put U.S. credibility on the line in the Third World—the Reagan administration was "quite prepared to send arms to friendly governments."[42]

Thus Ethiopia's attack on Somalia was "just the kind of test the Reagan administration welcomed" to prove that "the United States could be counted on and to demonstrate to Ethiopia that [Washington's] restraint in arming Somalia [should not] be construed as a sign of weakness."[43] To create maximum publicity to make this point, eight U.S. military air transports arrived at Mogadishu airport at midday with the July consignment of arms, and Washington allowed the Somali government to announce the impending U.S. airlift.[44] Despite Ethiopia's threats to break diplomatic relations, the Reagan administration went ahead with the emergency arms airlift.[45] Siad Barre, of course, contributed to the perception that U.S. credibility was on the line by depicting the joint Ethiopian-SSDF incursion as part of a Soviet-backed plot to threaten the survival of a pro-Western government: accusing the Russians, Cubans, East Germans, South Yemenis, and the Libyans of directing this military aggression.[46]

MIDDLE EAST DIVERSIONS

While the Reagan administration was prepared to assist Somalia repel what it viewed as a Soviet-instigated attack by the Ethiopians and SSDF, Siad Barre would not be able to blackmail the Americans into overreacting by threatening defection to another arms supplier. In the first place, Mogadishu had no other choice when it came to the two superpowers, given the Soviet investment in Ethiopia. Second, the conflict in Somalia was overshadowed by the ongoing war between Iran and Iraq in the Persian Gulf, and the Israeli invasion of Lebanon in June 1982. With a major personnel change taking place at the Department of State in early July, as George Shultz replaced Alexander Haig as secretary of state, coupled with these developments in the Middle East, it was not surprising that the U.S. response was delayed and temperate in its execution.

A prompt and positive U.S. response was necessary for political and psychological purposes rather than for any impact it would have on the ground. Between 1979 and 1983, Somalia imported $580 million worth of arms, of which only $30 million came from the United States.[47] So in the short term, even after the United States got involved on the ground in Somalia, U.S. weapons would make up only a small portion of what the Somalis added to their arsenal. During this period, Mogadishu's two most important sources of supply were Italy and China, who delivered $410 million and $50 million worth of arms, respectively.[48]

However, unlike the situation in 1977–1978, when the world's attention was focused on the Horn, this latest in a series of border clashes went largely unnoticed. Somalia's arms and financial supporters had become too involved in their own affairs to be of much help to Mogadishu. The fall of the shah of Iran was a particularly hard blow; the Iranian arms connection had proven especially useful, though futile, during the 1977–1978 Ogaden War. Given the implacable hostility toward the United States of the new Islamic government in Teheran, the Iranian option was closed after Somalia agreed to become a part of Washington's Southwest Asia base network. Then in October 1980, having failed to score a quick victory over Iran after crossing the Shatt al-Arab the previous month, Iraq ceased oil shipments to Somalia—shipments that had totaled $17 million per month on a concessionary sales basis.[49] Baghdad's decision may also have been affected by its displeasure with Mogadishu's pro-U.S. alignment, fearing that Somalia might be used as a staging area by the U.S. Rapid Deployment Force (RDF) for unwanted interference in Middle Eastern affairs.[50] This concern was not wholly without foundation; even high-ranking Saudi officials believed that the RDF was more likely to be used to seize rather than defend the oil fields.[51]

The outbreak of war in the Persian Gulf also diverted the attentions of Saudi Arabia, which had been so instrumental in building the anti-Soviet consensus in the Red Sea region at the end of the 1970s.[52] Between early February and late May 1981, Riyadh became involved in forming the Gulf Cooperation Council (GCC). Then, at the end of the year, an Iranian-backed plot to overthrow the government of Bahrain and destabilize the Saudi kingdom was uncovered. The Horn of Africa receded further into the background as the Saudis became increasingly absorbed in trying to prevent an Iranian victory over Iraq. In the Red Sea, Saudi Arabia was most concerned with the situation in the Yemens, where fighting had broken out in March 1982 between the Saudi-supported North Yemeni (YAR) government and the radical, PDRY-backed National Democratic Front (NDF) insurgents. Thus, the situation in the Horn was little more than a distracting side show for the Saudis.

Mogadishu's long-term relationship with Egypt was both a blessing and a bane at this time. Siad Barre's support of the Camp David peace process and the March 1979 Egyptian-Israeli peace treaty ensured that Israel would not oppose U.S. arms transfers to Somalia. But Riyadh's decision to join ranks with sixteen other Arab countries and the PLO, and to cease economic assistance to Egypt, as well as break off diplomatic relations with Cairo following the March 1979 Baghdad Conference, meant that Mogadishu would not be able to depend upon Egyptian aid.[53] Moreover, in the spring of 1982 Egypt became absorbed with the diplomatic initiatives of Riyadh and Baghdad to bring Cairo back into the Arab fold and to persuade President Mubarak to send Egyptian troops to Iraq. Security issues at the southern end of the Red Sea were not at the top of Cairo's agenda, either.

Thus, between September 1980 and July 1982 the Persian Gulf war completely overshadowed what was transpiring in the Horn of Africa. While between 1979 and 1982 Mogadishu had been able to purchase several hundred million dollars' worth of arms, mostly from Italy, Siad Barre needed the psychological support of an interested outside backer on the ground in Somalia. But on the very day (July 14, 1982) that Somalia informed Washington of the Ethiopian incursion, Iran launched a major counteroffensive against Iraq. Moreover, on June 6 Israel had invaded Lebanon, a move that American policy makers struggled to resolve throughout the rest of the summer. Now, virtually ignored because of the Persian Gulf conflict and Middle East situation, Siad Barre was in no position to threaten defection to another arms supplier.

RAS BANAS, DIEGO GARCIA, AND THE SUDANESE OPTIONS

Washington's response to the fighting in Somalia was quite temperate despite the involvement of Ethiopian forces. Ten days passed between the date of the Somali request (July 14) and the first arms delivery (July 24). In this instance, the Reagan administration did little more than try to stabilize the situation. Some critics in Congress feared that Somalia might use the incident to expand the conflict into Ethiopia. In any event, given U.S. options elsewhere, there was no reason to rush blindly to Somalia's aid.

Washington's cautious approach reflected declining interest in Somalia as a strategic asset. It was questionable whether Somali facilities would be needed to execute U.S. military options in Southwest Asia. The port and air facilities at Berbera would be only marginally useful in most contingencies. Moreover, the United States could conduct military operations from other sites in the southern Red Sea area and contain radical influence in northeast Africa without running the political risks associated with Somalia.

However, not all U.S. officials were suffering from buyer's remorse. At the Pentagon the U.S.-Somalia arms-for-access arrangement a real bargain; in relative terms, U.S. security assistance (or the rent paid to Mogadishu) amounted to "peanuts."[54] Moreover, the United States was getting a lot for those peanuts. Berbera's location at the mouth of the Bab al-Mandab and across the Gulf of Aden from the Arabian Peninsula, not to mention its 15,000-foot concrete runway and natural harbor, and Mogadishu's position on the Indian Ocean near the main sea lanes, were ideally situated to support the deployment of the RDF, sea control operations in the Indian Ocean and the Red Sea, and long-range reconnaissance missions in peacetime.[55] While some critics noted that Berbera was too distant from the Strait of Hormuz (1,350 miles) to be of significant value in supporting Persian Gulf military operations, it was more than 1,000 miles closer to the Persian Gulf than Diego Garcia and Mombasa. Moreover, if the United States chose to sealift supplies into the Persian Gulf, Berbera would be less prone to sea lane or choke-point disruption than Egyptian military facilities.

But Berbera was also very vulnerable to attack.[56] Directly across the Gulf of Aden, the Russians maintained access to South Yemen's port of Aden. Five hundred miles to the east, the Soviet Union was building a base on Socotra Island (PDRY). Berbera was less than 150 miles from the Ethiopian border. If a Persian Gulf conflict were to escalate horizontally and superpower client states were to come under attack, Berbera would be one of the least defensible facilities.

Moreover, there seemed to be little reason to run political risks in Somalia, given the growing redundancy of U.S. bases in Southwest Asia. While Somali military facilities gave the United States greater flexibility, they were not indispensable.[57] Long-range Pentagon military construction plans allocated only $24 million (out of $1.25 billion) to repair oil storage and other facilities at Berbera.[58] Somalia fell a distant fifth behind Diego Garcia, Egypt, Oman, and Kenya in dollar amounts requested by the Reagan administration for the region.[59] Lt. Gen. Ernest Graves, director of the International Security Assistance Agency, put the situation into perspective in testimony before the U.S. Senate Foreign Relations Committee in April 1981: "Berbera is important to us but considering the complex of bases we have in the area, it may not be as (important) as it was in the Russian network."[60]

The Carter Doctrine initially called for the United States to acquire base-access rights in three host countries—Somalia, Kenya, and Oman—to support U.S. naval deployments and the RDF.[61] Of these three agreements, the military sites in Oman, especially at Masirah Island, were considered most valuable, owing to their strategic location near the Strait of Hormuz.[62] But Oman's forward position also meant it might come under attack and be rendered inoperable early in a conflict. Relying on Oman was also politically risky; it would be susceptible to the pressures of Iran and other GCC members against its military relationship with the United States.

To expand its flexibility, in late 1980 the United States accepted Anwar Sadat's offer allowing U.S. forces to use Egyptian military facilities for deployment operations.[63] American military construction at Ras Banas, Egypt, on the Red Sea was expected to total over $522 million through FY 1985, making it the second most expensive project in Washington's Southwest Asia strategic network behind Diego Garcia.[64] Among the onshore facilities, Ras Banas was to become the centerpiece for U.S. military planning: it could serve as a rear staging area for Persian Gulf operations and as a potential forward staging site for other Middle Eastern–North African contingencies.[65] Flexibility was further enhanced by Egypt's willingness to allow deplotment of U.S. forces at its military facilities before committing them to combat or before the outbreak of hostilities.[66] The military utility of Ras Banas would be complemented by the political benefit of dealing with Egypt, a more independent-minded Middle Eastern state.

Following the events in Iran and Afghanistan, the United States accelerated military construction at Diego Garcia and the transformation of the island into a "major logistical support base."[67] For FY 1981–FY 1982, a military construction budget of approximately $370 million was authorized to expand the base.[68] Although Diego Garcia was the most distant of the Southwest Asia facilities, it was the only one under direct U.S. control. However, political issues threatened to complicate U.S. strategic planning involving the island base: legal controversies over the sovereignty of the Chagos Archipelago and the fate of the displaced Ilois inhabitants as well as the movement to demilitarize the Indian Ocean or declare the region a nuclear-free zone.[69] Nonetheless, U.S. military planning for Southwest Asia continued to revolve around Diego Garcia. It could become even more important if, as some analysts suggested, the United States were to rely more heavily or exclusively upon maritime prepositioning and capabilities to secure U.S. interests in the region.[70]

Somalia's declining political-strategic importance in the U.S. security calculation was affected most directly by the United States' decision to rely on Sudan for securing its interests in the Horn of Africa. The Carter administration had set this policy in motion by providing $65.4 million in security assistance in FY 1980 and by authorizing $82.3 million in SAP funds and approving $43 million worth of FMS cash sales to Khartoum for FY 1981.[71] U.S. emphasis on arms transfers and military support for Khartoum grew even more during the Reagan years. During FY 1982, the United States provided Sudan with SAP funds and approved FMS cash arms purchases valued at almost $300 million.[72] In early 1982 the administration proposed a FY 1983 SAP-FMS cash package worth more than $270 million.[73]

Sudan's emergence as Washington's leading SAP recipient in sub-Sahara Africa in the early 1980s was in part a reward for the stands taken by the Nimeiri government on global and regional issues. President Nimeiri's support for the Camp David accords and Egyptian-Israeli peace process, his adoption of a forceful anti-Soviet, antiradical stance in the Red Sea region, and his moderating influence in the Horn of Africa had impressed both the Carter and Reagan administrations.[74] In supporting Sudan, the United States also demonstrated an acute sensitivity to Egypt's traditional concerns about preventing threats to the flow of the Nile waters and the need to secure its southern buffer zone.[75] Cairo's concerns gave a more ominous meaning to Libyan interference in Chad and Sudan in 1981–1982. As for the Horn itself, exercising the Sudanese option offered a way to counter Soviet influence in Ethiopia without having to arm Somalia. Moreover, arming Sudan, and Kenya as well, would not be so provocative politically within the African regional context.

From a strategic point of view, there was little reason for the United States to rush to Siad Barre's aid in July 1982, given the marginal utility of Somali military facilities. Washington had no interest in picking up where the Soviets had left off and turning Somalia into a major overseas military site. There were other more attractive locations, geographically and politically, from which to choose in the region. Egypt and Oman were nearer to areas where U.S. forces might be deployed in a crisis. Diego Garcia and Kenya, in serving as rear staging sites for the RDF, offered a political security not available in Somalia. While Washington did wish to keep Somalia out of Moscow's hands and provide some insurance against potential military contingencies, in the final analysis, Somalia's strategic marginality justified a cautious response.

FROM IRREDENTISM TO COUNTERINSURGENCY

By 1982 Somalia had virtually collapsed economically and politically.[76] As a result of the continuing guerrilla conflict in the Ogaden, Somalia was confronting a mounting refugee problem. Addis Ababa had adopted what appeared to be a policy of depopulation to suppress Somali dissent in the Ogaden.[77] However, the refugee crisis tended to exacerbate existing political and economic problems. The economy had stagnated, government institutions were in a state of paralysis, and Siad Barre had tribalized Somali politics in order to survive in power.[78]

After assuming power in 1969, Siad Barre continued to cite the revolution to legitimize his government.[79] Power lay in the hands of the Somali president, who headed the Supreme Revolutionary Council and controlled Somalia's only legal party, the Somali Revolutionary Socialist party (SRSP). Individual liberties were subordinated to the needs of the state and tight controls were placed on civil and political rights.[80] Open criticism of the government was not permitted, and dissenters risked arbitrary arrest.[81] There were "unsubstantiated" reports of torture; political dissenters were not always accorded fair trials; and some civilian government officials overthrown in 1969, including a former prime minister, were political prisoners.[82] To carry out this repression, Siad Barre had created (with Soviet and East European assistance) a pervasive security apparatus, the National Security Service (NSS).

In 1979 a new constitution was adopted that confirmed existing state institutions, provided some guarantees of individual rights, and called for the establishment that December of a people's assembly with tightly circumscribed functions.[83] Even after a parliament was elected in 1980, real authority continued to be in Siad Barre's hands. In October 1980, Barre declared a state of emergency and suspended constitutional guarantees on the grounds of domestic economic inefficiency, corruption, and external threats.[84] At the time the Somali Salvation Front (SSF) was carrying out sporadic bombings in Mogadishu, and the government was trying to cope with hundreds of thousands of Somali refugees who had fled the Ogaden.[85] The state of emergency remained in effect, and Barre ruled through presidential decrees, until February 1982. Nonetheless, U.S. officials did not feel that Barre's declared state of emergency was accompanied by any additional repressive measures.[86]

While the Reagan administration did not seem appalled by the human rights situation in Somalia, by 1982 the State Department was becoming concerned about Siad Barre's exclusionary clan politics. Although all major Somali clans were represented in the government, the military, and the SRSP, Siad's small Mareehan clan enjoyed disproportionate representation and political influence.[87] Siad also had the support of the Ogadeeni clan, which like the Mareehan were strongly represented in these institutions. The Dulbahante clan completed the triumvirate of Siad's core support, collectively known as the "MOD connection."[88]

Clan rivalries, inherent in Somali's sociopolitical landscape, were exacerbated by Siad Barre's manipulation of clan divisions and interests. Although opposition to Siad's rule extended across clan lines, only the Majeerteen and Isaaq dissidents fielded active resistance units.[89] Operating in the northern border area of Somalia was the Somali National Movement (SNM), an Isaaq-based clan group founded in London in 1979 that moved its headquarters to Addis Ababa in June 1982. The Somali Salvation Democratic Front (SSDF), a Majeerteen-based clan group, was responsible for the June 1982 border incursion. This intrusion prompted Siad Barre to declare a state of emergency in the central region under attack, conscript recruits for the armed forces, and confiscate property for the war effort.[90]

While the Reagan administration seemed most concerned about Siad Barre's manipulation of clan rivalries and the external threat posed by a heavily armed, Soviet-backed Ethiopia, the U.S. Congress began to focus attention on the human rights situation in Somalia. Between November 1981 and March 1982, a series of hearings were held before several subcommittees of the House of Representatives Committee on Foreign Affairs concerning the implementation of congressionally mandated human rights provisions, in which Somalia figured prominently.[91] In a statement submitted by Congressman Toby Moffett, which drew upon recent reports by Amnesty International, Siad Barre's government was described as showing a "blatant disregard for the needs and rights of its citizens." He advised the United States to "think twice before aligning [itself] with that government."[92] It would be "folly" to depend upon such an inherently unstable repressive government; by helping "the unpopular, opportunistic and corrupt Barre regime," the United States would "be repeating the mistakes [it] made in propping up such tyrants as Shah Mohammed Reza Pahlavi of Iran and Anastasio Somoza of Nicaragua."[93] Siad Barre was a notorious opportunist who had "no real love for the West, and [could not] be relied upon as an ally."[94] The United States would be wise to "move slowly and carefully in dealing with a government which may be overthrown by a growing opposition, or which may abandon us to any power which makes a better offer."[95]

While those voicing human rights concerns on Capitol Hill certainly appeared sincere, Siad Barre and the Reagan administration may have detected a hidden agenda: using this issue to keep U.S. weapons out of Somalia. To ensure that Barre understood what was happening, in January 1982 the U.S. ambassador in Mogadishu reminded the Somali government of Washington's commitment to human rights and congressional interest in the status of Somalia's political prisoners.[96] In February, on the eve of his visit to the United States, Siad released several prominent political prisoners, including former Prime Minister Ibrahim Egal. During Siad's stay in Washington, the administration expressed its support for the release of political prisoners and urged continued progress in this regard. However, in June, Barre ordered the arrest and investigation of one of the released prisoners and six other high-ranking government officials for crimes against the state.[97]

As a result of this political repression and exploitation of clan rivalries, Siad Barre faced growing opposition. Barre became the symbol of all that was wrong with Somalia. He was seen as being nothing more than a clan leader using divide-and-rule tactics and repression to perpetuate his own rule and the interests of his clan.[98] By the end of 1981, ridding Somalia of Siad Barre had become the focus of editorials and articles in the American-based journal *Horn of Africa*.[99] Both the SNM and the SSDF were committed to the violent overthrow of Siad Barre's clan-based regime.[100] Thus, Mogadishu's security agenda, at least temporarily, had been diverted from pursuing irredentist claims in the Ogaden to waging a counterinsurgency campaign inside Somalia to ensure the survival of an authoritarian regime.[101]

Therefore, Siad had to be careful not to push the United States too hard on the military aid issue; the Americans might decide to stay clear of the deteriorating situation in Somalia. Barre's repression of religious leaders and civilian demonstrators in the north, as well as the use of arms to suppress dissent among Somali clans along the Ethiopian border, had edged Somalia closer to the brink of full-scale civil war.[102] Moreover, the deposition of Siad Barre would not necessarily harm U.S. interests. By remaining on the sidelines, the United States could perhaps maintain its position in Somalia after Barre passed from the scene. A passive U.S. response to the Ethiopian intrusion might even cause the collapse of Siad's government or prompt the Somali military to act against him.

Thus, a positive U.S. response to Somalia's July 1982 arms request carried an important symbolic political meaning for Siad Barre. American support in this situation would help to bolster Barre's position, at least to the extent that it would create the impression that his continuation in power was a vital prerequisite for U.S. aid to Somalia. Even if the United States had no interest in helping Siad survive politically, to maintain influence in a post-Barre Somalia, the United States would need to make some gesture of support for Somalia's territorial integrity. Still, Siad could not ask the Americans for too much; if he scared them away, he would be left facing alone what was in essence a threat to his rule.

ILLUSION OF CONTROL

When the Ethiopian and SSDF forces invaded Somalia, a significant change in attitude had occurred among some high-ranking and mid-level analysts in the Defense and State departments regarding the arming of Somalia. Although the Reagan administration recognized that it had inherited a very delicate situation in Somalia, there was a growing confidence that Mogadishu could be controlled. Because the situation in Somalia was deteriorating, and the balance of forces in the Horn of Africa heavily favored Addis Ababa, Mogadishu would apparently be highly dependent upon the United States.[103] The military imbalance in the Horn would deter another Somali invasion of Ethiopia and would also allow Washington to contain the Somalis.[104]

American policy makers premised their optimistic assessment upon the notion that the modest "defensive" American security assistance program planned for Somalia would come nowhere near matching what the Soviets had been doing in Ethiopia.[105] Somalia could not pose an offensive threat; it was no match for Ethiopia's army, now stocked with over a thousand tanks, artillery pieces, and several dozen modern combat aircraft.[106] The United States could only "do band-aids for Somalia" with the money it was giving Mogadishu.[107] At best, U.S. aid might make future Ethiopian ventures into Somalia more costly.[108] In fact, given what the Soviet Union was doing in Ethiopia, some Pentagon officials believed that U.S. aid for Somalia was inadequate.[109]

American military officials intimately involved in overseeing the Somali SAP felt that it would be some time before Mogadishu possessed the military capability to pose a threat to anyone in the region.[110] It would take three to five years to have some impact on the ground and five to ten years to cause a major turnaround in the program. Defense Department analysts saw such a gap between Ethiopia and Somalia that they felt there was nothing the United States could do in the next five years to cause Ethiopia to fear Somalia's conventional capability.[111] American officials did not expect a repeat of the 1977–1978 Ogaden War. Not only were the Somalis incapable of successfully waging war, but also there was no opportunity, as there had been during the tumultuous years of the Ethiopian revolution.[112]

As a result of Somalia's weak military posture in the region, the Reagan administration was less leery of placing arms in Somalia. It was believed that Mogadishu's actions could be controlled in the short run. Moreover, the longer the United States maintained a political-military foothold in Somalia, according to one line of reasoning, the better chance it stood of preventing the Somalis from going back into Ethiopia—or, for that matter, Kenya or Djibouti.[113] If the United States could keep the Somali Army out of the Ogaden for a generation, the Somali irredentist problem in the Horn might solve itself.[114] But to acquire this longer-term leverage over Mogadishu, the United States would have to start putting arms into Somalia.

Critics argued that once American weapons arrived, it would be impossible to extricate the United States from a difficult situation in Somalia without suffering some negative political fallout.[115] It would be easier to withhold or withdraw U.S. support before the United States started using Berbera or putting arms on the ground.[116] If Ethiopia attacked or bombed Berbera and the Americans defended themselves, they risked being drawn into fighting Somalia's war. Skeptics at the Africa Bureau and on Capitol

Hill believed that the United States should delay the transfer of arms to Somalia as long as possible to test the seriousness of Mogadishu's pledge to stay out of the Ogaden.[117] Thus, the main argument in Washington against arming Somalia was the risk of suffering a foreign policy humiliation by abandoning an arms client in the face of certain defeat by a Soviet-backed state.

What was largely absent from this debate was a concern for the implications of sending arms to a Somali government engaged in suppressing human rights and waging a counterinsurgency war. Instead, the possibility that Ethiopia and Somalia might fight a protracted, proxy guerrilla war, while refraining from sending their forces across the border, was foremost in the minds of U.S. officials.[118] The decision to send arms to Somalia implied that as long as these weapons were used to stabilize the situation inside Somalia and not to extend the fighting into Ethiopia, Washington would not question their use.

For the most part, Africa Bureau officials were still not confident about the U.S. military role in Somalia.[119] Africanists at the State Department still hoped to salvage something in Ethiopia. Despite the Soviet bear hug of Addis Ababa, U.S. military aid to Somalia would endanger more important long-term relationships with Ethiopia and Kenya. While Addis Ababa's opinion might not have mattered so much in Washington, Nairobi's view of the Somalis was important and quite well known: "We know our neighbor. . . . As soon as the weapons are delivered, they'll be in the Ogaden."[120] Comments by Somali defense officials to their U.S. counterparts did little to dispel the notion that Somalia posed a threat to its neighbors. One Somali military official derisively dismissed Kenya's paranoia by observing that one Somali soldier was the equal of ten Ethiopian soldiers, and one Ethiopian soldier was equal to ten Sudanese soldiers, and one Sudanese soldier was equal to ten Kenyan soldiers—the Kenyans were afraid of everything.[121] While the boast that one Somali soldier was the equal of 1,000 Kenyan soldiers may have amused Pentagon officials, it was not the sort of anecdote to inspire confidence in Somalia at the Africa Bureau or on Capitol Hill.

The U.S. decision to implement the emergency airlift in July 1982 was based on the belief that by making an arms commitment to Somalia, through the 1980 arms-for-access accord, the United States had already placed its credibility on the line.[122] What gave this argument greater legitimacy and momentum was Addis Ababa's accelerating move toward the radical camp as a result of its associations with the Soviet Union, and more recently with the PDRY and Libya. Some administration officials outside the Africa Bureau began to question whether it really made a difference what happened to U.S.-Ethiopia relations.[123] If Addis Ababa did not like what Washington was doing in Somalia, that was "too bad for Ethiopia."[124] Besides, Ethiopia now appeared to be threatening Somalia's security by supporting Somali dissidents, so why should Washington hold back on arms shipments to Mogadishu.[125] With the concurrence of the State Department, the U.S. chargé in Addis Ababa, David Korn, warned the Ethiopian government following the arms airlift to Somalia that summer that "if fighting continued, the United States would move to arm Somalia beyond anything contemplated up to that time."[126]

Even before the June 1982 Ethiopian incursion, some officials at the Defense Department and the State Department's Policy Planning Staff felt that the United States needed to be moving ahead in Somalia.[127] Mogadishu should be rewarded for supporting Washington's Southwest Asia strategy. As an additional rationale for moving ahead, Ethiopian-backed aggression and Addis Ababa's alignment with radical forces in the region actively engaged in undermining U.S. interests posed a threat. Given Somalia's long-term military vulnerability, the United States could move forward with its plan to arm Mogadishu "defensively" and not get its fingers burned in the process. Simple arithmetic and a bit of optimism suggested that the United States could control Mogadishu's irredentist ambitions. The United States established a kind of crude balance: Somalia would not be armed to such an extent that it could threaten Ethiopia, while Addis Ababa knew aggression against Somalia would result in increased U.S. arms transfers to Mogadishu.

CONCLUSION: FORCED HAND

There was a twofold purpose to Washington's "great stall" policy toward Somalia between August 1980 and July 1982. It offered the opportunity to test Siad Barre's sincerity in promising to keep the Somali military out of the Ogaden. Until Washington felt more confident about Somalia keeping its ambitions in check, the stall also precluded what the critics feared would be an irreversible security commitment whereby U.S. credibility would be placed on the line prematurely in a very uncertain situation. Thus, until the 1982 crisis, the slow-moving U.S. arms transfers process allowed Washington to buy time.

Ronald Reagan's decision to end the "great stall" was predicated upon a determination to blunt radical advances and the destabilization campaign against pro-Western states in the region. The availability of alternative base sites in Sudan, Egypt, Kenya, and Diego Garcia, coupled with the fact that Somalia could not threaten to defect to the Soviet Union, allowed the United States to respond in a somewhat tempered manner. However, the administration felt compelled to accelerate delivery of U.S. military equipment to Somalia because of its own globalist obsession with containment and maintaining U.S. credibility in the region, not because of any overriding strategic rationale. Given Washington's perception of the situation; the administration convinced itself that something had to be done to contain what was viewed as a Soviet-backed radical challenge. Moreover, after the charges hurled by the Republicans at Jimmy Carter over the desertion of the shah of Iran, the Reagan administration was not going to be accused of abandoning a state the United States had signed a military agreement with and which was now under siege by radical forces. Besides, since Reagan had taken office, the Somalis had kept their word and stayed out of the Ogaden. So it was time for the United States to fulfill its obligation and reward Mogadishu for good behavior.

Except for a slightly speeded-up timetable, the United States did not do anything not already planned for Somalia. Siad Barre had a weak hand to play vis-à-vis the United States, given Somalia's vulnerability to external attack and the externally supported internal challenge to Siad's rule. Although Somalia had no trouble obtaining arms from non-U.S. sources, in contrast to the Ogaden War of 1977–1978, Mogadishu's traditional Middle Eastern friends showed little interest in the affair. Their concern with the Persian Gulf conflict and the Israeli invasion of Lebanon highlighted the importance of having a superpower backer that could respond to simultaneous crises. Mogadishu could take some satisfaction in the Reagan administration's increased SAP funding for Somalia at this time. However, because for three years the Somalis had been unable to alter the basic negative perception of them on Capitol Hill and among working-level officials at the State Department, Siad Barre had little choice but to accept what the Americans were willing to offer during this crisis.

As a result of this crisis, Washington was forced to begin placing arms in Somalia. Until the Ethiopian incursion, U.S. policy was based on the assumption that Ethiopia and Somalia would engage in a proxy destabilization campaign in which their common border would be respected. This low-intensity struggle was a fact of life that might continue indefinitely. But so long as Ethiopia and Somalia kept their military forces on their own side of the border and U.S. weapons did not find their way into the hands of the WSLF, there was no reason to do anything out of the ordinary. However, now that Ethiopia had violated Washington's tacit rules of behavior, there was no longer any reason to hold back arms from Somalia. Ethiopia's military encroachment was taken as a signal that it was time for the United States to meet its security obligation to Somalia. Moreover, the administration believed that by carefully increasing or decreasing the flow of arms into Somalia, U.S. policy could deter aggression by either Somalia or Ethiopia.[128]

12

The 1990 Base Access Renegotiation

In the aftermath of the U.S. emergency arms airlift to Somalia in the summer of 1982, Mogadishu became the beneficiary of one of the largest U.S. security assistance programs ever put together for a sub-Sahara African state. Washington's initial two-year (FY 1980–FY 1981) $45 million SAP commitment was dwarfed by the aid amounts promised to Somalia throughout the mid-1980s.[1] During the next five-year period (FY 1982–FY 1986), U.S. security assistance to Somalia totaled over $266 million, including $114 million in grant military assistance, $4.3 million for an IMET program that trained more than 230 Somali military students, $128 million in Economic Support Funds (ESF), and $20 million in FMS financing credits. The United States also guaranteed more than $172 million worth of FMS cash sales. Although Washington had placed restrictions on the transfer of "offensive" weaponry to Somalia, a condition it had never imposed on Ethiopia. Nonetheless, over seven years the U.S. committed almost $500 million worth of military resources to Mogadishu—more than $100 million above what the United States had supplied to Addis Ababa during the course of their twenty-five-year arms partnership.

While Jimmy Carter had started the United States down the road to arming Somalia, Ronald Reagan accelerated the process with no apologies. The Reagan administration freely used arms transfers to support friendly Third World governments. Moreover, in the era of the Reagan Doctrine, covert and overt aid to anticommunist insurgent movements in Afghanistan, Angola, Cambodia, and Nicaragua was used to contain and roll back the spread of Soviet influence. Although Ethiopia was not officially a selected target of the Reagan Doctrine, a militant policy of containment was being applied in the Horn of Africa by arming Somalia, Sudan, and Kenya. Through 1986 these three countries accounted for well over half of U.S. security assistance provided to sub-Sahara Africa. Together they received an overall average of $500 million in security assistance annually.[2]

But as a result of the fiscal crisis confronting Washington, Congress began reducing the administration's foreign affairs budget. For FY 1987 approximately 25 percent of the $22.6 billion request was cut, resulting in more than $3 billion in SAP reductions.[3] Except for several key countries (specifically, Egypt and Israel, whose funds were earmarked by Congress), this action resulted in cuts of 50–60 percent in most foreign aid programs.[4] In the case of Somalia, the $67 million security assistance program proposed by the executive branch for FY 1987 was cut to $25 million. The more realistic $46.25 million budget request for FY 1988 was trimmed to $31.5 million. In early 1988 the administration had submitted a $41.1 million FY 1989 SAP proposal, and a request to allow an additional $15 million in FMS cash arms transfers. Following congressional budget hearings that spring, Somalia was expected to receive an estimated $26.65 million in SAP funds, including only $2.5 million in MAP assistance, and guarantees to purchase $10 million worth of military equipment through FMS cash sales.

However, by the fall of 1988 human rights considerations were weighing heavily in Washington's security calculation in the Horn. Near the end of May, the Somali National Movement (SNM) had launched a new offensive in the north of Somalia. The military response ordered by Siad Barre was brutal: as many as 10,000 people were killed over the next two months, most of them civilians.[5] As a result of government repression in the north, as well as in the south, an estimated 110,000 refugees, mostly members of the Isaaq clan, fled into Ethiopia. Somali government forces were reported to have committed massacres, summary executions, and indiscriminate killings and bombardment of the local population.[6]

In mid-July the U.S. House Subcommittee on Africa heard testimony on the human rights situation in Somalia and what the executive branch was doing to dissociate the United States from the "war against civilians."[7] Certain U.S. actions suggested that the United States was siding with the Somali government in this internal conflict. On June 29 a ship carrying U.S. rifles and grenade launchers, part of an arms consignment under the MAP agreement, had arrived at Berbera. Berbera itself had come under attack by SNM forces and was being used by Somali aircraft to bomb Hargeisa and Burao. In a controversial action that had the effect of boosting the Somali government's military capability in the northern war zone (although the administration defended it as normal procedure under MAP), an American military team repaired the Somali Army's communication site at Hargeisa, which was damaged in the fighting. U.S. policy appeared to reinforce Siad Barre's harsh response and belief that his government was the "only alternative to chaos."[8] Human rights organizations charged that the United States should exercise whatever leverage it had to rein in Somalia's army and security forces, and urged that Mogadishu be pressured to allow international relief agencies to treat civilians and to permit international human rights organizations and foreign journalists to report on the situation.[9] According to Human Rights Watch, "There should be no further military assistance to the Somali government."[10]

By the end of September 1988, the SNM attempt to seize the north and overthrow Siad Barre had failed. While sporadic fighting continued around Hargeisa and near Berbera, the SNM and the Isaaq clan were "badly shaken by the ferocity of the government response" and forced to revert to a policy of limited and largely ineffectual guerrilla warfare.[11] However, the battle continued in Washington, as thirty-five members of Congress called for a suspension of all U.S. aid to Somalia pending a thorough investigation and a move by Mogadishu toward reconciliation with the north.[12] Congress withheld the $2.5 million in MAP and $9 million of a $21 million reprogramming request in ESF funds obligated for FY 1989, along with $7 million from some $15 million in unused ESF from FY 1988.[13]

Despite the continuing problems in Somalia and heightened consciousness on Capitol Hill of the human rights record of the Barre regime, in spring 1989 the executive branch submitted to Congress a security assistance package for FY 1990 giving Mogadishu $20 million in ESF, $1.2 million for the IMETP, and $15 million in FMS financing credits, as well as guaranteeing $10 million in FMS cash sales. The newly elected Bush administration was also pressing Congress to release the entire package of suspended aid, which, added to the FY 1990 SAP request, would total $55 million.[14] Conversely, Congress pressured the executive branch to suspend indefinitely ESF support as well as MAP aid. In the spring of 1989 the Bush administration released some aid, although it agreed that other assistance should be held up until further steps were taken regarding human rights and national reconciliation.[15] Mogadishu would eventually receive the frozen FY 1988 and FY 1989 ESF funds, which allowed Mogadishu to repay $15 million of the amount owed to the IMF.[16] In sum, for FY 1988 and FY 1989, Somalia received a total of $48.25 million in ESF, $1.9 million for the IMETP, and $5.5 million in MAP.[17] But opponents of U.S. aid to Somalia were now calling on the administration to invoke section 502B of the Foreign Assistance Act prohibiting military aid and ESF to governments consistently engaged in gross violations of human rights.[18]

Following the freeze in U.S. aid in fall 1988, Siad Barre apparently flinched. He created a national reconciliation commission, publicly committed his government to the rehabilitation of the north, released several hundred political prisoners, and invited in the human rights organization

Amnesty International.[19] Critics saw this as a ploy to keep Western aid flowing to Somalia.[20] Reports surfaced that Barre's National Security Service continued to detain Isaaqs and that the Somali Air Force occasionally bombed Hargeisa, a provincial capital in the north.[21] However, by the spring of 1989 there was only small-scale and scattered fighting in the north. By beating back the SNM challenge, Siad could relax his repressive tactics and steer the international focus, especially that of Mogadishu's aid donors, away from the human rights situation in Somalia.

But in mid-July 1989, riots broke out in Mogadishu after the arrest of Moslem religious leaders alleged to have incited the July 9 assassination of the Roman Catholic bishop of Mogadishu.[22] The violence left several hundred people dead. Government forces used armored personnel carriers and jeeps with heavy machine guns to clear the streets. In the wake of the rioting, forty-six civilians were taken to a beach and executed. The U.S. Congress now forced the Bush administration to suspend all aid to Somalia, except for a token IMET program. Consequently, the $2.5 million in FY 1989 MAP funds would be canceled and everything except for a small IMET program (estimated at $796,000) was gutted from the FY 1990 SAP budget.

This legislative-initiated action against Somalia occurred a year before the U.S.-Somalia base-access agreement was to expire. The 1980 accord called for five-year review periods and stipulated that at the end of ten years (in Somalia's case August 1990), if the agreement had not been renegotiated it would continue in force with the provision that either party could terminate the agreement after a year's notice.[23] It had been expected that sometime in late 1989 or 1990 U.S. and Somali officials would negotiate a new arrangement. Congress had been reminded of this in the spring of 1989.[24] However, budget constraints and human rights questions arising from the political situation in Somalia tied the administration's hands. In the spring of 1990, the Bush administration presented to Congress the FY 1991 SAP proposal, in which only a $900,000 IMET program was requested for Somalia, justified on the grounds that U.S. military and technical training would "continue to expose Somali officers to U.S. values of respect for human rights."[25]

The ten-year anniversary of the arms-for-access agreement passed with neither side raising any objections, meaning the base agreement would remain in force through at least August 1991. Washington maintained access to Berbera at virtually no cost, as Siad Barre concentrated on saving his own neck. In material terms, it was a one-sided arrangement favoring the United States. On the other hand, as long as Siad Barre could survive in power without U.S. aid, American influence was quite limited.

SOMALI-ETHIOPIAN RAPPROCHEMENT

Washington's limited ability to force a change in Siad Barre's domestic policies stemmed in part from Somalia's altered security environment. The primary threat to Siad Barre's government was now internal. Barre's security agenda had shifted from preserving Somalia's territorial integrity from Ethiopian encroachments and the liberation of the Ogaden to ensuring his own political survival. With the United States no longer willing or able to support his regime, Barre had little reason not to crush this political challenge with every means at his disposal. The fate of the shah of Iran, who in the end was pressured by the Americans not to turn the Iranian military loose on his civilian opponents, was not lost on Siad Barre.

The transformation of Mogadishu's security agenda began with a meeting between Ethiopia's Mengistu Haile Mariam and Siad Barre in Djibouti on January 18–19, 1986.[26] The two leaders agreed to establish a joint consultative commission to normalize Ethiopian-Somali relations. However, owing to Mengistu's demand for $1 billion in war compensation and Somalia's public renunciation of its claims on the Ogaden, the proxy war continued into 1988. Addis Ababa supported the Somali Salvation Democratic Front (SSDF) and the Somali National Movement (SNM). Mogadishu financed and provided a safe haven for the Western Somali Liberation Front (WSLF).

However, both governments were coming under increasing military pressure. Throughout 1987 the Eritrean People's Liberation Front (EPLF) and the Tigrean People's Liberation Front (TPLF) scored significant military successes against Ethiopian forces and consolidated their gains in Ethiopia's northeast corner. At the end of 1986, the Ethiopian-backed SNM launched a new military campaign in the north of Somalia that resulted in fighting between Ethiopian and Somali forces in February 1987. One consequence of this clash was to disrupt talks between Ethiopia's and Somalia's foreign ministers as part of the joint consultative commission.

By this time both governments were physically exhausted by their conflict and failed attempts to suppress internal insurgencies. In the spring of 1987, Mengistu retracted his two preconditions, asking only that Somalia act in a more conciliatory manner.[27] In the spirit of détente, Addis Ababa tacitly allowed Somali forces to attack SNM bases located inside Ethiopia, while Siad Barre disbanded the Mogadishu-controlled WSLF. Finally on April 3, 1988, a peace treaty was signed calling for the mutual withdrawal of forces from the Ethiopian-Somali border area, a reopening of diplomatic relations, and the cessation of support for each other's dissidents.[28] It was also believed that by a "secret clause" Siad Barre agreed to accept the existing border and, in essence, to renounce Somali claims on the Ogaden.[29]

The Ethiopian-Somali peace agreement of 1988 was the action of two governments exhausted by international and internal wars.[30] While they chose to resolve their external conflict, both governments refused to compromise with internal opponents. Somalia, of course, could always resume the Ogaden struggle. But the stakes were too high for internal compromise, given the possible consequences of a political settlement with domestic opponents. For Ethiopia, it might mean the disintegration of the state and possibly Mengistu's ouster. Peace in Somalia could probably come only if Siad Barre were removed from power, and even then interclan rivalries threatened to divide the country.

Mengistu, in particular, felt extremely vulnerable.[31] In mid-March 1988, the EPLF had scored a major victory against the Ethiopian Army at Afabet. The Eritrean resistance was now fielding 18,000 soldiers organized into twelve regular brigades, backed up by 20,000 militias. Moreover, after two years of poor relations, the EPLF and the TPLF had recently agreed to coordinate their activities. The TPLF had 25,000 regular soldiers and regional militias under its command. By reaching agreement with Somalia, Mengistu could release some of his forces from the south and east and send them north. Mengistu was also under another kind of pressure to react: Moscow was growing impatient with Ethiopia's failure to resolve the war in Eritrea militarily or politically, and the Soviet ambassador had informed Addis Ababa in April 1988 that when the current five-year Soviet-Ethiopian arms agreement expired in 1991, large-scale military shipments would cease.[32] This message was repeated during Mengistu's July visit to the Soviet Union.[33] If Mengistu wished to preserve the unity of the Ethiopian state, he needed to win the war in Eritrea quickly.

Ironically, the Ethiopian-Somali rapprochement exacerbated Somalia's internal problems. The May 1988 SNM offensive was apparently a desperate gamble to gain a stronghold inside Somalia before the insurgents were kicked out of Ethiopia.[34] They had nowhere else to go except Somalia. Whereas in the past Siad had depicted the SNM and SSDF as Ethiopian puppets guilty of treason, following the SNM attack Barre sought to portray the insurgents as northern secessionists who were betraying the pan-Somali heritage.[35] Of course, Siad had opened himself to charges of betrayal by signing the peace agreement with Ethiopia.

The international stage was now secondary to the local Somali context for Siad Barre's political maneuverings. While acquiring arms from external sources remained a concern, the peace treaty allowed Siad to focus on isolating his domestic opposition and consolidating his support along clan lines. Foreign opinion mattered little in this struggle for power. Because

Ethiopia and Libya had ended their support for the SNM, and none of the other clan-based movements that emerged in 1989—the Hawiye-based United Somali Congress (USC) and the Ogadeen-based Somali Patriot Movement (SPM)—had foreign backers, Siad thought he could outgun his internal opponents.

Thus, as long as the peace agreement with Ethiopia held, the U.S. security connection was of little value to Siad Barre. No doubt the peace was fragile. Both sides accused the other of violating the agreement. Ethiopia had reportedly held discussions in 1989 with the United Somali Congress about providing support and allowing base sites to be established in Ethiopia.[36] But Barre apparently felt secure enough to pursue his internal security agenda without fear of external attack, and without U.S. support. In fact, continued dependence on U.S. security assistance might do more harm than good to Siad's domestic agenda, given U.S. attempts to restrain his actions.

THE END OF THE COLD WAR

Through the end of 1987, the Reagan administration viewed the Third World as an arena in which to confront the Soviet Union and play out the East-West struggle. This attitude was founded on a belief that since the 1950s the Soviets had expanded their influence and established military footholds in the Third World by promoting instability and exploiting internal conflicts.[37] Quite simply, Moscow and Washington held vastly different interpretations of the rules of the road for U.S.-Soviet competition in the Third World.[38] Three of the lessons the Reagan administration drew from Soviet expansion in the 1970s were that (1) countering the spread of Soviet power required the United States to "resist provocative Soviet action on the ground—with sufficient resources and, if necessary, by force"; (2) negotiation with the Soviet Union on regional issues would work only if Moscow knew that a use of force would not yield easy gains; and (3) Third World nationalism could be used to contain the Soviet Union and to reverse its gains.[39]

While the Reagan administration welcomed some of Mikhail Gorbachev's fresh ideas after his ascent to power in March 1985, especially his desire to use Soviet influence to resolve outstanding regional disputes, Soviet foreign policy in the Third World appeared fundamentally unchanged.[40] Moscow continued to support friendly regimes in Afghanistan, Angola, Cambodia, Nicaragua, Ethiopia, Vietnam, and North Korea. In March 1986, Assistant Secretary for African Affairs Chester Crocker declared, "Soviet/Libyan/Cuban adventurism operates in Africa just as it does in Afghanistan, Nicaragua, and the Middle East."[41] It followed from this logic that the United States should rid the African continent of "outside subversive influence and aggression" and in preventing "its use as a base for anti-Western propaganda and activities."[42] Thus, the Reagan administration would not hesitate "to provide military assistance to our friends when threatened by external aggression," as proved by the U.S. response to Libyan incursions against Chad, and would justify the FY 1987 Security Assistance Program for sub-Sahara Africa on the grounds that the Soviet Union, Cuba, and Libya posed a danger to the continent.[43]

In Somalia, U.S. security assistance was deemed "vital" for the government's ability to "control its borders and manage its own destiny," especially while Mogadishu remained engaged in a residual border conflict with Ethiopia.[44] Although the FY 1987 SAP budget was presented to Congress shortly after the 1986 meeting between Mengistu and Siad in Djibouti, SSDF forces still occupied two Somali villages, and the Ethiopian-backed SNM periodically engaged in border harassment against Somalia. Nonetheless, the administration claimed credit for facilitating negotiations between the antagonists. Chester Crocker argued that "the careful balance of our assistance to Somalia over the past several years" which gave Mogadishu a defensive capability, coupled with Washington's refusal to support Somalia's actions against Ethiopian territory, created an atmosphere in which Mengistu and Siad could meet to solve the Ethiopian-Somali dispute.[45] The Reagan administration believed that arming Somalia had contributed to peace and security in the Horn of Africa, even if it had accelerated the arms buildup in the region. As rationalization, Michael Armacost, undersecretary for political affairs at the State Department, explained that the United States could not rely exclusively on nonmilitary means to contain Soviet military intervention in the Third World because of Moscow's "excessive" reliance upon military power and force to pursue its objectives.[46]

The confrontational philosophy and logic underlying the Reagan Doctrine and U.S. policy toward the Third World was reassessed following the December 1987 meeting between Ronald Reagan and Mikhail Gorbachev. At this meeting the two leaders signed the Intermediate-range Nuclear Force (INF) treaty, which eliminated a whole category of nuclear weapons in Europe. By the time George Bush became president in January 1989, the old premises underlying U.S. policy toward the Soviet Union and superpower confrontation in the Third World had become outmoded. During Bush's first year and a half in office, a series of developments occurred that would affect the U.S. assessment of threat in the Horn of Africa. More generally, Soviet military forces completed their withdrawal from Afghanistan in February 1989, and European conventional arms reduction talks resumed in Geneva the following month. At the end of the year, a breakthrough occurred in the talks regarding Namibia's independence (which it received in 1990) and the withdrawal of Cuban military forces from Angola. In the Horn itself, the Cuban military presence in Ethiopia had decreased significantly since 1985, and at the end of 1989 the Soviet Union withdrew half of its military advisers from Ethiopia.[47] By mid-1989 the United States and the Soviet Union were in agreement that some formula had to be found that would guarantee Ethiopia's territorial unity while respecting the rights of the Eritreans.[48] Despite the superpowers' desire to see an end to the Eritrean conflict, the Ethiopians and Eritreans considered their respective goals to be incompatible and felt no compulsion in the short term to bend to Soviet or American pressure.

On the other hand, Moscow had tired of Mengistu's waste of Soviet resources in Eritrea. After the EPLF captured the port of Massawa in February 1990, the Soviet Union made no move to intervene or to relieve the besieged Ethiopian forces in Asmara. In June 1990, both Washington and Moscow pressured Mengistu to allow the delivery and dispersal of famine relief supplies to the civilian population in Eritrea through the port of Massawa, which was being bombed daily by the Ethiopian Air Force.[49] That spring Moscow had told Mengistu once again that Soviet military aid would be cut the following year.[50] The cold war in the Horn of Africa had apparently come to an end.

U.S. security assistance to Somalia as well as to Sudan and Kenya had been important to the extent that the USSR's effort in Ethiopia was effective.[51] Through the mid-1980s Addis Ababa appeared to be very confident politically and militarily, backed to the hilt by the Soviet Union, and willing to take risks. But with the insurgencies in Eritrea and Tigre gaining ground and Moscow's backing away from its carte blanche arms commitment, Ethiopia no longer seemed to pose a threat to anyone. Consequently, Somalia, Sudan, and Kenya all lost value as political-strategic counterweights to Ethiopia. As long as the Soviet Union remained absorbed in resolving its own internal political and economic problems, dealing with the disintegration of the East bloc and pursuing a cooperative relationship with the United States, there was no reason for Washington to risk becoming mired in Somalia's internal affairs by continuing security assistance to the Barre government.

Until Iraq's invasion of Kuwait in early August 1990, regional threats to U.S. interests also appeared to have dissipated. The U.S. bombing run over Libya in April 1986 had apparently put Qaddafi back in his box. Whereas the Reagan administration had cited the Libyan and Ethiopian threat to regional security as a justification for SAP assistance to Somalia and Sudan throughout most of the 1980s, by the end of the decade, no mention was made of this threat.[52] Instead, Libya was competing in a more overt and "legitimate" fashion by supplying arms and financial aid to the governments of Sudan and Somalia, rather than trying to topple them. Baghdad, too, had been busy throughout the 1980s developing ties with states in the Red Sea region, including Sudan, Djibouti, Yemen, and Somalia. Saddam Hussein's emergence as the new post-cold war enemy of the United States in the wake of Iraq's 1990 invasion of Kuwait, however, did not produce any immediate or appreciable change in American threat assessments in the Red Sea or in U.S. policy toward Somalia.[53]

With the end of the cold war, the overall strategic value of African territory had depreciated considerably.[54] Hence the game of playing the two superpowers off against one another was no longer a viable strategy. Africa's greatest product was now refugees, an abundance of which could be found in the Horn.[55] Despite the Persian Gulf crisis involving Iraq and Kuwait, nothing had happened in the area to suggest that U.S. interests were threatened in Somalia.[56] In late August and early September 1990, the strategic threat posed by Iraq was not expected to last, necessitating a dramatic change in the United States' relationship with Mogadishu, unlike the Soviet invasion of Afghanistan in 1979.[57] The Bush administration did not demand immediate resumption of military aid to Somalia, as there was no threat to U.S. interests to justify such a change in policy. Thus, ten years after the signing of the U.S.-Somali arms-for-base-access accord, Washington's perception of threat had changed so dramatically that Somalia's capacity to exploit and manipulate U.S. strategic vulnerability was virtually nil.

THE LIBYAN CONNECTION

By 1989, Mogadishu's strategy of manipulating Washington's sense of strategic vulnerability had lost much, if not all, of its impact. Thus any Somali threat of defection would be empty. The Soviets had nothing to give and would not jump in blindly. With Moscow reducing its involvement in Ethiopia, it would be unlikely to embrace Somalia. To maintain a favorable balance of power vis-à-vis his internal opponents, Siad Barre was forced to turn to what many in Washington considered an unsavory assortment of friends to procure arms and assistance.

Even before the 1988 freeze and 1989 suspension of U.S. security assistance, Somalia's military dependence upon the United States was marginal. Between 1982 and 1986, during the peak years of SAP funding for Somalia, U.S. arms transfers accounted for only 22 percent ($70 million) of the $315 million worth of arms imported by Mogadishu.[58] Among the Western powers, Italy had been most forthcoming; the Italians had delivered 100 M-47 tanks in 1983, though they rebuffed a Somali inquiry about acquiring more modern and sophisticated Leopard tanks in 1987.[59] While some U.S. military aid was in the pipeline in the fall of 1989, no arms or ammunition were delivered after the aid suspension took effect.[60]

In October 1988 Libya emerged as the primary supplier of small arms to Somalia.[61] After war erupted in the north of Somalia in May 1988, Siad Barre made an urgent appeal to the United States and Great Britain for military supplies. Both nations refused. The United States did allow delivery in June of weapons in the MAP pipeline, but that was the last arms shipment to Somalia. In August, Siad sent his son General Maslah Mohamed Siad, commander-in-chief of the armed forces, to Moscow and Tripoli in search of aid. The Soviets also refused. On the other hand, Colonel Qaddafi, looking toward enhanced Libyan influence in Somalia by terminating aid to the SNM and SSDF in 1985—which also paved the way for restoring diplomatic relations between Tripoli and Mogadishu that same year—moved to fill this void.

In early October 1988, two planeloads of light arms arrived in Somalia from Libya. Reports also surfaced that a shipment of heavy weapons had been sent by the Libyans.[62] In early 1989 there were rumors that Libya had supplied chemical weapons to Somalia.[63] The State Department "categorically" denied this allegation.[64] If it were true, Somali forces would probably kill themselves with them, as they did not have the training or technical expertise to use these weapons.[65] But it was known that Somalia had received a shipment of napalm canisters, possibly from Libya.[66] Qaddafi was no doubt motivated to deliver arms to Siad Barre, as well as to provide oil at concessional rates, to expand Libyan influence in Africa, while Somalia had joined the ranks of international pariahs with nowhere else to go for aid.

Siad Barre also entered into rather unsavory dealings with two other pariahs on the African scene—the government of South Africa and Rhodesian mercenaries. In mid-1985 reports began to circulate of Somali military relations with South Africa.[67] During the fighting in the north in mid-1988, the Somali government hired ex–Rhodesian Air Force pilots flying British Hawker Hunter aircraft to carry out bombing missions over Hargeisa—an order refused by one Somali pilot who then defected.[68] Some in Congress suspected that South Africa had facilitated this Rhodesian connection with Somalia.[69] Again, the only thing Mogadishu had in common with South Africa and the Rhodesians was their pariah status in Africa. Siad believed that any opportunity was worth seizing in order to survive.

Mogadishu's decade-long policy of arms diversification allowed Siad Barre to continue the suppression of the north despite the U.S. aid freeze.

However, Washington's punitive act did make life more difficult. If U.S. security assistance had been kept at the levels provided through the mid-1980s, the Somali Army perhaps would have been able to deal with the opposition more effectively and decisively.[70] As it was, ammunition was sometimes scarce, and morale in some units of the Somali military was quite low.[71] Siad was paying a price for his repressive policies, though perhaps only a small one whose cumulative effect might not be felt for years.

Despite continuing diplomatic rebuffs by Washington, Siad did not threaten U.S. access to Berbera. The connection was still too good to be jeopardized. Even if aid had not been frozen (and later suspended) because of the budget crisis, Washington had little to give Somalia on a bilateral basis. Nevertheless, a positive relationship with the United States gave Somalia access to international financial institutions.[72] In May 1988 Somalia had been barred from borrowing from the International Monetary Fund (IMF) because of overdue payments on previous loans totaling about $37 million.[73] The United States had released $15 million in ESF so Somalia could repay some of this debt and be eligible for future loans. However, in January 1989 the United States openly supported a move by the UN High Commissioner for Refugees to withhold food aid from Somalia after six months of warning the government to cease using Somali refugees to fight against the SNM.[74] Later that year, the United States supported a $70 million loan from the World Bank, which was part of $200 million of World Bank loans pending for Somalia.[75] The African Development Bank was also planning to provide $25 million as part of an agricultural stabilization package.[76] Human rights advocates claimed that multilateral development aid was playing a critical role in keeping Barre's regime afloat and that Washington should use its influence to squeeze this source dry.[77] It was suggested that Congress invoke section 701 of the International Financial Institution Act to prevent multilateral aid to systematic violators of human rights such as Siad Barre's regime.[78]

While multilateral aid continued, the future of U.S.-Somalia bilateral aid relations was quite dim, even if Siad were to clean up his act. In the spring of 1989, the Bush administration had requested $14.5 million for development assistance (DA) and PL 480 funds for FY 1990. A year later the administration proposed $8 million in DA and PL 480 funds for FY 1991. But by the summer of 1990, Somalia was in danger of falling victim to the Brooke amendment, which forbade giving aid to countries more than one year in arrears on loan repayments to the United States. Mogadishu needed to pay back $12 million in loans to be eligible for $5 million in U.S. aid.[79] Obviously, Mogadishu had little incentive to evade the Brooke amendment. Thus, unless the U.S. government came forward with a major aid package, the financial component of the American connection was worthless.

Thus, by the end of 1989 Siad Barre had few friends—except Libya—who would come forward with aid.[80] Moscow was unable to help. Until Siad Barre undertook domestic reforms, the United States had little to offer. While Mogadishu could acquire weapons from other countries, such as China, Libya, and Iraq, who were less concerned about the political and human rights situation in Somalia, Siad Barre was doing little to enhance his image in Washington by keeping company with such governments. Besides, Libya and Iraq were not the Soviet Union. Even immediately after Iraq's invasion of Kuwait, U.S. officials felt no compulsion to get into a bidding war over Somalia. Regarding the U.S.-Somalia base-access agreement, Mogadishu was in a weak bargaining position. It was better for the Somalis not to rock the boat.[81]

DECLINING STRATEGIC ASSETS AND OPTIONS

When the U.S.-Somalia base-access agreement came up for renewal in August 1990, there was already a movement in Washington pressing for a reassessment of U.S. strategic interests in Southwest Asia should be analyzed in light of the changes in U.S.-Soviet relations.[82] How important were these facilities now that the Russians had withdrawn from Afghanistan and the Soviet threat to the Persian Gulf had dissipated? What was the strategic significance of Somalia? Given the U.S. budget crisis and the declining Soviet menace, Washington might take this opportunity to cut back on its foreign commitments and obligations. However, such a study kept being put off; no one in the executive branch really wanted to do it.[83] One reason may have been the Pandora's box it would have opened if Congress got involved in the study.

It was no secret that influential congressional committees had little love for Siad Barre—or Somalia for that matter—and might use the opportunity to terminate the base-access agreement with Mogadishu. In the House Subcommittee on Africa, there was a feeling that Somalia had never been strategically important.[84] Acquiring access to Berbera had been a "symbolic post-Iran thing," advanced to get access and keep the Russians out, but little more.[85] There were other sites in the region—in Egypt, Oman, and Diego Garcia—from which to respond to major interventions. Moreover, as proved by the reaction in Riyadh to the Iraqi invasion of Kuwait, Saudi military facilities would be made available and even a U.S. ground presence in Saudi Arabia would be allowed if there was a direct threat to the Saudi Kingdom and Persian Gulf oil. The Iraq-Kuwait crisis also demonstrated that NATO forces and bases would support U.S. military operations in such an "out-of-area" contingency. Even in a minor contingency, Somalia was unnecessary, as U.S. aircraft carriers could be used to deal with the situation. In peacetime, not much had been going on at Berbera. Only a few planes, mostly UN emergency aircraft, used the airfield.[86] Critics viewed the continuation of the U.S.-Somalia base deal as an example of bureaucratic momentum: the Pentagon's inability to break with a precedent.[87]

For the Pentagon, Somalia was a convenience, but one to which the United States should keep negotiated access if possible.[88] While the facilities at Berbera were "not wonderful," they were "good."[89] Berbera was also "the best in terms of proximity and access to the Bab al-Mandab."[90] There was a reasonable airfield at Berbera that could be used if the need arose. As for Berbera's vulnerability, the facilities "would be vulnerable if the Somali military was not strong enough to repel insurgent attacks," or could be threatened by Ethiopia if Addis Ababa turned its attention from its own civil war and violated the 1988 peace agreement.[91]

In any event, Somalia gave the Central Command (CENTCOM), which was responsible for responding to contingency crises in Southwest Asia, flexibility. Since CENTCOM required access facilities to accomplish its mission, the United States needed a continued presence in Somalia. From the military perspective, access to Berbera was important, though in protecting U.S. interests there the Pentagon had to be careful not to run afoul of Congress or send the wrong message to Somalia. But as long as the United States did not contribute to Somalia's political problems and Mogadishu left the aid issue alone, it was worth keeping U.S. military options open.

American military planning for Somalia had originally taken place in the context of U.S.-Soviet relations. Even then, little was done at Berbera. While Iraq's invasion of Kuwait might have provoked renewed interest in the strategic importance of Somalia, working-level officials in the executive branch and congressional staffers were not impressed.[92] By the time the ten-year renewal date arrived, Somalia was being perceived only in terms of political developments in the country, not in a broader regional strategic context.

The United States seemed to assume that if the political costs of association with Mogadishu got too high, it could cut loose without any perceptible loss. The fact that the United States did not seek to extend its access rights beyond the one-year notification period (in contrast to the three-year, approximately $800 million, military base agreement negotiated with the Philippines in 1988), highlighted the ascendance of political considerations over a strategic rationale.[93] But in holding the line on aid suspension and not seeking a long-term guarantee to Somali military facilities, the United States seemed to be writing off the strategic value of the entire Horn of Africa. Not only Somalia, but also Sudan and Kenya found themselves at odds with Washington.

Sudan had been the linchpin for U.S. policy in northeast Africa and the recipient of the largest U.S. SAP package for sub-Sahara Africa throughout most of the 1980s. By 1990, however, its relationship with the United States had degenerated to a state worse than that between Washington and Mogadishu. Measured in terms of SAP funding for Sudan, Khartoum's decline as a U.S. regional ally began shortly after the fall of the Nimeiri government in April 1985. As a result of the renewed north-south civil war, human rights abuses associated with the war, Khartoum's budding relationship with Libya, and concern about Islamic fundamentalist influence in the government—issues that, with the exception of Libya, had arisen during Nimeiri's last year in power—U.S. security assistance dropped dramatically in the later 1980s.[94] Sudan, which had been given more than $100 million in SAP funding annually from FY 1982 to FY 1985, received approximately $27 million in FY 1986, $6 million in FY 1987, $15 million in FY 1988, and $13 million in FY 1989.[95] For FY 1990 and FY 1991, the United States was expected to provide a total of only $1.5 million in IMETP funds in order to expose the Sudanese officer corps "to U.S. values including human rights."[96]

Moreover, new U.S. military and economic assistance was barred to Sudan because of the Brooke amendment and because in June 1989 the military government of General Omer Hassan Ahmed al-Beshir overthrew the duly elected government of Prime Minister Sadiq al-Mahdi. With this action, Khartoum violated section 513 of the Foreign Assistance Act forbidding aid to military regimes that gain power by overthrowing a democratic government.[97] Like the Barre government, the Beshir government did not seem so much interested in U.S. aid, given the restrictions that might be placed on the prosecution of the civil war against the southern insurgents—the Sudanese Peoples Liberation Front (SPLF)—and its ability to attract support from other sources, most notably Libya and Iraq. While some prepositioning of U.S. military equipment was allowed under Nimeiri, by the end of 1990 it had all been removed. As in the case of Somalia, the U.S. strategic interest in Sudan was driven by the threat posed by the Soviet Union, Libya, and Ethiopia in northeast Africa.[98] Because this threat had diminished, so had the perceived value of Sudan.

American relations with Kenya began to go sour in the spring of 1990, at about the time that the U.S.-Kenya base-rights agreement was due to expire. Through FY 1990, declining U.S. security assistance to Mombasa had largely reflected budgetary constraints. As a result of decaying relations with Khartoum and Mogadishu at the end of the 1980s, Mombasa had emerged as the leading recipient of U.S. security assistance in sub-Sahara Africa. Kenya, seen as a model for economic management and political development in Africa, was a favorite aid recipient among liberals in Congress.[99]

However, throughout the first half of 1990 Kenya's economic and political performance deteriorated. President Daniel Moi's government was becoming increasingly repressive. In July 1990 it had cracked down on proponents of multiparty democracy. By August 1990 there was deep unhappiness on Capitol Hill concerning Kenya.[100] There was some question whether the remainder of the $16.175 million security assistance package proposed by the executive branch for FY 1991 would depend on Kenya's progress in human rights and opening up the political system, and whether $10 million in FMS concessional grant funds obligated for FY 1990 would be frozen.

A congressional threat to go after Kenya would not be taken so stoically by the Department of Defense. Kenya provided highly valued military facilities for U.S. naval fleet rotations in the Indian Ocean, and offered the closest "civilized" liberty port in the area.[101] While liberals in Congress would not favor cutting economic aid, some human rights crusaders might want to maintain pressure on Kenya.[102] Conversely, the Defense Department did not feel this was the time to "rock the boat with the Kenyans."[103] But outside the Pentagon, access to Kenyan facilities was "not worth a hill of beans."[104] Even after Iraq's invasion of Kuwait, the United States was getting to the Persian Gulf, conducting maritime intercept operations in the Red Sea, and implementing the blockade at the Bab al-Mandab without Kenya. Although the Kenyans had made some noise about renegotiating the base-access accord, by the end of the summer of 1990 no formal request had been made.[105] As in the case of Somalia, the United States did not press for a review, and the agreement with Kenya continued on a one-year notification basis.

While U.S. relations with Somalia, Sudan, and Kenya had deteriorated, Ethiopia sought to improve ties with Washington. Following the election of George Bush, and after a midyear trip to Moscow during which the Soviets reiterated the decision to retrench their military presence in the Horn, Mengistu suggested that he hoped for better diplomatic relations with the United States, then being conducted at the subambassadorial level.[106] Prior dealings with the United States would be forgotten, like "something that happens between two countries, as it does between members of a family."[107] With the situation in Eritrea becoming more desperate, and after surviving a coup attempt in May 1989, Mengistu hoped to reach a quid pro quo with the Americans—upgraded diplomatic relations in return for U.S. and Western aid.[108]

Although the Ethiopians agreed to participate in peace talks with the Eritreans, coordinated by former president Jimmy Carter, during the fall of 1989, and held discussions with U.S. Assistant Secretary of State for Africa Herman Cohen in Addis Ababa in August 1989, and in Washington in March and May 1990, these maneuvers failed. Instead, Washington used the issue of upgrading diplomatic relations to pressure Mengistu to allow the distribution of food aid through the Eritrean-controlled port of Massawa.[109] In reversing the quid pro quo equation, the Bush administration made the point that improving U.S.-Ethiopia diplomatic relations was less important to the United States than to Ethiopia. Addis Ababa, not Washington, would have to make the concessions.

Thus, Somalia was not alone in being rebuffed by the United States. Because of negative attitudes toward the Somalis in Washington, the United States was more willing to go after Somalia than Sudan or Kenya or even Ethiopia. Nonetheless, the targeting of African states by Washington not only reflected the diminished value of territory in Africa and a growing consciousness of human rights and political issues, but also would free up scarce resources to divert to what were viewed as "more worthy people [states]" such as Poland.[110] Given the relative nature of regional priorities, the Africanist community was afraid that what little interest there was in Africa was declining even further.[111] Thus, the United States' unspoken threat in dealing with Somalia and other African countries was not simply one of defection, but of complete disengagement, if the financial and political costs of continued engagement became too high.

CIVIL WAR IN SOMALIA

By the fall of 1989, political authority in Somalia had broken down. Government forces were engaged in almost daily fighting. Anarchy reigned in Mogadishu. Even the bedrock of Siad Barre's support, the MOD connection, was coming unraveled. Amid this internal disintegration, and what most observers saw as the gradual collapse of the Barre regime, neither the government nor the opposition directly threatened U.S. interests.[112] Both seemed willing to allow the United States to stay on the sidelines and come in later once the domestic situation improved.

Despite the growing opposition, Siad Barre held to his belief that only he could hold Somalia together. He had scored one success with the collapse of the SSDF. Ethiopia had started clamping down on the SSDF in late 1985, arresting its leaders and attacking SSDF camps to seize sophisticated weapons provided by Libya.[113] Several hundred SSDF fighters took advantage of a presidential amnesty to lay down arms and return to Somalia. Although at the end of 1988 about 1,000 SSDF soldiers were still in Ethiopian camps and were reported to possess impressive stocks of Libyan-supplied arms and ammunition, the last reported SSDF military raids occurred in early 1987.[114]

However, in the fall of 1988 there were signs that the MOD connection was breaking up. During the fighting against the SNM in 1988, several Dulbahante generals refused to serve in the north.[115] Until December 1988, Siad Barre had used the Ogadeen clan—former commandos of the WSLF and refugees forcibly conscripted into the army—to fight the SNM.[116] But in March 1989 a small-scale mutiny occurred among Ogadeeni troops, protesting the demotion of the defense minister, an Ogadeeni, who was then arrested in July. By the fall of 1989, a new Ogadeeni-based anti-Siad organization had been created—the Somali Patriot Movement (SPM). Some of the Ogadeen defectors believed that Siad had betrayed their cause by signing the 1988 peace agreement with Ethiopia, while some military leaders were displeased by the president's telling them how to fight in the north the previous year.[117] Thus, by the end of 1989 the Ogadeen clan, once among the most loyal to Siad, had split up, with one faction backing the government and the other siding with the SPM.[118]

In January 1989 another opposition movement dedicated to the termination of Siad Barre's rule, the United Somali Congress (USC), was founded in Rome by members of the Hawiye clan who had left the SNM.[119] A number of Hawiye had joined the SNM in late 1988 after leaving the moribund SSDF. While some remained with the SNM, those who left were concerned about their minority status within the Isaaq-dominated movement. Despite this split in the opposition, USC leaders established a committee in March 1989 to negotiate a merger with the SNM. At the time, the USC appeared too weak to launch an effective guerrilla struggle on its own. But it had a strong base of support in central Somalia and maintained ties to the aboveground political opposition, such as the so-called Somali Manifesto Group.[120]

The Somali Manifesto Group posed perhaps the most unique challenge to Siad's rule because it was an aboveground, nonviolent movement. It began in May 1990 when a group of 110 Somali elders published a scathing indictment of Siad's rule entitled Somali Manifesto I.[121] The ten-page document criticized the Barre government for corruption and maladministration, creating economic disaster, and human rights abuses. To address these problems, the elders called for a *shir*—a traditional conference of leading political, tribal, religious, and business leaders from all regions of the country—to be held on neutral ground (Djibouti, Saudi Arabia, Egypt, or Italy) to agree on common principles for a new constitution and to form a caretaker government until free elections could be held. At first Siad tried to ignore it; then on June 11 the government arrested forty-six prominent citizens associated with the manifesto. They were brought to trial before a National Security Court in mid-July on charges that could have brought the death penalty. However, demonstrations in Mogadishu forced the government to dismiss its case after a four-hour trial and to free the prisoners. The Somali Manifesto Group then began acting as a quasi-political party.[122]

In confronting opposition, Siad Barre's greatest strength continued to be the weakness of his fragmented opponents.[123] Despite the clans' dislike for Barre's regime, clan rivalries were even more virulent. Although agreeing that Siad must be removed from power, the opposition shared no consensus about Somalia's political future.[124] Siad, in true Machiavellian fashion, encouraged these rivalries by financing and supplying weapons to militias set up by the elders of various clans.[125]

Many Somalis associated with major clans, such as the Dir and Daarood, saw the opposition groups as purely self-interested and thus did not lend their support.[126] The Isaaqs were viewed as uninterested in the pan-Somali issue and ambitious to dominate the Somali political scene once again. In contrast, liberating the Ogaden seemed to be at the top of the agenda for the Ogadeen-based SPM. The Hawiye, who had relatively little power in previous governments, were fearful of being excluded again and desired to protect their business interests. While clan chauvinism fueled the opposition to Siad's rule, it also prolonged his stay in power.[127]

However, to keep all this together and to ensure that his own clan did not move against him, on August 29, 1989, Siad agreed to the creation of a multiparty system, with restrictions, and to hold elections in February 1991. Although the decision by the central committee of the ruling Somali Revolutionary Socialist Party (SRSP) was made to look as if it were Siad Barre's idea, it was reportedly forced on him by members of the presidential clan, the Mareehan.[128] The SRSP ruling committee had presented the proposal in June, when Siad rejected it. However, despite a "loyal bodyguard" of thousands of troops, continuing defections (by the Ogadeeni, in particular) apparently convinced Barre that he needed to take some dramatic action. However, Siad's idea of "multiparty" elections was to create three factions within the SRSP—an idea unacceptable to his opponents.[129]

As of fall 1990, the United States had emerged with its reputation basically intact among all parties. Washington maintained regular diplomatic relations with the Somali government. An exiled leader of the SPM in San'a, Yemen, was a former ambassador to the United States, and likely to be favorably disposed toward Washington.[130] While it was a "deep dark question" in the 1980s as to the SNM's stand toward the West because of the SNM's tactic of being all things to all people—communists for the East bloc, Islamic fundamentalists for the Iranians and some Arab countries, and capitalists for the West—they seemed well disposed toward the United States, as did the USC.[131] Discussions between the SNM and the United States had been ongoing since at least 1988.[132]

The Somali Manifesto Group was of particular interest to the United States because it seemed to offer a peaceful path to resolving Somalia's political difficulties. Moreover, the Manifesto Group was considered very pro-West and pro–United States, especially so as the result of the U.S. stance during their stay in jail.[133] A statement drafted by the State Department calling for their release, arguing that their arrest contradicted a government statement that it would tolerate peaceful opposition, was published in Mogadishu, and then copied by the thousands and distributed with much red, white, and blue fanfare. Subsequently, the U.S. government maintained contacts with the Somali Manifesto Group in Somalia and the United States.

Hence, the Somali political debate was focused on internal issues, not Somalia's foreign policy. In late summer 1990, the United States was not threatened with expulsion from Berbera by either the government or the opposition—a threat made by Somali insurgents back in 1982. The United States would be welcome in a post-Siad Somalia as long as it kept its distance from the Barre government. Siad Barre could perhaps take solace in that the Americans were not acting overtly against him. Thus, the political situation in Somalia was so precarious in 1990 that the question of U.S. access to Berbera was the least of anyone's worries.

CONGRESS AND SIAD: A PERSONAL THING

The aid debate in Washington weighed against Siad Barre and Somalia. There was little doubt that Congress would deny funding to Somalia without major changes in its human rights record and progress toward national reconciliation. Even the U.S. executive branch agreed that the Somali government had not done enough in these areas. But in Congress the question of aid for Somalia took on the appearance of a personal vendetta against Siad Barre.

At the forefront of the political battle in Washington against aid to Siad Barre's government was the House Subcommittee on Africa, chaired by Howard Wolpe, one of the most vocal critics of aid to the Somali government and a skeptic regarding Berbera's strategic value. The Africa subcommittee was by no means monolithic. Dan Burton, a conservative congressman from Indiana, often criticized his committee for attacking friends, such as Somalia and Kenya, for human rights abuses and ignoring similar problems in Ethiopia and Mozambique—a contention Wolpe denied.[134] During the subcommittee's July 1988 hearing on the reported massacres and indiscriminate killings in the north of Somalia, Burton counseled that the United States should not "go off half-cocked and start blaming the Somali government."[135] However, Burton came across as someone unwilling to accept the end of the cold war. The majority sentiment of the Africa subcommittee was captured by Howard Wolpe during the FY 1990–91 hearings on foreign assistance for Africa in the spring of 1989: "I hope that we can begin to understand these issues in broader terms and take them out of the context of cold war rhetoric and east-west paradigms because I think that's wholly irrelevant to the issues we're trying to address in the continent."[136]

Besides the generally anti-Somalia and anti-Siad views of Congress, in dealing with the United States over the past decade the Somalis had not proved very adept at public relations.[137] They had convinced very few American officials that U.S. interests in the Horn of Africa would be best served by a security link with Somalia. Most Somali crusaders in Washington had been motivated by short-term strategic reasons related to the cold war, not by any enduring sympathy for the Somalis. Now, this pressure point was gone.

Moreover, unlike Ethiopia, the Somalis could not count on any influential pressure group assisting their cause. The Israelis had again become involved in the Horn of Africa after Mengistu restored diplomatic relations with Israel in November 1989. This move apparently assumed a quid pro quo—Israeli military assistance in exchange for Ethiopia's help in the emigration of some 15,000 Falashas (Ethiopian Jews) to Israel.[138] Israel was also protecting its own strategic interest in denying the Red Sea coastline to the Eritreans and Arabs. In pursuit of that objective, Israel reportedly supplied cluster bombs and was preparing to provide Kfir fighter aircraft to Addis Ababa to use in the war against the Eritreans.[139] After the Eritrean victory at Massawa in February 1990, the Israelis began pressuring the United States for talks at the foreign minister level with the Ethiopians and to seize the opportunity to regain influence in Ethiopia now that the Soviet Union was cutting back its once sizable support for Mengistu.[140] Although the Bush administration refused to replace the Soviets in Ethiopia or alter its insistence that Addis Ababa should negotiate an end to the war in Eritrea, Ethiopia still had politically powerful friends operating in Washington on its behalf. Somalia did not.

Mogadishu's public relations problem, however, was not limited to a visceral dislike of Somalia and absence of effective lobbying on Capitol

Hill. Even if political conditions in Somalia changed, the executive branch would face an uphill battle in getting anything for the Somalis so long as Siad Barre remained in power. Influential members of Congress personally disliked Barre.[141] Not only was he not trusted, but also he was seen as guilty of human rights violations.

By the fall of 1989, the Somali government had virtually no support in Washington. Members of Congress were out to thwart military and economic aid to Barre's government.[142] Moreover, even if Siad left the scene, it was doubtful that Congress would want to help Somalia. In contrast to providing aid for Israel or Eastern Europe, there was nothing to be gained politically by helping Somalia.

The State Department's attitude was less personal; its mission was to conduct business with all kinds of governments. Although in September 1989 State Department officials still maintained that Berbera was "important to [U.S.] interests" as a staging point for Southwest Asia, pressure was being exerted on Somalia in the wake of the July 1989 riots and violence in Mogadishu.[143] Following the execution of forty-six Somalis allegedly involved in the rioting, the U.S. embassy in Mogadishu was instructed by the State Department to put Somalia on notice that the United States expected full protection of civil liberties and human rights.[144] According to Assistant Secretary of State Richard Schifter, Somalia was left in no doubt that unless these abuses stopped its relationship with the United States would change.[145] The Gersony Report, investigating Somalia's human right situation between May 1988 and March 1989 and released in September 1989, confirmed that several thousand Somali civilians had been killed by government forces during this period. It was highly critical of government abuses committed in the north to suppress the SNM insurgency and attempts to blame the Mosques for assassinating the Roman Catholic bishop of Mogadishu.[146]

Although the Africa Bureau wanted to provide humanitarian and development aid to Somalia, it had never desired a military involvement in Somalia because of Mogadishu's irredentist claims in the region.[147] Because of U.S. budgetary problems and continuing violence and human rights abuses in Somalia, the State Department could do little anyway. It saw three possible scenarios for the resumption of aid to Somalia.[148] First, a peaceful transition would occur, perhaps based on the Somali Manifesto, bringing democratic elections and Siad Barre's resignation, and a new request would be submitted to Congress. Second, the armed opposition would defeat the government and a coalition would take control—a situation requiring further assessment. Third, the war would drag on, Siad would either step down or die, and the president's son or another member of the Mareehan would succeed, in which case the United States would likely remain on the sidelines.

The Defense Department was more willing to continue a working relationship with Somalia. There was no question that the Somali government, not the United States, was at fault for the suspension of U.S. aid, and only Somalia could reverse the situation.[149] However, even this cloud had a silver lining: the IMET program, built up considerable goodwill between U.S. and Somali military officers.[150] Knowledgeable insiders in Washington believed that no matter what happened, the present senior corps of Somali military officials would retain influence.[151] It was important not to alienate them. Thus, the one program the executive branch continued to press for during this period (FY 1990–FY 1991) was the IMETP, which was justified on the grounds that it would "expose Somali officers to U.S. values of respect for human rights."[152] Besides, the IMET program was so small that Congress would probably leave it alone—an estimated $796,000 for FY 1990 and a proposed $900,000 program for FY 1991.

The debate in Washington was heavily skewed against Somalia. Even if it wanted to, the executive branch could not negotiate a new long-term base deal with Mogadishu, given the mood in Congress. On Capitol Hill, Siad's government was viewed as politically and economically bankrupt.[153] State Department and Pentagon officials also did not think much of Siad's style of rule either. Only the Pentagon raised a rather weak voice to advocate minimal security assistance for Mogadishu: if the U.S. military did not have Somalia, where would it go? However, by August 1990 the strategic sacrifice of possibly losing Berbera was outweighed by the political and moral costs of maintaining a security assistance relationship with Somalia.

SUSPENDING THE GAME

As the ten-year anniversary of the arms-for-base-access accord came and went, U.S. aid remained suspended. The civil war in Somalia raged on as Siad Barre continued to hold power. The United States still retained access rights to Berbera. In material terms it was a one-sided exchange favoring Washington.

Siad Barre essentially had no leverage to force Washington to choose between supporting his government or losing strategic base-access rights in Somalia. Barre was in no position to make threats, given the internal situation in Somalia. Yet, given the fragmentation of the opposition and the willingness of others (such as Libya) to help him, Barre perhaps could do without U.S. support. However, Siad could not afford to antagonize the

United States; it was better for Washington to remain a neutral observer in Somalia's civil war than to provide support to an opposition apparently willing to keep the strategic relationship with the Americans intact. If Mogadishu wished to avert further international isolation, it would have to accept this unprofitable exchange.

While the United States could not force Siad to undertake internal reforms, it could resist Somali pressures or threats of blackmail concerning Berbera. The end of the cold war between East and West had a profound impact on how Washington viewed Africa. As a consequence of this diminished perception of threat, not only Somali military facilities, but also other sites in northeast Africa lost much of their value. Despite worsening relations with Kenya and Sudan, Washington's narrowed choice of options meant less in light of the new political-military relationship developing between the United States and the Soviet Union. Finally, the balance of opinion in the legislative branch and executive branch favored at best a wait-and-see approach, if not complete disengagement from Somalia. Marginal strategic benefits were far outweighed by the political costs.

In contrast to the U.S.-Ethiopia military relationship, which grew stronger until the overthrow of Haile Selassie in 1974, the U.S.-Somalia relationship made few advances under Siad Barre. Somalia was still viewed with suspicion by U.S. policy makers. A "Somalia imperative" never developed at the Africa Bureau or Pentagon, beyond the debatable notion that Berbera possessed some strategic value. Without that rationale, it was difficult to justify aid to a government guilty of gross human rights violations. Even after Kagnew Station had been phased out and Addis Ababa was cited for human rights abuses, the attitude still prevailed that the United States should keep the lines of communication open to Ethiopia, even with Mengistu in charge. No such optimism colored the policy debate in Washington in 1989–1990 concerning aid to Somalia. Despite ten years of military relations, attitudes toward Somalia generally had changed very little, and in fact had hardened against Siad Barre.

Conclusion

On 4 January 1991, while world attention was focused on the Persian Gulf and counting down the days to George Bush's January 15 ultimatum for Saddam Hussein to withdraw Iraqi forces from Kuwait, a U.S. Navy Seals team arrived in Somalia.[1] Their mission was to ensure the safe evacuation of the U.S. embassy in Mogadishu. By the evening of January 6, the U.S. embassy, which had already come under small arms fire and had been hit by bazookas, was evacuated. A week later the Italian embassy, the last open foreign embassy in Mogadishu, had also closed down.

The embassy evacuations were brought on by the fierce fighting that had erupted in Mogadishu at the end of December 1990 between the forces of the United Somali Congress (USC) and Somali military units, including the presidential guard (Red Berets), that had remained loyal to Siad Barre.[2] Half the city of Mogadishu was destroyed in the fighting. From the presidential palace Siad's forces randomly shelled the city and outlying areas for weeks, while street battles consumed the capital. Thousands were killed, mostly civilians, in the fighting. Electricity, water, and telephone links to the outside world were knocked out, and there were food shortages. Mogadishu's gothic Catholic cathedral was hit by grenades and burned. The U.S. embassy, along with many other foreign embassies, was blown apart by bazookas and looted by the Somali Army following the American evacuation. Civilians who had not fled the city were buying weapons in the street to fend for themselves and survive this anarchy.

Amid the rubble, Siad Barre made one last attempt to salvage the situation diplomatically. On January 24 he appointed a new government—led by Omar Arteh Ghaleb, a nationally known political figure from the Isaaq clan—and agreed to step down as president if the rebels accepted a truce. Siad's deal was rejected. As the presidential palace came under siege, Siad and his top aides were forced to move to a fortified bunker near the Mogadishu airport. With the arrival of forces from the Somali

Patriot Movement (SPM), the noose tightened, forcing Siad into a humiliating withdrawal. Finally, on January 27 the USC rebels declared victory.

Amid the jubilation there remained a pervasive fear that the civil war was not yet completely over. Initially it was reported that Siad Barre and his entourage had slipped into Kenya, having been promised safe passage by the Kenyan government, and from there Siad would retire to Abu Dhabi in the United Arab Emirates.[3] But instead Siad and his top aides fled in a large armored convoy to the deposed president's hometown of Garbaharre, 300 kilometers northwest of Mogadishu, perhaps in order to regroup for a new round of fighting.[4] Given the general belief outside the president's own Mareehan clan that Siad Barre's twenty-one-year reign had brought Somalia nothing but economic hardships, military setbacks, and political fragmentation, it is hard to imagine any significant role for Siad in Somalia's future, especially given his age and poor health.[5] The Mareehan as a clan, however, may not necessarily be out of the game if traditional Somali clan rivalries resurface in post-Siad Somalia, as they are likely to do.

Even without Siad Barre to contend with, the new USC (Hawiye) dominated interim government will have a long road to travel, not only in rebuilding Somalia but also in bringing peace, stability, and democracy to this war-ravished country. After claiming victory, the USC called for the formation of a broad-based democratic government of national reconciliation and a multiparty system.[6] Ali Mahdi Mohammed, a member of the USC's Mogadishu-based Executive Committee, was sworn in as interim president on January 28, and he appointed Omar Arteh Ghalib as prime minister. Drawing upon the platform enunciated in the May 1990 Somali Manifesto I, the new president called for the convention of a *shir* (a traditional meeting of clan elders) to be held in February 1991. The *shir*, to include all clans, would be responsible for drafting a new constitution and seeking a formula for national reconciliation. U.S. State Department analysts viewed the USC-appointed government as moderate and democratic, because of its ties to the much-respected Manifesto Group. As the most conciliatory of the three main rebel movements because of its multiclan affiliations, it seemed to offer Somalia perhaps its best chance for peace.[7] Unfortunately, as of July 1991 the USC's call for a unity conference has been rejected by the SPM and SNM.

However, a closer examination of the post-Siad political scene in Somalia leads to a dismal projection. The USC is itself divided.[8] Although predominantly a Hawiye movement, the USC is fractured along subclan lines: the principal contenders are the Abgal Hawiye, who are numerous in and around Mogadishu and control the Mogadishu-based USC Executive Committee, of which President Ali Madhi Mohammed is a member, as are many signatories of Somali Manifesto I, and the Habr Gidir Hawiye, some of whom remained associated with the Somali National Movement (SNM), while others joined the Rome-based faction of the USC. Besides the Abgal, with nine subgroups, and the Habr Gidir, with five subgroups, there are four other Hawiye subclans, adding to the confusion.

In the south, the SPM and Daarood-based Somali National Front (SNF)—a group seen by some as a stalking horse for Siad Barre—continue to oppose the USC-dominated government in Mogadishu.[9] While there is at least one Ogadeeni minister in the new government, the SPM has demanded a greater share of political power.[10] Whereas for the Hawiye-based USC government the Ogaden issue is viewed with antipathy, it remains a fundamental part of the Ogadeen (SPM) and Daarood (SNF) agenda. Despite calls for moderation by Somali political leaders, the continued interclan fighting in the south seems to be favored by the populace, as there are old scores to settle; consequently, a new stream of refugees, mostly from the Daarood clan, are flowing into Kenya and the Ogaden.[11]

Like the SPM, the Isaaq-based SNM believes it has earned the right to have a major voice in the distribution of power because it had been in the field waging its war against the government throughout the 1980s and had borne the brunt of Siad's military crackdowns, especially in 1988. Thus, the SNM also views the USC as something of an usurper. The USC organization had only been created in 1989, and as late as mid-1990 was thought to be the weakest militarily and posing the least threat to Siad's rule of the three insurgency movements.[12] However, the USC was politically well positioned since its main base of clan support was in the center of the country, an area including Mogadishu. Nonetheless, the SNM and SPM feel that it was only owing to their persistent efforts that Siad Barre's government was worn down to a point of exhaustion, thus allowing the USC to seize power. So even though several Isaaqs were appointed to the interim government, including the prime minister, the fact that no other northern clans were represented, coupled with traditional northern suspicion of the south, resulted in a break between north and south.

Following the fall of Siad and the collapse of the Somali Army, the Isaaq-based SNM went about consolidating control in the north and establishing a regional administration. At first the SNM talked of moving the Somali capital from Mogadishu to a more central location.[13] However, the SNM agenda remained quite distinct from that of the southern clans—it would just as soon see the Ogaden issue disappear and wanted to reverse what northern clans believed had been years of discrimination against the north and domination by the south. Subsequently, the SNM renounced the 1960 act of Somali union and in May declared the Republic of Somaliland in the north, whose administrative lines were essentially the same as the old British Somaliland. While it was not clear if other northern clans agreed with this move, at least among the Isaaq popular opinion favored secession.[14] This seemed to be a replay of the situation in December 1960 when the Somali constitution was overwhelmingly adopted in the south, but stiffly opposed in the north. The basic attitude in the north was that southern clans and Italian rule and intervention—in propping up Siad Barre by supplying arms—had ruined Somalia.[15] Future association with the south would be on their terms.

Although the political leadership in the south is working to establish ties with the north, there is a feeling of bitterness among the general population toward the north. The SNM is seen as having betrayed the pan-Somali national cause. While many in the south would favor going to war to maintain Somalia's unity, logistically war between north and south seems unlikely, given the 300-mile gap between the two sides.[16] The popular movement at this time has been toward greater clannishness and fragmentation. Conceivably, Somalia could be sliced into three or four big chunks—a SNM-controlled north, the USC in Mogadishu and surrounding areas, and smaller areas under the control of the SPM and SNF.[17]

U.S. policy toward Somalia through the first half of 1991 was to encourage the factions to talk and get together through the auspices of the OAU, Egypt, or others, although the chances of success were not seen as great.[18] The declaration of the Republic of Somaliland by the SNM was greeted with a "big yawn" at the Department of State. Washington was "not impressed" and refused to support or condone the secession.[19] For the most part, there was only a limited role the United States could play, anyway. The $35 million U.S. embassy in Mogadishu had been destroyed, so there had been no American diplomatic presence in Somalia since early January. Thus, most of the information provided to Washington was second-hand and at times suspect.[20] Still, political analysts in Washington did ponder the question: what role would the Somali Army or Islamic fundamentalists play in post-Siad Somalia?[21]

More important for U.S. analysts, Somalia was no longer regarded as a strategic piece of property. Berbera had been abandoned by the Americans in December, and the storage tanks at the port had been emptied of fuel for use in the Persian Gulf war. Basically, Somalia was seen as "a total write-off"—it had been torn apart by years of civil war and insoluble interclan rivalries, was economically bankrupt, and had now lost all strategic value. The Bush administration did propose $300,000 in IMETP funding for FY 1992 to train sixteen Somali military students in the United States, but this was contingent on the resumption of normal bilateral relations with the new government. While $10 million in aid was released in spring 1991 to help Somalis who had fled the civil war, in this alphabet-soup land of rival clan-based factions, Washington's only interest was a humanitarian one.

THE UNITED STATES AND THE HORN OF AFRICA IN THE 1990S

The deteriorating political situation in Somalia over the past three years and continuing uncertainty about the new Somali government, the fall of the Mengistu government in Ethiopia, the end of the cold war, and the war in the Persian Gulf—which culminated in Iraq's defeat on February 28—have created a vastly changed security environment. Mengistu and Siad had both got on board George Bush's "new world order" bandwagon. Throughout the late summer and fall of 1990, Siad Barre followed the lead of Egypt and Saudi Arabia in the Arab League by voting to condemn Iraq's invasion of Kuwait and supported the introduction of Western forces into the Arabian peninsula. Reportedly, Somalia was handsomely rewarded with a $70 million cash payoff by Saudi Arabia and the United Arab Emirates.[22]

Ethiopia played a supporting role at the UN security council, voting with the United States to condemn the invasion of Kuwait and to impose sanctions against Iraq, and then in December supporting the UN Security Council's Resolution 678 authorizing the use of force to expel Iraq from Kuwait. Addis Ababa's announcement at the beginning of November 1990 that all Ethiopian Jews were free to emigrate to Israel—ending what many interpreted as Ethiopia's crude game of trading Ethiopian Jews for sophisticated arms from Israel—also improved relations between Ethiopia and the United States.[23] As a payoff, the United States, with the blessing of the Soviet Union, agreed to a more active role in mediating a settlement of the Ethiopian-Eritrean civil war.[24] On February 22, 1991, more than a year after the collapse of the negotiations sponsored by former president Jimmy Carter between the Ethiopian government and the Eritrean insurgents, a new round of peace talks was convened in Washington under State Department auspices, mediated by Herman Cohen, assistant secretary of state for African affairs.[25] Following the breakdown of these talks, the Bush administration in April sent a special envoy, Rudy Boschwitz, to raise the issue of Mengistu's resigning to achieve peace in Ethiopia.[26] Finally, in May, spurred by a desire to get the remaining Falashas out of Ethiopia before Addis Ababa fell to advancing Ethiopian People's Revolutionary Democratic Front (EPRDF) forces, and to avoid a catastrophe such as that suffered by the Kurds in Iraq, the Bush administration persuaded Mengistu to leave Ethiopia and the rebel forces to hold their advance until the Falasha evacuation was completed.[27] Herman Cohen then brokered an agreement that allowed the EPRDF to enter Addis Ababa and assume control in order to preserve "law and order."[28] The United States thereby acted as the "midwife" at the creation of a new Ethiopia—one that had been abandoned by the Soviet Union and which, except for its location across the Red Sea from Saudi Arabia, was of no direct strategic value to the United States.[29]

While the United States appreciated Somalia's and Ethiopia's political support at the Arab League and United Nations during the Gulf crisis, the war highlighted the fact that, strategically, regional threats to U.S. interests could be handled without using military facilities in the Horn. The economic embargo of Iraq, which included maritime sea-intercept operations in the Red Sea, was successfully conducted without using Berbera. With Addis Ababa torn by civil war and its Red Sea coastline largely under the control of insurgents, Ethiopia was a nonfactor in the strategic equation. When war broke out, U.S. naval vessels continued to operate in the Red Sea by using Saudi and Egyptian facilities. An American attack submarine in the Red Sea even got involved in the fighting by firing a Tomahawk missile at Iraq. Much as the critics of the 1980 U.S.-Somali arms-for-access deal had predicted in the event of a serious military threat in the Persian Gulf, everything in the region was opened up to the United States, negating the importance of Berbera. Turkey allowed U.S. jets to launch attacks against Iraq from its military bases; U.S. ground forces were "invited" into Saudi Arabia (which had apparently reached a secret agreement with Washington in the 1980s to construct military bases, command-and-control centers, and to allow the prepositioning of U.S. equipment at these secret sites) and other neighboring countries; and B-52 bombing runs were conducted from Diego Garcia. Moreover, after the U.S.-Iraq War ended, the United States was offered permanent basing rights in the Persian Gulf, further reducing the strategic value of Somali or Ethiopian military facilities. Another indicator of decreased U.S. strategic interest in the Horn of Africa is that while base-access accords with Somalia and Kenya were allowed to lapse into the one-year notification provision, a new ten-year access agreement was signed with Oman in December 1990.

While the United States did not need to use Berbera during the Persian Gulf buildup and six-week war, some analysts still believe that Berbera might prove useful given a different contingency.[30] The fact that the Somalis had granted the United States extraordinary access to the port weighs into this assessment. On the other hand, the prevailing feeling at the State Department is that, given the political situation in Somalia, the United States did not need such access.[31] It takes essentially no interest in Somalia, except of a humanitarian nature. Somalia could go down the tubes and it would not adversely affect the U.S. strategic posture in the region. Moreover, Berbera had suffered damage as a result of the civil war, and given the uncertainty of the situation, why should the United States go in there and repair facilities that might be blown up again?

Besides, Kenya appeared to offer all the access the United States would require to deal with potential contingencies in East Africa.[32] Mombasa's strategic significance in a Persian Gulf contingency had no doubt also decreased as a result of the Gulf crisis and war. The anticipated postwar U.S. security framework for the Persian Gulf—an increased naval presence in the Persian Gulf and access to bases in the affected area—would see to that. However, there were certain contingencies in which Kenya could, and did prove to be of value. The evacuation of the U.S. embassy in Khartoum in January 1991, after security threats arising from Sudan's alignment with Iraq, was conducted from Kenya. Furthermore, if something had gone wrong with the evacuation of the U.S. embassy in Mogadishu, there was an alternate plan to use Kenya.[33] Thus, even though U.S. security assistance to Kenya had been frozen by Congress in early July 1990 because of human rights violations, State Department officials were confident that given the pro-Western orientation of the Kenyan government, use of Kenya's military facilities would not be denied the United States. Strategically, Kenya was not absolutely necessary, but it would assure power projection in East Africa.[34]

The FY 1992 security assistance proposal presented to Congress in spring 1991 is quite revealing as to U.S. strategic interests in the post–cold war, post–Gulf war world order.[35] Sub-Sahara Africa ranks at the bottom of the Security Assistance Program's list of regional priorities. The Bush administration requested just under $62 million for the entire region, about one-sixth the amount for East Asian and Pacific countries and one-sixteenth of that for Latin America—the other two regions perennially at the bottom of the roster. However, some $1 billion in development and economic assistance was also proposed for Africa, which underscores a significant shift in how the United States intends to support African governments.

In the Horn itself, the only security assistance of any significance was that proposed for Djibouti ($5,175,000) and Kenya ($5,100,000), placing them second and third, respectively, in the region behind Namibia ($5,180,000). Because of continuing human rights violations in Kenya, it was questionable whether the $4 million portion of Foreign Military Financing (FMF) grant aid requested for Nairobi would pass through

Congress.[36] Only token IMET programs ($300,000) were planned for Somalia and Sudan, ranking them behind at least a dozen other SAP recipients in Africa. Washington's disenchantment and detachment from events in these two countries is further emphasized by the fact that of the $1 billion in FY 1992 development and economic aid proposed for Africa, none was requested for Somalia, and only $1 million for Sudan. Even before the fall of Mengistu, the executive branch requested $11,200,000 in PL 480 funds for Ethiopia.

U.S.-Ethiopia relations can be expected to improve in the 1990s if the government of Meles Zenawi fulfills its promise to return the economy to a free market and to promote democracy, and does not fall into the trap of renewing the war in Eritrea. Although the Tigrean leadership, including Zenawi, had at one point espoused a rigid Albanian-style communist doctrine, that has been cast off and the EPRDF has professed a commitment to democracy and free enterprise.[37] As a sign of its commitment to democracy, the EPRDF government agreed to allow EPLF and OLF participation and to hold national elections for a constituent assembly to decide Ethiopia's future by mid-1992. The Bush administration immediately drew a very clear and firm line with Zenawi: "No democracy, no cooperation."[38] One wonders, however, how far that cooperation will extend, given the fact that in the words of one high-ranking State Department official: "There are no geopolitical stakes in Ethiopia or the Horn of Africa anymore."[39]

Perhaps the most perplexing political question confronting American policy makers in the Horn of Africa concerns the fate of Eritrea. Following the collapse of the Ethiopian army in May 1991, the EPLF established a provisional administration in Eritrea. Assistant Secretary Herman Cohen sparked several days of anti-U.S. protests in Addis Ababa following a comment he made on May 28 supporting Eritrea's right to decide its own future.[40] Such a concept—allowing for the possibility of Eritrean independence—is not accepted in Addis Ababa, especially by the Amharas. While Mengistu was bad and brought ruin to Ethiopia, he was committed to Ethiopian unity and was respected as a nationalist.

While the EPRDF government and the United States have come out publicly in favor of an independence referendum in Eritrea, both parties believe that Ethiopia and Eritrea should remain united, or tied together in some formal political or economic union.[41] For its part, the EPLF has not shown much interest in power sharing in Addis Ababa. Although Isaias Afwerki, chairman of the EPLF, attended the reconciliation conference held in Addis Ababa in July 1991, apparently to emphasize Eritrea's separate status he did not sit with the other delegates.[42] While Afwerki has indicated that the EPLF would delay the referendum for up to two years to allow the situation to stabilize in Ethiopia, there is little doubt that the Eritreans will choose independence when given the chance. Memories of the last independence referendum held in Eritrea in 1962, which was fixed by Haile Selassie, certainly color the Eritrean perspective. This time around, however, the EPLF controls Ethiopia's Red Sea coastline and the situation on the ground, which grants it considerable leverage vis-à-vis Addis Ababa. Although the United States has shown a more realistic attitude toward the possibility of Eritrea's secession so not to give rise to any undesired speculation, State Department officials are closed-mouthed concerning under what conditions the United States would recognize an Eritrean declaration of independence.

Given the general mistrust of Somalia's ultimate regional ambitions, it seems unlikely that U.S.-Somali military relations will return to the situation that pertained in the 1980s, of massive levels of security assistance. At best Somalia might expect minimum aid, such as funding for military training (IMETP) and internal security. However, since Somalia has run afoul of the Brooke amendment, having fallen some $13 million in arrears in loan repayments, such aid will not be forthcoming. This, unfortunately, holds up the transfer of development assistance to Somalia—though it should be noted that Washington wiped out Egypt's military debt and helped reduce Cairo's $50 billion foreign debt by one-third in appreciation of Egypt's participation in the U.S.-led Gulf coalition.[43] For the near future, U.S. involvement in Somalia will be limited to providing emergency and humanitarian aid, and observing events from afar. At this point, chaos seems to be the order of the day in Somalia.

THE LESSONS OF U.S. SECURITY RELATIONS IN THE HORN

In considering the more general ramifications for supplier-recipient relations based on the U.S. experience in the Horn of Africa, there are several points to be noted. First, while there are economic incentives to sell arms to recipients who can afford to pay cash, where strategic rationales are the lone motive for a supplier—as in the case of the Horn—there will be a direct correlation between the supplier's perception of threat and its vulnerability to manipulation and reluctance to threaten defection. Second, the above formulation will be strengthened if unique assets are at stake in the recipient country, or muted if comparable alternatives are available. Third, the intensity of the game-playing will vary according to the weight of the domestic political debate toward engagement or defection. Thus, a supplier's influence vis-à-vis an arms client can be increased by reaching some accommodation or rules of understanding with its primary adversary, by developing redundant capabilities, or by responding to countervailing domestic political pressures. Of course, these actions may be beyond the control of any state.

In their dealings with the United States, Ethiopia and Somalia present two contrasting pictures of how to win friends within, and exert influence over, a reluctant supplier. First, if internal or regional conflict cannot be contained or eliminated in the client nation, it must be exploited so as to place a supplier's credibility on the line. Ethiopia did this with regard to Eritrea and the Ogaden by playing on the theme of defending Ethiopian unity. Somalia failed to do so because of the aggressive and destabilizing nature of Somali irredentism. As a result, the superpowers have been reluctant to become involved in Somalia because they have little to gain and much to lose, politically and militarily, by associating with an aggressor.

Second, a client's threats of defection carry little weight if global competition is muted or one's assets are deemed expendable or at high risk. Recipients interested in an enduring relationship with a supplier need to look beyond their own short-term strategic value to a supplier. It is important to develop a base of political support among influential political groups in supplier countries who can serve as advocates, especially in the permanent bureaucracy. Viewed in this light, the decade-long U.S.-Somalia security relationship appears to be an aberration. Where recipients do not confront immediate high-level threats, time, patience, and public relations may be their best allies and resources for acquiring long-term influence. With the end of the cold war, recipients states will be more pressed than ever to acquire scarce resources from retrenching great powers.

In arms relations between great power suppliers and small power recipients in the Horn of Africa, the manipulation of weakness and the threat of defection may have lost most of their utility as bargaining tools. Arms transfers are unlikely to reemerge as a modus operandi for the superpowers in the conduct of relations in the Horn. Indeed, military disengagement will become more attractive in light of the declining Soviet threat, budgetary problems in Washington, and the continuing instability and seemingly intractable conflicts in the Horn. Although the United States still maintains a strategic interest in the Horn, in terms of protecting SLOCs and the oil lanes, supporting Egypt's efforts to protect its southern flank and the Nile waters, and blunting destabilization activities aimed at Saudi Arabia and other pro-Western states, with the Soviet Union detaching itself from the influence game and pursuing a policy of cooperation with the United States, the threat to these interests appears marginal at best.

Arms transfers will continue to play a central role in the security calculations of Ethiopia and Somalia as long as their internal conflicts remain unresolved. Consequently, they will have to look to the middle powers, such as Israel, Libya, Egypt, Iran, or perhaps Iraq to meet their requirements. In the new global security setting, arms transfers will play only a minor role in U.S. and Soviet calculations and involvement in the Horn of Africa. The United States will maintain and wield influence in the region more effectively through its influence in international financial institutions and by extending bilateral development assistance. Other powers with more direct stakes in regional security issues have already begun, and likely will continue, to fill the arms void left by the superpowers. Of course, U.S. policy could abruptly change owing to the emergence of a new external threat or resulting from the loss of access to military facilities in the Persian Gulf.

Thus, in this altered global security environment, the manipulation of weakness and the threat of defection will have less meaning in U.S.-Horn relations. This type of game-playing may occur instead at the regional level, as Ethiopia and Somalia seek to exploit the Arab-Israeli conflict, or intra-Arab rivalries and alignments to their advantage. But, in the absence of a direct military threat to U.S. interests, there is no need for Washington to develop strategic options. One cannot manipulate weakness if one's target does not perceive a threat. One cannot threaten defection if the target state feels it has nothing to lose and questions what the defector stands to gain.

The United States is no longer strictly bound by the rules of the supplier-recipient bargaining game. Essentially, the game board has changed to Washington's advantage. Consequently, this may be the end of an era of high-profile military relations between the United States and the countries of the Horn of Africa. Perhaps it is the beginning of a new era based on economic development, human rights, and political reform.

Appendix

Notes

Index

Appendix

Table 1 U.S. Security Assistance to Other Countries, FY 1955–FY 1992
(in thousands of dollars)

	Near East and South Asia	*Europe and Canada*	*East Asia and Pacific*
1955–1969	2,903,884	18,545,047	14,690,588
1970–1979	13,599,445	2,823,977	17,011,070
FY 1980	2,913,915	678,813	394,951
FY 1981	3,588,420	840,566	376,446
FY 1982	4,141,393	1,218,789	425,656
FY 1983	5,474,477	1,640,003	483,600
FY 1984	5,635,420	1,790,935	506,090
FY 1985	5,119,675	2,070,935	578,670
FY 1986	4,935,620	2,086,140	584,050
FY 1987	6,136,690	2,118,660	600,140
FY 1988	5,928,730	1,882,670	351,910
FY 1989	5,818,880	1,143,920	313,140
FY 1990	5,873,275	1,151,195	445,105
FY 1991	5,808,855	1,121,320	412,775
FY 1992	5,527,971	1,226,440	352,895

Sources: See U.S. Department of Defense and U.S. Department of State, *Congressional Presentation for Security Assistance Programs,* for FY 1981, 479–511; and FY 1980–FY 1992.

	Africa	*South and Central American Republics*	*Total Worldwide*[1]
1955–1969	181,472	984,653	40,529,145
1970–1979	353,575	835,681	34,990,872
FY 1980	148,750	38,734	4,235,600
FY 1981	189,399	91,609	5,163,000
FY 1982	441,555	212,625	6,868,700
FY 1983	567,910	414,639	8,743,874
FY 1984	611,345	609,350	9,239,532
FY 1985	603,130	1,097,890	9,470,360
FY 1986	681,525	1,189,825	9,477,160
FY 1987	611,950	1,301,710	10,859,080
FY 1988	213,235	971,575	9,453,261
FY 1989	165,305	744,620	8,292,189
FY 1990	165,275	744,600	8,505,409
FY 1991	92,100	948,190	8,458,200
FY 1992	61,945	994,050	8,244,661

Note: Figures for 1955–1979 represent the total for MAP, FMS financing, and IMETP for this period. Figures for FY 1980–1992 are proposed amounts.

1. Includes nonregional assistance.

Table 2 U.S. Arms Transfers to Ethiopia, FY 1953–FY 1977
(in thousands of dollars)

	MAP	*IMETP*	*IMETP Students*	*ESF*	*FMS Financing*	*FMS Cash*
1953–1969	123,444	15,878	2,793	—	—	717
FY 1970	9,307	1,181	154	—	—	6
FY 1971	10,497	1,261	140	—	—	—
FY 1972	9,420	1,208	160	—	—	10
FY 1973	8,687	670	158	—	—	—
FY 1974	9.885	797	148	—	11,000	6,272
FY 1975	10,892	738	129	—	25,000	17,301
FY 1976	2,805	775	184	—	—	110,596
FY 1977	838	199	46	—	—	6
Security assistance program terminated						
1953–1977	185,774	22,707	3,912	—	36,000	134,907

Source: U.S. Department of Defense and U.S. Department of State, *Congressional Presentation for Security Assistance Programs, FY 1981,* 479–511.

Table 3 U.S. Arms Transfers to Somalia, FY 1980–FY 1992
(in thousands of dollars)

	MAP	*IMETP*	*IMETP Students*	*ESF*	*FMS Financing*	*FMS Cash*
FY 1980	—	—	—	5,000	20,000	—
FY 1981	—	380	21	—	20,000	41,104
FY 1982	15,000	440	26	20,000	10,000	45,394
FY 1983	15,000	601	32	21,000	10,000	8,653
FY 1984	32,000	993	47	35,000	—	24,252
FY 1985	33,000	1,132	72	30,000	—	32,941
FY 1986	19,140	1,106	57	22,011	—	20,264
FY 1987	7,500	707	16	17,125	—	18,511
FY 1988	5,500	989	56	25,000	—	4,998
FY 1989	—	900	42	23,250	—	10,000
FY 1990	—	—	—	—	—	—
FY 1991	—	—	—	—	—	—
FY 1992[1]	—	300	16	—	—	—

Source: U.S. Department of Defense and U.S. Department of State, *Congressional Presentation for Security Assistance Programs,* FY 1980–FY 1992.

1. Proposed amounts.

Table 4 U.S. Arms Transfers to Somalia, FY 1980–FY 1992: Requests and Appropriations
(in millions of dollars)

	Executive Branch Requests		*Legislative Branch Appropriations*	
	SAP	*FMS Cash*	*SAP*	*FMS Cash*
FY 1980	—	—	25.0	—
FY 1981	.084	—	20.380	41.104
FY 1982	40.350	20.0	45.440	45.394
FY 1983	55.550	30.0	46.601	8.653
FY 1984	76.000	50.0	67.993	24.252
FY 1985	76.250	30.0	64.132	32.941
FY 1986	76.250	30.0	42.257	20.264
FY 1987	67.150	20.0	25.332	18.511
FY 1988	46.250	15.0	31.489	4.998
FY 1989	41.100	15.0	23.250	10.000
FY 1990	36.200	10.0	—	—
FY 1991	.900	—	—	—
FY 1992	.300	—	—[1]	—

Source: U.S. Department of Defense and U.S. Department of State, *Congressional Presentation for Security Assistance Programs,* for FY 1980–FY 1992.

1. Decision pending in Congress.

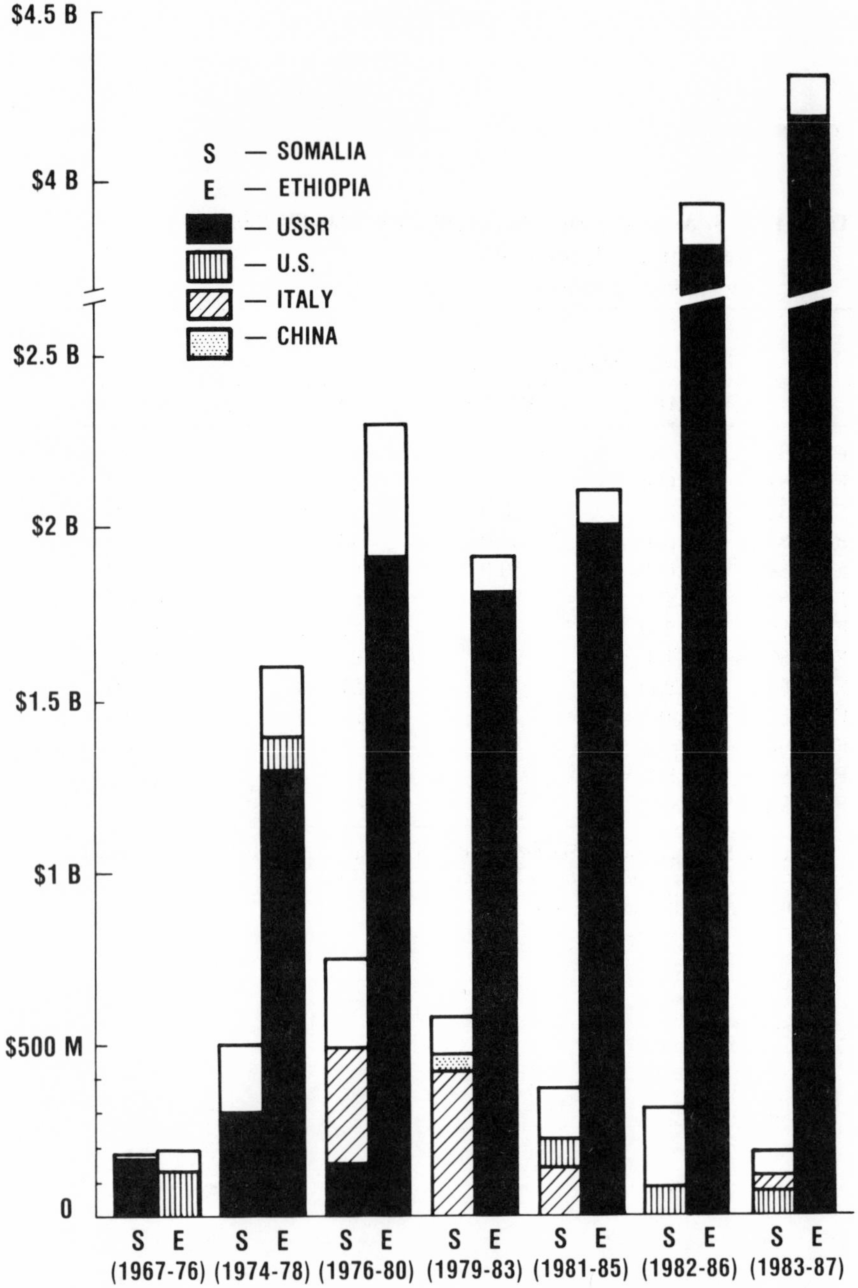

Source: U.S. Department of State, ACDA, *World Military Expenditures and Arms Transfers.*

Figure 1 Arms Exports to the Horn of Africa, 1967–1987

Notes

Introduction

1. See George Washington, "Farewell Address (September 17, 1796)," *Messages and Papers of the Presidents*, 213–24. Washington's comments on foreign affairs, here quoted, are extracted from 220–24.

2. Zbigniew Brzezinski placed the Horn of Africa in an "arc of crisis" that stretched from the Horn through the Middle East to Afghanistan. See George Lenczowski, "The Arc of Crisis: Its Central Sector," *Foreign Affairs* 57 (Spring 1979), 796–820.

3. The most recent data available from the U.S. Department of State, Arms Control and Disarmament Agency (ACDA), shows the Soviet Union providing Somalia with over $300 million worth of arms between 1967 and 1978, and Ethiopia with some $7 billion worth of weaponry between 1977 and 1986. See Appendix, figure 1. A more current estimate places Soviet arms transfers to Ethiopia between 1977 and 1990 at over $11 billion. See Jane Perlez, "On the Ethiopian Front, Rebel Confidence Rises," *New York Times*, February 14, 1990.

4. The assumptions underlying the supplier-recipient "exchange theory" are based upon the liberalism model presented in Robert Gilpin, *U.S. Power and the Multinational Corporation* (New York: Basic Books, 1975), 25–33; and the national interests model formulated in Theodore Moran, *Multinational Corporations and the Politics of Dependence: Copper in Chile* (Princeton, N.J.: Princeton University Press, 1974), 172–80. Also see Robert Packenham, *Liberal America and the Third World* (Princeton, N.J.: Princeton University Press, 1973), 4–5; Joan Nelson, *Aid, Influence and Foreign Policy* (New York: Macmillan, 1968), 91–128; C. R. Mitchell, *The Structure of International Conflict* (New York: St. Martin's Press, Inc., 1981), 17–25; Francis West, "The U.S. Security Assistance Program: Giveaway or Bargain?" *Strategic Review* 11 (Winter 1983), 50–56; and Andrew Pierre, *The Global Politics of Arms Sales* (Princeton, N.J.: Princeton University Press, 1982), 19–27.

5. The concept of "client dependence" in arms supplier-recipient relations draws upon the Marxism model in Gilpin, *U.S. Power and the Multinational Corporation*, 25–33; and the balance of power model in Moran, *Multinational Corporations and the Politics of Dependence: Copper in Chile*, 157–69. Also see Robert Keohane and Joseph Nye, *Power and Interdependence* (Boston: Little, Brown, 1977), 8–19; Mitchell, *The Structure of International Conflict*, 17–25; Johan Galtung, "A Structural Theory of Imperialism," *Journal of Peace Research* 8, no. 2 (1971), 81–117; T. Dos Santos, "The Structure of Dependence," *American*

Economic Review 60 (May 1974), 231–36; Richard Vengroff, "Dependency and Underdevelopment in Black Africa: An Empirical Test," *Journal of Modern African Studies* 15 (1977), 613–30; and Steve Weissman, ed., *The Trojan Horse: A Radical Look at Foreign Aid* (San Francisco: Ramparts Press, 1974).

6. The concept of "donor dependence" in supplier-recipient relations is influenced by the mercantilist model in Gilpin, *U.S. Power and the Multinational Corporation*, 25–33; and the economic nationalist model in Moran, *Multinational Corporations and the Politics of Dependence: Copper in Chile*, 119–52. Also see Keohane and Nye, *Power and Interdependence*, 17–25; Leslie Gelb, with Richard Betts, *The Irony of Vietnam: The System Worked* (Washington, D.C.: Brookings, 1979); J. William Fulbright, *The Arrogance of Power* (New York: Random House, 1966); U.S. Senate, *Security Agreements and Commitments Abroad*, Report to the Committee on Foreign Relations, 91st Cong., 2d sess. (Washington, D.C.: GPO, 1970); J. M. Healey and A. G. Coverdale, "Foreign Policy and British Bilateral Aid: A Comment on McKinlay and Little," *British Journal of Political Science* 11 (January 1981), 123–27; Pierre, *The Global Politics of Arms Sales*, 14–19; William Lewis, "Political Influence: The Diminished Capacity," in *Arms Transfers in the Modern World*, ed. Stephanie Neuman and Robert Harkavy (New York: Praeger Special Studies, 1980); David Baldwin, "Foreign Aid, Intervention and Influence," *World Politics* 21 (April 1969), 425–47; Thomas Wheelock, "Arms for Israel: The Limits of Leverage," *International Security* 2 (Fall 1979), 123–37; Robert Keohane, "The Big Influence of Small Allies," *Foreign Policy* 2 (Spring 1971), 161–82; and Yaacov Bar-Simon-Tov, "Alliance Strategy: U.S.-Small Allies Relationships," *Journal of Strategic Studies* 3 (September 1986), 202–16.

7. See Keohane and Nye, *Power and Interdependence*, 8–19; Pierre, *The Global Politics of Arms Sales*, 3–14; Kenneth Waltz, *Theory of International Politics* (Reading, Mass.: Addison-Wesley Publishing, Co., 1979), 129–60; Jonathan Stramseth, "Unequal Allies: Negotiations Over U.S. Bases in the Philippines," *Journal of International Affairs* 43 (Summer/Fall 1989), 161–88; and William Habeeb, *Power and Tactics in International Negotiations: How Weak States Bargain With Strong Nations* (Baltimore: Johns Hopkins University Press, 1988), 1–31.

8. States that behave as rational actors will choose the minimax strategy. See Graham Allison, *Essence of Decision* (Boston: Little, Brown, 1971), 32–35.

9. See Michael Ward and Lewis House, "A Theory of the Behavioral Power of Nations," *Journal of Conflict Resolution* 32 (March 1988), 3–36, esp. 6–11.

10. A succinct summary of the balance of interests model is presented in Richard Betts, *Nuclear Blackmail and Nuclear Balance* (Washington, D.C.: Brookings, 1987), 14–15. The bargaining strategy of "strength through weakness" is also argued in Thomas Schelling, *The Strategy of Conflict* (New York: Oxford University Press, 1960), 94–96.

11. The importance of manipulating threat perceptions is a central feature in Robert Jervis, *Perception and Misperception in International Politics* (Princeton, N.J.: Princeton University Press, 1976). The strategy of manipulating risk and utility perceptions in adversarial bargaining relationships is discussed in Glenn Snyder and Paul Diesing, *Conflict Among Nations* (Princeton, N.J.: Princeton University Press, 1977), 195–207.

12. Presumably governments will perform an analysis of short-term and long-term political, economic, and military costs and benefits. For the outline of one such model, see Geoffrey Kemp, with Steven Miller, "The Arms Transfers Phe-

nomenon," in *Arms Transfers and American Foreign Policy*, ed. Andrew Pierre (New York: New York University Press, 1979), 15–97, esp. 65–86.

13. This is based upon the five variables—systemic, individual, societal, role and governmental—identified by James Rosenau, "Pre-theories and Theories of Foreign Policy," in *Approaches to Comparative and International Politics*, ed. R. Barry Farrell (Evanston, Ill.: Northwestern University Press, 1966), 27–92.

14. David Easton's discussion [*A Systems Analysis of Political Life* (New York: Wiley, 1965)] of the personal, ideological, and structural sources of internal legitimacy also seems to capture the various bonds of legitimacy that may exist between two arms partners. Many of these ideas are embodied in the bureaucratic politics and the organizational process models presented in Allison, *Essence of Decision*. Also see Morton Halperin, *Bureaucratic Politics and Foreign Policy* (Washington, D.C.: Brookings, 1974); and Harold Seidman, *Politics, Position, and Power*, 2d ed. (London: Oxford University Press, 1976), 121–60. Thomas Schelling observed (*The Strategy of Conflict*, 29) that a bargaining agent (i.e. institution) has an incentive structure that differs from that of principles (i.e., leadership).

15. Disruption avoidance and incrementalism are prominent features of bureaucratic decision making. Abrupt policy changes seem more likely to occur where there is an absence of a structural bond between two states, since individuals who are advocates may be removed from power and governments which are ideologically incompatible with their current arms partner may come to power. An excellent case study of the strength and durability of personal, ideological and structural sources of legitimacy in a domestic political setting may be found in Michael Hudson, *Arab Politics: The Search for Legitimacy* (New Haven, Conn.: Yale University Press, 1977).

16. See the discussion of the elements of power in Hans Morgenthau, *Politics Among Nations*, 5th ed. (New York: Random House, 1973), 112–49. Also see David Baldwin, "Internation Influence Revisited," *Journal of Conflict Resolution* 15 (December 1971), 471–86.

17. See Marshall Singer, *Weak States in a World of Powers* (New York: The Free Press, 1972), 310–64; Charles Lockhart, *Bargaining in International Conflicts* (New York: Columbia University Press, 1979), 89–94, 108–14; Mitchell, *The Structure of International Conflict*, 15–46. This idea also relates to the concept of the "infungibility" of power in David Baldwin, "Power Analysis and World Politics: New Trends Versus Old Tendencies," *World Politics* 31 (January 1979), 161–94.

18. See Charles Hermann, "International Crisis as a Situational Variable," in *International Politics and Foreign Policy*, ed. James Rosenau (New York: Free Press, 1969), 409–21; Oli Holsti, *Crisis, Escalation, and War* (Montreal: McGill-Queen's University Press, 1972); and Howard Raiffa, *The Art and Science of Negotiation* (Cambridge, Mass.: Harvard University Press, 1982), 16.

19. SIPRI (Stockholm International Peace Research Institute), *The Arms Trade With the Third World* (New York: Humanities Press, 1971), 68–69.

20. Again, a cost-benefit analysis would be performed by each state to determine whether the advantages of defection would outweigh the costs of remaining in a relationship. See Kemp, with Miller, "The Arms Transfer Phenomenon," 65–86. A state may engage in "blocking" tactics to prevent the defection of a partner (Lockhart, *Bargaining in International Conflicts*, 101).

21. Creating strategic-military redundancy is not without costs. It not only requires a greater financial investment, but it may result in a "commitment-

capability" gap. See Halperin, *Bureaucratic Politics and Foreign Policy*, 56–60; and Leslie Gelb, "How Many Crises Are Too Many to Handle?" *New York Times*, August 14, 1983. The great powers' tendency toward, and the dangers arising from strategic overstretch are analyzed in Paul Kennedy, *The Rise and Fall of the Great Powers* (New York: Random House, 1987).

22. SIPRI, *The Arms Trade With the Third World*, 62–68.

23. Rosenau's model frames this discussion of internal variables ("Pre-theories and Theories of Foreign Policy," 27–92).

24. For a provocative analysis of the impact of the existence and nonexistence of countervailing domestic powers and pressures in a pluralist political system, see E. E. Schattschneider, *The Semi-Sovereign People* (New York: Holt, Rinehart and Winston, 1960), 20–46. Countervailing power may assume various constitutional and extraconstitutional guises in Third World political systems—the military, students, opposition movements, political parties, labor unions, intraparty factional disputes, protests and demonstrations, assassinations or insurgencies.

25. For a description of the dynamics underlying these two bargaining games, see Snyder and Diesing, *Conflict Among Nations*, 95–96, 107–22.

26. One might assume that the other partner will learn as the game progresses and is repeated. See Jervis, *Perception and Misperception in International Politics*, 217–82. The danger in using this strategy is that like the "boy who cried wolf" once too often, and perhaps at an inopportune time when the manipulator's threat is real, its partner will not take the threat seriously.

Chapter 1. U.S. Security Calculation in the Horn of Africa

1. U.S. arms transfers are grouped into two categories: FMS Cash Sales and the Security Assistance Program.

2. The Security Assistance Program (SAP) has five components: (1) FMS Financing (credit sales), (2) Military Assistance Program (MAP), (3) Economic Support Funds (ESF), (4) International Military Education and Training Program (IMETP), and (5) Peace-Keeping Operations (PKO).

3. For a legislative history of executive branch requests, and legislative appropriations and authorizations for the various components of the Security Assistance Program FY 1950–FY 1991, see U.S. Departments of Defense and State, *Congressional Presentation for Security Assistance Programs, FY 1992* (Washington, D.C.: GPO, 1990), 60–67.

4. Appendix, table 2.

5. See *Congressional Presentation for Security Assistance Programs, FY 1981* (Washington, D.C.: GPO, 1980), 479–511.

6. Ibid.

7. Ibid.

8. Appendix, table 3.

9. Ibid.

10. See Appendix, tables 1 and 3.

11. In the past, Congress has imposed a $25 million limit on MAP and a $40 million limit on total arms transfers, including cash sales to Africa. See U.S. House of Representatives, *Policy Toward Africa for the Seventies*, Hearings before the Subcommittee on Africa of the Committee on Foreign Affairs, 91st Cong., 2d sess. (Washington, D.C.: GPO, 1970), 194.

12. Officials at the Department of State Policy Planning Staff and Bureau for

Politico-Military Affairs and at the Department of Defense International Security Agency expressed similiar ideas on the objective strategic value of the Horn during interviews conducted in Washington, D.C., in April and June 1982.

13. J. Bowyer Bell, *The Horn of Africa: Strategic Magnet in the Seventies* (New York: Crane, Russak, 1973), 8–9.

14. Eritrea served as a rear supply and repair station for the Allied North African campaign in World War II. See John Rasmusen, *A History of Kagnew Station and American Forces in Eritrea* (Arlington, Va.: U.S. Army Security Agency, Information Division, 1973), 21. Moreover, the U.S. Navy's current "offensivist" maritime strategy might involve the Horn in a European conflict if Washington decided to execute preemptive strikes against Soviet Third World client states located along SLOCs, or as a precaution to secure the southern flank of North African and Middle Eastern staging areas in the event of a NATO defeat in the European land-air war. See Stephen Cimbala, "Extended Deterrence and Nuclear Escalation: Options in Europe," *Armed Forces and Society* 15 (Fall 1988), 9–31.

15. This assessment is based upon (1) the carrying capacity of oil pipelines being constructed across the Arabian Peninsula from Saudi Arabia's oil-producing eastern provinces to shipping terminals on the Red Sea, (2) the construction of pipelines from Iraq and Kuwait to Saudi Red Sea ports, and (3) the development of new oil fields in the Yemens. See "Red Sea: The Middle East's Next Troublespot," *The World Today* 44 (May 1988), 76–77. Also see Eric Watkins, "Tight Straits: The Red Sea Oil Route," *Middle East International* 373 (13 April 1990), 19.

16. See John Gaddis, *The United States and the Origins of the Cold War, 1941–1947* (New York: Columbia University Press, 1972).

17. See "X" [George Kennan], "The Sources of Soviet Conduct," *Foreign Affairs* 25 (1947), 566–82.

18. For globalists, North-South relations are a function of East-West relations. See Robert Tucker, "Reagan's Foreign Policy," *Foreign Affairs* 68 (1988/89), 19–21. Also see the address by Undersecretary for Political Affairs Michael Armacost, "U.S.-Soviet Relations: Coping With Conflicts in the Third World," *Current Policy* 879 (September 26, 1986).

19. Gamal Nasser's Arab nationalist ideology was perceived as an anti-Western challenge. Many of Nasser's ideas are espoused today by the Ba'athist governments in Syria and Iraq, as well as by Muammar Qaddafi's government in Libya. See Michael Hudson, *Arab Politics: The Search for Legitimacy* (New Haven, Conn.: Yale University Press, 1977). The Islamic fundamentalist movement, most particularly as represented by the followers of Iran's Ayatollah Khomeini, is heavily anti-Western. See R. K. Ramazani, *Revolutionary Iran* (Baltimore: Johns Hopkins University Press, 1988), 19–31.

20. For a summary of the regionalist critique of U.S. policy in the Third World, see Helen Kitchen, ed., "Options for U.S. Policy Toward Africa," *AEI Foreign Policy and Defense Review* 1 (1979), 2–76; and Charles Kupchan, "American Globalism in the Middle East: The Roots of Regional Security Policy," *Political Science Quarterly* 103 (Winter 1988/89), 585–611.

21. In May 1990 the YAR and PDRY merged into one state.

22. See Victor Levine, "The African-Israeli Connection 40 Years Later," *Middle East Review* 21 (Fall 1988), 12–17; and Mitchell Bard, "The Evolution of Israel's Africa Policy," *Middle East Review* 21 (Winter 1988/89), 21–28.

23. For an overview of U.S. policy in the Middle East, see Steven Spiegel, *The Other Arab-Israeli Conflict* (Chicago: University of Chicago Press, 1985); and

George Lenczowski, *American Presidents and the Middle East* (Durham, N.C.: Duke University Press, 1990).

24. This was true particularly after the June 1967 Arab-Israeli War, when many Arab governments broke diplomatic relations with Washington.

25. This notion was conveyed by a State Department official (interview, Washington, D.C., June 1982). U.S. thinking on this point has been influenced by the writings of Admiral Alfred Mahan. See Phillip Crowl, "Alfred Thayer Mahan: The Naval Historian," in *Makers of Modern Strategy*, ed. Peter Paret (Princeton, N.J.: Princeton University Press, 1986), 444–77.

26. This builds upon David Easton's idea of personal legitimacy in *A Systems Analysis of Political Life*.

27. Richard Nixon noted this particular distinction during Haile Selassie's July 1969 state visit to the United States. See *Public Papers of the President: Richard Nixon, 1969* (Washington, D.C.: GPO, 1971), 501–05.

28. See *New York Times*, February 19, 1964, 15.

29. See U.S. Senate, *Security Agreements and Commitments Abroad*, Report to the Committeee on Foreign Relations by the Subcommittee on U.S. Security Agreements and Commitments Abroad, 91st Cong., 2d sess. (Washington, D.C.: GPO, 1970). Some of the current congressional criticisms of SAP are summarized in Claiborne Pell, "Problems in Security Assistance," *Journal of International Affairs* 40 (Summer 1986), 33–42.

30. See U.S. Department of State, Bureau of Public Affairs, "The Fiscal Threat to U.S. Foreign Policy," *Current Policy* 877. See Mark Schneider, "A New Administration's New Policy: The Rise to Power of Human Rights," in *Human Rights and U.S, Foreign Policy*, ed. Peter Brown and Douglas MacLean (Lexington, Mass.: Lexington Books, 1979), 3–13. Since the mid-1970s the U.S. Congress has required the Department of State to present annual human rights reports for specific countries. In the case of the Horn, the linkage between arms transfers and human rights was expounded explicitly in 1977. U.S. Senate, *The International Security Assistance and Arms Export Control Act of 1977*, S. Rept. 95–195, Committee on Foreign Relations, 95th Cong., 1st sess. (Washington, D.C.: GPO, 1977), 2–3.

31. See Alton Frye, "Congress: The Virtues of its Vices," *Foreign Policy* 3 (Summer 1971), 108–25; and Paul Wanke, with Edward Luck, "American Arms Transfers: Policy and Process in the Executive Branch," in *Arms Transfers and American Foreign Policy*, ed. Andrew Pierre (New York: New York University Press, 1979), 193–94.

32. This view was conveyed to the author by a staff member of the U.S. Senate Foreign Relations Committee, interview, Washington, D.C., June 1982. Also see Richard Moose, with Daniel Spiegel, "Congress and Arms Transfers," in *Arms Transfers and American Foreign Policy*, ed. Pierre, 242.

33. Foreign aid has traditionally been one of the least favored programs on Capitol Hill and among the American public. In a nationwide New York Times/CBS News Poll conducted May 22–24, 1990, 83 percent of those polled would find a reduction in foreign aid acceptable (*New York Times*, May 27, 1990, A24).

34. This point was made to the author by a staff member of the U.S. Senate Foreign Relations Committee, interview, Washington, D.C., June 1982. Moreover, the legislative branch generally has given the executive branch much of what it has requested in the way of security assistance. See the summary of SAP amounts

requested, appropriated, and authorized in the Congressional Presentation for Security Assistance Programs, FY 1991, 60–64.

35. See Martin Weil, "Can the Blacks Do for Africa What the Jews Did for Israel?" *Foreign Policy* 15 (Summer 1974), 109–30; Donald McHenry, "Captive of No Group," *Foreign Policy* 15 (Summer 1974), 142–49; and Kenneth Longmeyer, "Black American Demands," *Foreign Policy* 60 (Fall 1985), 3–16.

36. See Edmond Keller, "Black Americans and U.S. Policy Toward the Horn of Africa," *Transafrica Forum* 2 (Fall 1984), 15–25.

37. This has not proved true, however, in the case of the U.S.-Israeli arms relationship.

38. See Halperin, *Bureaucratic Politics and Foreign Policy* (Washington, D.C.: Brookings, 1974), 26–28, 63–83.

39. Ibid., 243–45. Also see Harold Seidman, *Politics, Position, and Power*, 2d ed. (London: Oxford University Press, 1976), 121–60; and Graham Allison, *Essence of Decision* (Boston: Little, Brown, 1971), 67–96.

40. Generally the debate has been between "globalists" and "regionalists." For an overview of both positions, see Kitchen, ed. "Options for U.S. Policy Toward Africa," 2–76. Also see Noel Koch, "U.S. Security Assistance To The Third World: Time for a Reappraisal," *Journal of International Affairs* 40 (Summer 1986), 43–57.

41. See Halperin, *Bureaucratic Politics and Foreign Policy*, 56–60; and Leslie Gelb, "How Many Crises Are Too Many to Handle?" *New York Times*, August 14, 1983. This issue has been more broadly addressed in Paul Kennedy, *The Rise and Fall of the Great Powers* (New York: Random House, 1987).

42. See Halperin, *Bureaucratic Politics and Foreign Policy*, 63–83.

43. Francis West, Jr., "The U.S. Security Assistance Program: Giveaway or Bargain?" *Strategic Review* 11 (Winter 1983), 50–53; and U.S. Department of State, Bureau of Public Affairs, "Meeting Our Foreign Policy Goals," *Current Policy*, no. 1054.

44. Halperin, *Bureaucratic Politics and Foreign Policy*, 38.

45. These divisions became quite evident during the course of interviews conducted with officials in the State and Defense departments, as well as interviews held with former ambassadors assigned to the Horn of Africa. Also see Halperin, *Bureaucratic Politics and Foreign Policy*, 36–38; William Bacchus, "Foreign Affairs Officials: Professionals Without Professions?" *Public Administration Review* 37 (November/December 1977), 641–50; Andrew Scott, "The Department of State: Formal Organization and Informal Culture," *International Studies Quarterly* 13 (March 1969), 1–18; and Koch, "U.S. Security Assistance To The Third World," 46–48.

46. See Halperin, *Bureaucratic Politics and Foreign Policy*, 63–66.

47. Ibid., 38. This point was noted by several State Department officials during interviews conducted in April and June 1982.

48. See Scott, "The Department of State," 1–18. This perspective was expressed in interviews by more than one U.S. official who had served in the field.

49. The effect of SOPs on the formulation and conduct of U.S. policy is widely discussed in the bureaucratic politics literature. See Halperin, *Bureaucratic Politics and Foreign Policy*, 28–40; Allison, *Essence of Decision*, 83–89; and Seidman, *Politics, Position, and Power*, 121–60. For a more general survey, see Charles Perrow, *Complex Organizations: A Critical Essay* (Glenview, Ill.: Scott, Foresman, 1972).

50. Some analysts such as Jeane Kirkpatrick, President Reagan's UN ambassador, have attempted to distinguish between "authoritarian" governments of the right and "totalitarian regimes" of the left to justify such a policy. See Jeane Kirkpatrick, "Dictatorships and Double Standards," *Commentary* 68 (November 1979), 34–45.

51. The bureaucratic code of conduct encourages its members to "play the game, don't rock the boat, don't make waves, minimize risk-taking." The result is a bias against innovation in the policy-making process, and a tendency toward incremental or slow evolutionary change in policy. See Morton Halperin, *Bureaucratic Politics and Foreign Policy*, 55.

Chapter 2. The National Security Calculation of Ethiopia and Somalia

1. See U.S. Department of State, Arms Control and Disarmament Agency (ACDA), *World Military Expenditures and Arms Transfers (WMEAT), 1967–1976* (Washington, D.C.: GPO, 1978), 85; and U.S. Department of State, ACDA, *WMEAT, 1987* (Washington, D.C.: GPO, April 1988), 58.

2. See *WMEAT, 1967–1976*, 104; and *WMEAT, 1987*, 76.

3. *WMEAT, 1987*, 5.

4. In 1985 Ethiopia ranked twenty-ninth in the world (*WMEAT, 1967–1976*, 42; *WMEAT, 1987*, 58).

5. This averaged out to about 18.5 percent annually between 1967 and 1974, and 21 percent annually between 1975 and 1984 (*WMEAT, 1967–1976*, 61; *WMEAT, 1987*, 58, 76).

6. *WMEAT, 1967–1976*, 61; *WMEAT, 1987*, 76.

7. See *WMEAT, 1967–1976*, 129; *WMEAT, 1987*, 100.

8. See *WMEAT, 1967–1976*, 148.

9. *WMEAT, 1987*, 118.

10. See Appendix, figure 1.

11. Ibid.

12. Ibid.

13. The refugee crisis in the Horn of Africa is discussed in "6,000,000 Displaced in the Horn of Africa: A White Paper," *Horn of Africa* 4, no. 1 (1981); ibid., 2, no. 4 (1979).

14. While the French make good jet fighters (the Mirage jet) and the Italians tanks (Leopard), the United States and the Soviet Union can do it all. Moreover, the West Europeans can not produce sophisticated weapons at reasonable unit cost. Though the Soviets have the advantage in the speed of delivery and lower costs, the Americans give development assistance, ESF support, and military construction, and are more maintenance conscious. Overall, Washington and Moscow account for a majority of sophisticated weapons transferred to the Third World. See U.S. Department of State, *Conventional Arms Transfers in the Third World 1972–1981*, Special Report No. 102 (August 1982).

15. See Edmond Keller, "Revolution, Class and the National Question: The Case of Ethiopia," *Northeast African Studies* 2, no. 3 (1980/81); ibid., 3, no. 1 (1981), 43–68; John Harbeson, "Ethiopia and the Horn of Africa," ibid., 1, no. 1 (1979), 27–44; and Teshome Wagaw, "Emerging Issues of Ethiopian Nationalities: Cohesion or Disintegration," ibid., 2, no. 3 (1980/81); and ibid., 3, no. 1 (1981), 69–75.

16. Robert Gorelick, "Pan-Somali-ism vs. Territorial Integrity," *Horn of Africa* 3, no. 4 (1980/81), 31–36.

17. See Bereket Habte-Selassie, *Conflict and Intervention in the Horn of Africa* (New York: Monthly Review Press, 1980), 48–73; Basil Davidson, Lionel Cliffe, and Bereket Habte-Selassie, eds., *Behind the War in Eritrea* (Nottingham: Bertrand Russell House, 1980); Don Connell, "The Birth of the Eritrean Nation," *Horn of Africa* 3, no. 1 (1980), 14–24; Richard Sherman, "The Rise of Eritrean Nationalism," *Northeast African Studies* 2, no. 3 (1980/81); ibid., 3, no. 1 (1981), 121–29; and Tekie Fessehatzion, "The Eritrean Struggle for Independence and National Liberation," *Horn of Africa* 1, no. 2 (1978), 29–34.

18. See Tigray People's Liberation Front, *Tigray: A Nation in Struggle* (Khartoum: October 1979); Habte-Selassie, *Conflict and Intervention in the Horn of Africa*, 86–96; Patrick Gilkes, *The Dying Lion* (New York: St. Martin's Press, 1975), 175–91; Solomon Inquai, "The Hidden Revolution in Tigray," *Horn of Africa* 4, no. 3 (1981), 27–31; and "An Interview With TPLF," ibid., 32–35.

19. See "The Oromos: Voice Against Tyranny—Document 1971," *Horn of Africa* 3, no. 3 (1980), 15–23; "Ethiopia's Hidden War: The Oromo Liberation Struggle—Interview With the OLF," ibid., 5, no. 1 (1982), 62–67; Richard Greenfield and Mohammed Hassan, "Interpretation of Oromo Nationalism," ibid., 3, no. 3 (1980), 6–9; see also the interview with a member of the central committee of the OLF, "Oromia Speakes," ibid., 3, no. 3 (1980), 24–28; Patrick Gilkes, *The Dying Lion*, 205–15; and Habte-Selassie, *Conflict and Intervention in the Horn of Africa*, 86, 123–24.

20. See Gerard Chaliant, "The Horn of Africa's Dilemma," *Foreign Policy* 30 (Spring 1978), 116–31.

21. See Republic of Somalia, Ministry of Foreign Affairs, Public Relations Sector, *The Somali People's Quest for Unity* (Mogadiscio: September 1965).

22. In October 1981 the Somali Salvation Front (SSF) joined with the Somali Workers party (SWP) and the Somali Democratic Liberation Front (SDLF) to form the Somali Salvation Democratic Front (SSDF). See Bernd Debysmann, "Instability Reigns on the Horn of Africa," *Los Angeles Times*, December 5, 1981. The SSDF drew much of its support from the Hawiye clan in the south of Somalia. The SSDF is now virtually moribund, since many defectors have accepted Mogadishu's offer of amnesty. See "Somalia: Wounded North, bruised South," *Africa Confidential* 29 (18 November 1988). At the end of 1989, the Somali National Movement (SNM) was the main opposition group and was engaged in operations to seize the north of Somalia. See "Somalia: Showdown in the North," *Africa Confidential* 29 (29 July 29 1988); "Somalia: Generals fall out," ibid., 29 (23 September 1988); and "Support for Barre declines as Somali civil war intensifies," *Africa Report*, September/October 1989, 8–9. In 1990 the SNM was joined in armed rebellion by the United Somali Congress (USC) and the Somali Patriotic Movement (SPM).

23. The Ethiopia-Somalia rapprochement began in January 1986 with a meeting in Djibouti between Siad Barre and Colonel Mengistu. Talks broke down in February 1987 due to the activities of the Ethiopia-based SNM. Then in the spring of 1987 the WSLF supposedly was disbanded. Finally in April 1988 the agreement was signed between Addis Ababa and Mogadishu. However, the Ogadeeni clans feared that Siad had sold out the Ogaden and have opposed the agreement. See "Somalia: The president delegates," *Africa Confidential* 28 (1 April 1987); and "Somalia: Under Fire," ibid., 29 (28 April 1988).

24. Some claim that in the 1980s the EPLF became a "pawn of imperialism" by accepting arms from the United States and Saudi Arabia. See Tesfatsion Medhanie, *Eritrea: Dynamics of a National Question* (Amsterdam: B.R. Gruner, 1986). According to Philip Caputo, the genesis for his 1980 novel *Horn of Africa* about a covert CIA operation to arm "Eritrean" rebels against the Marxist-Leninist government in Addis Ababa was based on a real incident.

25. See Keller, "Revolution, Class and the National Question," 47–49.

26. Ibid., 49. Also see Mordechai Abir, *Ethiopia: The Era of the Princes* (London: Longmans, Green, 1968).

27. Keller, "Revolution, Class and the National Question," 50–51; Harold Marcus, *The Life and Times of Menelik II: Ethiopia 1844–1913* (Oxford: Clarendon Press, 1975), 77–110.

28. See Tom Farer, *War Clouds on the Horn of Africa: The Widening Storm*, 2d ed. (New York: Carnegie Endowment for International Peace, 1979), 13–16.

29. John Spencer, "A Reassessment of Ethiopian-Somali Conflict," *Horn of Africa* 1, no. 3 (1978), 23; also see Sven Rubenson, *The Survival of Ethiopian Independence* (New York: Holmes & Meier, 1976), 82–90, 389–98.

30. Nuruddin Farah, "Which Way to the Sea, Please?" *Horn of Africa* 1, no. 4 (1978), 31–36; John Harbeson, "Ethiopia and the Horn of Africa," 27–28.

31. Farah, "Which Way to the Sea, Please?" 31–36; Harbeson, "Ethiopia and the Horn of Africa," 27–28.

32. There is a vast literature on this subject. See for example Farer, *War Clouds on the Horn of Africa*, 69–127; Somali Republic, Ministry of Foreign Affairs, *The Somali People's Quest for Unity*; Gorelick, "Pan-Somali-ism vs. Territorial Integrity," 31–36; Saadia Touval, *Somali Nationalism* (Cambridge, Mass.: Harvard University Press, 1963); and Said Yusuf Abdi, "Self-Determination for Ogaden Somalis," *Horn of Africa* 1, no. 1 (1978), 20–25.

33. See I. M. Lewis, *The Modern History of Somaliland: From Nation to State* (New York: Praeger, 1965), 40–62; Touval, *Somali Nationalism*, 30–48; and Somali Republic *The Somali People's Quest for Unity*, 5–6.

34. Lewis, *The Modern History of Somaliland*, 56–62; Abdulqawi Yusuf, "The Anglo-Ethiopian Treaty of 1897 and the Somali-Ethiopian Dispute," *Horn of Africa* 3, no. 1 (1980), 38–42.

35. See Yusuf, "The Anglo-Ethiopian Treaty of 1897"; and also Somali Republic, *The Somali People's Quest for Unity*, 5.

36. For further information on the division and administration of the Somalilands by these four powers, see Lewis, *The Modern History of Somaliland*; Touval, *Somali Nationalism*; and Virginia Thompson and Richard Adloff, *Djibouti and the Horn of Africa* (Stanford, Calif.: Stanford University Press, 1968).

37. Accounts of Hassan's military exploits against the Italians, British, and the Ethiopians can be found in Touval, *Somali Nationalism*, 51–60; Farer, *War Clouds on the Horn of Africa*, 79–82; and Abdi Sheikh-Abdi, "Sayyid Mohamed Abdille Hassan and the Current Conflict on the Horn," *Horn of Africa* 1, no. 2 (1978), 61–65.

38. Touval, *Somali Nationalism*, 61–66.

39. For an account of this period, see John Drysdale, *The Somali Dispute* (New York: Praeger, 1964), 74–87; and Richard Pankhurst, "Decolonization of Ethiopia, 1940–1955," *Horn of Africa* 1, no. 4 (1978), 10–16.

40. After the end of World War II, the British government was in favor of uniting the Ogaden Somalis with those in British and Italian Somalilands. British

Foreign Minister Ernest Bevin had proposed in 1946 that British Somaliland, Italian Somaliland, and the adjacent part of Ethiopia should be lumped together as a trust territory, but only if Ethiopia agreed. Then in 1948 London tried to purchase the southern and western grazing lands of the Ogaden from Ethiopia. Haile Selassie refused this offer. Nonetheless these British actions raised Ethiopian suspicions about London's ultimate intentions. See Farer, *War Clouds on the Horn of Africa*, 85.

41. Ibid., 13–16.

42. Quoted in David Laitin and Said Samatar, *Somalia: Nation in Search of a State* (Boulder, Colo.: Westview Press, 1987), 90.

43. Some suppliers try to diversify by choosing different suppliers for each major weapons class—i.e., tanks, jet fighters, etc. See Michael Mihalka, "Supplier-Client Patterns in Arms Transfers: The Developing Countries, 1967–1976," in *Arms Transfers in the Modern World*, ed. Stephanie Neuman and Robert Harkavy (New York: Praeger Special Studies, 1980), 50. For the effect international crises may have on decision making, see Charles Hermann, "International Crisis as a Situational Variable," in *International Politics and Foreign Policy*, ed. James Rosenau (New York: Free Press, 1969), 409–21; and SIPRI, *The Arms Trade With the Third World* (New York: Humanities Press, 1971), 68–69.

44. *WMEAT, 1967–1976*, 159.

45. Ethiopia's central government military expenditures are calculated from *WMEAT, 1967–1976*, 42; and *WMEAT, 1987*, 58.

46. See U.S. Department of State, ACDA, *WMEAT, 1969–1978* (Washington, D.C.: GPO, 1980), 161.

47. See Jane Perlez, "On the Ethiopian Front, Rebel Confidence Rises," *New York Times*, February 14, 1990.

48. See Appendix, figure 1.

49. See for example Victor Levine, "The African-Israeli Connection 40 Years Later," *Middle East Review* 21 (Fall 1988), 12–17; and Mitchell Bard, "The Evolution of Israel's Africa Policy," ibid., 21 (Winter 1988/89), 21–28.

50. This policy has been termed the "deus ex machina" syndrome—when confronted by an overwhelming force invite in an external power to assist in one's defense. See Spencer, "A Reassessment of Ethiopian-Somali Conflict," 23–30.

51. See SIPRI, *The Arms Trade With the Third World*, 653–55; and Marina Ottaway, *Soviet and American Influence in the Horn of Africa* (New York: Praeger Special Studies, 1982), chaps. 9–10.

52. *WMEAT, 1967–1976*, 159.

53. See Steven David, "Realignment in the Horn: The Soviet Advantage," *International Security* 4 (Fall 1979), 69–90.

54. Italy, in particular, has been called upon to share this burden in supplying Somalia with arms. Between 1976 and 1985 Italy provided Mogadishu with approximately $500 million worth of arms (*WMEAT, 1971–1980*, 117; *WMEAT, 1986*, 143).

55. This estimate is derived from the Appendix, figure 1.

56. Somalia's central government military expenditures are calculated from *WMEAT, 1967–1976*, 61; and *WMEAT, 1987*, 76.

57. See Appendix, table 3.

58. Egypt for example delivered twenty Soviet-built T-55 tanks to Somalia in 1982. See SIPRI, *World Armaments and Disarmament: SIPRI Yearbook, 1983* (London: Taylor & Francis, 1983), 332.

59. See James Rosenau, "Pre-Theories and Theories of Foreign Policy," in *Approaches to Comparative and International Politics*, ed. Barry Farrell (Evanston: Ill.: Northwestern University Press, 1966), 27–92.

60. See W. Howard Wriggins, *The Ruler's Imperative: Strategies for Political Survival in Asia and Africa* (New York: Columbia University Press, 1969).

61. This is a major theme in Niccolò Machiavelli's *The Prince*.

62. Kenneth Redden, *The Legal System of Ethiopia* (Charlottesville, Va.: Michie, 1968), 99–130.

63. See Habte-Selassie, *Conflict and Intervention in the Horn of Africa*, 11–18.

64. For a discussion of Haile Selassie's fasination with the United States, see John Spencer, *Ethiopia at Bay* (Algonac, Mich.: Reference Publishers, 1984), 102.

65. The Dergue's Proclamation No. 1 on September 12, 1974, suspended the 1955 Constitution and announced the motto "Ethiopia Tikdem (first)." See Paul Brietzke, *Law, Development, and the Ethiopian Revolution* (Lewisburg, Pa.: Bucknell University Press, 1982), 181–83.

66. For an analysis of Mengistu's rise to power, see Pliny the Middle-Aged, "The PMAC: Origins and Structure, Part I," *Ethiopianist Notes* 2, no. 3 (1978/79), 1–18; and Pliny the Middle-Aged, "The PMAC: Origins and Structure, Part II," *Northeast African Studies* 1, no. 1 (1979), 1–20.

67. For a discussion of the PMAC's relations with the west bloc, east bloc, and Ethiopia's neighbors, see Olusola Ojo, "Ethiopia's Foreign Policy Since the 1974 Revolution," *Horn of Africa* 3, no. 4 (1980/81), 3–11. For a profile of Mengistu, see David Korn, *Ethiopia, the United States, and the Soviet Union* (Carbondale and Edwardsville: Southern Illinois University Press, 1986), 105–15.

68. See the discussion on Ethiopia in U.S. Department of State, *Country Reports on Human Rights Practices for 1988*, Report to the Committee on Foreign Relations of the U.S. Senate and the Committee on Foreign Affairs of the U.S. House of Representatives, 100th Cong., 2d sess. (Washington, D.C.: GPO, February 1989).

69. For a discussion of the application of Marxist-Leninist principles in Somalia, see David Laitin, "Somalia's Military Government and Scientific Socialism," in *Socialism in Sub-Saharan Africa*, ed. Carl Rosberg and Thomas Callaghy (Berkeley: Institute of International Studies, University of California, 1979), 174–206.

70. Ottaway, *Soviet and American Influence in the Horn of Africa*, 34–44; and "Supping With the Devil," *Economist* 272 (15 September 1979), 58–60. This point was also made in an interview with Richard Moose, who held extensive meetings with Siad Barre in the spring of 1978 (interview, Alexandria, Va., June 8, 1982).

71. For a discussion of Somali society and culture, see Laitin and Samatar, *Somalia: Nation in Search of a State*, 21–47. The Somali population is 99 percent Sunni Muslim and fall under the Shafi'ite school of Islamic law.

72. Ibid.

73. Ibid., 78–81.

74. A large number of Ogadeeni soldiers in the Somali Army have been recruited from the Western Somali Liberation Front, which was disbanded in 1987. Recruitment along clan lines has not been confined to the Ogadeeni and has blurred the distinction between regular units and clan militias. See "Somalia: The rise of the Ogadeni," *Africa Confidential* 30 (20 January 1989). By the latter half of 1989 substantial elements among the Ogadeeni, a major force in the army had

moved into open opposition against Siad Barre and the Mareehan. See "Somalia: The end in sight for Siad," ibid., 30 (September 8, 1989).

75. Laitin and Samatar, *Somalia: Nation in Search of a State*, 154–63.

76. Ibid., 92–94.

77. Siad Barre used tribalistic techniques to hold onto power (ibid., 90–91). The MOD connection began to fall apart as a result of the civil war in the north. See "Somalia: Generals fall out." In late 1989 some analysts were begininng to predict that the end was in sight for Siad Barre's rule. See "Somalia: The end in sight for Siad," *Africa Confidential* 30 (8 September 1989); and "Support for Barre declines as Somali civil war intensifies," *Africa Report* (September/October 1989), 8–9.

78. At the end of February 1991 a meeting of Somali elders was to establish a democratic parliamentary system. However, Siad Barre was regrouping his forces in the south, apparently not giving up the struggle for power. Moreover, the picture was further clouded in mid-January 1991, shortly before Siad's fall from power, by reports that another liberation front, based in the Issa clan, was being established in Djibouti ("Somalia: Divide to Rule," *Africa Confidential* 32 [14 January 1991]).

Chapter 3. The 1953 Arms-for-Bases Exchange

1. See U.S. Department of State, "Mutual Defense Assistance Agreement: United States-Imperial Ethiopian Government," *United States Treaties and Other International Agreements*, vol. 4, pt. 1 (1953), 422–26; and U.S. Department of State, "Utilization of Defense Installations Within Empire of Ethiopia," ibid., vol. 5, pt. 1 (1954), 750–61.

2. U.S. Department of State, *Foreign Relations of the United States (FRUS), 1952–1954* 11:419–20.

3. Ibid., 11:419–20, 423–24.

4. Ibid., 11:427–28. The U.S. ambassador to Ethiopia suggested in October 1952 that the provision of a military training mission would probably result in the speedy signing of a base agreement.

5. Ibid., 11:428–30.

6. Ibid.

7. Ibid., 11:433–35.

8. Ibid.

9. Ibid. Also see Harold Marcus, *Ethiopia, Great Britain, and the United States, 1941–1974* (Berkeley and Los Angeles: University of California Press, 1983), 89.

10. *FRUS, 1952–1954* 11:426–28. Colonel Query, a former U.S. military attache to Addis Ababa, suggested that twelve to fifteen advisers would be an appropriate number.

11. Ibid., 11:433–34.

12. Ibid., 11:435–37.

13. Ibid., 11:437–38.

14. See John Spencer, *Ethiopia at Bay* (Algonac, Mich.: Reference Publications, 1984), 263–68.

15. *FRUS, 1952–1954* 11:450–51.

16. Ibid., 11:445–48. The problems with U.S. military assistance to Ethiopia

were discussed at an 8 April 1953 meeting at Assistant Secretary of State Byroade's office.

17. Ibid., 442–49.

18. For a background discussion of the events leading up to federation and its aftermath, see Tekie Fessehatzion, "The International Dimensions of the Eritrean Question," *Horn of Africa* 6, no. 2 (1983), 7–24.

19. Spencer, *Ethiopia at Bay*, 266.

20. Marcus, *Ethiopia, Great Britain, and the United States*, 85.

21. *FRUS, 1943* 4:103–08.

22. *FRUS, 1945* 8:6. Haile Selassie argued that although in the short-term the railroad connecting Addis Ababa and the port at Djibouti satisfied Ethiopian interests, in the long-term Ethiopia required a port in Eritrea.

23. See U.S. Department of Defense, Joint Strategic Plans Committee, "Estimate of Probable Developments in the World Situation Up to 1957," December 11, 1947, *Declassified Documents Quarterly Catalog (DDQC), 1975* 1 (1976), 75B.

24. Ibid.

25. Central Intelligence Agency, "Significant Considerations Regarding the Disposition of the Italian African Colonies," July 25, 1947, *DDQC, 1978* 4 (1979), 335 B.

26. See U.S. Department of State, Bureau of Near Eastern Affairs, "Regional Security Arrangements in the Eastern Mediterranean and Near Eastern Areas," May 11, 1950, *DDQC, 1975* 1 (1976), 27B.

27. Ibid.

28. Ibid.

29. Nadav Safran, *Saudi Arabia: The Ceaseless Quest for Security* (Ithaca, N.Y.: Cornell University Press, 1988), 66.

30. The United States, Great Britain, and France issued the Tripartite Declaration in 1950 which was aimed at limiting Western arms shipments to the Middle East. Steven Spiegel, *The Other Arab-Israeli Conflict* (Chicago: University of Chicago Press, 1985), 46–47.

31. William Polk, *The Arab World* (Cambridge, Mass.: Harvard University Press, 1980), 320–24.

32. U.S. Department of State, Office of Intelligence Research, Intelligence Report No. 5980, "The British Position in the Middle East," October 2, 1952, *DDQC, 1978* 4 (1979), 415A.

33. *FRUS, 1942* 4:104–05.

34. *FRUS, 1943* 4:89–92.

35. The British had established what was tantamount to a protectorate over Ethiopia. State Department officials expressed their concern over this internal political development to British Foreign Secretary Eden in mid-1942. See John Spencer, *Ethiopia, the Horn of Africa, and U.S. Policy* (Cambridge, Mass.: Institute for Foreign Policy Analysis, 1977), 9; Marcus, *Ethiopia, Great Britain, and the United States*, 39.

36. See Spencer, *Ethiopia, the Horn of Africa, and U.S. Policy*, 8–17; and Richard Pankhurst, "Decolonization of Ethiopia, 1940–1955," *Horn of Africa* 1, no. 4 (1978), 13–15.

37. *FRUS, 1944* 5:74.

38. *FRUS, 1943* 4:96–98; Spencer, *Ethiopia, the Horn of Africa, and U.S. Policy*, 11.

39. *FRUS, 1944* 5:74–75.

40. Ibid., 5:73–74.
41. *FRUS, 1950* 5:1698–99.
42. *FRUS, 1947* 5:521, 597.
43. Ibid.
44. Ibid., 5:521. Following approval of the sale, it was reported by Ethiopian sources that the Soviets had offered to make a gift of certain quantities of arms, munitions, and other materials of war, including heavy equipment. The State Department then began to study the possibility of indicating to the Ethiopian government that any sale of U.S. arms to Ethiopia would be conditional on the refusal of the Soviet offer.
45. Marcus, *Ethiopia, Great Britain, and the United States,* 58.
46. Spencer, *Ethiopia at Bay,* 266.
47. Ibid.
48. Ibid., 103.
49. This analysis was made by the U.S. Minister in Ethiopia Felix Cole in early 1947. See Marcus, *Ethiopia, Great Britain, and the United States,* 53. One might consider, however, that Cole was not well liked by the Ethiopians and according to John Spencer (*Ethiopia at Bay,* 168) had made U.S.-Ethiopia relations difficult. Acting Secretary of State Joseph Grew, moreover, had required Addis Ababa to accept Cole's credentials.
50. *FRUS, 1952–1954* 11:438–42.
51. Ibid. The vote went overwhelmingly in favor of the United States.
52. See C. L. Sulzberger, "Ethiopia Approves Area Defense Pact," *New York Times,* December 21, 1952.
53. U.S. Senate, *Ethiopia and the Horn of Africa,* Hearings before the Subcommittee on African Affairs of the Committee on Foreign Relations, 94th Cong., 2d sess. (Washington, D.C.: GPO, 1976), 27; and Spencer, *Ethiopia at Bay,* 266–67.
54. *FRUS, 1952–1954* 11:429. The treaty did not enter into force until 8 October 1953.
55. Eritrea was distant enough from the combat zone in Libya and Egypt to be safe from ground attack yet close enough that damaged aircraft could be shipped down the Red Sea, repaired, and returned to the fighting with a minimal amount of delay. Massawa had the best harbor conditions in the Red Sea and was close enough to Alexandria to give direct support to the British Mediterranean Fleet, and far enough away to be safe from Rommel's short-range bombers. Massawa's importance was highlighted by the fact that at one point in 1942 it was the single operative Allied base in the Middle East. See John Rasmusen, *A History of Kagnew Station and American Forces in Eritrea* (Arlington, Va.: U.S. Army Security Agency, Information Division, 1973), 21, 27–37. Moreover, the Italians had used Eritrea to launch an air attack on Bahrain in October 1940. See Irvine Anderson, *Aramco: The United States and Saudi Arabia* (Princeton, N.J.: Princeton University Press, 1981), 111.
56. Rasmusen, *A History of Kagnew Station,* 27–37.
57. Ibid., 42. Also see John Spencer's testimony in U.S. Senate, *Ethiopia and the Horn of Africa,* 26.
58. Rasmusen, *A History of Kagnew Station,* 42; and U.S. Senate, *Ethiopia and the Horn of Africa,* 26.
59. Marcus, *Ethiopia, Great Britain, and the United States,* 82.
60. Ibid., 83.
61. Ibid.

62. Ibid.

63. Philip Jessup, *The Birth of Nations* (New York: Columbia University Press, 1974), 220.

64. Ibid.

65. Marcus, *Ethiopia, Great Britain, and the United States*, 84. Washington feared that a formal agreement would be misunderstood by London and embarrass Rome.

66. Quoted in ibid., 84.

67. Jessup, *The Birth of Nations*, 248.

68. For an account of the U.S. role at the United Nations in bringing about federation see Jessup, *The Birth of Nations*. See Richard Sherman, "The Rise of Eritrean Nationalism," *Northeast African Studies* 2, no. 3 (1980/81); ibid., 3, no. 1 (1981), 121–29.

69. Spencer, *Ethiopia at Bay*, 102.

70. Ibid., 102–03.

71. One critic has argued that Washington simply washed its hands of the whole affair. See Thomas Coffey, *Lion by the Tail* (New York: Viking, 1974), 170.

72. *FRUS, 1935* 1:776–77, 807–10.

73. Marcus, *Ethiopia, Great Britain, and the United States*, 58.

74. Spencer, *Ethiopia at Bay*, 265–66.

75. *FRUS, 1949* 4:1798. The $200,000 in funds were to be used in Ethiopia for (1) the delivery of real property and improvements, (2) education and cultural programs of benefit to both countries, and (3) defraying U.S. government expenses.

76. Why else would Haile Selassie keep bringing in Americans such as John Spencer, Albert Garretson, and later Donald Paradis to serve as legal advisors? See Spencer, *Ethiopia at Bay*, 103.

77. *FRUS, 1952–1954* 11:435–37.

78. Spencer, *Ethiopia at Bay*, 266–68. With the benefit of 20/20 hindsight, Spencer feels he would have better served the Ethiopians by opposing the agreements.

79. Ibid.

80. *FRUS, 1950* 5:1698–99.

81. Ibid., 5:1701–02.

82. Ibid.

83. Ibid. U.S. embassy officials were aware of the emperor's apprehensions. One source of information for the U.S. embassy on this matter was Albert H. Garretson, a U.S. citizen serving as a legal advisor to the Ethiopian Ministry of Foreign Affairs.

84. Marcus, *Ethiopia, Great Britain, and the United States*, 57. This also puzzled British officials.

85. *FRUS, 1950* 5:1701–02.

86. Ibid.

87. Marcus, *Ethiopia, Great Britain, and the United States*, 86. Also see U.S. Department of Defense, Joint Strategic Plans Committee, "Desirability of Providing U.S. Military Mission to Ethiopia," July 21, 1951, *DDQC, 1978* 4 (1979), 364C.

88. See U.S. Department of Defense, JSPC, "Desirability of Providing U.S. Military Mission to Ethiopia."

89. Marcus, *Ethiopia, Great Britain, and the United States*, 86–87.

90. Ibid., 87.

91. For the contents of the Bolte report, see U.S. Department of Defense, JSPC, "Desirability of Providing U.S. Military Mission to Ethiopia."
92. Ibid.
93. Marcus, *Ethiopia, Great Britain, and the United States*, 87.
94. See the memorandum for Admiral Radford in U.S. Department of Defense, Joint Chiefs of Staff, "Military Aid to Ethiopia," June 25, 1956, *DDQC, 1980* 6 (1981), 147B.
95. Spencer, *Ethiopia at Bay*, 102.
96. *FRUS, 1952–1954* 11:438–45.

Chapter 4. The 1957 Expanded Base Rights Negotiations

1. U.S. Department of State, *Foreign Relations of the United States (FRUS), 1952–1954* 11:451–52.
2. Ibid.
3. Ibid.
4. Ibid., 11:456–58.
5. Ibid., 11:456–69.
6. Ibid., 11:474–76. This point was made during a follow-up discussion on 7 July 1954.
7. Ibid., 11:461.
8. Ibid., 11:468.
9. Ibid.
10. For a discussion of the problems these issues posed for the United States, see Steven Spiegel, *The Other Arab-Israeli Conflict* (Chicago: University of Chicago Press, 1985), 61–83.
11. *FRUS, 1955–1957* 18:331–39. Also see U.S. Department of Defense, Joint Chiefs of Staff, "Memorandum for the Chairman, JCS from the Deputy Director of Intelligence of the Joint Staff—Ethiopia," June 27, 1956, *Declassified Documents Quarterly Catalog (DDQC), 1980* 6 (1981), 148A.
12. *FRUS, 1955–1957* 18:331–39.
13. *Public Papers of the President, Dwight D. Eisenhower, 1957* (Washington, D.C.: GPO, 1958), 197–98.
14. Ibid.
15. See Thomas Brady, "Nixon Requests Base in Ethiopia," *New York Times*, March 13, 1957.
16. *FRUS, 1955–1957* 18:339–43.
17. Ibid., 18:342.
18. See International Cooperation Agency, "Report to the President of the Vice-President's Visit to Africa," January 30, 1958, *DDQC, 1978* 3 (1979), 133A.
19. *FRUS, 1955–1957* 18:348–49.
20. National Security Council, Operations Coordinating Board, "Progress Report on U.S. Policy Toward Ethiopia—NSC 5615/1," May 29, 1957, *DDQC, 1986* 12 (1987), 430.
21. Ibid.
22. *FRUS, 1955–1957* 18:350–51. One news report had the emperor requesting approximately $80 million in military aid. See Homer Bigart, "Selassie Charges Egyptians Try Subversion in Ethiopia," *New York Times*, February 16, 1957.
23. *FRUS, 1955–1957* 18:350–51.

24. Ibid.
25. Ibid.
26. Ibid.
27. Ibid., 18:357–60. The termination of the negotiations was noted in the December 18, 1957, Progress Report on NSC 5615/1.
28. See U.S. Embassy, Addis Ababa, "Defense Problems of Ethiopia," March 12, 1957, *DDQC, 1978* 3 (1979), 133A.
29. Ibid.
30. This idea became incorporated in the Bevin Plan. See Saadia Touval, *Somali Nationalism* (Cambridge, Mass.: Harvard University Press, 1963), 78–83; and John Drysdale, *The Somali Dispute* (New York: Praeger, 1964), 65–73.
31. Drysdale, *The Somali Dispute*, 82–83.
32. This issue was raised by the Ethiopians during the 1954 military discussions. See *FRUS, 1952–1954* 11:461–67. More than two years later it was still a general consideration in the U.S. Statement of Policy on Ethiopia, NSC 5615/1. See *FRUS, 1955–1957* 18:336.
33. The emperor felt that Cairo's propaganda campaign had tapered off a bit after the Suez crisis, but he expected it to increase once Nasser was less preoccupied. See Bigart, "Selassie Charges Egyptians Try Subversion in Ethiopia."
34. Donald Paridis, interview, Washington, D.C., 26 April 1982.
35. U.S. Department of State, Office of Intelligence Research, "Intelligence Report No. 7129," January 10, 1956, *DDQC, 1979* 5 (1980), 447A.
36. A draft statement of U.S. policy toward Ethiopia, NSC 5615, was completed on 23 October 1956. See National Security Council, "U.S. Policy Toward Ethiopia—NSC 5616," October 23, 1956, *DDQC, 1986* 12 (1987), 427. The National Security Council was briefed on NSC 5615/1 on 4 November; it was discussed again at the 15 November meeting; and after some minor revisions was adopted as NSC 5615/1 on 19 November 1956. See *FRUS, 1955–1957* 18:331–39.
37. NSC, Operations Coordinating Board, "Progress Report on U.S. Policy Toward Ethiopia—NSC 5615/1."
38. U.S. Department of State, "Memorandum of Conversation at Walter Reed Hospital," November 12, 1956, *DDQC, 1987* 13 (1988), 2086.
39. ICA, "Report to the President of the Vice-President's Visit to Africa."
40. U.S. Embassy, Addis Ababa, "Defense Problems of Ethiopia."
41. Ibid.
42. Ibid.
43. Imperial Ethiopian Government, Ministry of Foreign Affairs, "Memorandum," March 12, 1957, *DDQC, 1978* 4 (1979), 133A.
44. Ibid. Two weeks before Nixon's visit, the United States had sat quietly on the sidelines, and for a few days even opposed Ethiopia before helping to defeat an anti-Ethiopian resolution at the UN General Assembly.
45. Ibid.
46. William Polk, *The Arab World* (Cambridge, Mass.: Harvard University Press, 1980), 323–25.
47. The affected states were Syria, Saudia Arabia, and Jordan.
48. See Miles Copeland, *The Game of Nations* (New York: Simon and Schuster, 1969), 170–224.
49. Polk, *The Arab World*, 331–32.
50. U.S. Department of Defense, Joint Chiefs of Staff, Joint Committee on

Progress for Military Assistance, "Military Aid for the Middle East," February 1, 1957, *DDQC, 1980* 6 (1981), 153B.

51. NSC, "Progress Report on U.S. Policy Toward Ethiopia—NSC 5615/1."
52. NSC, "U.S. Policy Toward Ethiopia—NSC 5615."
53. U.S. Embassy, Addis Ababa, "Defense Problems of Ethiopia."
54. NSC, "U.S. Policy Toward Ethiopia—NSC 5615."
55. *FRUS 1955–1957* 18:350–51.
56. Ibid.
57. U.S. Embassy, Addis Ababa, "Defense Problems of Ethiopia."
58. *FRUS, 1955–1957* 18:342, 348–49. DoD contended that 85.3 percent of the equipment had been delivered.
59. U.S. Department of Defense, "Memorandum—Ethiopia," June 27, 1956.
60. *FRUS, 1955–1957* 18:328.
61. Ibid., 18:348–49. Also see U.S. Embassy, Addis Ababa, "Defense Problems of Ethiopia."
62. U.S. Embassy, Addis Ababa, "Defense Problems of Ethiopia."
63. *FRUS, 1955–1957* 18:348–49.
64. U.S. Embassy, Addis Ababa, "Defense Problems of Ethiopia."
65. Ibid.
66. Ibid.
67. Ibid.
68. U.S. Department of Defense, "Memorandum—Ethiopia," June 27, 1956.
69. *FRUS, 1955–1957* 18:331–34.
70. Ibid.
71. Ibid., 18:350–51.
72. Ibid., 18;331–39.
73. U.S. Department of Defense, Joint Chiefs of Staff, Joint Logistic Plans Committee, "Base Requirements for U.S. Forces Deployed in the Middle East in Support of CINCSPECOMME Operation Plan 215–56," November 21, 1956, *DDQC, 1980* 6 (1981), 153A.
74. Ibid.
75. *FRUS, 1955–1957* 18:334–39.
76. Ibid.
77. Ibid.
78. Department of Defense, "Memorandum—Ethiopia," June 27, 1956.
79. *FRUS, 1955–1957* 18:351–53. When the question of developing facilities in Eritrea first came up in U.S.-Ethiopia discussions in 1954, the Americans told the Ethiopians to go to the IBRD for aid to develop the Port of Assab. The IBRD reportedly asked Ethiopia why it simply did not use the French Port of Djibouti. This shocked the IEG, which felt that Ethiopia had lost the Italian War of 1935 because of the blockage imposed at Djibouti.
80. See U.S. Embassy, Addis Ababa, "Defense Problems of Ethiopia"; and Imperial Ethiopian Government, Ministry of Foreign Affairs, "Memorandum," March 12, 1957.
81. Ibid. This argument is presented in the both the U.S. embassy report and IEG memorandum.
82. U.S. Embassy, Addis Ababa, "Defense Problems of Ethiopia."
83. Ibid.
84. Ibid.

85. Ibid.
86. *FRUS, 1955–1957* 18:351–53.
87. Ibid.
88. NSC, "U.S. Policy Toward Ethiopia—NSC 5615."
89. *FRUS, 1955–1957* 18:327–29, 337–38.
90. NSC, "U.S. Policy Toward Ethiopia—NSC 5615."
91. U.S. Department of Defense, "Military Aid Programs for the Middle East."
92. U.S. Department of Defense, JCS, Joint Middle East Planning Committee, "A Study of the Military Implications of the House Joint Resolution 117 for the Middle East Area," May 29, 1957, *DDQC, 1980* 6 (1981), 155A.
93. *FRUS, 1955–1957* 18:325–27.
94. See U.S. Department of Defense, JCS, "Military Aid for Ethiopia," June 25, 1956, *DDQC, 1980* 6 (1981), 147B.
95. Ibid.
96. See Harold Marcus, *Ethiopia, Great Britain, and the United States, 1941–1974* (Los Angeles: University of California Press, 1983), 93.
97. NSC, "U.S. Policy Toward Ethiopia—NSC 5615."
98. *FRUS, 1955–1957* 18:325–27.
99. Ibid.
100. Ibid.
101. Ibid., 18:327–29.
102. Ibid.
103. Ibid.
104. NSC, "U.S. Policy Toward Ethiopia—NSC 5615."
105. *FRUS, 1955–1957* 18:329–30.
106. Ibid., 331–39.
107. See George Lenczowski, *American Presidents and the Middle East* (Durham, N.C.: Duke University Press, 1990), 52–64.

Chapter 5. The 1960 "Secret" Commitment

1. National Security Council (NSC), "U.S. Policy on the Horn of Africa," January 10, 1961, *Declassified Documents Quarterly Catalog (DDQC), 1982* 8 (1983), 2233.
2. U.S. Department of State, "Memorandum for the President—Meeting with Ethiopian Deputy Prime Minister Aklilou Abte-Wold," September 25, 1960, *DDQC, 1982* 8 (1983), 164.
3. U.S. Senate, *United States Security Agreements and Commitments Abroad: Ethiopia, Part 8*, Hearings before the U.S. Security Agreements and Commitments Abroad Committee of the Committee on Foreign Affairs, 91st Cong., 2d sess. (Washington, D.C.: GPO, 1970), 1904–05.
4. This estimate is based on information contained in NSC, "U.S. Policy on the Horn of Africa"; and U.S. Department of State and U.S. Department of Defense, *Congressional Presentation for Security Assistance Programs, FY 1981* (Washington, D.C.: GPO, 1980), 479–511. The United States programmed $30.8 million worth of MAP funds to Ethiopia through FY 1958, $13.5 million in aid was provided in FY 1959–FY 1960. This amount ($44.3 million) was then deducted from approximately $204 million in MAP and IMETP funds provided to Ethiopia between FY 1953–FY 1975, for a total of $160 million for FY 1961–FY 1975. Subsequently, U.S. military aid was drastically decreased.

5. U.S. Senate, *United States Security Agreements and Commitments Abroad, Ethiopia, Part 8*, 1904–05.
6. Ibid. Edward Korry, the U.S. ambassador to Ethiopia (1963–67), also gave it this minimalist interpretation (interview, Stonington, Conn., February 6, 1982).
7. U.S. Senate, *United States Security Agreements and Commitments Abroad, Ethiopia, Part 8*, 1888. This argument was advanced by Senators Stuart Symington and William Fulbright.
8. View expressed by Donald Paradis, interview, Washington, D.C., April 26, 1982.
9. This was how Edward Korry felt the Department of State viewed it.
10. See Yonas Kebede, "The Legal Aspect of Ethiopian-Somali Dispute," *Horn of Africa* 1, no. 1 (1978), 26–31; and Abdulqawi Yusuf, "The Anglo-Abyssinian Treaty of 1897 and the Somali-Ethiopian Dispute," ibid., 3, no. 1 (1980), 38–42.
11. Kebede, "The Legal Aspect of Ethiopian-Somali Dispute." Also see Michael Reisman, "The Case of Western Somaliland: An International Legal Perspective," *Horn of Africa* 1, no. 3 (1978), 13–22.
12. Reisman, "The Case of Western Somaliland."
13. U.S. Department of State, *Foreign Relations of the United States (FRUS), 1955–1957* 18:346–48.
14. U.S. Department of State, "Memorandum for Brig.-General A. J. Goodpaster, the White House," July 31, 1958, *DDQC, 1976* 2 (1977), 67E. This memo contained a message to President Eisenhower from Haile Selassie.
15. Ibid.
16. Cited in Said Yusuf Abdi, "Self-determination for Ogaden Somalis," *Horn of Africa* 1, no. 1 (1978), 20–25.
17. Ibid.
18. Ibid.
19. David Laitin and Said Samatar, *Somalia: Nation in Search of a State* (Boulder, Colo.: Westview Press, 1987), 63–65.
20. Ibid., 72–77.
21. Cited in Raymond Thurston, "The United States, Somalia and the Crisis in the Horn," *Horn of Africa* 1, no. 2 (1978), 11–20. When the constitution was ratified in June 1961 it received overwhelming approval in the south, but less than 50 percent support in the north. Dissatisfaction with the constitution was one of the causes for the aborted coup in the north in December 1961. See Laitin and Samatar, *Somalia*, 70–72.
22. See Thurston, "The United States, Somalia and the Crisis in the Horn."
23. NSC, "U.S. Policy Toward the Near East—NSC 5820/1," November 4, 1958, *DDQC, 1980* 6 (1981), 386B.
24. Ibid.
25. Ibid.
26. Ibid.
27. See Madeleine Kalb, *The Congo Cables* (New York: Macmillan, 1982), 3–16.
28. Quoted in ibid., 29.
29. See ibid., esp. 139–49. A divergence in U.S. and UN objectives in the Congo began to occur toward the end of 1960.
30. U.S. Department of State, "Memorandum for the President."
31. See U.S. Department of Defense, Office of the Chief of Naval Operations, Office of Naval Intelligence, "Reply to ONI Study 4–58—Opportunities for Com-

munist Penetration of Ethiopia and the Horn of Africa," March 26, 1958, *DDQC, 1981* 7 (1982), 476B.

32. Ibid.

33. NSC, Operations Coordinating Board, "Progress Report on U.S. Policy Toward Ethiopia—NSC 5615/1," July 9, 1958, *DDQC, 1986* 12 (1987), 433.

34. Ibid.

35. See White House, "Staff Notes No. 621," August 27, 1959, *DDQC, 1983* 9 (1984), 1428.

36. Ibid. Also see U.S. Department of State, Bureau of Intelligence and Research, "The Ethiopia-Soviet Bloc Agreements: A Preliminary Appraisal," September 4, 1959, *DDQC, 1980* 6 (1981), 195C.

37. See U.S. Department of State, "The Ethiopia-Soviet Bloc Agreements."

38. Ibid.

39. Ibid.

40. See U.S. House of Representatives, *The Middle East, Africa, and Inter-American Affairs, Volume XVI*, Selected Executive Session Hearings of the Committee on Foreign Affairs, 1951–1956 (Washington, D.C.: GPO, 1980), 335–36.

41. Ibid.

42. Related to the author by Arthur Richards, interview, Washington, D.C., June 10, 1982.

43. *FRUS, 1955–1957* 18:339–43.

44. Ibid.

45. Lawrence Freedman, *The Evolution of Nuclear Strategy* (New York: St. Martin's, 1981), 227.

46. Ibid., 165–71.

47. White House, "Memorandum for the President," July 19, 1960, *DDQC, 1982* 8 (1983), 163.

48. Harold Marcus, *Ethiopia, Great Britain, and the United States, 1941–1974* (Los Angeles: University of California Press, 1983), 110.

49. This point was made to the author by two men who interacted quite frequently with Haile Selassie—Edward Korry in his capacity as U.S. ambassador and Donald Pardis, who served as a legal adviser in the Ethiopian Ministry for Foreign Affairs in the 1950s and 1960s.

50. *FRUS, 1955–1957* 18:332.

51. U.S. Department of Defense, JCS, Joint Committee on Progress for Military Assistance, "Military Aid Programs for the Middle East," February 1, 1957, *DDQC, 1980* 6 (1981), 153B.

52. NSC, "U.S. Policy Toward Ethiopia—NSC 5615," October 23, 1956, *DDQC, 1986* 12 (1987), 427.

53. *FRUS, 1955–1957* 18:332.

54. See James Dugan and Laurence Lafore, *Days of Emperor and Clown* (Garden City, N.Y.: Doubleday, 1973).

55. U.S. Embassy, Addis Ababa, "Defense Problems of Ethiopia," March 12, 1957, *DDQC, 1978* 3 (1979), 133A.

56. Ibid.

57. See *FRUS, 1955–1957* 18:357–60; and *DDQC, 1986* 12 (1987), 431. These sources contain the NSC, Operations Coordinating Board, "Progress Report on U.S. Policy Toward Ethiopia—NSC 5615/1," December 18, 1957.

58. Ibid.

59. Ibid.

60. Ibid.
61. Ibid.
62. Ibid.
63. Ibid.
64. Ibid. Also see U.S. Embassy, Addis Ababa, "Defense Problems of Ethiopia."
65. NSC, Operations Coordinating Board, "Progress Report on U.S. Policy Toward Ethiopia—NSC 5615/1," July 9, 1958, *DDQC, 1986* 12 (1987), 433.
66. NSC, "U.S. Policy on the Horn of Africa."
67. At the end of 1955 a U.S. MAAG officer in the field suggested that four "commands" could be created at the same budgetary level since Ethiopian divisions were smaller than their U.S. counterparts. See *FRUS, 1955–1957* 18:325–27.
68. Ibid., 18:348–49.
69. Ibid., 18:357–60.
70. Ibid.
71. Ibid.
72. Ibid., 18:331–34.
73. International Cooperation Agency, "Report to the President of the Vice-President's Visit to Africa (February 28–March 21, 1957)," January 30, 1958, *DDQC, 1978* 3 (1979), 133A.
74. Ibid.
75. See Russell Baker, "U.S. Is Becoming Africa-Conscious," *New York Times*, March 24, 1957.
76. Although in the fall of 1960 Ethiopia for the first time did not support the U.S. position regarding China, causing a minor diplomatic crisis. However, the previous April Haile Selassie made "an important sacrifice" in reversing his support for a twelve-mile territorial sea. See U.S. Department of State, "Memorandum for the President—Acknowledgement of Message from the Emperor of Ethiopia," *DDQC, 1982* 8 (1983), 162.
77. Ibid.
78. Ronald Segal, *African Profiles* (Baltimore, Md.: Penguin Books, 1962), 245–46.
79. Ibid., 270.
80. U.S. Department of State, "Memorandum for the President."
81. This analysis projected events into 1962. NSC, "National Security Implications of Future Developments Regarding Africa," *DDQC, 1980* 6 (1981), 370A.

Chapter 6. The 1966 F-5 Freedom Fighter Transfer

1. The Foreign Assistance Act of 1961 replaced the Mutual Security Act. The Alliance for Progress was launched in Latin America, the Agency for International Development (AID) was created to administer economic aid, and greater emphasis was placed on development capital and technical assistance at the start of the Kennedy administration. See Charles Kegley, Jr., and Eugene Wittkopf, *American Foreign Policy: Pattern and Process* (New York: St. Martin's, 1979), 90–91.
2. See Chester Bowles Papers, Box 311, Folder 675, New Haven, Conn.: Yale University. This includes an "Incoming Telegram from New Delhi," February 24, 1962.
3. Ibid.
4. See U.S. Senate, *United States Security Agreements and Commitments Abroad: Ethiopia, Part 8*, Hearings before the Subcommittee on U.S. Security

Agreements and Commitments Abroad of the Committee on Foreign Relations, 91st Cong., 2d sess. (Washington D.C.: GPO, 1970), 1906–07.

5. See the Addis Ababa embassy/MAAG message in U.S. Department of State, "Force Goal Discussions and Future of MAP Ethiopia," December 18, 1963, *Declassified Documents Quarterly Catalog (DDQC), 1978* 4 (1979), 74A.

6. Edward Korry, interview, Stonington, Conn., February 6, 1982.

7. See U.S. Senate, *United States Security Agreements and Commitments Abroad: Ethiopia, Part 8*, 1906–07.

8. See Tom Farer, *War Clouds on the Horn of Africa: The Widening Storm*, 2d ed. (New York: Carnegie Endowment for International Peace, 1979), 115–16; and Harold Nelson, ed., *Somalia: A Country Study* (Washington, D.C.: GPO, 1982), 258.

9. See Farer, *War Clouds on the Horn of Africa*, 115; Irving Kaplan, *Area Handbook for Somalia* (Washington, D.C.: GPO, 1977), 310–11; and I. M. Lewis, *The Modern History of Somaliland: From Nation to State* (New York: Praeger, 1965), 183–95.

10. See Farer, *War Clouds on the Horn of Africa*, 115; and Nelson, ed., *Somalia*, 258. According to Edward Korry, the U.S. embassy in Addis Ababa objected on the grounds that the United States would have to raise the ante in Ethiopia (interview).

11. See Stockholm International Peace Research Institute (SIPRI), *The Arms Trade with the Third World* (New York: Humanities Press, 1971), 654–55.

12. U.S. Department of State, "Incoming Telegram from Addis Ababa," December 11, 1963, *DDQC, 1977* 3 (1978), 226B.

13. U.S. Department of State, "Incoming Telegram from Addis Ababa," February 19, 1964, *DDQC, 1977*, 121E.

14. Ibid.

15. Ibid.

16. U.S. Department of State, "Incoming Telegram from Addis Ababa," January 1, 1964, *DDQC, 1977*, 226D.

17. Ibid.

18. Ibid.

19. This was contained in information sent from the U.S. United Nations mission to the U.S. embassies in Addis Ababa and Mogadishu. U.S. Department of State, "Ethiopia-Somalia Border Incident," February 10, 1964, *DDQC, 1977*, 121C.

20. The IEG had asked through the U.S. embassy that the ban on the airlift of ammunition be rescinded immediately. U.S. Department of State, "Incoming Telegram from Addis Ababa," March 17, 1964, *DDQC, 1977*, 227A.

21. U.S. Department of State, "Incoming Telegram from Addis Ababa," March 31, 1964, *DDQC, 1977*, 324E.

22. See ibid.; also see U.S. Department of State, "Outgoing Telegram to Addis Ababa," April 1, 1964, *DDQC, 1977*, 324F; U.S. Department of State, "Incoming Telegram from Addis Ababa," April 4, 1964, *DDQC, 1977*, 325A.

23. U.S. Department of State, "Incoming Telegram from Mogadishu," May 30, 1964, *DDQC, 1977*, 122C.

24. Ibid. So argued the Mogadishu embassy.

25. Ibid.

26. Ibid.

27. Ibid.

28. See the message sent by Ambassador Edward Korry, "U.S. Policy in the

Horn of Africa," with regard to the National Policy Paper on Ethiopia issued in December 1963. U.S. Department of State, "Incoming Telegram from Addis Ababa," April 22, 1964, *DDQC, 1977*, 325B.

29. Ibid.

30. Ibid.

31. See Steven Spiegel, *The Other Arab-Israeli Conflict*, (Chicago: University of Chicago Press, 1985), 94–117.

32. Ibid., 118–65.

33. See White House, "Neutralism and Foreign Aid: Or Belgrade Reconsidered," September 27, 1961, *DDQC, 1979* 5 (1980), 466C.

34. U.S. Department of State, "Guidelines for Policy and Operations—Africa," March 1962, *DDQC, 1978*, 392B.

35. Ibid. Also see U.S. Department of Defense, "Memorandum for the Secretary of Defense from the JCS, Subject: U.S. Policy Toward Portugal and the Republic of South Africa," July 10, 1963, *DDQC, 1979*, 263A.

36. Ibid.

37. U.S. Department of State, "Guidelines for Policy and Operations—Africa."

38. The Chester Bowles Papers contains the report of Bowles's October 15–November 9, 1962, fact-finding trip to Africa.

39. See Chester Bowles Papers, "Incoming Telegram from New Delhi," February 24, 1962.

40. Korry, interview. See U.S. Department of State, "Incoming Telegram from Addis Ababa," February 19, 1964.

41. Korry, interview.

42. Donald Paradis helped draft the OAU Charter (interview, Washington, D.C., April 26, 1982).

43. See U.S. Senate, *United States Security Agreements and Commitments Abroad: Ethiopia, Part 8*, 1935.

44. U.S. Department of State, "Incoming Telegram from Addis Ababa," December 17, 1964, *DDQC, 1977*, 123A.

45. U.S. Department of State, "U.S. Relations with the Sudan," *DDQC, 1983* 9 (1983), 2710. Note: no date appears on this document, but it appears to have been prepared after the May 1965 elections in Sudan.

46. According to the U.S. embassy. See U.S. Department of State, "Incoming Telegram from Addis Ababa," December 17, 1964.

47. Ibid.

48. Ibid.

49. U.S. Department of State, "Guidelines for Policy and Operations—Africa."

50. Ibid.

51. Ibid.

52. Ibid.

53. Ibid.

54. U.S. Department of Defense, "Memorandum," July 10, 1963.

55. See John Rasmusen, *A History of Kagnew Station and American Forces in Eritrea* (Arlington, Va.: U.S. Army Security Agency, Information Division, 1973), 57–59.

56. It was suggested that the operation be associated with a "peaceful" project such as Telstar. See U.S. Department of State,"Incoming Telegram from Addis Ababa," April 22, 1964.

57. Edward Korry, interview.

58. U.S. Department of State, "Incoming Telegram from Addis Ababa," April 22, 1964.

59. Ibid.

60. Ibid.

61. Ibid.

62. Ibid.

63. For this assessment, see U.S. General Accounting Office, "Furnishing of Military Assistance to Ethiopia in Excess of the Country's Ability to Effectively Utilize the Equipment," May 5, 1964, *DDQC, 1979*, 39B.

64. For a detailed account and analysis of the 1960 coup attempt see Harold Marcus, *Ethiopia, Great Britain, and the United States, 1941–1974* (Los Angeles: University of California Press, 1983), esp. 133–35.

65. Ibid., 169.

66. Ibid.

67. In an interview, Don Paradis noted that the coup did create a climate whereby the IEG seriously considered internal reforms in order to prevent another coup. Paradis devoted 75 percent of his time during his last seven years in Ethiopia, in the capacity of legal advisor, pushing for reform (interview).

68. See U.S. Department of State, "Incoming Telegram from Addis Ababa," December 17, 1964.

69. Edward Korry, interview.

70. U.S. Department of State, "Incoming Telegram from Addis Ababa," December 17, 1964.

71. Ibid.

72. Ibid.

73. So it seemed to the U.S. embassy (U.S. Department of State, "Incoming Telegram from Addis Ababa," February 19, 1964).

74. Ibid.

75. Ibid.

76. SIPRI, *Arms Trade Registers* (Cambridge, Mass.: MIT Press, 1975), 168.

77. See U.S. Senate, *United States Security Agreements and Commitments Abroad: Ethiopia, Part 8*, 1906–07.

78. For Ambassador Korry's rebuttal of the Drew Pearson article, see U.S. Department of State, "Incoming Telegram from Addis Ababa," July 4, 1964, *DDQC, 1976* 2 (1977), 67F.

79. Ibid.

80. U.S. Department of State, "Incoming Telegram from Addis Ababa," September 18, 1964, *DDQC, 1977*, 122D.

81. The U.S. embassy felt Washington should reopen the whole issue of MAP to Ethiopia. See U.S. Department of State, "Force Goal Dicussions and Future of MAP Ethiopia," December, 18, 1963. This assessment was confirmed by the GAO in "Furnishing of Military Assistance to Ethiopia."

82. Ambassador Korry suggested that Washington substitute F-86 fighters modified to include sidewinder capacity or U.S. Navy A–40s or some similar low supersonic attack fighter in place of the F-5s. See U.S. Department of State, "Force Goal Discussions and Future of MAP Ethiopia."

83. Ibid.

84. U.S. Department of State, "Incoming Telegram from Addis Ababa," April 22, 1964.

85. U.S. Department of State, "Incoming Telegram from Addis Ababa," September 18, 1964.

86. U.S. Department of State, "Outgoing Telegram to Addis Ababa," September 29, 1964, *DDQC, 1977*, 122F.

87. U.S. Department of State, "Incoming Telegram from Addis Ababa," December 17, 1964.

88. Korry, interview.

89. Ibid.

90. For a description of the Pentagon's MAP classification system, see U.S. Senate, *Foreign Assistance and Related Agencies Appropriations for 1962*, Hearings before the Committee of Appropriations, 87th Cong., 1st sess. (Washington, D.C.: GPO, 1961), 142.

91. See U.S. Department of State, "Incoming Telegram from Addis Ababa," October 15, 1964, *DDQC, 1977*, 122F.

92. See Edward Korry's testimony in U.S. Senate, *Ethiopia and the Horn of Africa*, Hearings before the Subcommittee on African Affairs of the Committee on Foreign Relations, 94th Cong., 2d sess. (Washington, D.C.: GPO, 1976), esp. 36.

93. See Chester Bowles Papers, "Incoming Telegram from New Delhi," February 24, 1962.

94. Korry, interview.

95. This was Korry's assessment of how the State Department was making policy (interview).

96. See SIPRI, *Arms Trade Registers*, 74–75.

97. According to Edward Korry, there was the fear of getting caught in the "big lie" (interview).

Chapter 7. The 1973 Arms Package Controversy

1. See SIPRI, *Arms Trade Registers: The Arms Trade With the Third World* (Stockholm: Stockholm International Peace Research Institute, 1975), 74–75.

2. See "Ethiopians Seeking New Arms From U.S.," *New York Times*, March 17, 1971; and Jim Hoagland and Lawrence Stern, "U.S. Aid to Ethiopia—From Emperor's Dentist to Jets," *Washington Post*, May 11, 1972.

3. See SIPRI, *SIPRI Yearbook, 1974* (Stockholm: Stockholm International Peace Research Institute, 1974), 233. The F-5 Freedom Fighter had a top speed of Mach 1.6, whereas the F-4 Phantom jet could travel at Mach 2.2. The F-4 export version was in production in 1973.

4. Ibid. It was expected that only 175 F-4 export models would be produced.

5. Ibid. The F-5 cost approximately $1.6 million, whereas the F-15A Eagle fighter cost $7 million and the F-14A Tomcat fighter used by the U.S. cost $11.4 million.

6. Ibid., 47–48. Third World states possessing supersonic aircraft—either the U.S.-made F-5 or the French Mirage V—were Israel (1956), UAR (1962), Algeria (1965), Iran (1965), Morocco (1965), Saudi Arabia (1966), Syria (1967), Jordan (1968), and Ethiopia (1967).

7. See U.S. Department of State and U.S. Department of Defense, *Congressional Presentation for Security Assistance Programs, FY 1981* (Washington, D.C.: GPO, 1980), 479–511.

8. See Colin Legum, ed., *Africa Contemporary Record (ACR), 1973–1974*,

B159; and Jim Hoagland, "Oil Find May Influence African Border Dispute," *Washington Post*, April 29, 1972.

9. I would like to thank Richard Remnek for a draft copy of his paper, "The Soviet-Somali Arms for Access Relationship," (October 22, 1981), which outlines the development of military relations between Moscow and Mogadishu.

10. John Spencer, *Ethiopia at Bay* (Algonac, Mich.: Reference Publications, 1984), 323.

11. Donald Petterson, "Ethiopia abandoned? An American perspective," *International Affairs* 62 (Autumn 1986), 628. Also see David Ottaway, "Ethiopia May Get Arms From China," *Washington Post*, December 30, 1973.

12. Spencer, *Ethiopia at Bay*, 323.

13. Ibid., 323–24.

14. This episode is pieced together from accounts found in Tom Farer, *War Clouds on the Horn of Africa: The Widening Storm*, 2d ed. (New York: Carnegie Endowment for International Peace, 1979), 118–20; and Ottaway, "Ethiopia May Get Arms From China."

15. See Farer, *War Clouds on the Horn of Africa*; and Ottaway, "Ethiopia May Get Arms From China."

16. Ibid.

17. Petterson, "Ethiopia abandoned?" 628.

18. Legum, ed., *ACR, 1973–1974*, B161.

19. Ibid., A50–51.

20. Ottaway, "Ethiopia May Get Arms From China."

21. The emperor replaced the official Eritrean languages of Tigrinya and Arabic with Amharic in the schools and local administration in 1957, and suppressed dissent against his edict. See Bereket Habte-Selassie, *Conflict and Intervention in the Horn of Africa* (New York: Monthly Review, 1980), 58–63.

22. The U.S. consul in Eritrea reported that IEG officials were bribing Eritrean assembly members for a favorable vote on union. He also warned that American indifference would be attributed to the desire not to risk tenure at Kagnew and would "hardly enhance our prestige" in Eritrea. See U.S. Department of State, "Dispatch to the State Department from the U.S. Consul (Matthew Looram) in Asmara," May 25, 1962, *Declassified Documents Quarterly Catalog (DDQC), 1979* 5 (1980), 75B.

23. Eric Pace, "Eritrean Rebels Said to Weaken," *New York Times*, September 27, 1968; and R. W. Apple. Jr., "Arab Arms Aid Revives Eritrean Insurgency," ibid., September 1, 1969.

24. Apple, "Arab Arms Aid Revives Eritrean Insurgency."

25. Ibid. Also see Pace, "Eritrean Rebels Said to Weaken."

26. "Brooklyn G.I. Slain in Ethiopia in Region of Guerrilla Activity," *New York Times*, January 22, 1971.

27. For an analysis of the political dynamics underlying the ELF-EPLF schism in the Eritrean Liberation Movement as well as the Arab support each group received, see Raman Bhardawi, "The Growing Externalization of the Eritrean Movement," *Horn of Africa* 2, no. 1 (1979), 19–27.

28. David Korn, *Ethiopia, the United States, and the Soviet Union* (Carbondale and Edwardsville: Southern Illinois University Press, 1986), 3.

29. Ibid, 3

30. Raymond Garthoff, *Detente and Confrontation* (Washington, D.C.: Brookings, 1985), 1–23, 69–105.

31. Henry Kissinger, *White House Years* (Boston: Little, Brown, 1979), 1297.

32. This was the central premise of the Nixon-Kissinger National Security Study memorandum of 1969 (NSSM–39) on southern Africa.

33. In his two voluminous memoirs *White House Years* and *Years of Upheaval*, Henry Kissinger makes almost no mention of Africa.

34. Kissinger, *White House Years*, 1292–93.

35. Ibid., 1293.

36. Ibid., 1292.

37. See Irving Kaplan, *Area Handbook for Somalia*, 2d ed. (Washington, D.C.: GPO, 1977), 323–25.

38. SIPRI, *The Arms Trade With the Third World* (New York: Humanities Press, 1971), 655.

39. Soviet arms exports to Somalia which totaled $18 million in 1964 and $12 million in 1965, amounted to only $5 million in 1966, zero in 1967, and $4 million in 1968. See U.S. Department of State, Arms Control and Disarmament Agency (ACDA), *World Military Expenditures and Arms Trade, 1963–1973* (Washington, DC: GPO, 1975), 55, 113.

40. See Gary Payton, "The Somali Coup of 1969: The Case for Soviet Complicity," *Journal of Modern African Studies* 18, no. 3 (1980), 502–04.

41. Ibid.

42. See Legum, ed., *ACR, 1970–1971*, B163.

43. Ibid. Also see Legum and Drysdale, eds., *ACR, 1969–1970*, B113; and Remnek, "The Soviet-Somali Arms for Access Relationship."

44. Legum, ed., *ACR, 1970–1971*, B163.

45. Remnek, "The Soviet-Somali Arms for Access Relationship," 5.

46. Ibid., 6.

47. Ibid., 23–24.

48. U.S. Senate, *United States Security Agreements and Commitments Abroad: Ethiopia, Part 8*, Hearings before the Subcommittee on U.S. Security Agreements and Commitments Abroad of the Committee on Foreign Affairs, 91st Cong., 2d sess. (Washington, D.C.: GPO, 1970), 1927.

49. Ibid., 1949.

50. Intelligence experts reportedly continued to decipher and analyze messages intercepted from Arab and East European countries. It was also widely believed that intelligence gathered at the station was turned over to Israel. See, "Phase-Out of Kagnew Base," *Middle East Report (MERIP)* 24 (January 1974), 28.

51. In December 1970 Washington announced plans to construct a radio communications center on Diego Garcia that would become operational in early 1973. The base formally opened with 274 personnel on March 23, 1973. According to Pentagon officials, Diego Garcia would close a gap in the U.S. worldwide strategic communications network. See John Finney, "U.S. Opens Small Post in Indian Ocean," *New York Times*, June 18, 1973. There was a predisposition on Capitol Hill to pursue a "Blue Water" strategy to move off land masses and onto the seas into an international situation where indigneous nationalism would not clash with U.S. interests. See U.S. Senate, *United States Security Agreements and Commitments Abroad: Ethiopia, Part 8*, 1910.

52. Hoagland and Stern, "U.S. Aid to Ethiopia."

53. John Rasmuson, *A History of Kagnew Station and American Forces in Eritrea* (Arlington, Va.: U.S. Army Security Agency, Information Division, 1973), 69.

54. Hoagland and Stern, "U.S. Aid to Ethiopia."
55. Ibid.
56. See U.S. Senate, *Foreign Assistance and Related Programs Appropriations, FY 1972*, Hearings before the Committee on Appropriations, 92d Cong., 1st sess. (Washington, D.C.: GPO, 1971), 489.
57. Appendix, table 2.
58. Ibid.
59. See Legum, ed., *ACR, 1973–1974*, A50.
60. Petterson, "Ethiopia abandoned?" 628.
61. See U.S. House of Representatives, *Foreign Assistance and Related Agencies Appropriations for 1971, Part I*, Hearings before a Subcommittee of the Committee on Appropriations, 91st Cong., 2d sess. (Washington, D.C.: GPO, 1970), 306.
62. Ibid.
63. See Frank van de Linden, *Nixon's Quest for Peace* (Washington, D.C.: Robert B. Luce, 1972), 13.
64. A number of observers held this view. See Legum and Drysdale, eds., *ACR, 1969–1970*, A41; and William Selover, "After the Rogers Jaunt," *Christian Science Monitor*, February 25, 1970.
65. See Secretary of State William Rogers's arrival statement in Addis Ababa on February 11, 1970, in U.S. Department of State, *Department of State Bulletin* 62 (March 23, 1970), 370.
66. Legum and Drysdale, eds. *ACR, 1969–1970*, A41.
67. Kissinger, *Years of Upheaval*, 122–27.
68. See *Public Papers of the President, Richard Nixon, 1969* (Washington, D.C.: GPO, 1971), 494–505.
69. Ibid.
70. *Public Papers of the President, Richard Nixon, 1973* (Washington, D.C.: GPO, 1975), 531–32.
71. Ibid.
72. Ibid.
73. Korn, *Ethiopia, the United States, and the Soviet Union*, 2–3.
74. See Charles Kegley, Jr., and Eugene Wittkopf, *American Foreign Policy: Pattern and Process* (New York: St. Martin's, 1979), 302–06.
75. See for example, J. William Fulbright, *The Arrogance of Power* (New York: Random House, 1966).
76. U.S. House of Representatives, *Policy Toward Africa for the 1970's*, Hearings before the Subcommittee on Africa of the Committee on Foreign Affairs, 91st Cong., 2d sess. (Washington, D.C.: GPO, 1970), 194.
77. A favorite target for congressional critics such as Otto Passman was the naval training ship HIMS *Ethiopia* referred to by Passman as the "emperor's yacht." See U.S. House of Representatives, *Foreign Assistance and Related Agencies Appropriations for 1969, Part I*, Hearings before a Subcommittee of the Committee on Appropriations, 90th Cong., 2d sess. (Washington, D.C.: GPO, 1968), 553; and U.S. House of Representatives, *Foreign Assistance and Related Agencies Appropriations for 1970, Part I*, Hearings before a Subcommittee of the Committee on Appropriations, 91st Cong., 1st sess. (Washington, D.C.: GPO, 1969), 765.
78. U.S. House of Representatives, *Foreign Assistance and Related Agencies Appropriations for 1970, Part I*, 613.
79. The legislative history of executive requests and legislative appropriations

and authorizations for Security Assistance Programs can be found in the annual editions of the *Congressional Presentation for Security Assistance Programs.* Through the 1950s, 1960s, and early 1970s the executive branch received a large percentage of what it requested.

80. President Kennedy's special envoy Chester Bowles was in Ethiopia on the eve of Addis Ababa's annexation of Eritrea and delivered a letter to Haile Selassie on behalf of the U.S. government—the letter's contents were not disclosed. In Bowles's private communications concerning his October 15–November 9, 1962, visit to Africa, no mention is made of the situation in Eritrea (Chester Bowles Papers, Box 311, Folder 675, New Haven, Conn.: Yale University).

81. Edward Korry, interview, Stonington, Conn., February 6, 1982.

82. This was so, according to Korry.

83. Related to the author by Edward Korry. Also see Thomas Powers, *The Man Who Kept the Secrets: Richard Helmes and the CIA* (New York: Knopf, 1979), 224–25.

84. See Neil G. Kotter, "The Over-Present Americans," *The Nation*, 204 (February 20, 1967), 236–39.

85. Ibid.

86. See U.S. Senate, *United States Security Agreements and Commitments Abroad: Ethiopia, Part 8*, 1935, 1949–50.

87. Ibid.

88. Ibid.

89. See Nancy Stein and Mike Klare, "Police Aid for Tyrants," in *The Trojan Horse*, ed. Steve Weissman (San Francisco: Ramparts Press, 1974), 232.

90. For an account of the Jackson kidnapping, see Georgie Anne Geyer, "Eritrea—A Name to Remember," *Progressive* 34 (June 1970), 24–26.

91. Ibid.

92. It was revealed in mid-February 1970 when Secretary of State William Rogers was in Addis Ababa. Charles Mohr, "An African Critic Exhorts Rogers," *New York Times*, February 13, 1970.

93. Geyer, "Eritrea," 53.

94. See U.S. Senate, *United States Security Agreements and Commitments Abroad: Ethiopia, Part 8*; U.S. Senate, *United States Security Agreements and Commitments Abroad: Broader Aspects of U.S. Commitments*, Hearings before the Subcommittee on U.S. Security Agreements and Commitments Abroad of the Committee on Foreign Relations, 91st Cong., 2d sess. (Washington, D.C.: GPO, 1971), 1; and U.S. Senate, *Security Agreements and Commitments Abroad*, Report to the Committee on Foreign Affairs by the Subcommittee on U.S. Security Agreements and Commitments Abroad, 91st Cong., 2d sess. (Washington, D.C.: GPO, 1970), 1.

95. Hoagland and Stern, "U.S. Aid to Ethiopia."

96. An American soldier was unintentionally killed by an ELF land mine placed along a road frequently used by the Ethiopian 2d Division. See "Brooklyn G.I. Slain in Ethiopia in Region of Guerrilla Activity." Due to repeated threats by the ELF to damage Kagnew, Brig. Gen. Robert Meyer, commander of the U.S. Strategic Communications Command, visited Kagnew in mid-March 1971 ("Ethiopians Seeking New Arms From U.S.," *New York Times*, March 17, 1971). The previous month Gen. William Westmoreland, army chief of staff, had visited Kagnew ("Westmoreland in Ethiopia," *New York Times*, February 4, 1971).

97. Two broader questions raised in the Senate hearings on Ethiopia were (1)

what should the public know? and (2) is U.S. foreign policy made in Washington or overseas by foreign governments? See U.S. Senate, *United States Security Agreements and Commitments Abroad: Ethiopia, Part 8*, 1900–01.

98. According to John Spencer, this rejection "marked the effective end of his reign" (*Ethiopia at Bay*, 323–24).

99. U.S. Senate, *Foreign Assistance and Related Programs Appropriations, FY 1973*, Hearings before the Committee on Appropriations, 92d Cong., 2d sess. (Washington, D.C.: GPO, 1972), 928–29.

100. See Appendix, table 2.

101. Kagnew's peak years of operation were 1961–1969.

Chapter 8. The 1977 Collapse of U.S.-Ethiopian Military Relations

1. For an analysis of the events leading up to the Wollo crisis and the IEG coverup, see Jack Shepherd, *The Politics of Starvation* (New York: Carnegie Endowment for International Peace, 1975). For a review of the revolution itself see Marina Ottaway and David Ottaway, *Ethiopia: Empire in Revolution* (New York: Africana Publishing, 1978), 1–13.

2. David Ottaway, "Ethiopia Gets New U.S. Arms," *Washington Post*, August 26, 1974.

3. Quoted in Donald Petterson, "Ethiopia abandoned? An American perspective," *International Affairs* 62 (Autumn 1986), 630.

4. Ibid.

5. Ibid.

6. Ibid., 630–31. For an excellent analysis of the problems plaguing U.S.-Ethiopia military relations between 1974 and 1977, see Baffour Agyeman-Duah, "The U.S. and Ethiopia: The Politics of Military Assistance," *Armed Forces & Society* 12 (Winter 1986), 287–07.

7. Petterson, "Ethiopia abandoned?" 633–34.

8. See Office of Management and Budget, "Memorandum for the President—Extension of Special Terms for Foreign Military Sales (FMS) Credits to Ethiopia," May 21, 1975, *Declassified Documents Quarterly Catalog (DDQC), 1989* 15 (1989), 429.

9. See National Security Council (NSC), "Memorandum for Secretary Kissinger—Presidential Determination on Credits for Ethiopia," June 21, 1975, *DDQC, 1989*, 335; and NSC, "Memorandum for Brent Scowcroft—Presidential Determination on Credits for Ethiopia," June 23, 1975, *DDQC, 1989*, 334.

10. White House, "Memorandum for the President from Henry Kissinger—Presidential Determination on Credits for Ethiopia," June 24, 1975, *DDQC, 1989*, 430.

11. White House, "Memorandum for the President from James Lynn, Executive Office of the President—Subject: Determination to Authorize the Provision of Sophisticated Weapon System to Ethiopia and Kenya," June 24, 1975," *DDQC, 1990* 16 (1990), 2860.

12. White House, "Memorandum for the President from Henry Kissinger—Subject: Determination to Authorize the Provision of Sophisticated Weapon System to Ethiopia and Kenya," July 9, 1975," *DDQC, 1990* 2861.

13. Petterson, "Ethiopia Abandoned?" 635.

14. Ibid.

15. Since the end of the Vietnam War, Henry Kissinger was troubled by the questions it raised about American power and resolve. Gerald Bender, "Kissinger

in Angola: Anatomy of Failure," in *American Policy in Southern Africa: The Stakes and the Stance*, ed. Rene Lemarchard (Washington, D.C.: University Press of America, 1978), 81.

16. Leslie H. Gelb, "U.S. Stung in Angola, Forges a Firm Africa Policy," *New York Times*, April 16, 1976.

17. Drew Middleton, "Cubans Reported in Red Sea Area," *New York Times*, April 5, 1976.

18. See David Ottaway, "U.S. Becoming Involved in African Arms Race," *Washington Post*, July 6, 1976.

19. Ibid.

20. Reported by John Darnton, "Ethiopian Moving to Break Old Link with U.S.," *New York Times*, April 25, 1977; and Marina Ottaway, *Soviet and American Influence in the Horn of Africa* (New York: Praeger, 1982), 108.

21. U.S. House of Representatives, *Foreign Assistance Legislation for FY 1978, Part 3*, Hearings before the Subcommittee on Africa of the Committee on International Relations, 95th Cong., 1st sess. (Washington, D.C.: GPO, 1977), 224–26.

22. Point made to the author by Jimmy Carter's assistant secretary of state for African affairs (Richard Moose, interview, Alexandria, Va., June 8, 1982).

23. See U.S. Senate, *The International Security Assistance and Arms Export Control Act of 1977*, S. Rept. 95–195, Committee on Foreign Relations, 95th Cong., 1st sess. (Washington, D.C.: GPO, 1977), 2–3.

24. Moose, interview.

25. Petterson, "Ethiopia abandoned?" 631–32.

26. Ibid., 633.

27. See Colin Legum, ed., *Africa Contemporary Record (ACR), 1974–1975*, B188. General Aman had served as a defense attache in Washington from May 1964 to July 1965 and had received a B.A. in government from Howard University. See Werner Wiskari, "Gen. Aman: Ethiopian of Many Roles," *New York Times*, September 13, 1974. The general was also seen as a major force behind the military reform movement. See David Ottaway, "What Future for Ethiopia," *Washington Post*, December 7, 1974.

28. Pliny the Middle-Aged, "The PMAC: Origins and Structure, Part I," *Ethiopianist Notes* 2, no. 3 (1978/79), 13.

29. Apparently Aman had proposed internal automony for all of Eritrea except the port of Assab and possibly a strip of land connecting Assab to the highlands. See Tom Farer, *War Clouds on the Horn of Africa: The Widening Storm*, 2d ed. (New York: Carnegie Endowment for International Peace, 1979), 41. Another source of tension within the PMAC was that Aman favored maintaining the U.S. arms connection, though he had warned Secretary Kissinger that Washington needed to increase grant military aid to Ethiopia. See Agyeman-Duah, "The U.S. and Ethiopia," 293.

30. Legum, ed. *ACR, 1974–1975*, B191.

31. Ibid., B184; and Pliny the Middle-Aged, "The PMAC: Origins and Structure, Part I," 13.

32. "The PMAC: Origins and Structure, Part I," 14. Also see Marina Ottaway and David Ottaway, *Ethiopia: Empire in Revolution*, 8.

33. Ottaway and Ottaway, *Ethiopia: Empire in Revolution*, 155–56; Legum, ed., *ACR, 1974–1975*, B192.

34. David Ottaway, "Aid is Key to Eritrea Outcome," *Washington Post*, February 9, 1975.

35. See U.S. House of Representatives, *U.S. Policy and Request for Sale of*

Arms to Ethiopia, Hearings before the Subcommittee on International Political and Military Affairs of the Committee on Foreign Affairs, 94th Cong., 1st sess. (Washington, D.C.: GPO, 1975).

36. David Ottaway, "U.S. Aid to Ethiopia Stalled After Killings," *Washington Post*, December 5, 1974. At the same time the U.S. military sought to avoid being drawn into the internal affairs of the PMAC. According to Brig. Gen. Harold Yow, chief of MAAG, in 1974 the U.S. MAAG in Addis Ababa adopted the policy to "stay out of all internal affairs," specifically the Eritrean conflict. In February 1975 MAAG paticipation in post-action critiques of Ethiopian combat operations was restricted. See Agyeman-Duah, "The U.S. and Ethiopia," 296–97.

37. Edward Mulcahy, acting assistant secretary of state for African affairs, noted that many of the Arab states supported a peaceful solution even if full independence was not granted to Eritrea. U.S. House of Representatives, *U.S. Policy and Request for Sale of Arms to Ethiopia*, 13.

38. David Binder, "Ethiopia Offered Munitions by U.S.," *New York Times*, March 18, 1975.

39. Official statement read to the press ("Ethiopia to Get U.S. Arms," *Washington Post*, March 18, 1975).

40. See U.S. House of Representatives, *The United States and the Persian Gulf*, Report of the Subcommittee on the Near East to the Committee on Foreign Affairs, 92d Cong., 2d sess. (Washington, D.C.: GPO, 1972), 12–13; and U.S. House of Representatives, *U.S. Interests and Policy Toward the Persian Gulf*, Hearings before the Subcommittee on the Near East of the Committee on Foreign Affairs, 92d Cong., 2d sess. (Washington, D.C.: GPO, 1972), 26.

41. U.S. House of Representatives, *U.S. Interests and Policy Toward the Persian Gulf*, 7–8.

42. Ibid.

43. Ibid., 25.

44. Ibid.

45. See U.S. House of Representatives, *The United States and the Persian Gulf*, 1. Assistant Secretary of State for Near Eastern and South Asian Affairs Joseph Sisco stated that as early as 1968 the State Department had been reviewing the situation in the Persian Gulf knowing that Great Britain would be vacating the area before the end of 1971. See U.S. House of Representatives, *U.S. Interests and Policy Toward the Persian Gulf*, 80.

46. U.S. House of Representatives, *Foreign Assistance and Related Agencies Appropriations for 1975*, Hearings before a Subcommittee on Appropriations, 93d Cong., 2d sess. (Washington, D.C.: GPO, 1974), 1096.

47. U.S. Senate, *Foreign Assistance and Related Programs Appropriations for 1975*, Hearings before the Committee on Appropriations, 93d Cong., 2d sess. (Washington, D.C.: GPO, 1974), 1058.

48. Ibid., 1154; See U.S. House of Representatives, *Foreign Assistance and Related Agencies Appropriations for 1975*, 1287.

49. See John Spencer's testimony in U.S. Senate, *Ethiopia and the Horn of Africa*, Hearings before the Subcommittee on African Affairs of the Committee on Foreign Relations, 94th Cong., 2d sess. (Washington, D.C.: GPO, 1976), 56.

50. U.S. House of Representatives, *U.S. Policy and Request for Sale of Arms to Ethiopia*, 6–7.

51. See L. Edgar Prina, "Schesinger's Mirage, Somali Semantics, and Signs of Permanency," *Sea Power* 18 (July 1975), 7; and Alvin Cottrell and R. M. Burrell,

"Soviet-U.S. Naval Competition in the Indian Ocean," *Orbis* 18 (Winter 1975), 1116.

52. See Prina, "Schesinger's Mirage," 7; and Cottrell and Burrell, "Soviet-U.S. Naval Competition," 1116.

53. U.S. Senate, *Ethiopia and the Horn of Africa*, 58. This opinion was expressed by Acting Assistant Secretary of State for African Affairs Edward Mulcahy in a meeting with Congressman Henry Reuss in November 1975.

54. See Dina Spechler, "The U.S.S.R. and Third World Conflicts," *World Politics* 38 (April 1986), 435–61.

55. See Ottaway, "Ethiopia Gets New U.S. Arms." Some analysts disputed Ottaway's critique which seemed to mirror the thinking in Addis Ababa. Instead Ethiopia's F-5s were comparable in performance to the MIG–21s. Although the MIG–21s possessed a speed advantage, the F-5s had greater range and versatility. The F-86 jets were assumed to be comparable to Somalia's MIG–15s and MIG–17s. See Irving Kaplan, *Area Handbook for Somalia*, 2d ed., (Washington, D.C.: GPO, 1977), 316.

56. Petterson, "Ethiopia abandoned?" 637.

57. Ibid., 636–37. See Harry Brind, "Soviet Policy in the Horn of Africa," *International Affairs* 60 (Winter 1983/84), 93.

58. See Petterson, "Ethiopia abandoned?" 637; and Brind, "Soviet Policy in the Horn of Africa," 93.

59. Pliny the Middle-Aged, "The PMAC: Origins and Structure, Part II," *Northeast African Studies* 1, no. 1 (1979), 10.

60. David Korn, *Ethiopia, the United States, and the Soviet Union* (Carbondale and Edwardsville: Southern Illinois University Press, 1986), 19, 91. After clashing with the EPRP in late 1976 and 1977, the Dergue would turn on Meison in September 1977.

61. John Markakis and Nega Ayele, *Class and Revolution in Ethiopia* (Nottingham: Russell Press, 1978), 163–64.

62. David Ottaway, "Ethiopia Says CIA Is Aiding Military Rulers' Internal Foes," *Washington Post*, October 8, 1976.

63. Some argue that Israel was simply used as a distraction by the Arab governments to ease African criticisms of their interventionist policies in the Horn. See Fred Halliday, "U.S. Policy in the Horn of Africa: Aboulia or Proxy Intervention," *Review of African Political Economy* 10 (September–December 1978), 24–25.

64. Donald Louchheim, "Ethiopia's Little War is Hard to Hide," *Washington Post*, April 30, 1967.

65. Legum, ed. *ACR, 1969–1970*, B112; Eric Pace, "Eritrean Liberation Group Is Pursuing Its Struggle at the U.N.," *New York Times*, December 15, 1971; Henry Tanner, "Sudan to Press for Indictments," ibid., March 13, 1973.

66. Edward Korry, interview, Stonington, Conn., February 6, 1982. For an account of a run-in Korry had with the CIA station chief in Addis Ababa, see Thomas Powers, *The Man Who Kept the Secrets: Richard Helms and the CIA* (New York: Knopf, 1979), 224–25. Moreover, by 1970 Israel maintained the second largest military presence in Ethiopia behind the United States. Legum, ed., *ACR, 1970–1971*, A68; Abel Jacob, "Israel's Military Aid to Africa," *Journal of Modern African Studies* 9, no. 2 (1971), 176.

67. According to Korry (interview).

68. Halliday, "U.S. Policy in the Horn of Africa," 24–25.

69. In mid-July 1977, Israel reportedly agreed to equip and train an Ethiopian

counterinsurgency task force of 15,000 soldiers. See J. Gus Liebenow, "The Caucus Race: The International Conflict in East Africa and the Horn," *American University Field Staff Reports*, July 1977, 9. Nonetheless, after the supposed break in relations Israel exported $4.4 million worth of goods to Ethiopia in 1975 and $4 million in the first four months of 1976 (Halliday, "U.S. Policy in the Horn of Africa," 24).

70. See U.S. Senate, *Ethiopia and the Horn of Africa*, 104–05; William Tuohy, "U.S., Russians Compete for Indian Ocean Role," *Los Angeles Times*, October 19, 1975; J. Bowyer Bell, "Bab El-Mandeb, Strategic Troublespot," *Orbis* 16, no. 4 (1973), 986; and James Fitzgerald, "Gunboat Diplomacy and the Horn," *Horn of Africa* 2, no. 2 (1979), 51.

71. Tel Aviv believed that the Arab states were attempting to turn the Red Sea into an "Arab lake" in order to further isolate Israel ("Israeli Drill in Red Sea," *New York Times*, February 21, 1975).

72. See the analysis of Edward Korry and John Spencer in U.S. Senate, *Ethiopia and the Horn of Africa*, 53–54, 103–04.

73. See ibid., 101–02, 105–06. Tom Farer refuted the "worst-case" scenario. Israel's June 1976 raid on Entebbe, Uganda also showed that the Israeli military could reach targets well beyond the Red Sea littoral. This demonstrated military capability to retaliate in any location would presumably serve as an adequate deterrent, unless the Arab states wished to risk the destruction of their oil facilities, ports, or airfields.

74. At an "authoritative-level" White House briefing in 1963, Edward Korry was told that the State Department presumed that Haile Selassie would either die or be overthrown during Korry's tenure as ambassador (Korry, interview).

75. Korn, *Ethiopia, the United States, and the Soviet Union*, 4–5.

76. See ibid., 5–7.

77. See, for example, Secretary of State for African Affairs David Newsom's statement in U.S. Senate, *United States Security Agreements and Commitments Abroad: Ethiopia, Part 8*, Hearings before the Subcommittee on U.S. Security Agreements and Commitments Abroad of the Committee on Foreign Affairs, 91th Cong., 2d sess. (Washington, D.C.: GPO, 1970), 1909; and Defense Secretary Melvin Laird's testimony in U.S. House of Representatives, *Foreign Assistance and Related Agencies Appropriations for 1972, Part I*, Hearings before a Subcommittee of the Committee on Appropriations, 92d Cong., 1st sess. (Washington, D.C.: GPO, 1971), 65.

78. See Pliny the Middle-Aged, "The PMAC: Origins and Structure, Part I," 1–18; and "The PMAC: Origins and Structure, Part II," 1–20." Also, Central Intelligence Agency, "Weekly Summary—Ethiopia: Rifts in the Military," October 11, 1974, *DDQC, 1990* 16 (1990), 615.

79. See Markakis and Ayele, *Class and Revolution in Ethiopia*, 127.

80. Ottaway and Ottaway, *Ethiopia: Empire in Revolution*, 139–40.

81. Ibid.

82. Korn, *Ethiopia, the United States, and the Soviet Union*, 16.

83. See ibid., 16–17; and Ottaway and Ottaway, *Ethiopia: Empire in Revolution*, 139–40. The "Peasant March" was an army of some 20,000–30,000 peasants from the northern provinces who were urged on by the pronouncements that they would be waging a "holy war" against the Muslim rebels in Eritrea. It met with military disaster.

84. See Pliny the Middle-Aged, "The PMAC: Origins and Structure, Part II," 5–7.

85. Korn, *Ethiopia, the United States, and the Soviet Union*, 103.

86. See ibid., 105–16.

87. State Department policy, nonetheless, was also defined by the policy of containment. For an analysis that emphasizes the predominance of globalist thinking in U.S. policy toward the Middle East see Charles Kupchan, "American Globalism in the Middle East: The Roots of Regional Security Policy," *Political Science Quarterly* 103 (Winter 1988/89), 585–611.

88. Petterson, "Ethiopia abandoned?" 631–32.

89. U.S. House of Representatives, *Foreign Assistance Legislation for FY 1978, Part 3*, 223–24.

90. Korn, *Ethiopia, the United States, and the Soviet Union*, 20.

91. U.S. House of Representatives, *Foreign Assistance Legislation for FY 1978, Part 3*, 283.

92. Ibid., 225; U.S. Senate, *The International Security Assistance and Arms Control Export Control Act of 1977*, S. Rept. 95–195, 27–28.

93. Korn, *Ethiopia, the United States, and the Soviet Union*, 20.

94. Henry Kissinger, *Years of Upheaval* (Boston: Little, Brown, 1982), 413.

95. Ibid.

96. Ibid., 412.

97. Ibid.

98. Kissinger challenged this charge (ibid., 374–413).

99. Following the execution of Major Sisay, the Dergue must have become rather paranoid over the real objectives behind U.S. policy toward Ethiopia, especially given Henry Kissinger's past dealings with leftist governments. For instance, in Chile Kissinger's 40 Committee had set a precedent in the early 1970s of providing covert "financial support [to] democratic political parties and media threatened with extinction" while Allende was president (ibid., 403).

100. See Jerel Rosati, *The Carter Administration's Quest for Global Community* (Columbia, S.C.: University of South Carolina Press, 1987), 39–57.

101. Ibid., 42.

102. Ibid., 44–49.

103. Jimmy Carter's rhetoric to change this negative reactive pattern of U.S. policy did not seem to be matched by his actions. See Charles Kegley, Jr., and Eugene Wittkopf, *American Foreign Policy: Pattern and Process* (New York: St. Martin's, 1979), 427–42. To gain an appreciation of the impact Carter's personal beliefs had upon his foreign policy decision making, see Jimmy Carter, *Keeping Faith* (New York: Bantam Books, 1982).

104. Adam Clymer, "Carter Talks on Arms Sales, South Africa," *The Sun*, July 30, 1976. For a discussion of the human rights movement in the U.S. Congress, see U.S. Senate, *Human Rights*, Hearing before the Subcommittee on Foreign Assistance of the Committee on Foreign Relations, 95th Cong., 1st sess. (Washington, D.C.: GPO, 1977), 1–7. During 1975–76 the U.S. Congress became very active in trying to achieve restraint in the sale of U.S. arms. Richard Moose and Daniel Spiegal, "Congress and Arms Transfers," in *Arms Transfers and American Foreign Policy*, ed. Andrew Pierre (New York: New York University Press, 1979), 228–60.

105. Noted in a confidential report. See U.S. Department of State, "Ethiopia," October 18, 1976, *DDQC,1989*, 151.

Chapter 9. The 1977–78 Ogaden War and the U.S. Arms Rebuff

1. Don Oberdorfer, "U.S. Offers Military Aid to Somalia," *Washington Post*, July 26, 1977.

2. Reported in David Korn, *Ethiopia, the United States, and the Soviet Union* (Carbondale and Edwardsville: Southern Illinois University Press, 1986), 32–33.
3. Quoted in Stanley Cloud, "With Jimmy from Dawn to Midnight," *Time*, April 18, 1977, 15.
4. See "Mogadishu Message," *Newsweek*, October 3, 1977. The link apparently was Dr. Kevin Cahill, a U.S. citizen and Siad Barre's personal physician. Korn, *Ethiopia, the United States, and the Soviet Union*, 36.
5. Cyrus Vance, *Hard Choices* (New York: Simon and Schuster, 1983), 73.
6. Ibid.
7. Ibid. Also see Donald Petterson, "Ethiopia abandoned? An American perspective," *International Affairs* 62 (Autumn 1986), 638.
8. Richard Moose, interview, Alexandria, Va., June 8, 1982.
9. John Loughran, interview, Washington, D.C., April 28, 1982.
10. Moose, interview.
11. Richard Burt, "Administration Ends U.S. Involvement in the Horn of Africa," *New York Times*, October 3, 1977. Somali positions also seemed to threaten Djibouti. See Jim Hoagland, "U.S., France Spurn Somalia's Plea for Urgent Arms Aid," *Washington Post*, September 1, 1977.
12. "Arms Offer to Somalia Suspended; U.S. Cites Ethiopian Fighting Role," *The Sun*, September 2, 1977.
13. Vance, *Hard Choices*, 73–74. This message was delivered by Philip Habib.
14. Paul Watson, "Arms and Aggression in the Horn of Africa," *Journal of International Affairs* 40 (Summer 1986), 166.
15. From the end of 1975 into the spring of 1978, ten of Ethiopia's fourteen provinces were in rebellion. See Gerard Chaliant, "The Horn of Africa's Dilemma," *Foreign Policy* 30 (Spring 1978), 116–31. Iraq would make much the same type of calculation when it decided to invade Iran in September 1980.
16. Watson, "Arms and Aggression in the Horn of Africa," 156–68. Also see Harry Brind, "Soviet Policy in the Horn of Africa," *International Affairs* 60 (Winter 1983/84), 85.
17. See U.S. House of Representatives, *Report of the Delegation to the Middle East and Africa*, Committee on Armed Services, 95th Cong., 1st sess. (Washington, D.C.: GPO, February 6, 1978), 25; "Soviet Arms Airlift to Ethiopia Violates Air Space of Pakistan," *Aviation Week & Space Technology*, December 19, 1977; and Nelsen Goodsell, "Castro's Troops to Ethiopia Restate Africa Commitment," *Christian Science Monitor*, December 20, 1977.
18. Vance, *Hard Choices*, 74.
19. See Raymond Garthoff, *Detente and Confrontation* (Washington, D.C.: Brookings Institution, 1985), 630–53.
20. Reported in Henry Trewhitt, "Somalia Promises Withdrawal," *The Sun*, March 10, 1978.
21. Watson, "Arms and Aggression in the Horn of Africa," 167.
22. Trewhitt, "Somalia Promises Withdrawal."
23. For an account of the "Red Terror" see Marina Ottaway and David Ottaway, *Ethiopia: Empire in Revolution* (New York: Africana Publishing, 1978), 146–48.
24. Comment made to the author by Tom Farer, interview, Camden, N.J., January 5, 1982.
25. Brind, "Soviet Policy in the Horn of Africa," 82–84; Watson, "Arms and Aggression in the Horn of Africa," 161.
26. Brind, "Soviet Policy in the Horn of Africa," 83.

27. Ibid.

28. See George Sheperd, "Dominance and Conflict in the Horn: Notes on U.S.-Soviet Rivalry," *Africa Today* 32 (3rd Quarter, 1985), 13–15.

29. Brind, "Soviet Policy in the Horn of Africa," 81. While much of Siad Barre's rhetoric was couched in Marxist-Leninist terms, Somalia's system of government bore only a superficial resemblance to the Soviet model.

30. See David Ottaway, "Moscow on a Tightrope in Somali-Ethiopian Dispute," *Washington Post*, August 7, 1977. This was suggested by the fact that the Soviets had resumed sending military supplies to Somalia in August 1977 apparently in order to dissuade Somalia from turning to the West for arms and to hedge their bet in case of a pro-Western coup in Ethiopia.

31. Brind, "Soviet Policy in the Horn of Africa," 83–86; Watson, "Arms and Aggression in the Horn of Africa," 165–70.

32. Watson, "Arms and Aggression in the Horn of Africa," 169–70.

33. Brind, "Soviet Policy in the Horn of Africa," 86.

34. Ibid., 86–89. One might also consider historical ties between Russia and Ethiopia, and a certain similarity in their history and background—czar and emperor, Orthodox and Coptic Christianity, and neofeudalism. Brind suggests that Marxist-Leninist considerations may not have been particularly important.

35. Ibid., 89. Also see Mohammed Ayoob, "The Super-Powers and Regional 'Stability': Parallel Responses to the Gulf and the Horn," *World Today* 35 (May 1979), 201.

36. See "Arms Offer to Somalia Suspended; U.S. Cites Ethiopian Fighting Role"; and John Darnton, "Russians in Somalia: Foothold in Africa Suddenly Shaky," *New York Times*, September 16, 1977.

37. Brind, "Soviet Policy in the Horn of Africa," 86–87.

38. Vance, *Hard Choices*, 72–75, 84–92.

39. See Daniel Southerland, "U.S. Foreign Policy Muddled?" *Christian Science Monitor*, December 19, 1977; and David Ottaway, "Struggle Over U.S. Africa Policy Pits Young Against Brzezinski," *Washington Post*, February 14, 1978.

40. Zbigniew Brzezinski, *Power and Principle* (New York: Farrar, Straus, Giroux, 1983), 178.

41. Ibid., 38.

42. No one took much notice of the Cubans when they first began arriving in Ethiopia during the late summer and early fall of 1977. See U.S. House of Representatives, *Report of the Delegation to the Middle East and Africa*, 25.

43. See Elizabeth Drew, "Brzezinski," *New Yorker*, May 1, 1978, 110. Brzezinski likened the situation in the Horn to the 1898 Fashoda incident between English and French expeditionary forces in the Sudan. In that case the English displaced the French. However, in this instance he felt that the first power to establish itself or preempt its rival would come out on top.

44. Brzezinski, *Power and Principle*, 178, 182.

45. Ibid.

46. Vance, *Hard Choices*, 72–75.

47. Ibid., 84–85.

48. Ibid., 47–48.

49. Ibid., 74.

50. Ibid., 74–75.

51. Ibid., 84–85.

52. Ibid., 72–75, 84–92.

53. Ibid., 85–86.
54. Ibid., 86.
55. Ibid. Also see Graham Hovey, "Contradictions Seen in U.S. African Policy," *New York Times*, February 12, 1978. The view of the State Department and most U.S. diplomats in East Africa was that no vital U.S. interest was at stake.
56. Brind, "Soviet Policy in the Horn of Africa," 86–89.
57. Sheperd, "Dominance and Conflict in the Horn," 14.
58. Ibid., 14.
59. David Willis, "Soviet African Policy on Verge of Failure," *Christian Science Monitor*, September 2, 1977.
60. See "Mogadishu Message."
61. See Arnaud De Borchgrave, "Crossed Wires," *Newsweek*, September 26, 1977.
62. Ibid.
63. Ibid.
64. David Lamb, "Soviets in Somalia Isolated by System They Helped Build," *Washington Post*, October 8, 1977.
65. Ibid.
66. Burt, "Administration Ends U.S. Involvement in Horn of Africa."
67. Brind, "Soviet Policy in the Horn of Africa," 86.
68. Ibid.
69. Ibid.
70. Ibid.
71. Vance, *Hard Choices*, 74.
72. Ibid.
73. Petterson, "Ethiopia abandoned?" 639–40.
74. Michael Parks, "Somalia, Ethiopia keeping arms dealers busy," *The Sun*, November 3, 1977.
75. See David Ottaway, "Somalia Said to Get French-Built Tanks," *Washington Post*, February 8, 1978; and "Airlift to Ethiopia," *Newsweek*, January 16, 1978.
76. Michael Getler, "Somalia-Egypt Arms Link Cited," *Washington Post*, January 24, 1978; Jay Ross and David Ottaway, "Egypt, Sudan Seen Pledging Military Help to Somalia," *Washington Post*, January 27, 1978.
77. Fred Halliday, "U.S. Policy in the Horn of Africa: Aboulia or Proxy Intervention," *Review of African Political Economy* 10 (September–December 1978), 8.
78. Petterson, "Ethiopia abandoned?" 638–41. This is how one well-informed U.S. official saw the situation. Petterson served as U.S. ambassador to Somalia from 1978 to 1982.
79. Vance, *Hard Choices*, 73.
80. David Ottaway, "Ethiopia Seeks to Heal Rift With U.S.," *Washington Post*, September 23, 1977.
81. Ibid.
82. Ibid.
83. Ibid. Also see Petterson, "Ethiopia abandoned?" 640; and Susanna McBee, "U.S. Denies It Encouraged Somali Aid to Ogaden Rebels," *Washington Post*, September, 20, 1977.
84. Ottaway, "Ethiopia Seeks to Heal Rift With U.S."
85. Ibid.
86. Ibid. Also see Petterson, "Ethiopia abandoned?" 640.
87. Ottaway, "Ethiopia Seeks to Heal Rift With U.S." Also see Petterson,

"Ethiopia abandoned?" 640. Washington claimed that Ethiopia owed more in unpaid loans than the amount Addis Ababa had spent on undelivered U.S. military equipment.

88. Ottaway, "Ethiopia Seeks to Heal Rift With U.S." This is what the Ethiopians claimed they wanted to do.

89. Burt, "Administration Ends U.S. Involvement in the Horn of Africa."

90. "Supplies for Ethiopia Withheld by U.S." *New York Times*, February 23, 1978.

91. Henry Bradsher, "Israel Helping Arm Ethiopia in Spite of U.S. Opposition," *Washington Star*, January 18, 1978; and "U.S. Must Decide on Ethiopian Arms," ibid., February 1, 1978.

92. Bradsher, "Israel Helping Arm Ethiopia in Spite of U.S. Opposition"; Dan Connell, Israelis Still Find Home in Ethiopia," *Washington Post*, October 1, 1977. Also see Michael Kaufman, "Ethiopia Shows Shot Down Somali Jet, Cache of Arms," *New York Times*, August 15, 1977. Addis Ababa suggested that the U.S. sell arms to Israel, which could then transfer weapons to Ethiopia.

93. Kaufman, "Ethiopia Shows Shot Down Somali Jet."

94. See U.S. House of Representatives, *Israel, Egypt, Sudan, Ethiopia, and Somalia*, Report of a Congressional Study Mission to Israel, Egypt, Sudan, Ethiopia, and Somalia (August 2–20, 1985), 99th Cong., 1st sess. (Washington, D.C.: GPO, 1986), 2.

95. Petterson, "Ethiopia abandoned?" 639–41.

96. Ibid., 640.

97. Reported in Bradsher, "U.S. Must Decide on Ethiopian Arms."

98. Petterson, "Ethiopia abandoned?" 641.

99. Ibid., 641; Vance, *Hard Choices*, 86.

100. Petterson, "Ethiopia abandoned?" 641. At the end of February 1977, in a minor exception to the arms embargo, the United States released twenty-three trucks and trailors and some spare parts for the Ethiopian Army. See Korn, *Ethiopia, the United States, and the Soviet Union*, 49–51.

101. Brzezinski, *Power and Principle*, 178–79.

102. See Lewis Diuguid, "Carter Promises Economic, Military Assistance to Kenya," *Washington Post*, March 3, 1978; and Robert Hecht, "Carter's Africa Policy—still outmoded," *Christian Science Monitor*, January 31, 1978.

103. Quoted in Borchgrave, "Crossed Wires."

104. Ibid.

105. Ibid. Matthew Nimetz, an aide to Secretary of State Vance, made this observation.

106. Quoted in an address by Secretary of State Cyrus Vance before the annual convention of the NAACP, July 1, 1977 (U.S. Department of State, *Department of State Bulletin*, August 1977).

107. According to the U.S. ambassador to Somalia, John Loughran (interview).

108. Jimmy Carter, *Keeping Faith: Memoirs of a President* (New York: Bantam Books, 1982), 20.

109. Ibid., 144.

110. Ibid., 143.

111. Loughran, interview. Carter's human rights message seemed to be directed toward the Palestinians too, though he was forced by domestic and Israeli criticism to back away from this stance. See William Polk, *The Arab World* (Cambridge, Mass.: Harvard University Press, 1980), 361–71.

112. Loughran, interview. Also see Jimmy Carter, *Keeping Faith*, 145.

113. Loughran, interview. Loughran reportedly held lengthy consultations in Washington, but not with the president. See Jonathan Randal, "Somalis Are United on Expelling Soviets," *Washington Post*, November 26, 1977.

114. Loughran, interview.

115. In the words of Siad Barre. See Randal, "Somalis Are United on Expelling Soviets."

116. Southerland, "U.S. Foreign Policy Muddled?"

117. See William Hyland, "U.S. Policy Options," *Washington Review*, Special supplement on the Horn of Africa, (May 1978), 23–30; and Helen Kitchen, ed., "The 'Afro-Centric' Perspective," *AEI Foreign Policy and Defense Review* 1, no. 1 (1979), 18–25.

118. See Hyland, "U.S. Policy Options," 23–30; and Kitchen, ed., "The 'Afro-Centric' Perspective," 18–25. Great power intervention would eventually run afoul of indigenous nationlism in the Horn, according to the area specialist school of thought. Also see Korn, *Ethiopia, the United States, and the Soviet Union*, 48–49.

119. Loughran, interview. Also see Raymond Thurston, "The United States, Somalia and the Crisis in the Horn," *Horn of Africa* 1, no. 2 (1978), 11–20. Thurston served as U.S. ambassador to Somalia from 1965 to 1968.

120. Loughran, interview.

121. Ibid.

122. See Edgar Prina, "Schesinger's Mirage, Somali Semantics, and Signs of Permanency," *Sea Power* 18 (July 1975), 7–9. For an analysis of Soviet naval activity at Berbera, see Dennis Chaplin, "Somalia and the Development of Soviet Activity in the Indian Ocean," *Military Review* 60 (July 1975), 3–9.

123. Francis Ofner, "Israel explains arms aid to Ethiopia," *Christian Science Monitor*, February 8, 1978. It was felt that Somalia only turned to the West for reasons of expediency after the Soviets opted for Ethiopia.

124. Apparently pursuing the Somali option in 1975 would have been a threat to gaining increased funding for Diego Garcia; thus it was rejected at the time. See U.S. Senate, *Multinational Corporations and U.S. Policy*, Hearings before the Subcommittee on Multinational Corporations of the Committee on Foreign Relations, 94th Cong., 2d sess. (Washington, D.C.: GPO, 1976), 430–40. Mogadishu had been sending signals to the U.S. government for several months before the Carter administration took an interest (Loughran, interview).

125. Drew, "Brzezinski," 115.

126. Ibid., 114.

127. To support Somalia would seemingly involve losing all hope of influencing the current Ethiopian government or its successor. See "Why the Horn Matters," *Economist* 266 (11 February 1978), 10–11.

128. See U.S. House of Representatives, *War in the Horn of Africa: A Firsthand Report on the Challenges for United States Policy*, Committee on International Relations, 95th Cong., 1st sess. (Washington, D.C.: GPO, 1978), 49.

129. The U.S. delegation visited Somalia in mid-November 1977 after the Soviets had been expelled. See U.S. House of Representatives, *Report of the Delegation to the Middle East and Africa*, 23–28.

130. Israel's concern that Somalia and Eritrea might form part of an Arab scheme to seize control of the Red Sea may have affected the judgment of the U.S. Congress. Israeli military aid to Addis Ababa continued throughout the Ogaden War. See Ofner, "Israel Explains Arms Aid to Ethiopia"; Jay Ross, "Dayan Dis-

closes Israel Is Selling Arms to Ethiopia," *Washington Post*, February 7, 1978; and "Why the Horn Matters." (already cited)

131. Vance, *Hard Choices*, 85–88.
132. Ibid., 87; Brzezinski, *Power and Principle*, 182.
133. Brzezinski, *Power and Principle*, 182–83.
134. Ibid.; Vance, *Hard Choices*, 87–88.
135. Vance, *Hard Choices*, 87.
136. Ibid.
137. Brzezinski, *Power and Principle*, 183.
138. Ibid.
139. Vance, *Hard Choices*, 87–88. Brzezinski stated in early March 1978 that the U.S. would deliberately slow down the SALT negotiations unless the Soviets showed more restraint in Africa. Vance believed that Brzezinski was setting an impossible objective of trying to eliminate Soviet-Cuban influence in Ethiopia and creating the perception that the U.S. had been defeated when instead the administration had achieved a successful outcome.

Chapter 10. The 1980 Arms-for-Base-Access Accord

1. Donald Petterson, "Ethiopia abandoned? An American perspective," *International Affairs* 62 (Autumn 1986), 642.
2. Ibid.
3. Richard Moose, interview, Alexandria, Va., June 8, 1982.
4. See "Somalia, U.S. Confer About Forces," *The Sun*, March 21, 1978; and David Ottaway, "Kenya Warns U.S. on Somalia Arms," *Washington Post*, April 13, 1978.
5. Petterson, "Ethiopia abandoned?" 642.
6. Moose, interview.
7. Petterson, "Ethiopia abandoned?" 642.
8. Sanford Ungar, "The Real Reasons For Our Africa Role," *Washington Post*, June 18, 1978.
9. "Double Reverse: How U.S. Policy on Africa Changed," *Washington Post*, June 25, 1978.
10. David Ottaway, "Saudis Score U.S. Failure to Challenge Cubans," *Washington Post*, May 15, 1978.
11. Ungar, "The Real Reasons For Our Africa Role"; Don Oberdorfer, "U.S. Revives Plan Extended Version Arms to Somalia," *Washington Post*, June 2, 1978; Graham Hovey, "Architects of U.S. African Policy Privately Worried by Carter's Attacks on Moscow," *New York Times*, June 14, 1978.
12. Henry Bradsher, "U.S. Faces Somali Aid Dilemma," *Washington Star*, June 3, 1978.
13. Ibid.
14. "U.S. Envoy in Somalia for Talks on Arms Aid," *The Sun*, October 21, 1978; Henry Bradsher, "Horn of Africa Rejects Superpower Prompting," *Washington Star*, November 1, 1978.
15. Petterson, "Ethiopia abandoned?" 642.
16. See Richard Burt, "U.S. Reappraises Persian Gulf Policies," *New York Times*, January 1, 1979; Bernard Weinraub, "Pentagon Is Urging Indian Ocean Fleet," *New York Times*, March 1, 1979; and Richard Burt, "U.S. Buildup Urged in the Persian Gulf," *New York Times*, June 28, 1979.

17. See David Halevy, "Soviet Airlift in Ethiopia, Aden Reported," *Washington Star*, September 23, 1979. According to Israeli analysts, it was a forceful demonstration of Soviet power projection capabilities.

18. See Oles Smolansky, "Soviet Interests in the Persian/Arabian Gulf," in *The Indian Ocean: Perspectives on a Strategic Arena*, ed. William Dowdy and Russell Trood (Durham, N.C.: Duke University Press, 1985), 468–72; and Dennis Ross, "Soviet Decisionmaking for the Middle East," in *Security in the Middle East*, ed. Samuel Wells and Mark Bruzonsky (Boulder, Colo.: Westview Press, 1987), 243–44.

19. Quoted in Walter Taylor, "Saudis Deepen Military Role in Red Sea Region," *Washington Star*, September 30, 1979.

20. According to a State Department official assigned to the Africa Bureau (interview, Washington, D.C., June 1982).

21. See Don Oberdorfer, "The Evolution of a Decision," *Washington Post*, January 24, 1980; and Richard Burt, "How U.S. Strategy Toward the Persian Gulf Region Evolved," *New York Times*, January 25, 1980. The Carter Doctrine was the product of a year of deliberations at the NSC and Pentagon.

22. See Richard Burt, "U.S. Wins Bases in Oman and Kenya," *New York Times*, April 22, 1980; and "U.S. Reassesses Need to Use Somali Base," *New York Times*, July 16, 1980.

23. Michael Getler, "Somalia Asks High Price for U.S. Access to Bases," *Washington Post*, April 22, 1980.

24. Burt, "U.S. Wins Bases in Oman and Kenya."

25. Negotiating with Siad Barre, according to one U.S. official, was like bargaining with "one of the world's greatest rug merchants." Washington would "have to walk away from the negotiations a few times before [picking] up that rug." See Daniel Southerland, "Haggling for Somalia Port Involves Money, Border War," *Christian Science Monitor*, April 21, 1980.

26. For a description of the facilities at Oman and Kenya, see James Wootten, *Regional Support Facilities for the Rapid Deployment Force*, Foreign Affairs and National Defense Division, Congressional Research Service (Washington, D.C.: GPO, March 25, 1982), 12–19, 23–25.

27. See "U.S. Reassesses Need to Use Somali Base"; Don Oberdorfer, "U.S., Somalia Move Toward Pact on Access to Military Facilities," *Washington Post*, August 12, 1980; and "Somalia Agrees to Let U.S. Use Ports, Airfields," ibid., August 22, 1980.

28. Petterson, "Ethiopia abandoned?" 642.

29. Wootten, *Regional Support Facilities*, 11. These conditions were built into all three of the base agreements to protect local prerogatives.

30. "Somali-backed Rebels Reviving Ogaden War Against Ethiopia," *The Sun*, February 3, 1979; "Somali Insurgents Harass Ethiopians," *Washington Post*, February 3, 1979.

31. See White Paper on Refugees in the Horn of Africa, "Somalia: One in Three a Refugee," *Horn of Africa* 4, no. 1 (1981), 46–51.

32. "Unfriendly and Wary Still," *Economist* 270, No. 7065 (29 January 1979), 56.

33. See U.S. Department of State, Arms Control and Disarmament Agency (ACDA), *World Military Expenditures and Arms Transfers, 1987* (Washington, D.C.: GPO, 1988), 58.

34. U.S. Department of State, ACDA, *World Military Expenditures and Arms Transfers, 1971–1980* (Washington, D.C.: GPO, 1983), 117.

35. Ibid., *1987*, 76.

36. Ibid., *1971–1980*, 117.

37. Quoted in "Another Place Kremlin Is Bogged Down," *U.S. News and World Report*, March 3, 1980.

38. The Africa Bureau believed that the Soviets would eventually burn their fingers in Ethiopia as long as the United States maintained a policy of noninvolvement in Somalia.

39. Moose, interview.

40. See Larry Bowman and Jeffrey Lefebvre, "The Indian Ocean: U.S. Military and Strategic Perspectives," in *The Indian Ocean: Perspectives on a Strategic Arena*, ed. Dowdy and Trood, 413–35.

41. See U.S. Senate, *United States Foreign Policy Objectives and Overseas Military Installations*, prepared for the Committee on Foreign Relations by the Foreign Affairs and National Defense Division, Congressional Research Service, Library of Congress, 96th Cong., 1st sess. (Washington, D.C.: GPO, April 1979), 2–4, 111–15.

42. For a description of the U.S. military buildup at Diego Garcia and the political-legal issues confronting Washington, see Joel Larus, "Diego Garcia: The Military and Legal Limitations of America's Pivotal Base in the Indian Ocean," in *The Indian Ocean: Perspectives on a Strategic Arena*, ed. Dowdy and Trood, 435–51; and Squadron Leader J. Clementson, "Diego Garcia," *Journal of the Royal United Services Institute* 126 (June 1981), 33–39.

43. See U.S. Senate, *United States Foreign Policy Objectives and Overseas Military Installations.*

44. Ibid., 88.

45. Ibid., 133.

46. Ibid., 87–88.

47. Larry Bowman, "African Conflict and Superpower Involvement in the Western Indian Ocean," in *The Indian Ocean in Global Politics*, ed. Bowman and Ian Clark (Boulder, Colo.: Westview Press, 1981), 93–97.

48. U.S. Senate, *United States Foreign Policy Objectives and Overseas Military Installations*, 127. The Suez Canal was closed between June 1967 and June 1975 without causing any serious economic and military consequences for the United States.

49. Don Oberdorfer, "The Evolution of a Decision," *Washington Post*, January 24, 1980.

50. See U.S. House of Representatives, *U.S. Interests in, and Policies Toward, the Persian Gulf, 1980*, Hearings before the Subcommittee on Europe and the Middle East, Committee on Foreign Affairs, 96th Cong., 2d sess. (Washington, D.C.: GPO, 1980), 26.

51. See Richard Burt, "Should U.S. Create Quick-Strike Force," *New York Times*, December 1, 1979. After the hostage crisis began, Brzezinski renewed his call for a "quick strike force".

52. See Stuart Auerbach, "Saudis Termed Responsive to U.S. Military Needs," *Washington Post*, February 6, 1980. U.S. officials conferred with the Saudis about the base-access strategy in early February 1980. While the Saudis approved of the idea, they were low-key about their support.

53. Wootten, *Regional Support Facilities*, 7. Diego Garcia is 3,000 miles from Teheran and 2,600 miles from Dhahran, Saudi Arabia.

54. Ibid., 7. Mombasa is 2,500 miles from the Strait of Hormuz.

55. Ibid., 12–19.

56. Bruce Kuniholm, "A Political/Military Strategy for the Persian Gulf," in *Security in the Middle East*, ed. Samuel Wells and Mark Bruzonsky (Boulder, Colo.: Westview Press, 1987), 329–32.

57. Wootten, *Regional Support Facilities*, 30–33.

58. See U.S. Senate, *Department of Defense Authorization for Appropriations for FY 1981, Part I*, Hearings before the Committee on Armed Services, 96th Cong., 2d sess. (Washington, D.C.: GPO, 1980), 484.

59. See Thomas Moorer and Alvin Cottrell, "The Search for U.S. Bases in the Indian Ocean: A Last Chance," *Strategic Review* 8 (Spring 1980), 31.

60. See Jeffrey Record, *The Rapid Deployment Force and U.S. Military Intervention in the Persian Gulf* (Cambridge, Mass.: Institute for Foreign Policy Analysis, February 1981); and Congressional Budget Office, *Rapid Deployment Forces: Policy and Budgetary Implications* (Washington, D.C.: GPO, February, 1983).

61. Wootten, *Regional Support Facilities*, 19–21.

62. See Raman Bhardwaj, "The Growing Externaliztion of the Eritrean Movement," *Horn of Africa* 2, no. 1 (1979), 24; and Tom Farer, *War Clouds on the Horn of Africa: The Widening Storm*, 2d ed. (New York: Carnegie Endowment for International Peace, 1979), 134–35.

63. Fred Halliday, "U.S. Policy in the Horn of Africa: Aboulia or Proxy Intervention," *Review of African Political Economy* 10 (September–December, 1978), 8–31; Peter Schwab, "Cold War on the Horn of Africa," *African Affairs* 77 (1979), 6–20.

64. U.S. Department of State, ACDA, *World Military Expenditures and Arms Transfers, 1967–1976* (Washington, D.C.: GPO, 1978), 159.

65. Ibid., *1971–1980*, 117.

66. U.S. House of Representatives, *War in the Horn of Africa: A Firsthand Report on the Challenges for United States Policy*, Committee on International Relations, 95th, 1st (Washington, D.C.: GPO, 1978), 50.

67. See Jerel Rosati, *The Carter Administration's Quest for Global Community* (Columbia, S.C.: University of South Carolina Press, 1987), 81–95.

68. Graham Hovey, "U.S. Moving Toward Military Ties With Somalia, Recognizing Risks," *New York Times*, February 10, 1980.

69. Rosati, *The Carter Administration's Quest*, 144.

70. Hovey, "U.S. Moving Toward Military Ties With Somalia."

71. Wootten, *Regional Support Facilities*, 20.

72. Richard Halloran, "U.S. Is Reported to Study Offer of a Somali Base," *New York Times*, December 23, 1979; and Christopher Wren, "Somalia Bargaining With U.S. on Bases," ibid., May 21, 1980.

73. Wootten, *Regional Support Facilities*, 21.

74. Ibid.

75. See U.S. House of Representatives, *Foreign Assistance and Related Programs Appropriations for 1981, Part 6*, Hearings before the Subcommittee on Foreign Operations Appropriations, 96th Cong., 2d sess. (Washington, D.C.: GPO, 1980), 185.

76. State Department official assigned to the Africa Bureau, interview, Washington, D.C., June 1982; Wootten, *Regional Support Facilities*, 8.

77. See Kenya SAP summary for FY 1955–FY 1979 in U.S. Department of Defense and U.S. Department of State, *Congressional Presentation for Security Assistance Programs, FY 1981* (Washington, D.C.: GPO, 1980).

78. See James Fitzgerald, "Gunboat Diplomacy and the Horn," *Horn of Africa* 2, no. 2 (1979), 49; and Dale Tahtinen, *Arms in the Indian Ocean: Interests and Challenges* (Washington, D.C.: American Enterprise Institute for Public Policy Research, 1977), 16–17.

79. See Sudan SAP summary for FY 1955–FY 1979 in *Congressional Presentation for Security Assistance Programs, FY 1981.*

80. Ibid.

81. See Sudan SAP summary for FY 1982 in *Congressional Presentation for Security Assistance Programs, FY 1982.*

82. See North Yemen and Djibouti SAP summary for FY 1955–FY 1979 in *Congressional Presentation for Security Assistance Programs, FY 1981.*

83. Ibid. See North Yemen SAP summary for FY 1981.

84. U.S. House of Representatives, *Foreign Assistance Legislation for Fiscal Years 1980–1981, Part 6,* Hearings before the Subcommittee on Africa of the Committee on Foreign Affairs, 96th Cong., 2d sess., (Washington, D.C.: GPO, 1980), 287.

85. Ibid., 269–92. One line of thinking went that if the U.S. were to increase its role in Ethiopia, and since Addis Ababa's foreign policy goals were primary defensive in nature, then it would reduce the need or make unnecessary large-scale arms transfers to Kenya and Sudan.

86. Harry Brind, "Soviet Policy in the Horn of Africa," *International Affairs* 60 (Winter 1983/84), 94.

87. Petterson, "Ethiopia abandoned?" 641.

88. Brind, "Soviet Policy in the Horn of Africa," 94.

89. Petterson, "Ethiopia abandoned?" 641.

90. Comment by staff member of U.S. Senate Armed Services Committee (interview, Washington, D.C., June 1982).

91. Richard Burt, "Brzezinski Seeking Stronger Influence," *New York Times,* November 5, 1979; and Rowland Evans and Robert Novak, "Brzezinski Gets His Say," *Washington Post,* November 2, 1979.

92. See Kathleen Teltsch, "Young, in U.N. Post a Year, Quieter but Still an Activist," *New York Times,* March 4, 1978; and Ungar, "The Real Reasons for Our Africa Role."

93. Hovey, "U.S. Moving Toward Military Ties With Somalia."

94. Moose, interview.

95. Ibid.

96. State Department official, interview, Washington, D.C., June 1982.

97. Ibid.

98. Moose, interview.

99. See Cord Meyer, "Ostriches in the Pentagon," *Washington Star* (June 21, 1980). Advocates argued that U.S. military aid could be separated from Somali irredentist claims by laying down strict conditions on Mogadishu not to use U.S. aid in the Ogaden.

100. Moose, interview.

101. See "Supping with the Devil," *Economist* 272 (15 September 1979).

102. "The Big White Book," *Economist* 272, No. 7094 (18 August 1979).

103. See Farer, *War Clouds on the Horn of Africa: The Widening Storm*, 141; and Georgie Anne Geyer, "Troubled Somalia Looks to Us, and We Look the Other Way," *Los Angeles Times*, October 15, 1979.

104. See Joseph Kraft, "Somalia's Case Against the U.S.," *Washington Post*, April 18, 1978.

105. Ibid.

106. Moose, interview.

107. Ibid.

108. The Somali army was not verified as being out of the Ogaden by the Carter administration until January 1981.

109. See U.S. House of Representatives, *Reprogramming Military Aid to Somalia*, Hearing before the Subcommittee on Africa, 96th, 2d sess. (Washington, D.C.: GPO, 1980), 18–19. Washington did not press Mogadishu on the issue of curtailing WSLF activities inside Ethiopia. The Africa Bureau would contend that the WSLF had a "good measure of autonomy from Mogadishu."

110. David Korn, *Ethiopia, the United States, and the Soviet Union* (Carbondale and Edwardsville: Southern Illinois University Press, 1986), 51.

111. Ibid.

112. Ibid., 51–53.

113. For an account of U.S. efforts to keep open the lines of communication, see ibid., 51–55.

114. Address by Secretary of State Cyrus Vance before the 58th annual meeting of the U.S. Jaycees (June 20, 1978). See U.S. Department of State, *Department of State Bulletin*, August 1978.

115. Andrew Young's statements are quoted in the *New York Times*, March 4, 1978 and September 22, 1978.

116. See ibid., March 4, 1978.

117. Statement by Assistant Secretary Richard Moose before the Subcommittee on Africa of the U.S. House of Representatives Committee on Foreign Affairs, February 14, 1979 (U.S. Department of State, *Department of State Bulletin*, April 1979).

118. Arguments against the Somali base access deal were pieced together from conversations held with Richard Moose and a staff member of the U.S. House of Representatives Subcommittee on Africa in June 1982. Also see Shimshon Zelnicker, "A Quest for a Foothold: The Big Powers in the Horn of Africa," in *Challenges in the Middle East: Regional Dynamics and Western Security*, ed. Nimrod Novik and Joyce Starr (New York: Praeger, 1981), 55–68.

119. According to a staff member of the U.S. House of Representatives Subcommittee on Africa (interview, Washington, D.C., June 1982).

120. Ibid. These are several possible military contingencies in which Somalia might be called upon to provide access for U.S. forces.

121. Moose, interview.

122. Ibid.

123. Ibid.

124. Ibid.

125. Statement by Richard Moose before the U.S. House of Representatives Subcommittee on Africa (February 28, 1979). U.S. Department of State, *Department of State Bulletin*, April 1979.

126. Moose, interview.

Chapter 11. The 1982 Emergency Arms Airlift

1. A good flow chart of the two-year arms ordering and delivery process can be found in U.S. Department of Defense and U.S. Department of State, *Congressional Presentation for Security Assistance Programs, FY 1988* (Washington, D.C.: GPO, 1987), 28.

2. Several Pentagon officials noted this to the author (interviews, Washington, D.C., April 26–29 and June 5–19, 1982).

3. Ibid.

4. George Wilson, "Indian Ocean Bases Plan Hits Snag," *Washington Post*, August 28, 1980.

5. Ibid.

6. Don Oberdorfer, "Somalia Vows No Forces in Ethiopia," *Washington Post*, September 6, 1980.

7. See George Wilson, "7 on Hill Panel Tell Muskie They Oppose Somalia Aid," *Washington Post*, August 30, 1980; and Michael Getler, "Hill May Block Somalian Base Pact," *Washington Post*, September 18, 1980.

8. Juan de Onis, "U.S. Arms Sale to Somalia is Conditionally Approved," *New York Times*, October 1, 1980.

9. Ibid.

10. David Korn, *Ethiopia, the United States, and the Soviet Union* (Carbondale and Edwardsville: Southern Illinois University Press, 1986), 56–57.

11. Ibid.

12. Ibid., 57.

13. See ibid., 59–71.

14. Ibid.

15. See Gerald Funk, "Some Observations on Strategic Realities and Ideological Red Herrings on the Horn of Africa," *CSIS African Notes* 1 (July 1, 1982); and Donald Petterson, "Ethiopia abandoned? An American perspective," *International Affairs* 62 (Autumn 1986), 642.

16. This assessment of U.S. policy was expressed to the author by an Eritrean who maintains wide contacts with the EPLF and State Department officials. Bereket Habte-Selassie (interview, Washington, D.C., June 16, 1982).

17. This description of U.S. policy was provided by a State Department official assigned to the Africa Bureau (interview, Washington, D.C., June 1982).

18. The actual amount provided to Somalia for FY 1982 is cited in *Congressional Presentation for Security Assistance Programs, FY 1984*, 285–87.

19. The amount proposed for FY 1983 is cited in *Congressional Presentation Presentation for Security Assistance Programs, FY 1983*, 373–75. This amount placed Somalia fourth in the Africa region behind Sudan, Kenya and Zimbabwe.

20. Richard Halloran, "U.S. Flying Arms to Somalia After Ethiopian Raids," *New York Times*, July 25, 1982.

21. See "U.S. Alerted by Somalia," *New York Times*, July 15, 1982; and Richard Halloran, "U.S. Flying Arms to Somalia After Ethiopian Raids."

22. See "Two House Members Urge Shultz To Develop Horn of Africa Policy," *New York Times*, July 27, 1982. The State Department completed a confidential review of political trends in the Horn early in the Fall of 1982. See Alan Cowell, "Ethiopian Drive Against Somalia Bogs Down," *New York Times*, October 8, 1982.

23. "Two House Members Urge Shultz To Develop Horn of Africa Policy."

24. "Somalis Report Vast U.S. Airlift," *New York Times*, August 27, 1982.

25. A top-ranking Somali official publicly complained, "The Sudanese cried war and they are getting their equipment. . . . We are still waiting. . . . Perhaps we didn't shout loud enough" (quoted in Ray Wilkinson, "Washington's Short Leash," *Newsweek*, January 11, 1982).

26. See David Laitin and Said Samatar, *Somalia: Nation In Search of a State* (Boulder, Colo.: Westview Press, 1987), 88–99.

27. This "stepping-stone" approach was a Soviet attempt to subvert U.S. allies according to two members of the Policy Planning Staff at the State Department (interview, Washington, D.C., June 1982).

28. Ibid. Also since the end of 1980 the Soviet anchorage in Ethiopia's Dahlak Islands in the Red Sea had been a cause for concern for it would facilitate Soviet naval deployments in the Indian Ocean. "New Soviet Anchorage Reported in Ethiopia Isles in Red Sea," *New York Times*, October 28, 1980.

29. Alexander Haig, *Caveat* (New York: Macmillan, 1984), 95.

30. Ibid.

31. Ibid., 96.

32. Ibid.

33. Ibid., 96, 107.

34. Ibid., 96.

35. Ibid., 88–89.

36. Ibid., 172.

37. Ibid., 170–71.

38. Ibid., 169–72.

39. Bernard Gwertzman, "U.S. Pledges to Aid Countries in Africa That Resist Libyans," *New York Times*, June 3, 1981.

40. See the statement by James Buckley, Under Secretary for Security Assistance, Science and Technology, before the U.S. Senate Foreign Relations Committee (July 28, 1981). U.S. Department of State, Bureau of Public Affairs, "Conventional Arms Transfers," *Current Policy*, no. 301.

41. See Chester Crocker and William Lewis, "Missing Opportunities in Africa," *Foreign Policy* 35 (Summer 1979), 142–61. Also see Stanley Macebuh, "Misreading Opportunities in Africa," ibid., 162–69.

42. Lee Games and Phil Mayers, "U.S. Not Reluctant to Send Arms to Africa, Envoy Says," *Honolulu Star-Bulletin*, August 29, 1981.

43. Korn, *Ethiopia, the United States, and the Soviet Union*, 77.

44. Ibid.

45. Ibid., 77–78.

46. Alan Cowell, "Ethiopian Drive Against Somalia Bogs Down,"; and "Somalia Reports an Incursion From Ethiopia," *New York Times*, July 15, 1982.

47. U.S. Department of State, Arms Control and Disarmament Agency (ACDA), *World Military Expenditures and Arms Transfers, 1985* (Washington, D.C.: GPO, 1985), 131.

48. Ibid.; Also see Korn, *Ethiopia, the United States, and the Soviet Union*, 58–59. Italy held a special interest in Ethiopia and Somalia going back to colonial days.

49. Gregory Jaynes, "A World Awash in other Problems All but Forgets Somalia's Refugees," *New York Times*, October 11, 1980.

50. James Wootten, *Regional Support Facilities for the Rapid Deployment Force*, Foreign Affairs and National Defense Division, Congressional Research

Service (Washington, D.C.: GPO, March 25, 1982), 10. Siad Barre denied in an interview with a Beirut newspaper that he would allow Somali facilities to be used in such a way. See "U.S.-Somali Pact Defended," *Washington Post*, October 1, 1980.

51. Wootten, *Regional Support Facilities*, 10.

52. See Nadav Safran, *Saudi Arabia: The Ceaseless Quest for Security* (Ithaca, N.Y.: Cornell University Press, 1988), 235–397.

53. Ibid., 262–64.

54. This opinion was expressed by State Department and Pentagon officials (interviews, in Washington, D.C., between April 26–29 and June 5–19, 1982).

55. Wootten, *Regional Support Facilities*, 20–21.

56. Ibid., 20.

57. Ibid., 8. Still, redundancy was important so the success of an operation would not hinge on access to a single facility. Some of the base access sites were simply backups in case the one best suited was not available for some reason.

58. Besides the $24 million requested for Somali military construction projects for FY 1982, the Pentagon had requested $400,000 in FY 1981, but did not expect to request any more funds for FY 1983. U.S. Senate, *Military Construction Authorization, Fiscal Year 1983*, Hearings before the Committee on Armed Services, 97th Cong., 1st sess. (Washington, D.C.: GPO, 1981), 322.

59. The FY 1982 military construction request for Southwest Asia totaled over $412 million: Diego Garcia—$237.8 million; Ras Banas—$106.4 million; Oman—$78.5 milliom; Lajes air base in the Azores—$46.6 million; Kenya—$26 million; and Somalia—$24 million. U.S. House of Representatives, *Military Construction Appropriations for FY 1983, Part 5*, Hearings before the Committee on Appropriations, 97th Cong., 2d sess. (Washington, D.C.: GPO, 1982), 265.

60. U.S. Senate, *Foreign Assistance Authorization for Fiscal Year 1982*, Hearings before the Committee on Foreign Relations, 97th Cong., 1st sess. (Washington, D.C.: GPO, 1981), 211.

61. For an analysis of the capabilities of these sites, see Wootten, *Regional Support Facilities*, 12–33.

62. Ibid., 12–19. Masirah Island lies 500 miles from the Strait of Hormuz.

63. Ibid., 25–30.

64. U.S. House of Representatives, *Military Construction Appropriations for FY 1983, Part 5*, 265 and 278. Pentagon officials estimated that total expenditures at Ras Banas would exceed $502 million through FY 1985.

65. Ibid., 267, 275.

66. Congressional Budget Office, *Rapid Deployment Forces: Policy and Budgetary Implications* (Washington, D.C.: GPO, February 1983), 59.

67. See U.S. House of Representatives, *Persian Gulf/Indian Ocean Military Construction Program and Defense Posture in the Pacific*, Hearings before the Subcommittee on Military Construction Appropriations of the Committee on Appropriations, 97th Cong., 1st sess. (Washington, D.C.: GPO, 1981), 193; Squadron Leader J. Clementson, "Diego Garcia," *Journal of the Royal United Services Institute* 126 (June 1981), 33; and Wootten, *Regional Support Facilities*, 30–33.

68. Wootten, *Regional Support Facilities*, 32. U.S. plans called for the "orderly expansion" of the base including (1) a deep water anchorage, (2) an extended 12,000-foot runway, (3) additional support buildings, and (4) an increased naval repair capability that would save ships having to travel 6,000 miles to Subic Bay in the Philippines for repair.

69. See Joel Larus, "Diego Garcia: The Military and Legal Limitations of America's Pivotal Base in the Indian Ocean," in *The Indian Ocean: Perspectives on a Strategic Arena*, ed. William Dowdy and Russell Trood (Durham, N.C.: Duke University Press, 1985), 435–51.

70. Wootten, *Regional Support Facilities*, 2–3. The maritime option was one of several alternatives being discussed in early 1982.

71. The actual amounts for FY 1980 are cited in *Congressional Presentation for Security Assistance Programs, FY 1982*, 351–53. The actual amounts for FY 1981 are cited in ibid., *FY 1983*, 379–81.

72. The actual amounts for FY 1982 are cited in ibid., *FY 1984*, 289–91.

73. See ibid., *FY 1983*, 379–81.

74. For an executive-branch summary of Sudan's importance in 1981–1982 see ibid., *FY 1982*, 351–53; and ibid., *FY 1983*, 379–81.

75. See "Egypt: Water Diplomacy," *Africa Confidential* 29 (March 18, 1988); and Alan Cowell, "Egypt's Friend in Need," *New York Times Magazine*, December 20, 1981.

76. Osman Mohamoud, "Somalia: Crisis and Decay in an Authoritarian Regime," *Horn of Africa* 4, no. 3 (1981), 7–11.

77. See White Paper, "Ogaden: The Land but Not the People," *Horn of Africa* 4, no. 1 (1981), 42–45.

78. Mohamoud, "Somalia," 7–11.

79. U.S. Department of State, *Country Reports on Human Rights Practices for 1982* (Washington, D.C.: GPO, 1983), 272.

80. Ibid.

81. Ibid.

82. Ibid., 226–27.

83. U.S. Department of State, *Country Reports on Human Rights Practices for 1981* (Washington, D.C.: GPO, 1982), 226.

84. Ibid.

85. Ibid.

86. Ibid.

87. Ibid., *1982*, 272.

88. Laitin and Samatar, *Somalia: Nation in Search of a State*, 92–94.

89. *Country Reports on Human Rights Practices for 1982*, 272.

90. Ibid., 272–73.

91. See statement of Congressman Toby Moffett in U.S. House of Representatives, *Implementation of Congressionally Mandated Human Rights Provisions (Volume II)*, Hearings before Subcommittees on Europe and the Middle East, on Asian and Pacific Affairs, on Human Rights and International Organizations, and on Africa of the Committee on Foreign Affairs, November 1981–March 1982 (Washington, D.C.: GPO, 1982).

92. Ibid.

93. Ibid.

94. Ibid.

95. Ibid.

96. Ibid., 335.

97. *Country Reports on Human Rights Practices for 1982*, 273.

98. "Somalia on the Brink of Civil War," *Horn of Africa* 6, no. 3 (1983/84), 40–42.

99. See the journal *Horn of Africa* in the 1981–83 period in which a number of

antigovernment articles, letters, and editorials were published, esp. Editorial, "Will President Barre's Tyranny Sink Somalia?" *Horn of Africa* 4, no. 4 (1981/82), 2.

100. The ideological platform of the SSDF is leftist in orientation, while that of the SNM has more of a religious and regionalist content. See Osman Mohamoud, "From Irredentism to Insurgency," *Horn of Africa* 5, no. 4 (1982/83), 26–31.

101. Ibid., 26–31.

102. "Somalia on the Brink of Civil War," 40.

103. State Department as well as Pentagon officials seemed quite aware of the potential explosiveness of the situation in the Horn (interviews conducted in Washington, D.C., April 26–29 and June 5–19, 1982).

104. Point made by two members of the Policy Planning Staff (interview, Washington, D.C., June 1982).

105. Ibid.

106. Korn, *Ethiopia, the United States, and the Soviet Union*, 78.

107. Defense Department officials (interviews, Washington, D.C., June 1982.

108. Korn, *Ethiopia, the United States, and the Soviet Union*, 78.

109. Defense Department officials (interviews, Washington, D.C., June 1982.

110. This represented the perspective of several Pentagon officials (interviews, Washington, D.C., June 1982).

111. Ibid.

112. Point made by a member of the Policy Planning Staff, State Department. (interview, Washington, D.C., June 1982).

113. This was the view of one official at the Africa Bureau (interview, Washington, D.C., June 1982).

114. Ibid.

115. See U.S. House of Representatives, *Reprogramming Military Aid to Somalia*, Hearing before the Subcommittee on Africa, 96th Cong., 2d sess. (Washington, D.C.: GPO, 1980), 5–8.

116. Ibid.

117. Ibid.

118. Ibid.

119. Pentagon officials noted this reluctance on the part of the Africa Bureau (interviews, Washington, D.C., June 1982).

120. Quoted in Jay Ross, "U.S. Arms Accord With Somalia Alarms Rival Neighbor Kenya," *Washington Post*, October 20, 1980.

121. Pentagon official (interview, Washington, D.C. June 1982).

122. Undersecretary of State Matthew Nimitz had made this argument. See U.S. House of Representatives, *Foreign Assistance and Related Programs Appropriations for 1981, Part 6*, Hearings before the House Appropriations Subcommittee on Foreign Operations Appropriations, 96th Cong., 2d sess. (Washington, D.C.: GPO, 1980), 195.

123. This view was expressed by Pentagon officials (interviews, Washington, D.C., June 1982).

124. Perspective of Pentagon official involved in the management of SAP (interview, Washington, D.C., April 1982).

125. Ibid.

126. Korn, *Ethiopia, the United States, and the Soviet Union*, 78.

127. Policy Planning Staff member (interview, Washington, D.C., June 1982).

128. Korn, *Ethiopia, the United States, and the Soviet Union*, 78.

Chapter 12. The 1990 Base Access Renegotiation

1. All SAP statistics cited for Somalia in this chapter are drawn from tables 3 and 4 in the Appendix.

2. The "actual" amounts obligated to Somalia, Kenya, and Sudan for FY 1980-FY 1986 can be found in U.S. Department of Defense and Department of State, *Congressional Presentation for Security Assistance Programs* for FY 1982 through FY 1988.

3. See address by Ronald Spiers, undersecretary for management (October 15, 1986), "The Fiscal Threat to U.S. Foreign Policy," *Current Policy,* no. 877.

4. Ibid.

5. U.S. House of Representatives, *Reported Massacres and Indiscriminate Killings in Somalia,* Hearings before the Subcommittee on Africa of the Committee on Foreign Affairs (July 14, 1988), 100th Cong., 2d sess. (Washington, D.C.: GPO, 1989), 19–21.

6. Ibid., 7–25. This is the testimony provided by Aryeh Neier, vice chairman, Human Rights Watch—"Human Rights in Somalia."

7. See ibid.

8. Ibid., 24.

9. Ibid., 24–25.

10. Ibid., 25.

11. See "Somalia: Generals fall out," *Africa Confidential* 29 (23 September 1988); and "Somalia: Wounded North, bruised South," ibid., 29 (18 November 1988).

12. "Somalia: Wounded North, bruised South."

13. See U.S. House of Representatives, *Foreign Assistance Legislation for Fiscal Years 1990–91 (Part 6),* Hearings and Markup before the Subcommittee on Africa of the Committee on Foreign Affairs (March 8–9 and April 25, 1989), 101st Cong., 1st sess. (Washington, D.C.: GPO, 1990), 217–18.

14. Ibid., 218.

15. Ibid., 396.

16. Ibid., 218.

17. Discussions with U.S. officials and accounts provided in public and congressional testimony present a somewhat confusing picture of just what Somalia received in actual SAP funding. I have cited the "actual" amounts given in the *Congressional Presentation for Security Assistance* for these years.

18. *Foreign Assistance Legislation for Fiscal Years 1990–91 (Part 6),* 218.

19. Ibid., 219.

20. U.S. House of Representatives, *Human Rights and Multilateral Aid to China and Somalia,* Hearings before the Subcommittee on International Development, Finance, Trade and Monetary Policy of the Committee on Banking, Finance and Urban Affairs (June 20, 1989), 101st Cong., 1st sess. (Washington, D.C.: GPO, 1989), 28.

21. "Somalia: The Mogadishu factor," *Africa Confidential* 29 (16 December 1988).

22. See "Somalia: Death in Mogadishu," ibid., 30 (28 July 1989).

23. This information was provided by a U.S. government source (interview). In cnducting research for this book and other related projects, I held ten telephone interviews with several State Department officials, as well as Pentagon, AID, and congressional staff sources between August 1989 and September 1990. Where

appropriate, I will give the approximate date of the interview; I will refer to each of these individuals as a "government source."

24. See *Foreign Assistance Legislation for Fiscal Years 1990–91 (Part 6)*, 395. Also see *Congressional Presentation for Security Assistance Programs, FY 1990*, 250.

25. *Congressional Presentation for Security Assistance Programs, FY 1991*, 253.

26. "Somalia: The president delegates," *Africa Confidential* 28 (1 April 1987); and "Ethiopia: Nationalities and the constitution," ibid., 28 (1 April 1987).

27. "Ethiopia: Nationalities and the constitution."

28. "Somalia: Under fire," *Africa Confidential* 29 (29 April 1988).

29. Ibid.

30. Government source (interview).

31. See "Ethiopia: A battle lost, a war in stalemate," *Africa Confidential* 29 (29 April 1988).

32. "Ethiopia: Mengistu soldiers on," ibid., 29 (1 July 1988).

33. "Ethiopia: Dark days for Mengistu," ibid., 30 (17 February 1989).

34. "Somalia: Feeling the pinch," ibid., 29 (17 June 1988).

35. "Somalia: Showdown in the north," ibid., 29 (29 July 1988).

36. See Daniel Compagnon, "The Somali Opposition Fronts: Some Comments and Questions," *Horn of Africa* 13, nos. 1–2 (1990), 34.

37. Address by Michael Armacost, undersecretary for political affairs (September 26, 1986), "U.S.-Soviet Relations: Coping With Conflict in the Third World," *Current Policy*, no. 879.

38. Ibid.

39. Ibid.

40. See address by Secretary of State George Shultz (April 14, 1986), "Moral Principles and Strategic Interests: The Worldwide Movement Toward Democracy," *Current Policy*, no. 820.

41. See Statement by Chester Crocker, assistant secretary for African affairs, before the Subcommittee on International Operations of the House Foreign Affairs Committee (March 18, 1986), "FY 1987 Assistance Request for Sub-Saharan African," *Current Policy*, no. 814.

42. Ibid.

43. Ibid.

44. Ibid.

45. Ibid.

46. See *Current Policy*, no. 879.

47. Caryle Murphy, "Ethiopian Army Dealt Setbacks by Guerrillas," *Washington Post*, April 9, 1990. Soviet advisers, which once numbered 2,000, no longer operated in Eritrea.

48. "Ethiopia: Talks start at last," *Africa Confidential* 30 (25 August 1989).

49. Clifford Krauss, "U.S. and Soviets Will Seek to Prevent Ethiopia Famine," *New York Times*, June 4, 1990.

50. "Ethiopian Army Dealt Setbacks by Guerrillas."

51. Analysis provided by government source (interview, January 1990).

52. See Somalia and Sudan justification for these years in *Congressional Presentation for Security Assistance Programs*.

53. This assessment is based upon conversations held with government sources (interviews, September 1990).

54. Comment by government source (interview, September 1990).

55. Ibid.
56. Ibid.
57. Ibid.
58. U.S. Department of State, Arms Control and Disarmament Agency (ACDA), *World Military Expenditures and Arms Transfers, 1987* (Washington, D.C.: GPO, April 1988), 127.
59. Paul Watson, "Arms and Aggression in the Horn of Africa," *Journal of International Affairs* 40 (Summer 1986), 172–73.
60. This was stated by the administration in response to a question posed by the House Subcommittee on Africa. See *Foreign Assistance Legislation for Fiscal Years 1990–91 (Part 6)*, 395.
61. Ibid, 133. See "Somalia: Wounded North, bruised South."
62. "Somalia: Wounded North, bruised South."
63. *Foreign Assistance Legislation for Fiscal Years 1990–91 (Part 6)*, 215.
64. Ibid. This assessment was reaffirmed by a government source (interview, September 1990).
65. Comment by government source (interview).
66. *Foreign Assistance Legislation for Fiscal Years 1990–91 (Part 6)*, 215.
67. *Reported Massacres and Indiscriminate Killings in Somalia*, 42–43.
68. Ibid.
69. Ibid.
70. Comment by government source (interview).
71. Ibid.
72. This point was made by several different government sources (interviews). It is also evidence by the fact that congressional hearings were held to examine this issue. See *Human Rights and Multilateral Aid to China and Somalia.*
73. See *New York Times*, May 11, 1988.
74. "U.N. Withholds Aid in Somalia Dispute," *New York Times*, January 28, 1989.
75. *Human Rights and Multilateral Aid to China and Somalia*, 1.
76. Ibid.
77. Ibid. See testimony of Holly Burthalter of Africa Watch.
78. Ibid., 7.
79. Information supplied by government source (interview).
80. Comment by government source (interview).
81. Ibid.
82. This information was related by government source (interview).
83. Ibid.
84. Comment by government source (interview).
85. Ibid.
86. Information provided by government source (interview).
87. Comment by government source (interview).
88. See *Foreign Assistance Legislation for Fiscal Years 1990–91 (Part 6)*, 396.
89. Comment by government source (interview).
90. *Foreign Assistance Legislation for Fiscal Years 1990–91 (Part 6)*, 396.
91. Ibid.
92. This is the impression given by several government sources (interviews).
93. For the size of the SAP package provided to the Philippines for the 1988–1991 miltary base agreement see *Congressional Presentation for Security Assistance Programs, FY 1991*, 233–35.

94. See Jeffrey Lefebvre, "Globalism and Regionalism: U.S. Arms Transfers to Sudan," *Armed Forces & Society* 17 (Winter 1991), 211–27.

95. See *Congressional Presentation for Security Assistance Programs* for Sudan for these three years.

96. See *Congressional Presentation for Security Assistance Programs, FY 1991*, 259.

97. Ibid.

98. Comment by government source (interview).

99. Ibid. Congress began to become troubled by the human rights situation in Kenya in the spring of 1989. See *Foreign Assistance Legislation for Fiscal Years 1990–91 (Part 6)*, 122–23. In early July 1990 U.S. military assistance to Kenya was frozen by Congress until the human rights situation improved.

100. Comment by government source (interview).

101. Ibid.

102. Ibid.

103. Ibid.

104. Ibid.

105. Ibid.

106. Jane Perlez, "Ethiopia's President Looks Toward Better U.S. Relations," *New York Times*, November 28, 1988.

107. Ibid.

108. John Goshko, "Top U.S. Officials Shun Ethiopia," *Washington Post*, March 30, 1990.

109. James Dorsey, "U.S. may let Ethiopia send envoy in deal for famine aid," *Washington Times*, April 19, 1990.

110. Comment by government source (interview).

111. Ibid.

112. One informed source wrote that a terminal air surrounded the government of Siad Barre in mid-1987. See "Somalia: Family feuds," *Africa Confidential* 28 (22 July 1987). This source then predicted in the Fall of 1989 that the end was in sight for Siad. See "Somalia: The end in sight for Siad," *Africa Confidential* 30 (8 September 1989).

113. See Compagnon, "The Somali Opposition Fronts," 35–37.

114. Ibid., 34–40.

115. "Somalia: Generals fall out," *Africa Confidential* 29 (23 September 1988).

116. This had the side effect of boosting the political power of the Ogadeen clan. "Somalia: The rise of the Ogadeni," *Africa Confidential* 30 (20 January 1989).

117. "Somalia: The end in sight for Siad."

118. Compagnon, "The Somali Opposition Fronts," 36–37.

119. Ibid., 35–37.

120. Assessment by government source (interview).

121. See Somali Elders, "An Open Letter to President Mohamed Siyaad Barre," *Horn of Africa* 13, nos. 1–2 (1990).

122. Information provided by government source (interview).

123. See Compagnon, "The Somali Opposition Fronts," 35–40.

124. Ibid., 41–46.

125. Ibid., 38.

126. Ibid.

127. Ibid., 42.

128. "Somalia: The end in sight for Siad." Siad Barre had been elected president

of Somali for a seven-year term in December 1986 with 99.92 percent of the vote. See "Somalia: The president delegates," *Africa Confidential* 28 (1 April 1987).

129. Assessment by government source (interview).

130. Government source (interview, September 1990).

131. *Reported Massacres and Indiscriminate Killings in Somalia*, 45–47.

132. Ibid., 45–47.

133. Government source (interview).

134. Burton had made this point in the spring of 1989. See *Foreign Assistance Legislation for Fiscal Years 1990–91 (Part 6)*, 358–60.

135. See *Reported Massacres and Indiscriminate Killings in Somalia*, 31.

136. *Foreign Assistance Legislation for Fiscal Years 1990–91 (Part 6)*, 333.

137. Comment by U.S. official, interview, Washington, D.C., June 1982.

138. Jane Hunter, "Israel and Ethiopia: Cluster bombs and Falashas," *Middle East International*, No. 368 (2 February 1990), 11–12.

139. Ibid.

140. "Top U.S. Officials Shun Ethiopia."

141. View of government source in executive branch (interview).

142. Ibid.

143. Quoted in Jane Perlez, "Report for U.S. Says Somali Army Killed 5,000 Unarmed Civilians," *New York Times*, September 9, 1989.

144. "Somalia Executes 46 After Rioting," *New York Times*, July 22, 1989.

145. Quoted in Holly Burkhalter, "Somalia's Massacres Aren't on TV," *New York Times*, August 13, 1989.

146. The report by Robert Gersony is quoted at some length in Compagnon, "The Somali Opposition Fronts," 32–33. Some aspects of the Gersony report were also relayed to the author by a government source (interview).

147. The fact that the executive branch still wanted to do something for Somalia was mentioned by a government source (interview).

148. Scenarios provided by government source (interview).

149. Comment by government source (interview).

150. Government source (interview).

151. Belief expressed by government source (interview).

152. See *Congressional Presentation for Security Assistance Programs, FY 1991*, 253.

153. View expressed by government source (interview).

Conclusion

1. Account provided by government source, executive branch (interview, February 1991).

2. The following account of the battle for Mogadishu was provided by ibid.; Jane Perlez, "Insurgents Claiming Victory in Somalia," *New York Times*, January 28, 1991; Jane Perlez, "Fighting Subsides in Somalia's Capital," ibid., January 29, 1991; "In Somalia, Graves, and Devastation," ibid., January 30, 1991; and "Somalia: Where do we go from here?" *Africa Confidential* 32 (8 February 1991).

3. Perlez, "Fighting Subsides in Somalia's Capital."

4. See "Somalia: Where do we go from here?"

5. Assessment provided by I. M. Lewis (in Perlez, "Fighting Subsides in Somalia's Capital").

6. See "Somalia: Where do we go from here?"
7. Government source, executive branch (interview, February 1991).
8. See "Somalia: Where do we go from here?"
9. Government source, executive branch (interview, May 1991).
10. See "Somalia: Where do we go from here?"
11. Government source, executive branch (interview, May 1991).
12. See "Somalia: Where do we go from here?"
13. See Jane Perlez, "2 Months After Ousting Despot, Somalia Faces Life as Abandoned Pawn," *New York Times,* April 4, 1991.
14. According to a government source, executive branch (interview, May 1991).
15. Ibid.
16. Ibid.
17. Scenario provided by government source, executive branch (interview, May 1991).
18. Ibid.
19. Point made by two government sources, executive branch (interviews, May 1991).
20. Government source, executive branch (interview, May 1991).
21. "Somalia: Where do we go from here?"
22. Government source, executive branch (interview), February 1991.
23. Clifford Krauss, "Ethiopia Says All Jews Are Free to Leave for Israel," *New York Times,* November 2, 1990.
24. Ibid.
25. See Clifford Krauss, "Ethiopia Talks to Resume, Under U.S. Leadership," *New York Times,* January 30, 1991; and Clifford Krauss, "Conflicting Peace Plans Offered in Ethiopia Strife," ibid., February 24, 1991.
26. Jane Perlez, "New View of Ethiopia," *New York Times,* May 31, 1991.
27. Ibid. Israel reportedly paid $35 million for their release. See Craig Whitney, "Ethiopian Seeks to Form Temporary Government," *New York Times,* May 29, 1991.
28. See "Ethiopian Seeks to Form Temporary Government."
29. Neil Lewis, "U.S. Plans to Be 'Midwife' to a New Rule in Ethiopia," *New York Times,* May 26, 1991.
30. Government source, executive branch (interview, February 1991).
31. A second government source, executive branch (interview, February 1991).
32. Analysis provided by government source, executive branch (interview, February 1991).
33. Ibid.
34. Ibid.
35. See U.S. Departments of Defense and State, *Congressional Presentation for Security Assistance Programs, FY 1992* (Washington, D.C.: GPO, 1991), 8–10, 311–17.
36. Government source, executive branch (interview, May 1991).
37. See Jane Perlez, "A Hard-Line Marxist Who Mellowed," *New York Times,* May 30, 1991.
38. Quoted in "Ethiopian Seeks to Form Temporary Government."
39. Quoted in Clifford Krauss, "Ethiopia and 3 Rebel Groups Look Toward U.S.-Led Peace Talks," *New York Times,* May 14, 1991.
40. See Craig Whitney, "Ethiopia Rebel Faction Is to Govern Separately," *New*

York Times, May 30, 1991; and Clifford Krauss, "Rioters in Addis Ababa Vent Their Anger on Americans," ibid., May 30, 1991.

41. Government source, executive branch (interview, May 1991).

42. See Jane Perlez, "Ethiopian Seeks to Form Temporary Government," *New York Times,* July 2, 1991.

43. "Egypt: The Gulf windfall," *Africa Confidential* 32 (8 February 1991).

Index

Index

Pitt Series in Policy and Institutional Studies
Bert A. Rockman, Editor

The Acid Rain Controversy
James L. Regens and Robert W. Rycroft

Affirmative Action at Work: Law, Politics, and Ethics
Bron Raymond Taylor

Agency Merger and Bureaucratic Redesign
Karen M. Hult

The Aging: A Guide to Public Policy
Bennett M. Rich and Martha Baum

Arms for the Horn: U.S. Security Policy in Ethiopia and Somalia, 1953–1991
Jeffrey A. Lefebvre

The Atlantic Alliance and the Middle East
Joseph I. Coffey and Gianni Bonvicini, Editors

The Budget-Maximizing Bureaucrat: Appraisals and Evidence
André Blais and Stéphane Dion

Clean Air: The Policies and Politics of Pollution Control
Charles O. Jones

The Competitive City: The Political Economy of Suburbia
Mark Schneider

Conflict and Rhetoric in French Policymaking
Frank R. Baumgartner

Congress and Economic Policymaking
Darrell M. West

Congress Oversees the Bureaucracy: Studies in Legislative Supervision
Morris S. Ogul

Democracy in Japan
Takeshi Ishida and Ellis S. Krauss, Editors

Demographic Change and the American Future
R. Scott Fosler, William Alonso, Jack A. Meyer, and Rosemary Kern

Economic Decline and Political Change: Canada, Great Britain, and the United States
Harold D. Clarke, Marianne C. Stewart, and Gary Zuk, Editors

Extraordinary Measures: The Exercise of Prerogative Powers in the United States
Daniel P. Franklin

Foreign Policy Motivation: A General Theory and a Case Study
Richard W. Cottam

"He Shall Not Pass This Way Again": The Legacy of Justice William O. Douglas
Stephen L. Wasby, Editor

Homeward Bound: Explaining Changes in Congressional Behavior
Glenn Parker

How Does Social Science Work? Reflections on Practice
Paul Diesing

Imagery and Ideology in U.S. Policy Toward Libya, 1969–1982
Mahmoud G. ElWarfally

The Impact of Policy Analysis
James M. Rogers

Iran and the United States: A Cold War Case Study
Richard W. Cottam

Japanese Prefectures and Policymaking
Steven R. Reed

Making Regulatory Policy
Keith Hawkins and John M. Thomas, Editors

Managing the Presidency: Carter, Reagan, and the Search for Executive Harmony
Colin Campbell, S.J.

Organizing Governance, Governing Organizations
Colin Campbell, S.J., and B. Guy Peters, Editors

Party Organizations in American Politics
Cornelius P. Cotter et al.

Perceptions and Behavior in Soviet Foreign Policy
Richard K. Herrmann

Pesticides and Politics: The Life Cycle of a Public Issue
Christopher J. Bosso

Policy Analysis by Design
Davis B. Bobrow and John S. Dryzek

The Political Failure of Employment Policy, 1945–1982
Gary Mucciaroni

Political Leadership: A Source Book
Barbara Kellerman, Editor

The Politics of Public Utility Regulation
William T. Gormley, Jr.

The Politics of the U.S. Cabinet: Representation in the Executive Branch, 1789–1984
Jeffrey E. Cohen

The Presidency and Public Policy Making
George C. Edwards III, Steven A. Shull, and Norman C. Thomas, Editors

Private Markets and Public Intervention: A Primer for Policy Designers
Harvey Averch

Public Policy in Latin America: A Comparative Survey
John W. Sloan

Roads to Reason: Transportation, Administration, and Rationality in Colombia
Richard E. Hartwig

Site Unseen: The Politics of Siting a Nuclear Waste Repository
Gerald Jacob

The Struggle for Social Security, 1900–1935
Roy Lubove

Tage Erlander: Serving the Welfare State, 1946–1969
Olof Ruin

Traffic Safety Reform in the United States and Great Britain
Jerome S. Legge, Jr.

Urban Alternatives: Public and Private Markets in the Provision of Local Services
Robert M. Stein

The U.S. Experiment in Social Medicine: The Community Health Center Program, 1965–1986
Alice Sardell